UNDOING GENDER

UNDOING GENDER

JUDITH BUTLER

ROUTLEDGE
NEW YORK AND LONDON

Published in 2004 by
Routledge
270 Madison Avenue
New York, NY 10016
www.routledge-ny.com

Published in Great Britain by
Routledge
2 Park Square
Milton Park
Abington, Oxfordshire, OX14 4RN, UK
www.routledge.co.uk

Printed in the United States of America on acid-free paper.

10 9 8 7 6 5 4 3

Library of Congress Cataloging in Publication Data

Butler, Judith.
    Undoing gender/by Judith Butler.
        p. cm.
    Includes bibliographical references and index.
    ISBN 0-415-96922-0 (alk. paper) – ISBN 0-415-96923-9 (pbk.: alk. paper)
        1. Sex role. 2. Gender identity, I. Title.
    HQ1075.B89 2004
    305.3–dc22   2003066872

ISBN 0-415-96922-0 (hb)
ISBN 0-415-96923-9 (pb)

For Wendy,
again and again

Acknowledgments

M y thanks go to Amy Jamgochian and Stuart Murray who helped at various stages to edit and compile these essays. I also thank Denise Riley whose conversation over these last years has moved my thinking in ways too many and too intricately to recount. I thank Gayle Salamon as well whose dissertation on embodiment and materiality has prompted my own re-thinking on such topics.

The essay "Beside Oneself" was given as part of the Amnesty Lecture Series on "Sexual Rights" at Oxford in the spring of 2002 and will appear in an Oxford publication of those lectures edited by Nicholas Bamforth. It contains material published in "Violence, Mourning, Politics," which first appeared in *Studies in Gender and Sexuality* 4:1 (2003). "Doing Justice to Someone" appeared in a different form in *GLQ* (7, no. 4, 2001). In revising the essay, I have incorporated suggestions made by Vernon Rosario and Cheryl Chase and am grateful to them both for the important perspectives they provided. "Gender Regulations" was commissioned by Gil Herdt and Catharine Stimpson for a forthcoming volume on "Gender" with the University of Chicago Press. "Undiagnosing Gender" is also in *Transgender Rights: Culture, Politics, and Law*, edited by Paisley Currah and Shannon Minter (Minneapolis: University of Minnesota Press, 2004). "Is Kinship Always Already Heterosexual" appeared first in *differences* (vol. 13, no. 1, spring 2002). "Longing for Recognition" appeared first in *Studies in Gender and Sexuality* (vol. 1, no. 3, 2000) and some parts of that essay appeared as well as "Capacity" in *Regarding Sedgwick*, edited by Stephen Barber (New York: Routledge, 2001). "Quandaries of the Incest Taboo" appeared in *Whose Freud? The Place of Psychoanalysis in Contemporary Culture*, edited by Peter Brooks and Alex Woloch (New Haven: Yale University Press, 2000). "Bodily Confessions" was given as a paper at the American Psychological Division Meetings (Division 39) in San Francisco in the spring of 1999. "The End of Sexual Difference?" appeared in different form in *Feminist Consequences: Theory for a New Century*, edited by Misha Kavka and Elizabeth Bronfen (New York: Columbia Univeristy Press, 2001). "The Question of Social Transformation" appeared in a longer version in Spanish in *Mujeres y transformaciones sociales*, with Lidia Puigvert and Elizabeth Beck Gernsheim (Barcelona: El Roure Editorial, 2002). "Can the 'Other' of Philosophy Speak?" was published in *Schools of Thought: Twenty-Five Years of Interpretive Social Science*, edited by Joan W. Scott and Debra Keates (Princeton: Princeton University Press, 2002) and appeared in a separate version in *Women and Social Transformation* (New York: Peter Lang Publishing, 2003).

CONTENTS

Introduction: Acting in Concert

The essays included here represent some of my most recent work on gender and sexuality focusing on the question of what it might mean to undo restrictively normative conceptions of sexual and gendered life. Equally, however, the essays are about the experience of *becoming undone* in both good and bad ways. Sometimes a normative conception of gender can undo one's personhood, undermining the capacity to persevere in a livable life. Other times, the experience of a normative restriction becoming undone can undo a prior conception of who one is only to inaugurate a relatively newer one that has greater livability as its aim.

If gender is a kind of a doing, an incessant activity performed, in part, without one's knowing and without one's willing, it is not for that reason automatic or mechanical. On the contrary, it is a practice of improvisation within a scene of constraint. Moreover, one does not "do" one's gender alone. One is always "doing" with or for another, even if the other is only imaginary. What I call my "own" gender appears perhaps at times as something that I author or, indeed, own. But the terms that make up one's own gender are, from the start, outside oneself, beyond oneself in a sociality that has no single author (and that radically contests the notion of authorship itself).

Although being a certain gender does not imply that one will desire a certain way, there is nevertheless a desire that is constitutive of gender itself and, as a result, no quick or easy way to separate the life of gender from the life of desire. What does gender want? To speak in this way may seem strange, but it becomes less so when we realize that the social norms that constitute our existence carry desires that do not originate with our individual personhood. This matter is made more complex by the fact that the viability of our individual personhood is fundamentally dependent on these social norms.

The Hegelian tradition links desire with recognition, claiming that desire is always a desire for recognition and that it is only through the experience of recognition that any of us becomes constituted as socially viable beings. That view has its allure and its truth, but it also misses a couple of important points. The terms by which we are recognized as human are socially articulated and changeable. And sometimes the very terms that confer "humanness" on some individuals are those that deprive certain other individuals of the possibility of achieving that status, producing a differential between the human and the less-than-human. These norms have far-reaching consequences for how we understand the model of the human entitled to rights or included in the participatory sphere of political deliberation. The human is understood differentially depending on its race, the legibility of that race, its morphology, the recognizability of that morphology, its sex, the perceptual verifiability of that sex, its ethnicity, the categorical understanding of that ethnicity. Certain humans are recognized as less than human, and that form of qualified recognition does not lead to a viable life. Certain humans are not recognized as human at all, and that leads to yet another order of unlivable life. If part of what desire wants is to gain recognition, then gender, insofar as it is animated by desire, will want recognition as well. But if the schemes of recognition that are available to us are those that "undo" the person by conferring recognition, or "undo" the person by withholding recognition, then recognition becomes a site of power by which the human is differentially produced. This means that to the extent that desire is implicated in social norms, it is bound up with the question of power and with the problem of who qualifies as the recognizably human and who does not.

If I am a certain gender, will I still be regarded as part of the human? Will the "human" expand to include me in its reach? If I desire in certain ways, will I be able to live? Will there be a place for my life, and will it be recognizable to the others upon whom I depend for social existence?

There are advantages to remaining less than intelligible, if intelligibility is understood as that which is produced as a consequence of recognition according to prevailing social norms. Indeed, if my options are loathsome, if I have no desire to be recognized within a certain set of norms, then it follows that my sense of survival depends upon escaping the clutch of those norms by which recognition is conferred. It may well be that my sense of social belonging is impaired by the distance I take, but surely that estrangement is preferable to gaining a sense of intelligibility by virtue of norms that will only do me in from another direction. Indeed, the capacity to develop a critical relation to these norms presupposes a distance from them, an ability to suspend or defer the need for them, even as there is a desire for norms that might let one live. The critical relation depends as well on a capacity, invariably collective, to articulate an alternative, minority version of sustaining norms or ideals that enable me to act. If I am someone who cannot *be* without *doing*, then the conditions of my doing are, in part, the conditions of my existence. If my doing is dependent on what is done to me or, rather, the ways in which I am done by norms, then the possibility of my persistence as an "I" depends upon my being able to do something with what is done with me. This does not mean that I can remake the world so that I become its maker. That fantasy of godlike power only refuses the ways we are constituted, invariably and from the start, by what is before us and outside of us. My agency does not consist in denying this condition of my constitution. If I have any agency, it is opened up by the fact that I am constituted by a social world I never chose. That my agency is riven with paradox does not mean it is impossible. It means only that paradox is the condition of its possibility.

As a result, the "I" that I am finds itself at once constituted by norms and dependent on them but also endeavors to live in ways that maintain a critical and transformative relation to them. This is not easy, because the "I" becomes, to a certain extent unknowable, threatened with unviability, with becoming undone altogether, when it no longer incorporates the norm in such a way that makes this "I" fully recognizable. There is a certain departure from the human that takes place in order to start the process of remaking the human. I may feel that without some recognizability I cannot live. But I may also feel that the terms by which I am recognized make life unlivable. This is the juncture from which critique emerges, where critique is understood as an interrogation of the terms by which life is constrained in order to open up the possibility of different modes of living; in other words, not to celebrate difference as such but to establish more inclusive conditions for sheltering and maintaining life that resists models of assimilation.

The essays in this text are efforts to relate the problematics of gender and sexuality to the tasks of persistence and survival. My own thinking has been influenced by the "New Gender Politics" that has emerged in recent years, a combination of movements concerned with transgender, transsexuality, intersex, and their complex relations to feminist and queer theory.[1] I believe, however, that it would be a mistake to subscribe to a progressive notion of history in which various frameworks are understood to succeed and supplant one another. There is no story to be told about how one moves from feminist to queer to trans. The reason there is no story to be told is that none of these stories are the past; these stories are continuing to happen in simultaneous and overlapping ways as we tell them. They happen, in part, through the complex ways they are taken up by each of these movements and theoretical practices.

Consider the intersex opposition to the widespread practice of performing coercive surgery on infants and children with sexually indeterminate or hermaphroditic anatomy in the name of normalizing these bodies. This movement offers a critical perspective on the version of the "human" that requires ideal morphologies and the constraining of bodily norms. The intersex community's resistance to coercive surgery moreover calls for an understanding that infants with intersexed conditions are part of the continuum of human morphology and ought to be treated with the presumption that their lives are and will be not only livable, but also occasions for flourishing. The norms that govern idealized human anatomy thus work to produce a differential sense of who is human and who is not, which lives are livable, and which are not. This differential works for a wide range of disabilities as well (although another norm is at work for invisible disabilities).

A concurrent operation of gender norms can be seen in the *DSM IV*'s Gender Identity Disorder diagnosis. This diagnosis that has, for the most part, taken over the role of monitoring signs of incipient homo-sexuality in children assumes that "gender dysphoria" is a psycholog-ical disorder simply because someone of a given gender manifests attributes of another gender or a desire to live as another gender. This imposes a model of coherent gendered life that demeans the complex ways in which gendered lives are crafted and lived. The diagnosis, however, is crucial for many individuals who seek insurance support for sex reassignment surgery or treatment, or who seek a legal change in status. As a result, the diagnostic means by which transsexuality is attributed implies a pathologization, but undergoing that pathologiz-ing process constitutes one of the important ways in which the desire to change one's sex might be satisfied. The critical question thus becomes, how might the world be reorganized so that this conflict can be ameliorated?

The recent efforts to promote lesbian and gay marriage also pro-mote a norm that threatens to render illegitimate and abject those sexual arrangements that do not comply with the marriage norm in either its existing or its revisable form. At the same time, the homo-phobic objections to lesbian and gay marriage expand out through the culture to affect all queer lives. One critical question thus becomes, how does one oppose the homophobia without embracing the marriage norm as the exclusive or most highly valued social arrangement for queer sexual lives? Similarly, efforts to establish bonds of kinship that are not based on a marriage tie become nearly illegible and unviable when marriage sets the terms for kinship, and kinship itself is collapsed into "family." The enduring social ties that constitute viable kinship in communities of sexual minorities are threatened with becoming unrecognizable and unviable as long as the marriage bond is the exclu-sive way in which both sexuality and kinship are organized. A critical relation to this norm involves disarticulating those rights and obliga-tions currently attendant upon marriage so that marriage might remain a symbolic exercise for those who choose to engage in it, but the rights and obligations of kinship may take any number of other forms. What reorganization of sexual norms would be necessary for those who live sexually and affectively outside the marriage bond or in kin relations to the side of marriage either to be legally and culturally recognized for the endurance and importance of their intimate ties or, equally important, to be free of the need for recognition of this kind?

If a decade or two ago, gender discrimination applied tacitly to women, that no longer serves as the exclusive framework for understanding its contemporary usage. Discrimination against women continues—especially poor women and women of color, if we consider the differential levels of poverty and literacy not only in the United States, but globally—so this dimension of gender discrimination remains crucial to acknowledge. But gender now also means gender identity, a particularly salient issue in the politics and theory of transgenderism and transsexuality. Transgender refers to those persons who cross-identify or who live as another gender, but who may or may not have undergone hormonal treatments or sex reassignment operations. Among transsexuals and transgendered persons, there are those who identify as men (if female to male) or women (if male to female), and yet others who, with or without surgery, with or without hormones, identify as *trans*, as transmen or transwomen; each of these social practices carries distinct social burdens and promises.

Colloquially, "transgender" can apply to the entire range of these positions as well. Transgendered and transsexual people are subjected to pathologization and violence that is, once again, heightened in the case of trans persons from communities of color. The harassment suffered by those who are "read" as trans or discovered to be trans cannot be underestimated. They are part of a continuum of the gender violence that took the lives of Brandon Teena, Mathew Shephard, and Gwen Araujo.[2] And these acts of murder must be understood in connection with the coercive acts of "correction" undergone by intersexed infants and children that often leave those bodies maimed for life, traumatized, and physically limited in their sexual functions and pleasures.

Although intersex and transsex sometimes seem to be movements at odds with one another, the first opposing unwanted surgery, the second sometimes calling for elective surgery, it is most important to see that both challenge the principle that a natural dimorphism should be established or maintained at all costs. Intersex activists work to rectify the erroneous assumption that every body has an inborn "truth" of sex that medical professionals can discern and bring to light on their own. To the extent that the intersex movement maintains that gender ought to be established through assignment or choice, but noncoercively, it shares a premise with transgendered and transsexual activism. The latter opposes forms of unwanted coercive gender assignment, and in this sense calls for greater claims of autonomy, a situation that parallels intersex claims as well. What precisely autonomy means, however, is complicated for both movements, since it turns out that choosing one's own body invariably means navigating among norms that are laid out in advance and prior to one's choice or are being articulated in concert by other minority agencies. Indeed, individuals rely on institutions of social support in order to exercise self-determination with respect to what body and what gender to have and maintain, so that self-determination becomes a plausible concept only in the context of a social world that supports and enables that exercise of agency. Conversely (and as a consequence), it turns out that changing the institutions by which humanly viable choice is established and maintained is a prerequisite for the exercise of self-determination. In this sense, individual agency is bound up with social critique and social transformation. One only determines "one's own" sense of gender to the extent that social norms exist that support and enable that act of claiming gender for oneself. One is dependent on this "outside" to lay claim to what is one's own. The self must, in this way, be dispossessed in sociality in order to take possession of itself.

One tension that arises between queer theory and both intersex and transsexual activism centers on the question of sex assignment and the desirability of identity categories. If queer theory is understood, by definition, to oppose all identity claims, including stable sex assignment, then the tension seems strong indeed. But I would suggest that more important than any presupposition about the plasticity of identity or indeed its retrograde status is queer theory's claim to be opposed to the unwanted legislation of identity. After all, queer theory and activism acquired political salience by insisting that antihomophobic activism can be engaged in by anyone, regardless of sexual orientation, and that identity markers are not prerequisites for political participation. In the same way that queer theory opposes those who would regulate identities or establish epistemological claims of priority for those who make claims to certain kinds of identities, it seeks not only to expand the community base of antihomophobic activism, but, rather, to insist that sexuality is not easily summarized or unified through categorization. It does not follow, therefore, that queer theory would oppose all gender assignment or cast doubt on the desires of those who wish to secure such assignments for intersex children, for instance, who may well need them to function socially even if they end up changing the assignment later in life, knowing the risks. The perfectly reasonable assumption here is that children do not need to take on the burden of being heroes for a movement without first assenting to such a role. In this sense, categorization has its place and cannot be reduced to forms of anatomical essentialism.

Similarly, the transsexual desire to become a man or a woman is not to be dismissed as a simple desire to conform to established identity categories. As Kate Bornstein points out, it can be a desire for transformation itself, a pursuit of identity as a transformative exercise, an example of desire itself as a transformative activity.[3] But even if there are, in each of these cases, desires for stable identity at work, it seems crucial to realize that a livable life does require various degrees of stability. In the same way that a life for which no categories of recognition exist is not a livable life, so a life for which those categories constitute unlivable constraint is not an acceptable option.

The task of all of these movements seems to me to be about distinguishing among the norms and conventions that permit people to breathe, to desire, to love, and to live, and those norms and conventions that restrict or eviscerate the conditions of life itself. Sometimes norms function both ways at once, and sometimes they function one way for a given group, and another way for another group. What is most important is to cease legislating for all lives what is livable only for some, and similarly, to refrain from proscribing for all lives what is unlivable for some. The differences in position and desire set the limits to universalizability as an ethical reflex. The critique of gender norms must be situated within the context of lives as they are lived and must be guided by the question of what maximizes the possibilities for a livable life, what minimizes the possibility of unbearable life or, indeed, social or literal death.

None of these movements is, in my view, postfeminist. They have all found important conceptual and political resources in feminism, and feminism continues to pose challenges to these movements and to function as an important ally. And just as it no longer works to consider "gender discrimination" as a code for discrimination against women, it would be equally unacceptable to propound a view of gender discrimination that did not take into account the differential ways in which women suffer from poverty and illiteracy, from employment discrimination, from a gendered division of labor within a global frame, and from violence, sexual and otherwise. The feminist framework that takes the structural domination of women as the starting point from which all other analyses of gender must proceed imperils its own viability by refusing to countenance the various ways that gender emerges as a political issue, bearing a specific set of social and physical risks. It is crucial to understand the workings of gender in global contexts, in transnational formations, not only to see what problems are posed for the term "gender" but to combat false forms of universalism that service a tacit or explicit cultural imperialism. That feminism has always countered violence against women, sexual and nonsexual, ought to serve as a basis for alliance with these other movements, since phobic violence against bodies is part of what joins antihomophobic, antiracist, feminist, trans, and intersex activism.

Although some feminists have worried in public that the trans movement constitutes an effort to displace or appropriate sexual difference, I think that this is only one version of feminism, one that is contested by views that take gender as an historical category, that the framework for understanding how it works is multiple and shifts through time and place. The view that transsexuals seek to escape the social condition of femininity because that condition is considered debased or lacks privileges accorded to men assumes that female-to-male (FTM) transsexuality can be definitively explained through recourse to that one framework for understanding femininity and masculinity. It tends to forget that the risks of discrimination, loss of employment, public harassment, and violence are heightened for those who live openly as transgendered persons. The view that the desire to become a man or a transman or to live transgendered is motivated by a repudiation of femininity presumes that every person born with female anatomy is therefore in possession of a proper femininity (whether innate, symbolically assumed, or socially assigned), one that can either be owned or disowned, appropriated or expropriated. Indeed, the critique of male-to-female (MTF) transsexuality has centered on the "appropriation" of femininity, as if it belongs properly to a given sex, as if sex is discretely given, as if gender identity could and should be derived unequivocally from presumed anatomy. To understand gender as a historical category, however, is to accept that gender, understood as one way of culturally configuring a body, is open to a continual remaking, and that "anatomy" and "sex" are not without cultural framing (as the intersex movement has clearly shown). The very attribution of femininity to female bodies as if it were a natural or necessary property takes place within a normative framework in which the assignment of femininity to femaleness is one mechanism for the production of gender itself. Terms such as "masculine" and "feminine" are notoriously changeable; there are social histories for each term; their meanings change radically depending upon geopolitical boundaries and cultural constraints on who is imagining whom, and for what purpose. That the terms recur is interesting enough, but the recurrence does not index a sameness, but rather the way in which the social articulation of the term depends upon its repetition, which constitutes one dimension of the performative structure of gender. Terms of gender designation are thus never settled once and for all but are constantly in the process of being remade.

The concept of gender as historical and performative, however, stands in tension with some versions of sexual difference, and some of the essays included here try to broach that divide within feminist theory. The view that sexual difference is a primary difference has come under criticism from several quarters. There are those who rightly argue that sexual difference is no more primary than racial or ethnic difference and that one cannot apprehend sexual difference outside of the racial and ethnic frames by which it is articulated. Those who claim that being produced by a mother and a father is crucial to all humans may well have a point. But are sperm donors or one-night stands, or indeed, rapists, really "fathers" in a social sense? Even if in some sense or under certain circumstances they are, do they not put the category into crisis for those who would assume that children without discernible fathers at their origin are subject to psychosis? If a sperm and egg are necessary for reproduction (and remain so)—and in that sense sexual difference is an essential part of any account a human may come up with about his or her origin—does it follow that this difference shapes the individual more profoundly than other constituting social forces, such as the economic or racial conditions by which one comes into being, the conditions of one's adoption, the sojourn at the orphanage? Is there very much that follows from the fact of an originating sexual difference?

Feminist work on reproductive technology has generated a host of ethical and political perspectives that have not only galvanized feminist studies but have made clear the implications for thinking about gender in relation to biotechnology, global politics, and the status of the human and life itself. Feminists who criticize technologies for effectively replacing the maternal body with a patriarchal apparatus must nevertheless contend with the enhanced autonomy that those technologies have provided for women. Feminists who embrace such technologies for the options they have produced nevertheless must come to terms with the uses to which those technologies can be put, ones that may well involve calculating the perfectibility of the human, sex selection, and racial selection. Those feminists who oppose technological innovations because they threaten to efface the primacy of sexual difference risk naturalizing heterosexual reproduction. The doctrine of sexual difference in this case comes to be in tension with antihomophobic struggles as well as with the intersex movement and the transgender movement's interest in securing rights to technologies that facilitate sex reassignment.

In each of these struggles, we see that technology is a site of power in which the human is produced and reproduced—not just the humanness of the child but also the humanness of those who bear and those who raise children, parents and nonparents alike. Gender likewise figures as a precondition for the production and maintenance of legible humanity. If there is important coalitional thinking to be done across these various movements, all of which comprise the New Gender Politics, it will doubtless have to do with presumptions about bodily dimorphism, the uses and abuses of technology, and the contested status of the human, and of life itself. If sexual difference is that which ought to be protected from effacement from a technology understood as phallocentric in its aims, then how do we distinguish between sexual difference and normative forms of dimorphism against which intersex and transgendered activists struggle on a daily basis? If technology is a resource to which some people want access, it is also an imposition from which others seek to be freed. Whether technology is imposed or elected is salient for intersex activists. If some trans people argue that their very sense of personhood depends upon having access to technology to secure certain bodily changes, some feminists argue that technology threatens to take over the business of making persons, running the risk that the human will become nothing other than a technological effect.

Similarly, the call for a greater recognition of bodily difference made by both disability movements and intersex activism invariably calls for a renewal of the value of life. Of course, "life" has been taken up by right-wing movements to limit reproductive freedoms for women, so the demand to establish more inclusive conditions for valuing life and producing the conditions for viable life can resonate with unwanted conservative demands to limit the autonomy of women to exercise the right to an abortion. But here it seems important not to cede the term "life" to a right-wing agenda, since it will turn out that there are within these debates questions about when human life begins and what constitutes "life" in its viability. The point is emphatically not to extend the "right to life" to any and all people who want to make this claim on behalf of mute embryos, but rather to understand how the "viability" of a woman's life depends upon an exercise of bodily autonomy and on social conditions that enable that autonomy. Moreover, as in the case with those seeking to overcome the pathologizing effects of a gender identity disorder diagnosis, we are referring to forms of autonomy that require social (and legal) support and protection, and that exercise a transformation on the norms that govern how agency itself is differentially allocated among genders; thus, a women's right to choose remains, in some contexts, a misnomer.

Critiques of anthropocentrism have made clear that when we speak about human life we are indexing a being who is at once human and living, and that the range of living beings exceeds the human. In a way, the term "human life" designates an unwieldy combination, since "human" does not simply qualify "life," but "life" relates human to what is nonhuman and living, establishing the human in the midst of this relationality. For the human to be human, it must relate to what is nonhuman, to what is outside itself but continuous with itself by virtue of an interimplication in life. This relation to what is not itself constitutes the human being in its livingness, so that the human exceeds its boundary in the very effort to establish them. To make the claim, "I am an animal," avows in a distinctively human language that the human is not distinct. This paradox makes it imperative to separate the question of a livable life from the status of a human life, since livability pertains to living beings that exceed the human. In addition, we would be foolish to think that life is fully possible without a dependence on technology, which suggests that the human, in its animality, is dependent on technology, to live. In this sense, we are thinking within the frame of the cyborg as we call into question the status of the human and that of the livable life.

The rethinking of the human in these terms does not entail a return to humanism. When Frantz Fanon claimed that "the black is not a man," he conducted a critique of humanism that showed that the human in its contemporary articulation is so fully racialized that no black man could qualify as human.[4] In his usage, the formulation was also a critique of masculinity, implying that the black man is effeminized. And the implication of that formulation would be that no one who is not a "man" in the masculine sense is a human, suggesting that both masculinity and racial privilege shore up the notion of the human. His formulation has been extended by contemporary scholars, including the literary critic Sylvia Wynter, to pertain to women of color as well and to call into question the racist frameworks within which the category of the human has been articulated.[5] These formulations show the power differentials embedded in the construction of the category of the "human" and, at the same time, insist upon the historicity of the term, the fact that the "human" has been crafted and consolidated over time.

The category of the "human" retains within itself the workings of the power differential of race as part of its own historicity. But the history of the category is not over, and the "human" is not captured once and for all. That the category is crafted in time, and that it works through excluding a wide range of minorities means that its rearticulation will begin precisely at the point where the excluded speak to and from such a category. If Fanon writes that "a black is not a man," who writes when Fanon writes? That we can ask the "who" means that the human has exceeded its categorical definition, and that he is in and through the utterance opening up the category to a different future. If there are norms of recognition by which the "human" is constituted, and these norms encode operations of power, then it follows that the contest over the future of the "human" will be a contest over the power that works in and through such norms. That power emerges in language in a restrictive way or, indeed, in other modes of articulation as that which tries to stop the articulation as it nevertheless moves forward. That double movement is found in the utterance, the image, the action that articulates the struggle with the norm. Those deemed illegible, unrecognizable, or impossible nevertheless speak in the terms of the "human," opening the term to a history not fully constrained by the existing differentials of power.

These questions form in part an agenda for the future that one hopes will bring a host of scholars and activists together to craft wide-ranging frameworks within which to broach these urgent and complex issues. These issues are clearly related to changes in kinship structure, debates on gay marriage, conditions for adoption, and access to reproductive technology. Part of rethinking where and how the human comes into being will involve a rethinking of both the social and psychic landscapes of an infant's emergence. Changes at the level of kinship similarly demand a reconsideration of the social conditions under which humans are born and reared, opening up new territory for social and psychological analysis as well as the sites of their convergence.

Psychoanalysis has sometimes been used to shore up the notion of a primary sexual difference that forms the core of an individual's psychic life. But there it would seem that sexual difference gains its salience only through assuming that sperm and egg imply heterosexual parental coitus, and then a number of other psychic realities, such as the primal scene and oedipal scenario. But if the egg or sperm comes from elsewhere, and is not attached to a person called "parent," or if the parents who are making love are not heterosexual or not reproductive, then it would seem that a new psychic topography is required. Of course, it is possible to presume, as many French psychoanalysts have done, that reproduction follows universally from heterosexual parental coitus, and that this fact provides a psychic condition for the human subject. This view proceeds to condemn forms of nonheterosexual unions, reproductive technology, and parenting outside of nuclear heterosexual marriage as damaging for the child, threatening to culture, destructive of the human. But this recruitment of psychoanalytic vocabularies for the purpose of preserving the paternal line, the transmission of national cultures, and heterosexual marriage is only one use of psychoanalysis, and not a particularly productive or necessary one.

It is important to remember that psychoanalysis can also serve as a critique of cultural adaptation as well as a theory for understanding the ways in which sexuality fails to conform to the social norms by which it is regulated. Moreover, there is no better theory for grasping the workings of fantasy construed not as a set of projections on an internal screen but as part of human relationality itself. It is on the basis of this insight that we can come to understand how fantasy is essential to an experience of one's own body, or that of another, as gendered. Finally, psychoanalysis can work in the service of a conception of humans as bearing an irreversible humility in their relations to others and to themselves. There is always a dimension of ourselves and our relation to others that we cannot know, and this not-knowing persists with us as a condition of existence and, indeed, of survivability. We are, to an extent, driven by what we do not know, and cannot know, and this "drive" (*Trieb*) is precisely what is neither exclusively biological nor cultural, but always the site of their dense convergence.[6] If I am always constituted by norms that are not of my making, then I have to understand the ways that constitution takes place. The staging and structuring of affect and desire is clearly one way in which norms work their way into what feels most properly to belong to me. The fact that I am other to myself precisely at the place where I expect to be myself follows from the fact that the sociality of norms exceeds my inception and my demise, sustaining a temporal and spatial field of operation that exceeds my self-understanding. Norms do not exercise a final or fatalistic control, at least, not always. The fact that desire is not fully determined corresponds with the psychoanalytic understanding that sexuality is never fully captured by any regulation. Rather, it is characterized by displacement, it can exceed regulation, take on new forms in response to regulation, even turn around and make it sexy. In this sense, sexuality is never fully reducible to the "effect" of this or that operation of regulatory power. This is not the same as saying that sexuality is, by nature, free and wild. On the contrary, it emerges precisely as an improvisational possibility within a field of constraints. Sexuality, though, is not found to be "in" those constraints as something might be "in" a container: it is extinguished by constraints, but also mobilized and incited by constraints, even sometimes requiring them to be produced again and again.

It would follow, then, that to a certain extent sexuality establishes us as outside of ourselves; we are motivated by an elsewhere whose full meaning and purpose we cannot definitively establish.[7] This is only because sexuality is one way cultural meanings are carried, through both the operation of norms and the peripheral modes of their undoing.

Sexuality does not follow from gender in the sense that what gender you "are" determines what kind of sexuality you will "have." We try to speak in ordinary ways about these matters, stating our gender, disclosing our sexuality, but we are, quite inadvertently, caught up in ontological thickets and epistemological quandaries. Am I a gender after all? And do I "have" a sexuality?

Or does it turn out that the "I" who ought to be bearing its gender is undone by being a gender, that gender is always coming from a source that is elsewhere and directed toward something that is beyond me, constituted in a sociality I do not fully author? If that is so, then gender undoes the "I" who is supposed to be or bear its gender, and that undoing is part of the very meaning and comprehensibility of that "I." If I claim to "have" a sexuality, then it would seem that a sexuality is there for me to call my own, to possess as an attribute. But what if sexuality is the means by which I am dispossessed? What if it is invested and animated from elsewhere even as it is precisely mine? Does it not follow, then, that the "I" who would "have" its sexuality is undone by the sexuality it claims to have, and that its very "claim" can no longer be made exclusively in its own name? If I am claimed by others when I make my claim, if gender is for and from another before it becomes my own, if sexuality entails a certain dispossession of the "I," this does not spell the end to my political claims. It only means that when one makes those claims, one makes them for much more than oneself.

1. Beside Oneself: On the Limits of Sexual Autonomy

What makes for a livable world is no idle question. It is not merely a question for philosophers. It is posed in various idioms all the time by people in various walks of life. If that makes them all philosophers, then that is a conclusion I am happy to embrace. It becomes a question for ethics, I think, not only when we ask the personal question, what makes my own life bearable, but when we ask, from a position of power, and from the point of view of distributive justice, what makes, or ought to make, the lives of others bearable? Somewhere in the answer we find ourselves not only committed to a certain view of what life is, and what it should be, but also of what constitutes the human, the distinctively human life, and what does not. There is always a risk of anthropocentrism here if one assumes that the distinctively human life is valuable—or most valuable—or is the only way to think the problem of value. But perhaps to counter that tendency it is necessary to ask both the question of life and the question of the human, and not to let them fully collapse into one another.

I would like to start, and to end, with the question of the human, of who counts as the human, and the related question of whose lives count as lives, and with a question that has preoccupied many of us for years: what makes for a grievable life? I believe that whatever differences exist within the international gay and lesbian community, and there are many, we all have some notion of what it is to have lost somebody. And if we've lost, then it seems to follow that we have had, that we have desired and loved, and struggled to find the conditions for our desire. We have all lost someone in recent decades from AIDS, but there are other losses that inflict us, other diseases; moreover, we are, as a community, subjected to violence, even if some of us individually have not been. And this means that we are constituted politically in part by virtue of the social vulnerability of our bodies; we are constituted as fields of desire and physical vulnerability, at once publicly assertive and vulnerable.

I am not sure I know when mourning is successful, or when one has fully mourned another human being. I'm certain, though, that it does not mean that one has forgotten the person, or that something else comes along to take his or her place. I don't think it works that way. I think instead that one mourns when one accepts the fact that the loss one undergoes will be one that changes you, changes you possibly forever, and that mourning has to do with agreeing to undergo a transformation the full result of which you cannot know in advance. So there is losing, and there is the transformative effect of loss, and this latter cannot be charted or planned. I don't think, for instance, you can invoke a Protestant ethic when it comes to loss. You can't say, "Oh, I'll go through loss this way, and that will be the result, and I'll apply myself to the task, and I'll endeavor to achieve the resolution of grief that is before me." I think one is hit by waves, and that one starts out the day with an aim, a project, a plan, and one finds oneself foiled. One finds oneself fallen. One is exhausted but does not know why. Something is larger than one's own deliberate plan or project, larger than one's own knowing. Something takes hold, but is this something coming from the self, from the outside, or from some region where the difference between the two is indeterminable? What is it that claims us at such moments, such that we are not the masters of ourselves? To what are we tied? And by what are we seized?

It may seem that one is undergoing something temporary, but it could be that in this experience something about who we are is revealed, something that delineates the ties we have to others, that shows us that those ties constitute a sense of self, compose who we are, and that when we lose them, we lose our composure in some fundamental sense: we do not know who we are or what to do. Many people think that grief is privatizing, that it returns us to a solitary situation, but I think it exposes the constitutive sociality of the self, a basis for thinking a political community of a complex order.

It is not just that I might be said to "have" these relations, or that I might sit back and view them at a distance, enumerating them, explaining what this friendship means, what that lover meant or means to me. On the contrary, grief displays the way in which we are in the thrall of our relations with others that we cannot always recount or explain, that often interrupts the self-conscious account of ourselves we might try to provide in ways that challenge the very notion of ourselves as autonomous and in control. I might try to tell a story about what I am feeling, but it would have to be a story in which the very "I" who seeks to tell the story is stopped in the midst of the telling. The very "I" is called into question by its relation to the one to whom I address myself. This relation to the Other does not precisely ruin my story or reduce me to speechlessness, but it does, invariably, clutter my speech with signs of its undoing.

Let's face it. We're undone by each other. And if we're not, we're missing something. If this seems so clearly the case with grief, it is only because it was already the case with desire. One does not always stay intact. It may be that one wants to, or does, but it may also be that despite one's best efforts, one is undone, in the face of the other, by the touch, by the scent, by the feel, by the prospect of the touch, by the memory of the feel. And so when we speak about *my* sexuality or *my* gender, as we do (and as we must) we mean something complicated by it. Neither of these is precisely a possession, but both are to be understood as *modes of being dispossessed*, ways of being for another or, indeed, by virtue of another. It does not suffice to say that I am promoting a relational view of the self over an autonomous one, or trying to redescribe autonomy in terms of relationality. The term "relationality" sutures the rupture in the relation we seek to describe, a rupture that is constitutive of identity itself. This means that we will have to approach the problem of conceptualizing dispossession with circumspection. One way of doing this is through the notion of ecstasy.

We tend to narrate the history of the broader movement for sexual freedom in such a way that ecstasy figures in the 60s and 70s and

persists midway through the 80s. But maybe ecstasy is more historically persistent than that, maybe it is with us all along. To be ec-static
means, literally, to be outside oneself, and this can have several meanings: to be transported beyond oneself by a passion, but also to be *beside
oneself* with rage or grief. I think that if I can still speak to a "we,"
and include myself within its terms, I am speaking to those of us who
are living in certain ways *beside ourselves*, whether it is in sexual passion, or emotional grief, or political rage. In a sense, the predicament
is to understand what kind of community is composed of those who
are beside themselves.

We have an interesting political predicament, since most of the time
when we hear about "rights," we understand them as pertaining to
individuals, or when we argue for protection against discrimination,
we argue as a group or a class. And in that language and in that context, we have to present ourselves as bounded beings, distinct, recognizable, delineated, subjects before the law, a community defined by
sameness. Indeed, we had better be able to use that language to secure
legal protections and entitlements. But perhaps we make a mistake if
we take the definitions of who we are, legally, to be adequate descriptions of what we are about. Although this language might well establish
our legitimacy within a legal framework ensconced in liberal versions
of human ontology, it fails to do justice to passion and grief and rage,
all of which tear us from ourselves, bind us to others, transport us,
undo us, and implicate us in lives that are not are own, sometimes
fatally, irreversibly.

It is not easy to understand how a political community is wrought
from such ties. One speaks, and one speaks for another, to another,
and yet there is no way to collapse the distinction between the other
and myself. When we say "we" we do nothing more than designate
this as very problematic. We do not solve it. And perhaps it is, and
ought to be, insoluble. We ask that the state, for instance, keep its laws
off our bodies, and we call for principles of bodily self-defense and
bodily integrity to be accepted as political goods. Yet, it is through the
body that gender and sexuality become exposed to others, implicated
in social processes, inscribed by cultural norms, and apprehended in
their social meanings. In a sense, to be a body is to be given over to
others even as a body is, emphatically, "one's own," that over which
we must claim rights of autonomy. This is as true for the claims made

by lesbians, gays, and bisexuals in favor of sexual freedom as it is for transsexual and transgender claims to self-determination; as it is for intersex claims to be free of coerced medical, surgical, and psychiatric interventions; as it is for all claims to be free from racist attacks, physical and verbal; and as it is for feminism's claim to reproductive freedom. It is difficult, if not impossible, to make these claims without recourse to autonomy and, specifically, a sense of bodily autonomy. Bodily autonomy, however, is a lively paradox. I am not suggesting, though, that we cease to make these claims. We have to, we must. And I'm not saying that we have to make these claims reluctantly or strategically. They are part of the normative aspiration of any movement that seeks to maximize the protection and the freedoms of sexual and gender minorities, of women, defined with the broadest possible compass, of racial and ethnic minorities, especially as they cut across all the other categories. But is there another normative aspiration that we must also seek to articulate and to defend? Is there a way in which the place of the body in all of these struggles opens up a different conception of politics?

The body implies mortality, vulnerability, agency: the skin and the flesh expose us to the gaze of others but also to touch and to violence. The body can be the agency and instrument of all these as well, or the site where "doing" and "being done to" become equivocal. Although we struggle for rights over our own bodies, the very bodies for which we struggle are not quite ever only our own. The body has its invariably public dimension; constituted as a social phenomenon in the public sphere, my body is and is not mine. Given over from the start to the world of others, bearing their imprint, formed within the crucible of social life, the body is only later, and with some uncertainty, that to which I lay claim as my own. Indeed, if I seek to deny the fact that my body relates me—against my will and from the start—to others I do not choose to have in proximity to myself (the subway or the tube are excellent examples of this dimension of sociality), and if I build a notion of "autonomy" on the basis of the denial of this sphere or a primary and unwilled physical proximity with others, then do I precisely deny the social and political conditions of my embodiment in the name of autonomy? If I am struggling *for* autonomy, do I not need to be struggling for something else as well, a conception of myself as invariably in community, impressed upon by others, impressing them as well, and in ways that are not always clearly delineable, in forms that are not fully predictable?

Is there a way that we might struggle for autonomy in many spheres but also consider the demands that are imposed upon us by living in a world of beings who are, by definition, physically dependent on one another, physically vulnerable to one another. Is this not another way of imagining community in such a way that it becomes incumbent upon us to consider very carefully when and where we engage violence, for violence is, always, an exploitation of that primary tie, that primary way in which we are, as bodies, outside ourselves, for one another.

If we might then return to the problem of grief, to the moments in which one undergoes something outside of one's control and finds that one is beside oneself, not at one with oneself, we can say grief contains within it the possibility of apprehending the fundamental sociality of embodied life, the ways in which we are from the start, and by virtue of being a bodily being, already given over, beyond ourselves, implicated in lives that are not our own. Can this situation, one that is so dramatic for sexual minorities, one that establishes a very specific political perspective for anyone who works in the field of sexual and gender politics, supply a perspective with which to begin to apprehend the contemporary global situation?

Mourning, fear, anxiety, rage. In the United States after September 11, 2001, we have been everywhere surrounded with violence, of having perpetrated it, having suffered it, living in fear of it, planning more of it. Violence is surely a touch of the worst order, a way in which the human vulnerability to other humans is exposed in its most terrifying way, a way in which we are given over, without control, to the will of another, the way in which life itself can be expunged by the willful action of another. To the extent that we commit violence, we are acting upon another, putting others at risk, causing damage to others. In a way, we all live with this particular vulnerability, a vulnerability to the other that is part of bodily life, but this vulnerability becomes highly exacerbated under certain social and political conditions. Although the dominant mode in the United States has been to shore up sovereignty and security to minimize or, indeed, foreclose this vulnerability, it can serve another function and another ideal. The fact that our lives are dependent on others can become the basis of claims for nonmilitaristic political solutions, one which we cannot will away, one which we must attend to, even abide by, as we begin to think about what politics might be implied by staying with the thought of corporeal vulnerability itself.

Is there something to be gained from grieving, from tarrying with grief, remaining exposed to its apparent tolerability and not endeavoring to seek a resolution for grief through violence? Is there something to be gained in the political domain by maintaining grief as part of the framework by which we think our international ties? If we stay with the sense of loss, are we left feeling only passive and powerless, as some fear? Or are we, rather, returned to a sense of human vulnerability, to our collective responsibility for the physical lives of one another? The attempt to foreclose that vulnerability, to banish it, to make ourselves secure at the expense every other human consideration, is surely also to eradicate one of the most important resources from which we must take our bearings and find our way.

To grieve, and to make grief itself into a resource for politics, is not to be resigned to a simple passivity or powerlessness. It is, rather, to allow oneself to extrapolate from this experience of vulnerability to the vulnerability that others suffer through military incursions, occupations, suddenly declared wars, and police brutality. That our very survival can be determined by those we do not know and over whom there is no final control means that life is precarious, and that politics must consider what forms of social and political organization seek best to sustain precarious lives across the globe.

There is a more general conception of the human at work here, one in which we are, from the start, given over to the other, one in which we are, from the start, even prior to individuation itself, and by virtue of our embodiment, given over to an other: this makes us vulnerable to violence, but also to another range of touch, a range that includes the eradication of our being at the one end, and the physical support for our lives, at the other.

We cannot endeavor to "rectify" this situation. And we cannot recover the source of this vulnerability, for it precedes the formation of "I." This condition of being laid bare from the start, dependent on those we do not know is, one with which we cannot precisely argue. We come into the world unknowing and dependent, and, to a certain degree, we remain that way. We can try, from the point of view of autonomy, to argue with this situation, but we are perhaps foolish, if not dangerous, when we do. Of course, we can say that for some this primary scene is extraordinary, loving, and receptive, a warm tissue of relations that support and nurture life in its infancy. For others, this is, however, a scene of abandonment or violence or starvation; they are bodies given over to nothing, or to brutality, or to no sustenance. No matter what the valence of that scene is, however, the fact remains that infancy constitutes a necessary dependency, one that we never fully leave behind. Bodies still must be apprehended as given over. Part of understanding the oppression of lives is precisely to understand that there is no way to argue away this condition of a primary vulnerability, of being given over to the touch of the other, even if, or precisely when, there is no other there, and no support for our lives. To counter oppression requires that one understand that lives are supported and maintained differentially, that there are radically different ways in which human physical vulnerability is distributed across the globe. Certain lives will be highly protected, and the abrogation of their claims to sanctity will be sufficient to mobilize the forces of war. And other lives will not find such fast and furious support and will not even qualify as "grievable."

What are the cultural contours of the notion of the human at work here? And how do the contours that we accept as the cultural frame for the human limit the extent to which we can avow loss as loss? This is surely a question that lesbian, gay, and bi-studies has asked in relation to violence against sexual minorities, and that transgendered people have asked as they have been singled out for harassment and sometimes murder, and that intersexed people have asked, whose formative years have so often been marked by an unwanted violence against their bodies in the name of a normative notion of human morphology. This is no doubt as well the basis of a profound affinity between movements centered on gender and sexuality with efforts to counter the normative human morphologies and capacities that condemn or efface those who are physically challenged. It must, as well, also be part of the affinity with antiracist struggles, given the racial differential that undergirds the culturally viable notions of the human—ones that we see acted out in dramatic and terrifying ways in the global arena at the present time.

So what is the relation between violence and what is "unreal," between violence and unreality that attends to those who become the victims of violence, and where does the notion of the ungrievable life come in? On the level of discourse, certain lives are not considered lives at all, they cannot be humanized; they fit no dominant frame for the human, and their dehumanization occurs first, at this level. This level then gives rise to a physical violence that in some sense delivers the message of dehumanization which is already at work in the culture.

So it is not just that a discourse exists in which there is no frame and no story and no name for such a life, or that violence might be said to realize or apply this discourse. Violence against those who are already not quite lives, who are living in a state of suspension between life and death, leaves a mark that is no mark. If there is a discourse, it is a silent and melancholic writing in which there have been no lives, and no losses, there has been no common physical condition, no vulnerability that serves as the basis for an apprehension of our commonality, and there has been no sundering of that commonality. None of this takes place on the order of the event. None of this takes place. How many lives have been lost from AIDS in Africa in the last few years? Where are the media representations of this loss, the discursive elaborations of what these losses mean for communities there?

I began this chapter with a suggestion that perhaps the interrelated movements and modes of inquiry that collect here might need to consider autonomy as one dimension of their normative aspirations, one value to realize when we ask ourselves, in what direction ought we to proceed, and what kinds of values ought we to be realizing? I suggested as well that the way in which the body figures in gender and sexuality studies, and in the struggles for a less oppressive social world for the otherwise gendered and for sexual minorities of all kinds, is precisely to underscore the value of being beside oneself, of being a porous boundary, given over to others, finding oneself in a trajectory of desire in which one is taken out of oneself, and resituated irreversibly in a field of others in which one is not the presumptive center. The particular sociality that belongs to bodily life, to sexual life, and to becoming gendered (which is always, to a certain extent, becoming gendered *for others*) establishes a field of ethical enmeshment with others and a sense of disorientation for the first-person, that is, the perspective of the ego. As bodies, we are always for something more than, and other than, ourselves. To articulate this as an entitlement is not always easy, but perhaps not impossible. It suggests, for instance, that "association" is not a luxury, but one of the very conditions and prerogatives of freedom. Indeed, the kinds of associations we maintain importantly take many forms. It will not do to extol the marriage norm as the new ideal for this movement, as the Human Rights Campaign has erroneously done.[1] No doubt, marriage and same-sex domestic partnerships should certainly be available as options, but to install either as a model for sexual legitimacy is precisely to constrain the sociality of the body in acceptable ways. In light of seriously damaging judicial decisions against second parent adoptions in recent years, it is crucial to expand our notions of kinship beyond the heterosexual frame. It would be a mistake, however, to reduce kinship to family, or to assume that all sustaining community and friendship ties are extrapolations of kin relations.

I make the argument in "Is Kinship Always Already Heterosexual" in this volume that kinship ties that bind persons to one another may well be no more or less than the intensification of community ties, may or may not be based on enduring or exclusive sexual relations, may well consist of ex-lovers, nonlovers, friends, and community members. The relations of kinship cross the boundaries between community and family and sometimes redefine the meaning of friendship as well. When these modes of intimate association produce sustaining webs of relationships, they constitute a "breakdown" of traditional kinship that displaces the presumption that biological and sexual relations structure kinship centrally. In addition, the incest taboo that governs kinship ties, producing a necessary exogamy, does not necessarily operate among friends in the same way or, for that matter, in networks of communities. Within these frames, sexuality is no longer exclusively regulated by the rules of kinship at the same time that the durable tie can be situated outside of the conjugal frame. Sexuality becomes open to a number of social articulations that do not always imply binding relations or conjugal ties. That not all of our relations last or are meant to, however, does not mean that we are immune to grief. On the contrary, sexuality outside the field of monogamy well may open us to a different sense of community, intensifying the question of where one finds enduring ties, and so become the condition for an attunement to losses that exceed a discretely private realm.

Nevertheless, those who live outside the conjugal frame or maintain modes of social organization for sexuality that are neither monogamous nor quasi-marital are more and more considered unreal, and their loves and losses less than "true" loves and "true" losses. The derealization of this domain of human intimacy and sociality works by denying reality and truth to the relations at issue.

The question of who and what is considered real and true is apparently a question of knowledge. But it is also, as Michel Foucault makes plain, a question of power. Having or bearing "truth" and "reality" is an enormously powerful prerogative within the social world, one way that power dissimulates as ontology. According to Foucault, one of the first tasks of a radical critique is to discern the relation "between mechanisms of coercion and elements of knowledge."[2] Here we are confronted with the limits of what is knowable, limits that exercise a certain force, but are not grounded in any necessity, limits that can only be tread or interrogated by risking a certain security through departing from an established ontology: "[N]othing can exist as an element of knowledge if, on the one hand, it . . . does not conform to a set of rules and constraints characteristic, for example, of a given type of scientific discourse in a given period, and if, on the other hand, it does not possess the effects of coercion or simply the incentives peculiar to what is scientifically validated or simply rational or simply generally accepted, etc."[3] Knowledge and power are not finally separable but work together to establish a set of subtle and explicit criteria for thinking the world: "It is therefore not a matter of describing what knowledge is and what power is and how one would repress the other or how the other would abuse the one, but rather, a nexus of knowledge-power has to be described so that we can grasp what constitutes the acceptability of a system . . . ."[4]

What this means is that one looks *both* for the conditions by which the object field is constituted, and for *the limits* of those conditions. The limits are to be found where the reproducibility of the conditions is not secure, the site where conditions are contingent, transformable. In Foucault's terms, "schematically speaking, we have perpetual mobility, essential fragility or rather the complex interplay between what replicates the same process and what transforms it."[5] To intervene in the name of transformation means precisely to disrupt what has become settled knowledge and knowable reality, and to use, as it were, one's unreality to make an otherwise impossible or illegible claim. I think that when the unreal lays claim to reality, or enters into its domain, something other than a simple assimilation into prevailing norms can and does take place. The norms themselves can become rattled, display their instability, and become open to resignification.

In recent years, the new gender politics has offered numerous challenges from transgendered and transsexual peoples to established feminist and lesbian/gay frameworks, and the intersex movement has rendered more complex the concerns and demands of sexual rights advocates. If some on the Left thought that these concerns were not properly or substantively political, they have been under pressure to rethink the political sphere in terms of its gendered and sexual presuppositions. The suggestion that butch, femme, and transgendered lives are not essential referents for a refashioning of political life, and for a more just and equitable society, fails to acknowledge the violence that the otherwise gendered suffer in the public world and fails as well to recognize that embodiment denotes a contested set of norms governing who will count as a viable subject within the sphere of politics. Indeed, if we consider that human bodies are not experienced without recourse to some ideality, some frame for experience itself, and that this is as true for the experience of one's own body as it is for experiencing another, and if we accept that that ideality and frame are socially articulated, we can see how it is that embodiment is not thinkable without a relation to a norm, or a set of norms. The struggle to rework the norms by which bodies are experienced is thus crucial not only to disability politics, but to the intersex and transgendered movements as they contest forcibly imposed ideals of what bodies ought to be like. The embodied relation to the norm exercises a transformative potential. To posit possibilities beyond the norm or, indeed, a different future for the norm itself, is part of the work of fantasy when we understand fantasy as taking the body as a point of departure for an articulation that is not always constrained by the body as it is. If we accept that altering these norms that decide normative human morphology give differential "reality" to different kinds of humans as a result, then we are compelled to affirm that transgendered lives have a potential and actual impact on political life at its most fundamental level, that is, who counts as a human, and what norms govern the appearance of "real" humanness.

Moreover, fantasy is part of the articulation of the possible; it moves us beyond what is merely actual and present into a realm of possibility, the not yet actualized or the not actualizable. The struggle to survive is not really separable from the cultural life of fantasy, and the foreclosure of fantasy—through censorship, degradation, or other means—is one strategy for providing for the social death of persons. Fantasy is not the opposite of reality; it is what reality forecloses, and, as a result, it defines the limits of reality, constituting it as its constitutive outside. The critical promise of fantasy, when and where it exists, is to challenge the contingent limits of what will and will not be called reality. Fantasy is what allows us to imagine ourselves and others otherwise; it establishes the possible in excess of the real; it points elsewhere, and when it is embodied, it brings the elsewhere home.

How do drag, butch, femme, transgender, transsexual persons enter into the political field? They make us not only question what is real, and what "must" be, but they also show us how the norms that govern contemporary notions of reality can be questioned and how new modes of reality can become instituted. These practices of instituting new modes of reality take place in part through the scene of embodiment, where the body is not understood as a static and accomplished fact, but as an aging process, a mode of becoming that, in becoming otherwise, exceeds the norm, reworks the norm, and makes us see how realities to which we thought we were confined are not written in stone. Some people have asked me what is the use of increasing possibilities for gender. I tend to answer: Possibility is not a luxury; it is as crucial as bread. I think we should not underestimate what the thought of the possible does for those for whom the very issue of survival is most urgent. If the answer to the question, is life possible, is yes, that is surely something significant. It cannot, however, be taken for granted as the answer. That is a question whose answer is sometimes "no," or one that has no ready answer, or one that bespeaks an ongoing agony. For many who can and do answer the question in the affirmative, that answer is hard won, if won at all, an accomplishment that is fundamentally conditioned by reality being structured or restructured in such a way that the affirmation becomes possible.

One of the central tasks of lesbian and gay international rights is to assert in clear and public terms the reality of homosexuality, not as an inner truth, not as a sexual practice, but as one of the defining features of the social world in its very intelligibility. In other words, it is one thing to assert the reality of lesbian and gay lives as a reality, and to insist that these are lives worthy of protection in their specificity and commonality; but it is quite another to insist that the very public assertion of gayness calls into question what counts as reality and what counts as a human life. Indeed, the task of international lesbian and gay politics is no less than a remaking of reality, a reconstituting of the human, and a brokering of the question, what is and is not livable? So what is the injustice opposed by such work? I would put it this way: to be called unreal and to have that call, as it were, institutionalized as a form of differential treatment, is to become the other against whom (or against which) the human is made. It is the inhuman, the beyond the human, the less than human, the border that secures the human in its ostensible reality. To be called a copy, to be called unreal, is one way in which one can be oppressed, but consider that it is more fundamental than that. To be oppressed means that you already exist as a subject of some kind, you are there as the visible and oppressed other for the master subject, as a possible or potential subject, but to be unreal is something else again. To be oppressed you must first become intelligible. To find that you are fundamentally unintelligible (indeed, that the laws of culture and of language find you to be an impossibility) is to find that you have not yet achieved access to the human, to find yourself speaking only and always *as if you were* human, but with the sense that you are not, to find that your language is hollow, that no recognition is forthcoming because the norms by which recognition takes place are not in your favor.

We might think that the question of how one does one's gender is a merely cultural question, or an indulgence on the part of those who insist on exercising bourgeois freedom in excessive dimensions. To say, however, that gender is performative is not simply to insist on a right to produce a pleasurable and subversive spectacle but to allegorize the spectacular and consequential ways in which reality is both reproduced and contested. This has consequences for how gender presentations are criminalized and pathologized, how subjects who cross gender risk internment and imprisonment, why violence against transgendered subjects is not recognized as violence, and why this violence is sometimes inflicted by the very states that should be offering such subjects protection from violence.

What if new forms of gender are possible? How does this affect the ways that we live and the concrete needs of the human community? And how are we to distinguish between forms of gender possibility that are valuable and those that are not? I would say that it is not a question merely of producing a new future for genders that do not yet exist. The genders I have in mind have been in existence for a long time, but they have not been admitted into the terms that govern reality. So it is a question of developing within law, psychiatry, social, and literary theory a new legitimating lexicon for the gender complexity that we have been living for a long time. Because the norms governing reality have not admitted these forms to be real, we will, of necessity, call them "new."

What place does the thinking of the possible have within political theorizing? Is the problem that we have no norm to distinguish among kinds of possibility, or does that only appear to be a problem if we fail to comprehend "possibility" itself as a norm? Possibility is an aspiration, something we might hope will be equitably distributed, something that might be socially secured, something that cannot be taken for granted, especially if it is apprehended phenomenologically. The point is not to prescribe new gender norms, as if one were under an obligation to supply a measure, gauge, or norm for the adjudication of competing gender presentations. The normative aspiration at work here has to do with the ability to live and breathe and move and would no doubt belong somewhere in what is called a philosophy of freedom. The thought of a possible life is only an indulgence for those who already know themselves to be possible. For those who are still looking to become possible, possibility is a necessity.

It was Spinoza who claimed that every human being seeks to persist in his own being, and he made this principle of self-persistence, the *conatus*, into the basis of his ethics and, indeed, his politics. When Hegel made the claim that desire is always a desire for recognition, he was, in a way, extrapolating upon this Spinozistic point, telling us, effectively, that to persist in one's own being is only possible on the condition that we are engaged in receiving and offering recognition. If we are not recognizable, if there are no norms of recognition by which we are recognizable, then it is not possible to persist in one's own being, and we are not possible beings; we have been foreclosed from possibility. We think of norms of recognition perhaps as residing already in a cultural world into which we are born, but these norms change, and with the changes in these norms come changes in what does and does not count as recognizably human. To twist the Hegelian argument in a Foucaultian direction: norms of recognition function to produce and to deproduce the notion of the human. This is made true in a specific way when we consider how international norms work in the context of lesbian and gay human rights, especially as they insist that certain kinds of violences are impermissable, that certain lives are vulnerable and worthy of protection, that certain deaths are grievable and worthy of public recognition.

To say that the desire to persist in one's own being depends on norms of recognition is to say that the basis of one's autonomy, one's persistence as an "I" through time, depends fundamentally on a social norm that exceeds that "I," that positions that "I" ec-statically, outside of itself in a world of complex and historically changing norms. In effect, our lives, our very persistence, depend upon such norms or, at least, on the possibility that we will be able to negotiate within them, derive our agency from the field of their operation. In our very ability to persist, we are dependent on what is outside of us, on a broader sociality, and this dependency is the basis of our endurance and survivability. When we assert our "right," as we do and we must, we are not carving out a place for our autonomy—if by autonomy we mean a state of individuation, taken as self-persisting prior to and apart from any relations of dependency on the world of others. We do not negotiate with norms or with Others subsequent to our coming into the world. We come into the world on the condition that the social world is already there, laying the groundwork for us. This implies that I cannot persist without norms of recognition that support my persistence: the sense of possibility pertaining to me must first be imagined from somewhere else before I can begin to imagine myself. My reflexivity is not only socially mediated, but socially constituted. I cannot be who I am without drawing upon the sociality of norms that precede and exceed me. In this sense, I am outside myself from the outset, and must be, in order to survive, and in order to enter into the realm of the possible.

To assert sexual rights, then, takes on a specific meaning against this background. It means, for instance, that when we struggle for rights, we are not simply struggling for rights that attach to my person, but we are struggling *to be conceived as persons*. And there is a difference between the former and the latter. If we are struggling for rights that attach, or should attach, to my personhood, then we assume that personhood as already constituted. But if we are struggling not only to be conceived as persons, but to create a social transformation of the very meaning of personhood, then the assertion of rights becomes a way of intervening into the social and political process by which the human is articulated. International human rights is always in the process of subjecting the human to redefinition and renegotiation. It mobilizes the human in the service of rights, but also rewrites the human and rearticulates the human when it comes up against the cultural limits of its working conception of the human, as it does and must.

Lesbian and gay human rights takes sexuality, in some sense, to be its issue. Sexuality is not simply an attribute one has or a disposition or patterned set of inclinations. It is a mode of being disposed toward others, including in the mode of fantasy, and sometimes only in the mode of fantasy. If we are outside of ourselves as sexual beings, given over from the start, crafted in part through primary relations of dependency and attachment, then it would seem that our being beside ourselves, outside ourselves, is there as a function of sexuality itself, where sexuality is not this or that dimension of our existence, not the key or bedrock of our existence, but, rather, as coextensive with existence, as Merleau-Ponty once aptly suggested.[6]

I have tried here to argue that our very sense of personhood is linked to the desire for recognition, and that desire places us outside ourselves, in a realm of social norms that we do not fully choose, but that provides the horizon and the resource for any sense of choice that we have. *This means that the ec-static character of our existence is essential to the possibility of persisting as human.* In this sense, we can see how sexual rights brings together two related domains of ec-stasy, two connected ways of being outside of ourselves. As sexual, we are dependent on a world of others, vulnerable to need, violence, betrayal, compulsion, fantasy; we project desire, and we have it projected onto us. To be part of a sexual minority means, most emphatically, that we are also dependent on the protection of public and private spaces, on legal sanctions that protect us from violence, on safeguards of various institutional kinds against unwanted aggression imposed upon us, and the violent actions they sometimes instigate. In this sense, our very lives, and the persistence of our desire, depend on there being norms of recognition that produce and sustain our viability as human. Thus, when we speak about sexual rights, we are not merely talking about rights that pertain to our individual desires but to the norms on which our very individuality depends. That means that the discourse of rights avows our dependency, the mode of our being in the hands of others, a mode of being with and for others without which we cannot be.

I served for a few years on the board of the International Gay and Lesbian Human Rights Commission, a group that is located in San Francisco. It is part of a broad international coalition of groups and individuals who struggle to establish both equality and justice for sexual minorities, including transgender and intersexed individuals as well as persons with HIV or AIDS.[7] What astonished me time and again was how often the organization was asked to respond to immediate acts of violence against sexual minorities, especially when that violence was not redressed in any way by local police or government in various places in the globe. I had to reflect on what sort of anxiety is prompted by the public appearance of someone who is openly gay, or presumed to be gay, someone whose gender does not conform to norms, someone whose sexuality defies public prohibitions, someone whose body does not conform with certain morphological ideals. What motivates those who are driven to kill someone for being gay, to threaten to kill someone for being intersexed, or would be driven to kill because of the public appearance of someone who is transgendered?

The desire to kill someone, or killing someone, for not conforming to the gender norm by which a person is "supposed" to live suggests that life itself requires a set of sheltering norms, and that to be outside it, to live outside it, is to court death. The person who threatens violence proceeds from the anxious and rigid belief that a sense of world and a sense of self will be radically undermined if such a being, uncategorizable, is permitted to live within the social world. The negation, through violence, of that body is a vain and violent effort to restore order, to renew the social world on the basis of intelligible gender, and to refuse the challenge to rethink that world as something other than natural or necessary. This is not far removed from the threat of death, or the murder itself, of transsexuals in various countries, and of gay men who read as "feminine" or gay women who read as "masculine." These crimes are not always immediately recognized as criminal acts. Sometimes they are denounced by governments and international agencies; sometimes they are not included as legible or real crimes against humanity by those very institutions.

If we oppose this violence, then we oppose it in the name of what? What is the alternative to this violence, and for what transformation of the social world do I call? This violence emerges from a profound desire to keep the order of binary gender natural or necessary, to make of it a structure, either natural or cultural, or both, that no human can oppose, and still remain human. If a person opposes norms of binary gender not just by having a critical point of view about them, but by incorporating norms critically, and that stylized opposition is legible, then it seems that violence emerges precisely as the demand to undo that legibility, to question its possibility, to render it unreal and impossible in the face of its appearance to the contrary. This is, then, no simple difference in points of view. To counter that embodied opposition by violence is to say, effectively, that this body, this challenge to an accepted version of the world is and shall be unthinkable. The effort to enforce the boundaries of what will be regarded as real requires stalling what is contingent, frail, open to fundamental transformation in the gendered order of things.

An ethical query emerges in light of such an analysis: how might we encounter the difference that calls our grids of intelligibility into question without trying to foreclose the challenge that the difference delivers? What might it mean to learn to live in the anxiety of that challenge, to feel the surety of one's epistemological and ontological anchor go, but to be willing, in the name of the human, to allow the human to become something other than what it is traditionally assumed to be? This means that we must learn to live and to embrace the destruction and rearticulation of the human in the name of a more capacious and, finally, less violent world, not knowing in advance what precise form our humanness does and will take. It means we must be open to its permutations, in the name of nonviolence. As Adriana Cavarero points out, paraphrasing Arendt, the question we pose to the Other is simple and unanswerable: "who are you?"[8] The violent response is the one that does not ask, and does not seek to know. It wants to shore up what it knows, to expunge what threatens it with not-knowing, what forces it to reconsider the presuppositions of its world, their contingency, their malleability. The nonviolent response lives with its unknowingness about the Other in the face of the Other, since sustaining the bond that the question opens is finally more valuable than knowing in advance what holds us in common, as if we already have all the resources we need to know what defines the human, what its future life might be.

That we cannot predict or control what permutations of the human might arise does not mean that we must value all possible permutations of the human; it does not mean that we cannot struggle for the realization of certain values, democratic and nonviolent, international and antiracist. The point is only that to struggle for those values is precisely to avow that one's own position is not sufficient to elaborate the spectrum of the human, that one must enter into a collective work in which one's own status as a subject must, for democratic reasons, become disoriented, exposed to what it does not know.

The point is not to apply social norms to lived social instances, to order and define them (as Foucault has criticized), nor is it to find justificatory mechanisms for the grounding of social norms that are extrasocial (even as they operate under the name of the social). There are times when both of these activities do and must take place: we level judgments against criminals for illegal acts, and so subject them to a normalizing procedure; we consider our grounds for action in collective contexts and try to find modes of deliberation and reflection about which we can agree. But neither of these is all we do with norms. Through recourse to norms, the sphere of the humanly intelligible is circumscribed, and this circumscription is consequential for any ethics and any conception of social transformation. We might try to claim that we must *first* know the fundamentals of the human in order to preserve and promote human life as we know it. But what if the very categories of the human have excluded those who should be described and sheltered within its terms? What if those who ought to belong to the human do not operate within the modes of reasoning and justifying validity claims that have been proffered by western forms of rationalism? Have we ever yet known the human? And what might it take to approach that knowing? Should we be wary of knowing it too soon or of any final or definitive knowing? If we take the field of the human for granted, then we fail to think critically and ethically about the consequential ways that the human is being produced, reproduced, and deproduced. This latter inquiry does not exhaust the field of ethics, but I cannot imagine a responsible ethics or theory of social transformation operating without it.

The necessity of keeping our notion of the human open to a future articulation is essential to the project of international human rights discourse and politics. We see this time and again when the very notion of the human is presupposed; the human is defined in advance, in terms that are distinctively western, very often American, and, therefore, partial and parochial. When we start with the human as a foundation, then the human at issue in human rights is already known, already defined. And yet, the human is supposed to be the ground for a set of rights and obligations that are global in reach. How we move from the local to the international (conceived globally in such a way that it does not recirculate the presumption that all humans belong to established nation-states) is a major question for international politics, but it takes a specific form for international lesbian, gay, bi-, trans-, and intersex struggles as well as for feminism. An anti-imperialist or, minimally, nonimperialist conception of international human rights must call into question what is meant by the human and learn from the various ways and means by which it is defined across cultural venues. This means that local conceptions of what is human or, indeed, of what the basic conditions and needs of human life are, must be subjected to reinterpretation, since there are historical and cultural circumstances in which the human is defined differently. Its basic needs and, hence, basic entitlements are made known through various media, through various kinds of practices, spoken and performed.

A reductive relativism would say that we cannot speak of the human or of international human rights, since there are only and always local and provisional understandings of these terms, and that the generalizations themselves do violence to the specificity of the meanings in question. This is not my view. I'm not ready to rest there. Indeed, I think we are compelled to speak of the human, and of the international, and to find out in particular how human rights do and do not work, for example, in favor of women, of what women are, and what they are not. But to speak in this way, and to call for social transformations in the name of women, we must also be part of a critical democratic project. Moreover, the category of women has been used differentially and with exclusionary aims, and not all women have been included within its terms; women have not been fully incorporated into the human. Both categories are still in process, underway, unfulfilled, thus we do not yet know and cannot ever definitively know in what the human finally consists. This means that we must follow a double path in politics: we must use this language to assert an entitlement to conditions of life in ways that affirm the constitutive role of sexuality and gender in political life, and we must also subject our very

categories to critical scrutiny. We must find out the limits of their inclu-
sivity and translatability, the presuppositions they include, the ways in
which they must be expanded, destroyed, or reworked both to encom-
pass and open up what it is to be human and gendered. When the United
Nations conference at Beijing met a few years ago, there was a discourse
on "women's human rights" (or when we hear of the International Gay
and Lesbian Human Rights Commission), which strikes many people
as a paradox. Women's human rights? Lesbian and gay human rights?
But think about what this coupling actually does. It performs the
human as contingent, a category that has in the past, and continues
in the present, to define a variable and restricted population, which
may or may not include lesbians and gays, may or may not include
women, which has several racial and ethnic differentials at work in its
operation. It says that such groups have their own set of human rights,
that what human may mean when we think about the humanness of
women is perhaps different from what human has meant when it has
functioned as presumptively male. It also says that these terms are
defined, variably, in relation to one another. And we could certainly
make a similar argument about race. Which populations have qualified
as the human and which have not? What is the history of this category?
Where are we in its history at this time?

I would suggest that in this last process, we can only rearticulate
or resignify the basic categories of ontology, of being human, of being
gendered, of being recognizably sexual, to the extent that we submit
ourselves to a process of cultural translation. The point is not to assim-
ilate foreign or unfamiliar notions of gender or humanness into our
own as if it is simply a matter of incorporation alienness into an established lexicon. Cultural translation is also a process of yielding our
most fundamental categories, that is, seeing how and why they break
up, require resignification when they encounter the limits of an
available episteme: what is unknown or not yet known. It is crucial to
recognize that the notion of the human will only be built over time in
and by the process of cultural translation, where it is not a translation
between two languages that stay enclosed, distinct, unified. But rather,
*translation will compel each language to change in order to apprehend
the other*, and this apprehension, at the limit of what is familiar,
parochial, and already known, will be the occasion for both an ethical
and social transformation. It will constitute a loss, a disorientation,

but one in which the human stands a chance of coming into being anew.

When we ask what makes a life livable, we are asking about certain normative conditions that must be fulfilled for life to become life. And so there are at least two senses of life, the one that refers to the minimum biological form of living, and another that intervenes at the start, which establishes minimum conditions for a livable life with regard to human life.[9] And this does not imply that we can disregard the merely living in favor of the livable life, but that we must ask, as we asked about gender violence, what humans require in order to maintain and reproduce the conditions of their own livability And what are our politics such that we are, in whatever way is possible, both conceptualizing the possibility of the livable life, and arranging for its institutional support? There will always be disagreement about what this means, and those who claim that a single political direction is necessitated by virtue of this commitment will be mistaken. But this is only because to live is to live a life politically, in relation to power, in relation to others, in the act of assuming responsibility for a collective future. To assume responsibility for a future, however, is not to know its direction fully in advance, since the future, especially the future with and for others, requires a certain openness and unknowingness; it implies becoming part of a process the outcome of which no one subject can surely predict. It also implies that a certain agonism and contestation over the course of direction will and must be in play. Contestation must be in play for politics to become democratic. Democracy does not speak in unison; its tunes are dissonant, and necessarily so. It is not a predictable process; it must be undergone, like a passion must be undergone. It may also be that life itself becomes foreclosed when the right way is decided in advance, when we impose what is right for everyone and without finding a way to enter into community, and to discover there the "right" in the midst of cultural translation. It may be that what is right and what is good consist in staying open to the tensions that beset the most fundamental categories we require, in knowing unknowingness at the core of what we know, and what we need, and in recognizing the sign of life in what we undergo without certainty about what will come.

2. Gender Regulations

At first glance, the term "regulation" appears to suggest the institutionalization of the process by which persons are made regular. Indeed, to refer to regulation in the plural is already to acknowledge those concrete laws, rules, and policies that constitute the legal instruments through which persons are made regular. But it would be a mistake, I believe, to understand all the ways in which gender is regulated in terms of those empirical legal instances because the norms that govern those regulations exceed the very instances in which they are embodied. On the other hand, it would be equally problematic to speak of the regulation of gender in the abstract, as if the empirical instances only exemplified an operation of power that takes place independently of those instances.

Indeed, much of the most important work with feminist and lesbian/gay studies has concentrated on actual regulations: legal, military, psychiatric, and a host of others. The kinds of questions posed within such scholarship tend to ask how gender is regulated, how such regulations are imposed, and how they become incorporated and lived by the subjects on whom they are imposed. But for gender to be regulated is not simply for gender to come under the exterior force of a regulation.[1] If gender were to exist prior to its regulation, we could then take gender as our theme and proceed to enumerate the various kinds of regulations to which it is subjected and the ways in which that subjection takes place. The problem, however, for us is more acute. After all, is there a gender that preexists its regulation, or is it the case that, in being subject to regulation, the gendered subject emerges, produced in and through that particular form of subjection? Is subjection not the process by which regulations produce gender?

It is important to remember at least two caveats on subjection and regulation derived from Foucaultian scholarship: (1) regulatory power not only acts upon a preexisting subject but also shapes and forms that subject; moreover, every juridical form of power has its productive effect; and (2) to become subject to a regulation is also to become subjectivated by it, that is, to be brought into being as a subject precisely through being regulated. This second point follows from the first in that the regulatory discourses which form the subject of gender are precisely those that require and induce the subject in question.

Particular kinds of regulations may be understood as instances of a more general regulatory power, one that is specified as the regulation of gender. Here I contravene Foucault in some respects. For if the Foucaultian wisdom seems to consist in the insight that regulatory power has certain broad historical characteristics, and that it operates on gender as well as on other kinds of social and cultural norms, then it seems that gender is but the instance of a larger regulatory operation of power. I would argue against this subsumption of gender to regulatory power that the regulatory apparatus that governs gender is one that is itself gender-specific. I do not mean to suggest that the regulation of gender is paradigmatic of regulatory power as such, but rather, that gender requires and institutes its own distinctive regulatory and disciplinary regime.

The suggestion that gender is a norm requires some further elaboration. A norm is not the same as a rule, and it is not the same as a law.[2] A norm operates within social practices as the implicit standard of *normalization*. Although a norm may be analytically separable from the practices in which it is embedded, it may also prove to be recalcitrant to any effort to decontextualize its operation. Norms may or may not be explicit, and when they operate as the normalizing principle in social practice, they usually remain implicit, difficult to read, discernible most clearly and dramatically in the effects that they produce.

For gender to be a norm suggests that it is always and only tenuously embodied by any particular social actor. The norm governs the social intelligibility of action, but it is not the same as the action that it governs. The norm appears to be indifferent to the actions that it governs, by which I mean only that the norm appears to have a status and effect that is independent of the actions governed by the norm. The norm governs intelligibility, allows for certain kinds of practices and action to become recognizable as such, imposing a grid of legibility on the social and defining the parameters of what will and will not appear within the domain of the social. The question of what it is to be outside the norm poses a paradox for thinking, for if the norm renders the social field intelligible and normalizes that field for us, then being outside the norm is in some sense being defined still in relation to it. To be not quite masculine or not quite feminine is still to be understood exclusively in terms of one's relationship to the "quite masculine" and the "quite feminine."

To claim that gender is a norm is not quite the same as saying that there are normative views of femininity and masculinity, even though there clearly are such normative views. Gender is not exactly what one "is" nor is it precisely what one "has." Gender is the apparatus by which the production and normalization of masculine and feminine take place along with the interstitial forms of hormonal, chromosomal, psychic, and performative that gender assumes. To assume that gender always and exclusively means the matrix of the "masculine" and "feminine" is precisely to miss the critical point that the production of that coherent binary is contingent, that it comes at a cost, and that those permutations of gender which do not fit the binary are as much a part of gender as its most normative instance. To conflate the definition of gender with its normative expression is inadvertently to reconsolidate the power of the norm to constrain the definition of gender. Gender is the mechanism by which notions of masculine and feminine are produced and naturalized, but gender might very well be the apparatus by which such terms are deconstructed and denaturalized. Indeed, it may be that the very apparatus that seeks to install the norm also works to undermine that very installation, that the installation is, as it were, definitionally incomplete. To keep the term "gender" apart from both masculinity and femininity is to safeguard a theoretical perspective by which one might offer an account of how the binary of masculine and feminine comes to exhaust the semantic field of gender. Whether one refers to "gender trouble" or "gender blending," "transgender" or "cross-gender," one is already suggesting that gender has a way of moving beyond that naturalized binary. The conflation of gender with masculine/feminine, man/woman, male/female, thus performs the very naturalization that the notion of gender is meant to forestall.

Thus, a restrictive discourse on gender that insists on the binary of man and woman as the exclusive way to understand the gender field performs a *regulatory* operation of power that naturalizes the hegemonic instance and forecloses the thinkability of its disruption.

One tendency within gender studies has been to assume that the alternative to the binary system of gender is a multiplication of genders. Such an approach invariably provokes the question: how many genders can there be, and what will they be called?[3] But the disruption of the binary system need not lead us to an equally problematic quantification of gender. Luce Irigaray, following a Lacanian lead, asks whether the masculine sex is the "one" sex, meaning not only "the one and only," but the one that inaugurates a quantitative apprach to sex. "Sex" in her view is neither a biological category nor a social one (and is thus distinct from "gender"), but a linguistic one that exists, as it were, on the divide between the social and the biological. "The sex which is not one" is thus femininity understood precisely as what cannot be captured by number.[4] Other approaches insist that "transgender" is not exactly a third gender, but a mode of passage between genders, an interstitial and transitional figure of gender that is not reducible to the normative insistence on one or two.[5]

Symbolic Positions and Social Norms

Although some theorists maintain that norms are always social norms, Lacanian theorists, indebted to the structuralism of Claude Lévi-Strauss, insist that symbolic norms are not the same as social ones, and that a certain "regulation" of gender takes place through the symbolic demand that is placed on psyches from their inception.

The "symbolic" became a technical term for Jacques Lacan in 1953 and became his own way of compounding mathematical (formal) and anthropological uses of the term. In a dictionary on Lacanian parlance, the symbolic is explicitly linked with the problem of regulation: "The symbolic is the realm of the Law which *regulates* desire in the Oedipus complex."[6] That complex is understood to be derived from a primary or symbolic prohibition against incest, a prohibition that makes sense only in terms of kinship relations in which various "positions" are established within the family according to an exogamic mandate. In other words, a mother is someone with whom a son and daughter do not have sexual relations, and a father is someone with whom a son and daughter do not have sexual relations, a mother is someone who only has sexual relations with the father, and so forth. These relations of prohibition are encoded in the "position" that each of these family members occupies. To be in such a position is thus to be in such a crossed sexual relation, at least according to the symbolic or normative conception of what that "position" is.

The consequences of this view are clearly enormous. In many ways the structuralist legacy within psychoanalytic thinking exerted a monumental effect on feminist film and literary theory, as well as feminist approaches to psychoanalysis throughout the disciplines. It also paved the way for a queer critique of feminism that has had, and continues to have, inevitably divisive and consequential effects within sexuality and gender studies. In what follows, I hope to show how the notion of culture that becomes transmuted into the "symbolic" for Lacanian psychoanalysis is very different from the notion of culture that remains current within the contemporary field of cultural studies, such that the two enterprises are often understood as hopelessly opposed. I also plan to argue that any claim to establish the rules that "regulate desire" in an inalterable and eternal realm of law has limited use for a theory that seeks to understand the conditions under which the social transformation of gender is possible. Another concern regarding the symbolic is that the prohibition of incest can be one of the motivations for its own transgression, which suggests that the symbolic positions of kinship are in many ways defeated by the very sexuality that they produce through regulation.[7] Lastly, I hope to show that the distinction between symbolic and social law cannot finally hold, that the symbolic itself is the sedimentation of social practices, and that radical alterations in kinship demand a rearticulation of the structuralist presuppositions of psychoanalysis, moving us, as it were, toward a queer poststructuralism of the psyche.

To return to the incest taboo, the question emerges: what is the status of these prohibitions and these positions? Lévi-Strauss makes clear in *The Elementary Structures of Kinship* that nothing in biology necessitates the incest taboo, that it is a purely *cultural* phenomenon. By "cultural," Lévi-Strauss does not mean "culturally variable" or "contingent," but rather according to "universal" laws of culture. Thus, for Lévi-Strauss, cultural rules are not alterable rules (as Gayle Rubin subsequently argued), but are inalterable and universal. The domain of a universal and eternal rule of culture—what Juliet Mitchell calls "the universal and primordial law"[8]—becomes the basis for the Lacanian notion of the symbolic and the subsequent efforts to divide the symbolic from both the biological and social domains. In Lacan, that which is universal in culture is understood to be its symbolic or linguistic rules, and these are understood to support kinship relations. The very possibility of pronominal reference, of an "I," a "you," a "we," and "they" appears to rely on this mode of kinship that operates in and as language. This is a slide from the cultural to the linguistic, one toward which Lévi-Strauss himself gestures toward the end of *The Elementary Structures of Kinship*. In Lacan, the symbolic becomes defined in terms of a conception of linguistic structures that are irreducible to the social forms that language takes. According to structuralist terms, it establishes the universal conditions under which the sociality, that is, communicability of all language use, becomes possible. This move paves the way for the consequential distinction between symbolic and social accounts of kinship.

Hence, a norm is not quite the same as "symbolic position" in the Lacanian sense, which appears to enjoy a quasi-timeless character, regardless of the qualifications offered in endnotes to several of Lacan's seminars. The Lacanians almost always insist that a symbolic position is not the same as a social one, that it would be a mistake to take the symbolic position of the father, for instance, which is after all the paradigmatically symbolic position, and mistake that for a socially constituted and alterable position that fathers have assumed throughout time. The Lacanian view insists that there is an ideal and unconscious demand that is made upon social life which remains irreducible to socially legible causes and effects. The symbolic place of the father does not cede to the demands for a social reorganization of paternity. Instead, the symbolic is precisely what sets limits to any and all utopian efforts to reconfigure and relive kinship relations at some distance from the oedipal scene.[9]

One of the problems that emerged when the study of kinship was combined with the study of structural linguistics is that kinship positions were elevated to the status of fundamental linguistic structures. These are positions that make possible the entry into language, and which, therefore, maintain an essential status with respect to language. They are, in other words, positions without which no signification could proceed, or, in different language, no cultural intelligibility can be secured. What were the consequences of making certain conceptions of kinship timeless, and then elevating them to the status of the elementary structures of intelligibility?

Although Lévi-Strauss purports to consider a variety of kinship systems, he does so in the service of delimiting those principles of kinship that assume cross-cultural status. What is offered by structuralism as a "position" within language or kinship is not the same as a "norm," for the latter is a socially produced and variable framework. A norm is not the same as a symbolic position. Moreover, if a symbolic position is more appropriately regarded as a norm, then a symbolic position is not the same as itself, but is, rather, a contingent norm whose contingency has been covered over by a theoretical reification that bears potentially stark consequences for gendered life. One might respond within the structuralist conceit with the claim, "But this is the law!" What is the status of such an utterance, however? "It is the law!" becomes the utterance that performatively attributes the very force to the law that the law itself is said to exercise. "It is the law" is thus a sign of allegiance to the law, a sign of the desire for the law to be the indisputable law, a theological impulse within the theory of psychoanalysis that seeks to put out of play any criticism of the symbolic father, the law of psychoanalysis itself. Thus, the status given to the law is, not surprisingly, precisely the status given to the phallus, where the phallus is not merely a privileged "signifier" within the Lacanian scheme but becomes the characteristic feature of the theoretical apparatus in which that signifier is introduced. In other words, the authoritative force that shores up the incontestability of the symbolic law is itself an exercise of that symbolic law, a further instance of the place of the father, as it were, indisputable and incontestable. Although there are, as Lacanians will remind us, only and always contestations of the symbolic, they fail to exercise any final force to undermine the symbolic itself or to force a radical reconfiguration of its terms.

The authority of the theory exposes its own tautological defense within the fact that the symbolic survives every and any contestation of its authority. It is not only a theory, that is, that insists upon masculine and feminine as symbolic positions which are finally beyond all contestation and which set the limit to contestation as such, but one that relies on the very authority it describes to shore up the authority of its own descriptive claims.

To separate the symbolic from the social sphere facilitates the distinction between the Law and variable laws. In the place of a critical practice that anticipates no final authority, and which opens up an anxiety-producing field of gendered possibilities, the symbolic emerges to put an end to such anxiety. If there is a Law that we cannot displace, but which we seek through imaginary means to displace again and again, then we know in advance that our efforts at change will be put in check, and our struggle against the authoritative account of gender will be thwarted, and we will submit to an unassailable authority. There are those who believe that to think that the symbolic itself might be changed by human practice is pure voluntarism. But is it? One can certainly concede that desire is radically conditioned without claiming that it is radically determined, and one can acknowledge that there are structures that make desire possible without claiming that those structures are timeless and recalcitrant, impervious to a reiterative replay and displacement. To contest symbolic authority is not necessarily a return to the "ego" or classical liberal notions of freedom, rather to do so is to insist that the norm in its necessary temporality is opened to a displacement and subversion from within.

The symbolic is understood as the sphere that regulates the assumption of sex, where sex is understood as a differential set of positions, masculine and feminine. Thus, the concept of gender, derived as it is from sociological discourse, is foreign to the discourse on sexual difference that emerges from the Lacanian and post-Lacanian framework. Lacan was clearly influenced by Lévi-Strauss's *The Elementary Structures of Kinship*, first published in 1947, approximately six years before Lacan uses the term.[10] In the Lévi-Straussian model, the position of man and woman is what makes possible certain forms of sexual exchange. In this sense, gender operates to secure certain forms of reproductive sexual ties and to prohibit other forms. One's gender, in this view, is an index of the proscribed and prescribed sexual relations by which a subject is socially regulated and produced.

According to Lévi-Strauss the rules that govern sexual exchange and which, accordingly, produce viable subject positions on the basis of that regulation of sexuality are distinct from the individuals who abide by those rules and occupy such positions. That human actions are regulated by such laws but do not have the power to transform the substance and aim of their laws appears to be the consequence of a conception of law that is indifferent to the content that it regulates. How does a shift from thinking about gender as regulated by symbolic laws to a conception of gender as regulated by social norms contest this indifference of the law to what it regulates? And how does such a shift open up the possibility of a more radical contestation of the law itself?

If gender is a norm, it is not the same as a model that individuals seek to approximate. On the contrary, it is a form of social power that produces the intelligible field of subjects, and an apparatus by which the gender binary is instituted. As a norm that appears independent of the practices that it governs, its ideality is the reinstituted effect of those very practices. This suggests not only that the relation between practices and the idealizations under which they work is contingent, but that the very idealization can be brought into question and crisis, potentially undergoing deidealization and divestiture.

The distance between gender and its naturalized instantiations is precisely the distance between a norm and its incorporations. I suggested above that the norm is analytically independent of its incorporations, but I want to emphasize that this is only an intellectual heuristic, one that helps to guarantee the perpetuation of the norm itself as a timeless and inalterable ideal. In fact, the norm only persists as a norm to the extent that it is acted out in social practice and reidealized and reinstituted in and through the daily social rituals of bodily life. The norm has no independent ontological status, yet it cannot be easily reduced to its instantiations; it is itself (re)produced through its embodiment, through the acts that strive to approximate it, through the idealizations reproduced in and by those acts.

Foucault brought the discourse of the norm into currency by arguing in *The History of Sexuality* (vol. 1), that the nineteenth century saw the emergence of the norm as a means of social regulation which is not identical with the operations of law. Influenced by Foucault, the sociologist, François Ewald, has expanded upon this remark in several essays.[26] Ewald argues that the action of the norm is at the expense of the juridical system of the law, and that although normalization entails an increase in legislation, it is not necessarily opposed to it, but remains independent of it in some significant ways ("Norms" 138). Foucault notes that the norm often appears in legal form, that the normative comes to the fore most typically in constitutions, legal codes, and the constant and clamorous activity of the legislature (Foucault, "Right of Death and Power Over Life"). Foucault further claims that a norm belongs to the arts of judgment, and that although a norm is clearly related to power, it is characterized less by the use of force or violence than by, as Ewald puts it, "an implicit logic that allows power to reflect upon its own strategies and clearly define its objects. This logic is at once the force that enables us to imagine life and the living as objects of power and the power that can take 'life' in hand, creating the sphere of the bio-political" ("Norms" 138).

For Ewald, this raises at least two questions, whether, for instance, modernity participates in the logic of the norm and what the relation between norms and the law would be.[12] Although the norm is sometimes used as synonomous with "the rule," it is clear that norms are also what give rules a certain local coherence. Ewald claims that the beginning of the nineteenth century inaugurates a radical change in the relationship between the rule and the norm ("Norms" 140), and that the norm emerges conceptually not only as *a particular variety of rules*, but also as *a way of producing them*, and as *a principle of valorization*.

In French, the term *normalité* appears in 1834, *normatif* in 1868, and in Germany at the end of the nineteenth century, we get the normative sciences (which, I gather, gets carried forward in the name of the division at the contemporary American Political Science Association meetings called "normative political theory"); the term "normalization" appears in 1920. For Foucault as well as Ewald, it corresponds to the normalizing operation of bureaucratic and disciplinary powers.

According to Ewald, the norm transforms constraints into a mechanism, and thus marks the movement by which, in Foucaultian terms, juridical power becomes productive; it transforms the negative restraints of the juridical into the more positive controls of normalization; thus the norm performs this transformative function. The norm thus marks and effects the shift from thinking power as juridical constraint to thinking power as (a) an organized set of constraints, and (b) as a regulatory mechanism.

Norms and the Problem of Abstraction

This then returns us to the question not only of how discourse might be said to produce a subject (something everywhere assumed in cultural studies but rarely investigated in its own right), but, more precisely, what in discourse effects that production. When Foucault claims that discipline "produces" individuals, he means not only that disciplinary discourse *manages* and *makes use of them* but that it also *actively constitutes them*.

The norm is a measurement and a means of producing a common standard, to become an instance of the norm is not fully to exhaust the norm, but, rather, to become subjected to an abstraction of commonality. Although Foucault and Ewald tend to concentrate their analyses of this process in the nineteenth century and twentieth century, Mary Poovey in *Making a Social Body* dates the history of abstraction in the social sphere to the late eighteenth century. In Britain, she maintains, "The last decades of the eighteenth century witnessed the first modern efforts to represent all or significant parts of the population of Britain as aggregates and to delineate a social sphere distinct from the political and economic domains" (8). What characterizes this social domain, in her view, is the entrance of quantitative measurement: "Such comparisons and measurement, of course, produce some phenomena as normative, ostensibly because they are numerous, because they represent an average, or because they constitute an ideal towards which all other phenomena move" (9).

Ewald seeks a narrower definition of the norm in order to understand its capacity to regulate all social phenomena as well as the internal limits it faces in any such regulation ("Power" 170–71). He writes:

> what precisely is the norm? It is the measure which simultaneously individualizes, makes ceaseless individualisation possible and creates comparability. The norm makes it possible to locate spaces, indefinitely, which become more and more discrete, minute, and at the same time makes sure that these spaces never enclose anyone in such a way as to create a nature for them,

since these individualising spaces *are never more than the expression of a relationship*, of a relationship which has to be seen indefinitely in the context of others. What is a norm? A principle of comparison, of comparability, a common measure, which is instituted in the pure reference of one group to itself, when the group has no relationship other than to itself, without external reference and without verticality. ("Norms" 173, my emphasis)

According to Ewald, Foucault adds this to the thinking of normalisation: "normative individualisation is not exterior. The abnormal does not have a nature which is different from that of the normal. The norm, or normative space, knows no outside. The norm integrates anything which might attempt to go beyond it—nothing, nobody, whatever difference it might display, can ever claim to be exterior, or claim to possess an otherness which would actually make it other" ("Norms" 173).

Such a view suggests that any opposition to the norm is already contained within the norm, and is crucial to its own functioning. Indeed, at this point in our analysis, it appears that moving from a Lacanian notion of symbolic position to a more Foucaultian conception of "social norm" does not augment the chances for an effective displacement or resignification of the norm itself.

In the work of Pierre Macheray, however, one begins to see that norms are not independent and self-subsisting entities or abstractions but must be understood as forms of action. In "Towards a Natural History of Norms," Macheray makes clear that the kind of causality that norms exercise is not transitive, but immanent, and he seeks recourse to Spinoza and Foucault to make his claim:

To think in terms of the immanence of the norm is indeed to refrain from considering the action of the norm in a restrictive manner, seeing it as a form of "repression" formulated in terms of interdiction exercised against a given subject in advance of the performance of this action, thus implying that this subject could, on his own, liberate himself or be liberated from this sort of control: the history of madness, just like that of sexuality, shows that such "liberation," far from suppressing the action of norms, on the contrary reinforces it. But one might also wonder if it is enough to denounce the illusions of this anti-repressive discourse in order to escape from them: does one not run the risk of reproducing them on another level, where they cease to be naive but where, though of a more learned nature, they still remain out of step in relation to the context at which they seem to be aiming? (185)

By maintaining that the norm only subsists in and through its actions, Macheray effectively locates action as the site of social intervention: "From this point of view it is no longer possible to think of the norm itself in advance of the consequences of its action, as being in some way behind them and independent of them; *the norm has to be considered such as it acts precisely in its effects* in such a way, not so as to limit the reality by means of simple conditioning, but in order to confer upon it the maximum amount of reality of which it is capable" (186, my emphasis).

I mentioned above that the norm cannot be reduced to any of its instances, but I would add: neither can the norm be fully extricated from its instantiations. The norm is not exterior to its field of application. Not only is the norm responsible for producing its field of application, according to Macheray (187), but *the norm produces itself in the production of that field.* The norm is actively conferring reality; indeed, only by virtue of its repeated power to confer reality is the norm constituted as a norm.

Gender Norms

According to the notion or norms elaborated above, we might say that the field of reality produced by gender norms constitutes the background for the surface appearance of gender in its idealized dimensions. But how are we to understand the historical formation of such ideals, their persistence through time, and their site as a complex convergence of social meanings that do not immediately appear to be about gender? To the extent that gender norms are *reproduced*, they are invoked and cited by bodily practices that also have the capacity to alter norms in the course of their citation. One cannot offer a full narrative account of the citational history of the norm: whereas narrativity does not fully conceal its history, neither does it reveal a single origin.

One important sense of regulation, then, is that persons are regulated by gender, and that this sort of regulation operates as a condition of cultural intelligibilty for any person. To veer from the gender norm is to produce the aberrant example that regulatory powers (medical, psychiatric, and legal, to name a few) may quickly exploit to shore up the rationale for their own continuing regulatory zeal. The question remains, though, what departures from the norm constitute something other than an excuse or rationale for the continuing authority of the norm? What departures from the norm disrupt the regulatory process itself?

The question of surgical "correction" for intersexed children is one case in point. There the argument is made that children born with irregular primary sexual characteristics are to be "corrected" in order to fit in, feel more comfortable, achieve normality. Corrective surgery is sometimes performed with parental support and in the name of normalization, and the physical and psychic costs of the surgery have proven to be enormous for those persons who have been submitted, as it were, to the knife of the norm.[13] The bodies produced through such a regulatory enforcement of gender are bodies in pain, bearing the marks of violence and suffering. Here the ideality of gendered morphology is quite literally incised in the flesh.

Gender is thus a regulatory norm, but it is also one that is produced in the service of other kinds of regulations. For instance, sexual harassment codes tend to assume, following the reasoning of Catharine MacKinnon, that harassment consists of the systematic sexual subordination of women at the workplace, and that men are generally in the position of harasser, and women, as the harassed. For MacKinnon, this seems to be the consequence of a more fundamental sexual subordination of women. Although these regulations seek to constrain sexually demeaning behavior at the workplace, they also carry within them certain tacit norms of gender. In a sense, the implicit regulation of gender takes place through the explicit regulation of sexuality.

For MacKinnon, the hierarchical structure of heterosexuality in which men are understood to subordinate women is what produces gender: "Stopped as an attribute of a person, sex inequality takes the form of gender; moving as a relation between people, it takes the form of sexuality. Gender emerges as the congealed form of the sexualization of inequality between men and women" (*Feminism Unmodified* 6–7).

If gender is the congealed form that the sexualization of inequality takes, then the sexualization of inequality precedes gender, and gender is its effect. But can we even conceptualize the sexualization of inequality without a prior conception of gender? Does it make sense to claim that men subordinate women sexually if we don't first have an idea of what men and women are? MacKinnon maintains, however, that there is no constitution of gender outside of this form of sexuality and, by implication, outside of this subordinating and exploitative form of sexuality.

In proposing the regulation of sexual harassment through recourse to this kind of analysis of the systematic character of sexual subordination, MacKinnon institutes a regulation of another kind: to have a gender means to have entered already into a heterosexual relationship of subordination; there appear to be no gendered people who are outside of such relationships; there appear to be no nonsubordinating heterosexual relations; there appear to be no nonheterosexual relations; there appears to be no same-sex harassment.

This form of reducing gender to sexuality has thus given way to two separate but overlapping concerns within contemporary queer theory. The first move is to separate sexuality from gender, so that to have a gender does not presuppose that one engages sexual practice in any particular way, and to engage in a given sexual practice, anal sex, for instance, does not presuppose that one is a given gender.[14] The second and related move within queer theory is to argue that gender is not reducible to hierarchical heterosexuality, that it takes different forms when contextualized by queer sexualities, indeed, that its binariness cannot be taken for granted outside the heterosexual frame, that gender itself is internally unstable, that transgendered lives are evidence of the breakdown of any lines of causal determinism between sexuality and gender. The dissonance between gender and sexuality is thus affirmed from two different perspectives; the one seeks to show possibilities for sexuality that are not constrained by gender in order to break the causal reductiveness of arguments that bind them; the other seeks to show possibilities for gender that are not predetermined by forms of hegemonic heterosexuality.[15]

The problem with basing sexual harassment codes on a view of sexuality in which gender is the concealed effect of sexualized subordination within heterosexuality is that certain views of gender and certain views of sexuality are reinforced through the reasoning. In MacKinnon's theory, gender is produced in the scene of sexual subordination, and sexual harassment is the explicit moment of the institution of heterosexual subordination. What this means, effectively, is that sexual harassment becomes the allegory for the production of gender. In my view, the sexual harassment codes become themselves the instrument by which gender is thus reproduced.

It is the regulation of gender, argues legal scholar Katherine Franke, that remains not only uninterrogated in this view, but unwittingly abetted. Franke writes:

> What is wrong with the world MacKinnon describes in her work is not exhausted by the observation that men dominate women, although that is descriptively true in most cases. Rather, the problem is far more systematic. By reducing sexism to only that which is done to women by men, we lose sight of the underlying ideology that makes sexism so powerful.... The subordination of women by men is part of a larger social practice that creates gendered bodies—feminine women and masculine men. ("What's Wrong With Sexual Harassment?" 761–62)

The social punishments that follow upon transgressions of gender include the surgical correction of intersexed persons, the medical and psychiatric pathologization and criminalization in several countries including the United States of "gender dysphoric" people, the harassment of gender-troubled persons on the street or in the workplace, employment discrimination, and violence. The prohibition of sexual harassment of women by men that is based on a rationale that assumes heterosexual subordination as the exclusive scene of sexuality and gender thus itself becomes a regulatory means for the production and maintenance of gender norms within heterosexuality.[16]

At the outset of this essay, I suggested several ways to understand the problem of "regulation." A regulation is that which *makes regular*, but it is also, following Foucault, a mode of *discipline and surveillance* within late modern forms of power; it does not merely constrict and negate and is, therefore, not merely a juridical form of power. Insofar as regulations operate by way of norms, they become key moments in which the ideality of the norm is reconstituted, its historicity and vulnerability temporarily put out of play. As an operation of power, regulation can take a legal form, but its legal dimension does not exhaust the sphere of its efficaciousness. As that which relies on categories that render individuals socially interchangeable with one another, regulation is thus bound up with the process of *normalization*. Statutes that govern who the beneficiaries of welfare entitlements will be are actively engaged in producing the norm of the welfare recipient. Those that regulate gay speech in the military are actively engaged in producing and maintaining the norm of what a man or what a woman will be, what speech will be, where sexuality will and will not be. State regulations on lesbian and gay adoption as well as single-parent adoptions not only restrict that activity, but refer to and reenforce an ideal of what parents should be, for example, that they should be partnered, and what counts as a legitimate partner. Hence, regulations that seek merely to curb certain specified activities (sexual harassment, welfare fraud, sexual speech) perform another activity that, for the most part, remains unmarked: the production of the parameters of personhood, that is, making persons according to abstract norms that at once condition and exceed the lives they make—and break.

3. Doing Justice to Someone: Sex Reassignment and Allegories of Transsexuality

I would like to take my point of departure from a question of power, the power of regulation, a power that determines, more or less, what we are, what we can be.[1] I am not speaking of power only in a juridical or positive sense, but I am referring to the workings of a certain regulatory regime, one that informs the law, and also exceeds the law. When we ask, what are the conditions of intelligibility by which the human emerges, by which the human is recognized, by which some subject becomes the subject of human love, we are asking about conditions of intelligibility composed of norms, of practices, that have become presuppositional, without which we cannot think the human at all. So I propose to broach the relationship between variable orders of intelligibility and the genesis and knowability of the human. And it is not just that there are laws that govern our intelligibility, but ways of knowing, modes of truth, that forcibly define intelligibility.

This is what Foucault describes as the politics of truth, a politics that pertains to those relations of power that circumscribe in advance what will and will not count as truth, which order the world in certain regular and regulatable ways, and which we come to accept as the given field of knowledge. We can understand the salience of this point when we begin to ask: What counts as a person? What counts as a coherent gender? What qualifies as a citizen? Whose world is legitimated as real? Subjectively, we ask: Who can I become in such a world where the meanings and limits of the subject are set out in advance for me? By what norms am I constrained as I begin to ask what I may become? And what happens when I begin to become that for which there is no place within the given regime of truth? This is what Foucault describes as "the desubjugation of the subject in the play of . . . the politics of truth" ("What is Critique?" 39).

Another way of putting this is the following: "what, given the contemporary order of being, can I be?" This question does not quite broach the question of what it is not to be, or what it is to occupy the place of not-being within the field of being. What it is to live, breathe, attempt to love neither as fully negated nor as fully acknowledged as being. This relationship, between intelligibility and the human is an urgent one; it carries a certain theoretical urgency, precisely at those points where the human is encountered at the limits of intelligibility itself. I would like to suggest that this interrogation has something important to do with justice. Justice is not only or exclusively a matter of how persons are treated or how societies are constituted. It also concerns consequential decisions about what a person is, and what social norms must be honored and expressed for "personhood" to become allocated, how we do or do not recognize animate others as persons depending on whether or not we recognize a certain norm manifested in and by the body of that other. The very criterion by which we judge a person to be a gendered being, a criterion that posits coherent gender as a presupposition of humanness, is not only one which, justly or unjustly, governs the recognizability of the human, but one that informs the ways we do or do not recognize ourselves at the level of feeling, desire, and the body, at the moments before the mirror, in the moments before the window, in the times that one turns to psychologists, to psychiatrists, to medical and legal professionals to negotiate what may well feel like the unrecognizability of one's gender and, hence, the unrecognizability of one's personhood.

I want to consider a legal and psychiatric case of a person who was determined without difficulty to be a boy at the time of birth, then determined again within a few months to be a girl, who decided in his teenage years to become a man. This is the story of David Reimer, whose situation is referred to as "the Joan/John case," one that was brought to public attention by the BBC and in various popular, psychological, and medical journals. I base my analysis on several documents: an article written by Dr. Milton Diamond, an endocrinologist, and the popular book *As Nature Made Him*, written by John Colapinto, a journalist for *Rolling Stone*, as well as several publications by John Money, and critical commentaries offered by Anne Fausto-Sterling and Suzanne Kessler in their important recent books.[2] David Reimer has now talked openly to the media and has chosen to live outside the pseudonym reserved for him by Milton Diamond and his colleagues. David became "Brenda" at a certain point in his childhood which I discuss below, and so instead of referring to him as Joan and John, neither of which is his name, I will use the name he uses.

David was born with XY chromosomes and at the age of eight months, his penis was accidentally burned and severed in the course of a surgical operation to rectify phimosis, a condition in which the foreskin thwarts urination. This is a relatively risk-free procedure, but the doctor who performed it on David was using a new machine, apparently one that he hadn't used before, one that his colleagues declared was unnecessary for the job. He had trouble making the machine work, so he increased the power to the machine to the point that it effectively burned away a major portion of the penis. The parents were, of course, appalled and shocked, and they were, according to their own description, unclear how to proceed. Then one evening, about a year after this event, they were watching television, and there they encountered John Money, talking about transsexual and intersexual surgery, offering the view that if a child underwent surgery and started socialization as a gender different from the one originally assigned at birth, the child could develop normally, adapt perfectly well to the new gender, and live a happy life. The parents wrote to Money and he invited them to Baltimore, and so David was subsequently seen at Johns Hopkins University, at which point the strong recommendation was made by Dr. John Money that David be raised as a girl. The parents agreed, and the doctors removed the testicles, made some preliminary preparation for surgery to create a vagina, but decided to wait until Brenda, the newly named child, was older to complete the task. So Brenda grew up as a girl, and was monitored often, given over on

a periodic basis to John Money's Gender Identity Institute for the purposes of fostering adaptation to being a girl. Then between the ages
of eight and nine, Brenda found herself developing the desire to buy
a toy machine gun. Between the ages of nine and eleven, she started
to make the realization that she was not a girl. This realization seems
to coincide with the desire to buy certain kinds of toys: more guns,
apparently, and some trucks. Although there was no penis, Brenda
liked to stand to urinate. And she was caught in this position once, at
school, and the other girls threatened to "kill" her if she continued.

At this point, the psychiatric teams that were intermittently monitoring Brenda's adaptation offered her estrogen, and she refused this.
Money tried to talk to her about getting a real vagina, and she refused;
in fact, she went screaming from the room. Money had her view sexually graphic pictures of vaginas. Money even went so far as to show
Brenda pictures of women giving birth, holding out the promise that
Brenda might be able to give birth if she acquired a vagina. And in a
scene that could have been the model for the recent film *But I'm a
Cheerleader!*[3] she and her brother were required to perform mock coital
exercises with one another, on command. They both later reported being
very frightened and disoriented by this demand and did not tell their
parents at the time. Brenda is said to have preferred male activities and
not to have liked developing breasts. And all of these attributions to
Brenda are made by another set of doctors, this time a team of psychiatrists at Brenda's local hospital. The local psychiatrists and medical professionals intervened in the case, believing that a mistake had been made
in sex reassignment here, and eventually the case was reviewed by
Milton Diamond, a sex researcher who believes in the hormonal basis
of gender identity and who has been battling Money for several years.
This new set of psychiatrists and doctors offered her the choice of changing paths, which she accepted. She started living as a boy, named David,
at the age of fourteen. At this point, David started requesting, and receiving, male hormone shots, and also had his breasts removed. A phallus,
so it was called by Diamond, was constructed for him between the age
of fifteen and sixteen. David, it is reported, does not ejaculate, although
he feels some sexual pleasure there; he urinates from its base. It is a phallus that only approximates some of its expected functions and, as we
shall see, enters David only ambivalently into the norm.

During the time that David was Brenda, Money continued to publish papers extolling the success of this sex reassignment case. The case was enormously consequential because Brenda had a brother for an identical twin, and so Money could track the development of both siblings and assume an identical genetic makeup for both of them. He insisted that both were developing normally and happily into their different genders. But his own recorded interviews, mainly unpublished, and subsequent research, have called his honesty into question. Brenda was hardly happy, refused to adapt to many so-called girl behaviors, and was appalled and angered by Money's invasive and constant interrogations. And yet, the published records from Johns Hopkins claim that Brenda's adaptation to girlhood was "successful," and immediately certain ideological conclusions followed. John Money's Gender Identity Clinic, which monitored Brenda often, concluded that Brenda's successful development as a girl "offers convincing evidence that the gender identity gate is open at birth for a normal child no less than for one born with unfinished sex organs or one who was prenatally over or underexposed to androgen, and that it stays open at least for something over a year at birth" (Money and Green, 299). Indeed, the case was used by the public media to make the case that what is feminine and what is masculine can be altered, that these cultural terms have no fixed meaning or internal destiny, and that they are more malleable than previously thought. Even Kate Millett cited the case in making the argument that biology is not destiny. And Suzanne Kessler also co-wrote with Money essays in favor of the social constructionist thesis. Later Kessler would disavow the alliance and write one of the most important books on the ethical and medical dimensions of sex assignment, *Lessons from the Intersexed*, which includes a trenchant critique of Money himself.

Money's approach to Brenda was to recruit male to female transsexuals to talk to Brenda about the advantages of being a girl. Brenda was subjected to myriad interviews, asked again and again whether she felt like a girl, what her desires were, what her image of the future was, whether it included marriage to a man. Brenda was also asked to strip and show her genitals to medical practitioners who were either interested in the case or monitoring the case for its adaptational success.

When this case was discussed in the press, and when psychiatrists and medical practitioners have referred to it, they have done so in order to criticize the role that John Money's institute played in the case and, in particular, how quickly that institute sought to use Brenda as an example of its own theoretical beliefs, beliefs about the gender neutrality of early childhood, about the malleability of gender, of the primary role of socialization in the production of gender identity. In fact, this is not exactly everything that Money believes, but I will not probe that question here. Those who have become critical of this case believe that it shows us something very different. When we consider, they argue, that David found himself deeply moved to become a boy, and found it unbearable to continue to live as a girl, we have to consider as well that there was some deep-seated sense of gender that David experienced, one that is linked to his original set of genitals, one that seems to be there, as an internal truth and necessity, which no amount of socialization could reverse. This is the view of Colapinto and of Milton Diamond as well. So now the case of Brenda/David is being used to make a revision and reversal in developmental gender theory, providing evidence this time for the reversal of Money's thesis, supporting the notion of an essential gender core, one that is tied in some irreversible way to anatomy and to a deterministic sense of biology. Indeed, Colapinto clearly links Money's cruelty to Brenda to the "cruelty" of social construction as a theory, remarking that Money's refusal to identify a biological or anatomical basis for gender difference in the early 1970s "was not lost on the then-burgeoning women's movement, which had been arguing against a biological basis for sex differences for decades." He claims that Money's published essays "had already been used as one of the main foundations of modern feminism" (69). He quotes *Time Magazine* as engaging in a similarly misguided appropriation of Money's views when they argued that this case "provides strong support for a major contention of women's liberationists: that conventional patterns of masculine and feminine behavior can be altered . . ."(69). Indeed, Colapinto proceeds to talk about the failure of surgically reassigned individuals to live as "normal" and "typical" women or men, arguing that normality is never achieved and, hence, assuming throughout the inarguable value of normalcy itself.

When Natalie Angier reported on the refutation of Money's theory in *The New York Times* (14 March 1997), she claimed that the story of David had "the force of allegory." But which force was that? And is this an allegory with closure? In that article, Angier reports that Diamond used the case to make an argument about intersexual surgery and, by implication, the relative success of transsexual surgery. Diamond argued, for instance, that intersexed infants, that is, those born with mixed genital attributes, generally have a Y chromosome, and the possession of the Y is an adequate basis for concluding that the child ought to be raised as a boy. As it is, the vast majority of intersexed infants are subjected to surgery that seeks to assign them to a female sex, since, as Cheryl Chase, points out, it is simply considered easier to produce a provisional vaginal tract than it is to construct a phallus. Diamond argues that these children should be assigned to the male sex, since the presence of the Y is sufficient grounds for the presumption of social masculinity.

In fact, Chase, the founder and director of the Intersexed Society of North America, voiced skepticism about Diamond's recommendations. Her view, defended by Anne Fausto-Sterling as well, is that although a child should be given a sex assignment for the purposes of establishing a stable social identity, it does not follow that society should engage in coercive surgery to remake the body in the social image of that gender. Such efforts at "correction" not only violate the child but lend support to the idea that gender has to be borne out in singular and normative ways at the level of anatomy. Gender is a different sort of identity, and its relation to anatomy is complex. According to Chase, a child upon maturing may choose to change genders or, indeed, elect for hormonal or surgical intervention, but such decisions are justified because they are based on knowing choice. Indeed, research has shown that such surgical operations have been performed without parents knowing, that such surgical operations have been performed without the children themselves ever having been truthfully told, and without waiting until the child is old enough to offer his or her consent. Most astonishing, in a way, is the mutilated state that these bodies are left in, mutilations performed and then paradoxically rationalized in the name of "looking normal," the rationale used by medical practitioners to justify these surgeries. They often say to parents that the child will not look normal, that the child will be ashamed in the locker room, the locker room, that site of prepubescent anxiety about impending gender developments, and that it would be better for the child to look normal, even when such surgery may deprive the person permanently of sexual function and pleasure. So, as some experts, such as Money, claim that the absence of the full phallus makes the social case for rearing the child as a girl, others such as Diamond argue that the presence of the Y is the most compelling evidence, that it is what is being indexed in persistent feelings of masculinity, and that it cannot be constructed away.

Thus, in the one case, how anatomy looks, how it appears to others, and to myself, as I see others looking at me—this is the basis of a social identity as woman or man. In the other case, how the genetic presence of the "Y" works in tacit ways to structure feeling and self-understanding as a sexed person is the basis. Money thus argues for the ease with which a female body can be surgically constructed, as if femininity was always little more or less than a surgical construction, an elimination, a cutting away. Diamond argues for the invisible and necessary persistence of maleness, one that does not need to "appear" in order to operate as the key feature of gender identity itself. When Angier asks Chase whether she agrees with Diamond's recommendations on intersexual surgery, Chase replies: "They can't conceive of leaving someone alone." Indeed, is the surgery performed in order to create a "normal-looking" body after all? The mutilations and scars that remain hardly offer compelling evidence that this is what the surgeries actually accomplish. Or are these bodies, precisely because they are "inconceivable," subjected to medical machinery that marks them for life?

Another paradox emerges here—one that I hope to write about further on another occasion—namely, the place of sharp machines, of the technology of the knife, in debates on intersexuality and transsexuality alike. If the David/Brenda case is an allegory, or has the force of allegory, it seems to be the site where debates on intersexuality (David is not an intersexual) and transsexuality (David is not a transsexual) converge. This body becomes a point of reference for a narrative that is not about this body, but which seizes upon the body, as it were, in order to inaugurate a narrative that interrogates the limits of the conceivably human. What is inconceivable is conceived again and again, through narrative means, but something remains outside the narrative, a resistant moment that signals a persisting inconceivability.

Despite Diamond's recommendations, the intersex movement has been galvanized by the Brenda/David case, able now to bring to public attention the brutality, coerciveness and lasting harm of the unwanted surgeries performed on intersexed infants. The point is to try to imagine a world in which individuals with mixed genital attributes might be accepted and loved without having to transform them into a more socially coherent or normative version of gender. In this sense, the intersex movement has sought to question why society maintains the ideal of gender dimorphism when a significant percentage of children are chromosomally various, and a continuum exists between male and female that suggests the arbitrariness and falsity of the gender dimorphism as a prerequisite of human development. There are humans, in other words, who live and breathe in the interstices of this binary relation, showing that it is not exhaustive; it is not necessary. Although the transsexual movement, which is internally various, has called for rights to surgical means by which sex might be transformed, it is also clear—and Chase underscores this—that there is also a serious and increasingly popular critique of idealized gender dimorphism within the transsexuality movement itself. One can see it in the work of Riki Wilchins, whose gender theory makes room for transsexuality as a transformative exercise, but one can see it perhaps most dramatically in Kate Bornstein, who argues that to go from F to M, or from M to F, is not necessarily to stay within the binary frame of gender, but to engage transformation itself as the meaning of gender. In some ways, it is Kate Bornstein who is now carrying the legacy of Simone de Beauvoir: If one is not born a woman, but rather becomes one, then becoming is the vehicle for gender itself. But why, we might ask, has David become the occasion for a reflection on transsexuality?

Although David comes to claim that he would prefer to be a man, it is not clear whether David himself believes in the primary causal force of the Y chromosome. Diamond finds support for his theory in David, but it is not clear that David agrees with Diamond. David clearly knows about the world of hormones, asked for them and takes them. David has learned about phallic construction from transsexual contexts, wants a phallus, has it made, and so allegorizes a certain transsexual transformation without precisely exemplifying it. He is, in his view, a man born a man, castrated by the medical establishment, feminized by the psychiatric world, and then enabled to return to who he is. But in order to return to who he is, he requires—and wants, and gets—a subjection to hormones and surgery. He allegorizes transsexuality in order to achieve a sense of naturalness. And this transformation is applauded by the endocrinologists on the case since they understand his appearance now to be in accord with an inner truth.

Whereas the Money Institute enlists transsexuals to instruct Brenda in the ways of women, and *in the name of normalization*, the endocrinologists prescribe the sex change protocol of transsexuality to David for him to reassume his genetic destiny, *in the name of nature*.

And though the Money Institute enlists transsexuals to allegorize Brenda's full transformation into a woman, the endocrinologists propose to appropriate transsexual surgery in order to build the phallus that will make David a more legible man. Importantly, it seems, the norms govern intelligible gender for Money are those that can be forcibly imposed and behaviorally appropriated, so the malleability of gender construction, which is part of his thesis, turns out to require a forceful application. And the "nature" that the endocrinologists defend also needs a certain assistance through surgical and hormonal means, at which point a certain nonnatural intervention in anatomy and biology is precisely what is mandated by nature. So in each case, the primary premise is in some ways refuted by the means by which it is implemented. *Malleability is, as it were, violently imposed. And naturalness is artificially induced.* There are ways of arguing social construction that have nothing to do with Money's project, but that is not my aim here. And there are no doubt ways of seeking recourse to genetic determinants that do not lead to the same kind of interventionist conclusions that are arrived at by Diamond and Sigmundsen. But that is also not precisely my point. For the record, though, the prescriptions arrived at by these purveyors of natural and normative gender in no way follow necessarily from the premises from which they begin, and that the premises with which they begin have no necessity of itself. (One might well disjoin the theory of gender construction, for instance, from the hypothesis of gender normativity and have a very different account of social construction than that offered by Money; one might allow from genetic factors without assuming that they are the only aspect of "nature" that one might consult to understand the sexed characteristics of a human: why is the "Y" considered the exclusive and primary determinant of maleness, exercising preemptive rights over any and all other factors?)

But my point in recounting this story to you and its appropriation for the purposes of gender theory is to suggest that the story as we have it does not actually supply evidence for either thesis, and to suggest that there may be another way of reading this story, one that neither confirms nor denies the theory of social construction, one that neither affirms nor denies gender essentialism. Indeed, what I hope to under-score here is the disciplinary framework within which Brenda/David develops a discourse of self-reporting and self-understanding, since it constitutes the grid of intelligibility by which his own humanness is both questioned and asserted. It seems crucial to remember, as one considers what might count as the evidence of the truth of gender, that Brenda/David was intensely monitored by psychological teams through childhood and adolescence, that teams of doctors observed her behav-ior, that teams of doctors asked her and her brother to disrobe in front of them so that genital development could be gauged, that there was the doctor who asked her to engage in mock coital exercises with her brother, to view the pictures, to know and want the so-called normalcy of unambiguous genitalia. There was an apparatus of knowledge applied to the person and body of Brenda/David that is rarely, if ever, taken into account as part of what David is responding to when he reports on his feelings of true gender.

The act of self-reporting and the act of self-observation takes place in relation to a certain audience, with a certain audience as the imag-ined recipient, before a certain audience for whom a verbal and visual picture of selfhood is being produced. These are speech acts that are very often delivered to those who have been scrutinizing, brutally, the truth of Brenda's gender for years. And even though Diamond and Sigmundsen and even Colapinto are in the position of defending David against Money's various intrusions, they are still asking David how he feels and who he is, trying to ascertain the truth of his sex through the discourse he provides. Because Brenda was subjected to such scrutiny and, most importantly, constantly and repeatedly subjected to a norm, a normalizing ideal that was conveyed through a plurality of gazes, a norm applied to the body, a question is constantly posed: Is this person feminine enough? Has this person made it to femininity? Is femininity being properly embodied here? Is the embodiment working? What evidence can be marshalled in order to know? And surely we must have knowledge here. We must be able to say that we know, and to communicate that in the professional journals, and justify our deci-sion, our act. In other words, these exercises interrogate whether the gender norm that establishes coherent personhood has been success-fully accomplished. The inquiries and inspections can be understood, along these lines, as the violent attempt to implement the norm, and the institutionalization of that power of implementation.

The pediatricians and psychiatrists who have revisited the case in recent years cite David's own self-description to support their point. David's narrative about his own sense of being male that supports the theory that David is really male, and that he was, even when he was Brenda, always male.

David tells his interviewers the following about himself:

> There were little things from early on. I began to see how different I felt and was, from what I was supposed to be. But I didn't know what it meant. I thought I was a freak or something . . . I looked at myself and said I don't like this type of clothing, I don't like the types of toys I was always being given. I like hanging around with the guys and climbing trees and stuff like that and girls don't like any of that stuff. I looked in the mirror and [saw] my shoulders [were] so wide, I mean there [was] nothing feminine about me. I [was] skinny, but other than that, nothing. But that [was] how I figured it out. [I figured I was a guy] but didn't want to admit it. I figured I didn't want to wind up opening a can of worms. (Diamond and Sigmundson, 299–300)

So now you read how David describes himself. And so, if part of my task here is to do justice, not only to my topic, but to the person I am sketching for you, the person around whom so much has been said, the person whose self-description and whose decisions have become the basis for so much gender theorizing, I must be careful in presenting these words. For these words can give you only something of the person I am trying to understand, some part of that person's verbal instance. Since I cannot truly understand this person, since I do not know this person, and have no access to this person, I am left to be a reader of a selected number of words, words that I did not fully select, ones that were selected for me, recorded from interviews and then chosen by those who decided to write their articles on this person for journals such as the *Archives of Pediatric Adolescent Medicine* (Volume 151, March 1997). So we might say that I am given fragments of the person, linguistic fragments of something called a person; what might it mean to do justice to someone under these circumstances? Can we?

On the one hand, we have a self-description, and that is to be honored. These are the words by which this individual gives himself to be understood. On the other hand, we have a description of a self that takes place in a language that is already going on, that is already saturated with norms, that predisposes us as we seek to speak of ourselves. Moreover, we have words that are delivered in the context of an interview, an interview which is part of the long and intrusive observational process that has accompanied Brenda's formation from the start. To do justice to David is, certainly, to take him at his word, and to call him by his chosen name, but how are we to understand his word and his name? Is this the word that he creates? Is this the word that he receives? Are these the words that circulate prior to his emergence as an "I" who might only gain a certain authorization to begin a self-description within the norms of this language? So that when one speaks, one speaks a language that is already speaking, even if one speaks it in a way that is not precisely how it has been spoken before. So what and who is speaking here, when David reports: "There were little things from early on. I began to see how different I felt and was, from what I was supposed to be."

This claim tells us minimally that David understands that there is a norm, a norm of how he was supposed to be, and that he has fallen short of the norm. The implicit claim here is that the norm is femininity, and he has failed to live up to that norm. And there is the norm, and it is externally imposed, communicated through a set of expectations that others have; and then there is the world of feeling and being, and these realms are, for him, distinct. What he feels is not in any way produced by the norm, and the norm is other, elsewhere, not part of who he is, who he has become, what he feels.

But given what we know about how David has been addressed, I might, in an effort to do justice to David, ask, what did Brenda see as Brenda looks at himself, feels as he feels himself, and please excuse my mixing of pronouns here, but matters are becoming changeable. When Brenda looks in the mirror and sees something nameless, freakish, something between the norms, is she not at that moment in question as a human, is she not the spectre of the freak against which and through which the norm installs itself? What is the problem with Brenda such that people are always asking to see her naked, asking her questions about what she is, how she feels, whether this is or is not the same as what is normatively true? Is that self-seeing distinct from the way s/he is seen? He seems clear that the norms are external to him, but what if the norms have become the means by which he sees, the frame for his own seeing, his way of seeing himself? What if the action of the norm is to be found not merely in the ideal that it posits, but in the sense of aberration and of freakishness that it conveys? Consider where precisely the norm operates when David claims, "I looked at myself and said I don't like this type of clothing." To whom is David speaking? And in what world, under what conditions, does not liking that type of clothing provide evidence for being the wrong gender? For whom would that be true? And under what conditions?

Brenda reports, "I didn't like the toys I was being given," and Brenda is speaking here as someone who understands that such a dislike can function as evidence. And it seems reasonable to assume that the reason Brenda understands this "dislike" as evidence of gender dystopia, to use the technical term, is that Brenda has been addressed time and again by those who make use of every utterance that Brenda makes about her experience as evidence for or against a true gender. That Brenda happens not to like certain toys, certain dolls, certain games, may be significant in relation to the question of how and with what Brenda likes to play. But in what world, precisely, do such dislikes count as clear or unequivocal evidence for or against being a given gender? Do parents regularly rush off to gender identity clinics when their boys play with yarn, or their girls play with trucks? Or must there already be a rather enormous anxiety at play, an anxiety about the truth of gender which seizes on this or that toy, this or that proclivity of dress, the size of the shoulder, the leanness of the body, to conclude that something like a clear gender identity can or cannot be built from these scattered desires, these variable and invariable features of the body, of bone structure, of proclivity, of attire?

So what does my analysis imply? Does it tell us whether the gender here is true or false? No. And does this have implications for whether David should have been surgically transformed into Brenda, or Brenda surgically transformed into David? No, it does not. I do not know how to judge that question here, and I am not sure it can be mine to judge. Does justice demand that I decide? Or does justice demand that I wait to decide, that I practice a certain deferral in the face of a situation in which too many have rushed to judgement? Might it not be useful, important, even just, to consider a few matters before we decide, before we ascertain whether it is, in fact, ours to decide.

Consider in this spirit, then, that it is for the most part the gender essentialist position that must be voiced for transsexual surgery to take place, and that someone who comes in with a sense of the gender as changeable will have a more difficult time convincing psychiatrists and doctors to perform the surgery. In San Francisco, FTM candidates actually practice the narrative of gender essentialism that they are required to perform before they go in to see the doctors, and there are now coaches to help them, dramaturgs of transsexuality who will help you make the case for no fee. Indeed, we might say that Brenda/David together went through two transsexual surgeries: the first based on a hypothetical argument about what gender should be, given the ablated nature of the penis; the second based on what the gender should be, based on the behavioral and verbal indications of the person in question. In both cases, certain inferences are made, ones that suggest that a body must be a certain way for a gender to work, another which says that a body must feel a certain way for a gender to work. David clearly came to disrespect and abhor the views of the first set of doctors and developed, we might say, a lay critique of the phallus to support his resistance:

Doctor said "it's gonna be tough, you're gonna be picked on, you're gonna be very alone, you're not gonna find anybody (unless you have vaginal surgery and live as a female)." And I thought to myself, you know I wasn't very old at the time, but it dawned on me that these people gotta be pretty shallow if that's the only thing they think I've got going for me; that the only reason why people get married and have children and have a productive life is because of what they have between their legs . . . If that's all they think of me, that they justify my worth by what I have between my legs, then I gotta be a complete loser. (301)

Here David makes a distinction between the "I" that he is, the person that he is, and the value that is conferred upon his personhood by virtue of what is or is not between his legs. He was wagering that he will be loved for something other than this or, at least, that his penis will not be the reason he is loved. He was holding out, implicitly, for something called "depth" over and against the "shallowness" of the

doctors. And so although David asked for and received his new status as male, has asked for and received his new phallus, he is also
something other than what he now has, and though he has undergone
this transformation, he refuses to be reduced to the body part that he
has acquired. "If that's all they think of me," he begins his sentence,
offering a knowing and critical rejoinder to the work of the norm.
There is something of me that exceeds this part, though I want this part,
though it is part of me. He does not want his "worth justified" by what
he has between his legs, and what this means is that he has another sense
of how the worth of the person might be justified. So we might say that
he is living his desire, acquiring the anatomy that he wants in order to
live his desire, but that his desire is complex, and his worth is complex.
And this is why, no doubt, in response to many of the questions that
Money posed: Do you want to have a penis? Do you want to marry a
girl? David often refused to answer the question, refused to stay in the
room where Money was, refused to visit Baltimore at all after a while.

David does not trade in one gender norm for another, not exactly.
It would be as wrong to say that he has simply internalized a gendered
norm (from a critical position) as it would be to say that he has failed
to live up to a gendered norm (from a normalizing, medical position),
since he has already established that what will justify his worth will be
the invocation of an "I" which is not reducible to the compatibility of
his anatomy with the norm. He thinks something more of himself than
what others think, he does not fully justify his worth through recourse
to what he has between his legs, and he does not think of himself as
a complete loser. Something exceeds the norm, and he recognizes its
unrecognizability. It is, in a sense, his distance from the knowably
human that operates as a condition of critical speech, the source of his
worth, as the justification for his worth. He says that if what those doctors believe were true, he would be a complete loser, and he implies
that he is not a complete loser, that something in him is winning.

But he is also saying something more—he is cautioning us against
the absolutism of distinction itself, for his phallus does not constitute
the entirety of his worth. There is an incommensurability between who
he is and what he has, an incommensurability between the phallus he
has and what it is expected to be (and in this way no different from
anyone with a phallus), which means that he has not become one with
the norm, and yet he is still someone, speaking, insisting, even referring to himself. And it is from this gap, this incommensurability,

between the norm that is supposed to inaugurate his humanness and the spoken insistence on himself that he performs that he derives his worth, that he speaks his worth. And we cannot precisely give content to this person at the very moment that he speaks his worth, which means that it is precisely the ways in which he is not fully recognizable, fully disposable, fully categorizable, that his humanness emerges. And this is important because we might ask that he enter into intelligibility in order to speak and to be known, but what he does instead, through his speech, is to offer a critical perspective on the norms that confer intelligibility itself. He shows, we might say, that there is an understanding to be had that exceeds the norms of intelligibility itself. And he achieves this "outside," we might speculate, by refusing the interrogations that besiege him, reversing their terms, and learning the ways in which he might escape. If he renders himself unintelligible to those who seek to know and capture his identity, this means that something about him is intelligible outside of the framework of accepted intelligibility. We might be tempted to say that there is some core of a person, and so some presumption of humanism, that emerges here, that is supervenient to the particular discourses on sexed and gendered intelligibility that constrain him. But that would mean only that he is denounced by one discourse only to be carried by another discourse, the discourse of humanism. Or we might say that there is some core of the subject who speaks, who speaks beyond what is sayable, and that it is this ineffability that marks David's speech, the ineffability of the other who is not disclosed through speech, but leaves a portentious shard of itself in its saying, a self that is beyond discourse itself.

But what I would prefer is that we might consider carefully that when David invokes the "I" in this quite hopeful and unexpected way, he is speaking about a certain conviction he has about his own lovability; he says that "they" must think he is a real loser if the only reason anyone is going to love him is because of what he has between his legs. The "they" is telling him that he will not be loved, or that he will not be loved unless he takes what they have for him, and that they have what he needs in order to get love, that he will be loveless without what they have. But he refuses to accept that what they are offering in their discourse is love. He refuses their offering of love, understanding it as a bribe, as a seduction to subjection. He will be and he is, he tells us, loved for some other reason, a reason they do not understand, and it is not a reason we are given. It is clearly a reason that is beyond the regime of reason established by the norms of sexology itself. We know only that he holds out for another reason, and that in this sense, we no longer know what kind of reason this is, what reason can be; he establishes the limits of what they know, disrupting the politics of truth, making use of his desubjugation within that order of being to establish the possibility of love beyond the grasp of that norm. He positions himself, knowingly, in relation to the norm, but he does not comply with its requirements. He risks a certain "desubjugation"—is he a subject? How will we know? And in this sense, David's discourse puts into play the operation of critique itself, critique which, defined by Foucault, is precisely the desubjugation of the subject within the politics of truth. This does not mean that David becomes unintelligible and, therefore, without value to politics; rather, he emerges at the limits of intelligibility, offering a perspective on the variable ways in which norms circumscribe the human. It is precisely because we understand, without quite grasping, that he has another reason, that he *is*, as it were, another reason, that we see the limits to the discourse of intelligibility that would decide his fate. David does not precisely occupy a new world, since he is still, even within the syntax which brings about his "I," still positioned somewhere between the norm and its failure. And he is, finally, neither one; he is the human in its anonymity, as that which we do not yet know how to name or that which sets a limits on all naming. And in that sense, he is the anonymous—and critical—condition of the human as it speaks itself at the limits of what we think we know.

Postscript: As this book was going to press in June of 2004, I was saddened to learn that David Reimer took his life at the age of 38. The New York Times obituary (5/12/04) mentions that his brother died two years earlier and that he was now separated from his wife. It is difficult to know what, in the end, made his life unlivable or why this life was one he felt was time to end. It seems clear, however, that there was always a question posed for him, and by him, whether life in his gender would be survivable. It is unclear whether it was his gender that was the problem, or the "treatment" that brought about an enduring suffering for him. The norms governing what it is to be a worthy, recognizable, and sustainable human life clearly did not support his life in any continuous or solid way. Life for him was always a wager and a risk, a courageous and fragile accomplishment.

4. Undiagnosing Gender

In recent years there have been debates about the status of the *Diagnostic and Statistical Manual of Mental Disorders'* (*DSM-IV*) diagnosis of gender identity disorder and, in particular, whether there are good reasons to keep the diagnosis on the books, or whether there are no longer very many good reasons. On the one hand, those within the GLBQTI community who want to keep the diagnosis argue that it offers certification for a condition, and facilitates access to a variety of medical and technological means for transitioning. Moreover, some insurance companies will only absorb some of the very high costs of sex change if they first can establish that the change is "medically necessitated." It is important, for these reasons, not to understand sex change surgery or hormonal usage as "elective surgery." Although one might want to say that it is a choice, even a choice of a dramatic and profound kind, for the purpose of the insurance allocation it has to be a medically conditioned choice. We can surely think for quite some time about what a medically conditioned choice actually is, but for the purpose of this argument it's important to distinguish between a choice conditioned by a diagnosis and one that is not. In the latter case, the choice to transition can include some or all of the following: the choice to live as another gender, to take hormonal surgery, to find and declare a name, to secure new legal status for one's gender, and to undergo surgery. If it is determined by psychological or medical professionals to be necessitated, that is, if it is determined that not undergoing this transition produces distress, maladaptation, and other forms of suffering, then it would seem to follow that the choice to transition is conceived as one that is embraced and condoned by medical professionals who have the person's ultimate well-being at issue. The "diagnosis" can operate in several ways, but one way it can and does operate, especially in the hands of those who are transphobic, is as an instrument of pathologization.

To be diagnosed with gender identity disorder (GID) is to be found, in some way, to be ill, sick, wrong, out of order, abnormal, and to suffer a certain stigmatization as a consequence of the diagnosis being given at all. As a result, some activist psychiatrists and trans people have argued that the diagnosis should be eliminated altogether, that transsexuality is not a disorder, and ought not to be conceived of as one, and that trans people ought to be understood as engaged in a practice of self-determination, an exercise of autonomy. Thus, on the one hand, the diagnosis continues to be valued because it facilitates an economically feasible way of transitioning. On the other hand, the diagnosis is adamantly opposed because it continues to pathologize as a mental disorder what ought to be understood instead as one among many human possibilities of determining one's gender for oneself.

One can see from the above sketch that there is a tension in this debate between those who are, for the purposes of the debate, trying to gain entitlement and financial assistance, and those who seek to ground the practice of transsexuality in a notion of autonomy. We might well hesitate at once and ask whether these two views are actually in opposition to one another. After all, one might argue, and people surely have, that the way that the diagnosis facilitates certain entitlements to insurance benefits,[1] to medical treatment, and to legal status, actually works in the service of what we might call transautonomy. After all, if I want to transition, I may well need the diagnosis to help me achieve my goal, and achieving my goal is precisely an exercise of my autonomy. Indeed, we can argue that no one achieves autonomy without the assistance or support of a community, especially if one is making a brave and difficult choice such as transitioning. But then we have to ask whether the diagnosis is unambiguously part of the "support" that individuals need in order to exercise self-determination with respect to gender. After all, the diagnosis makes many assumptions that undercut transautonomy. It subscribes to forms of psychological assessment which assume that the diagnosed person is affected by forces he or she does not understand It assumes that there is delusion or dysphoria in such people. It assumes that certain gender norms have not been properly embodied, and that an error and a failure have taken place. It makes assumptions about fathers and mothers, and what normal family life is, and should have been. It assumes the language of correction, adaptation, and normalization. It seeks to uphold the gender norms of the world as it is currently constituted and tends to pathologize any effort to produce gender in ways that fail to conform to existing norms (or, fails to conform to a certain dominant fantasy of what existing norms actually are). It is a diagnosis that has been given to people against their will, and it is a diagnosis that has effectively broken the will of many people, especially queer and trans youth.

So, it would seem that the debate is a very complex one, and that, in a way, those who want to keep the diagnosis want to do so because it helps them achieve their aims and, in that sense, realize their autonomy. And those who want to do away with the diagnosis want to do so because it might make for a world in which they might be regarded and treated in non-pathological ways, therefore enhancing their autonomy in important ways. I think we see here the concrete limits to any notion of autonomy that establishes the individual as alone, free of social conditions, without dependency on social instruments of various kinds. Autonomy is a socially conditioned way of living in the world. Those instruments, such as the diagnosis, can be enabling, but they can also be restrictive and often they can function as both at the same time.

On the face of it, it would seem that there are two different approaches to autonomy, but it is important to note that this is not only a philosophical problem to be answered in the abstract. To understand the difference between these views, we have to ask how the diagnosis is actually lived. What does it mean to live with it?[2] Does it help some people to live, to achieve a life that feels worth living? Does it hinder some people from living, make them feel stigmatized, and, in some cases, contribute to a suicidal conclusion? On the one hand, we ought not to underestimate the benefits that the diagnosis has brought, especially to trans people of limited economic means who, without the assistance of medical insurance, could not have achieved their goals. On the other hand, we ought not to underestimate the pathologizing force of the diagnosis, especially on young people who may not have the critical resources to resist this force. In these cases, the diagnosis can be debilitating, if not murderous. And sometimes it murders the soul, and sometimes it becomes a contributing factor in suicide. So, the stakes of this debate are high since it would seem, in the end, to be a matter of life and death, and for some the diagnosis seems to mean life, and for others, the diagnosis seems to mean death. For others too, it may well seem to be an ambivalent blessing or, indeed, an ambivalent curse.

In order to understand how these two understandable positions have emerged, let's consider first what the diagnosis consists of in the United States and, second, its history and present usages. A diagnosis of gender disorder has to conform to the sway of the *DSM-IV*'s definition of gender dysphoria.[3] The last revision to that set of definitions was instituted in 1994. For a diagnosis to be complete, however, psychological tests are needed along with "letters" from therapists providing a diagnosis and vouching that the individual in question can live and thrive in the new sexed identity. The 1994 definition is the result of several revisions, and probably needs to be understood as well in light of the American Psychiatric Association's (APA) decision in 1973 to get rid of the diagnosis of homosexuality as a disorder and its 1987 decision to delete "ego dystonic homosexuality," a remaining vestige from the earlier definition. Some have argued that the GID diagnosis took over some of the work that the earlier homosexuality diagnosis performed, and that GID became an indirect way of diagnosing homosexuality as a gender identity problem. In this way, the GID continued the APA's tradition of homophobia, but in a less explicit way. In fact, conservative groups that seek to "correct" homosexuality, such as the National Association of Research and Therapy of Homosexuality, argue that if you can identify GID in a child, there's a 75 percent chance that you can predict homosexuality in that person as an adult, a result which, for them, is a clear abnormality and tragedy. Thus, the diagnosis of GID is in most cases a diagnosis of homosexuality, and the disorder attached to the diagnosis implies that homosexuality remains a disorder as well.

The very way that groups such as these conceptualize the relationship between GID and homosexuality is very problematic. If we are to understand GID as based on the perception of enduring gendered traits of the opposite sex, that is, boys with "feminine" attributes, and girls with "masculine" attributes, then the assumption remains that boy traits will lead to a desire for women, and girl traits will lead to a desire for men. In both of these cases, heterosexual desire is presumed, where presumably opposites attract. But this is to argue, effectively, that homosexuality is to be understood as gender inversion, and that the "sexual" part remains heterosexual, although inverted. It is apparently rare, according to this conceptualization, that boy traits in a boy lead to desire for other boys, and that girl traits in a girl lead to desire for other girls. So the 75 percent of those diagnosed with GID are considered homosexual only if we understand homosexuality under the model of gender inversion, and sexuality under the model of heterosexual desire. Boys are still always desiring girls, and girls are still always desiring boys. If 25 percent of those diagnosed with GID do not become homosexual, that would seem to mean that they do not conform to the gender inversion model. But because the gender inversion model can only understand sexuality as heterosexuality, it would seem that the remaining 25 percent would be homosexual, that is, nonconforming to the model of homosexuality as inverted heterosexuality. Thus, we could argue, somehat facetiously, that 100 percent of those diagnosed with GID turn out to be homosexual!

Although the joke is irresistible to me only because it would so alarm the National Association of Research and Therapy of Homosexuality, it is important to consider, more seriously, how the map of sexuality and gender is radically misdescribed by those who think within these terms. Indeed, the correlations between gender identity and sexual orientation are murky at best: we cannot predict on the basis of what gender a person is what kind of gender identity the person will have, and what direction(s) of desire he or she will ultimately entertain and pursue. Although John Money and other so-called transpositionalists think that sexual orientation tends to follow from gender identity, it would be a huge mistake to assume that gender identity causes sexual orientation or that sexuality references in some necessary way a prior gender identity. As I'll try to show, even if one could accept as unproblematic what "feminine" traits are, and what "masculine" traits are, it would not follow that the "feminine" is attracted to the masculine, and the "masculine" to the feminine. That would only follow if we used an exclusively heterosexual matrix to understand desire. And actually, that matrix would misrepresent some of the queer crossings in heterosexuality, when for instance a feminized heterosexual man wants a feminized woman, in order that the two might well be "girls together." Or when masculine heterosexual women want their boys to be both girls and boys for them. The same queer crossings happen in lesbian and gay life, when butch on butch produces a specifically lesbian mode of male homosexuality. Moreover, bisexuality, as I've said before, can't be reducible to two heterosexual desires, understood as a feminine side wanting a masculine object, or a masculine side wanting a feminine one. Those crossings are as complex as anything that happens within heterosexuality or homosexuality. These kinds of crossings occur more often than is generally noted, and it makes a mockery of the transpositionalist claim that gender identity is a predictor of sexual orientation. Indeed, sometimes it is the very disjunction between gender identity and sexual orientation—the disorientation of the transpositionalist model itself—that constitutes for some people what is most erotic and exciting.

The way that the disorder has been taken up by researchers with homophobic aims presupposes the tacit thesis that homosexuality is the damage that will follow from such a sex change, but it is most important to argue that it is not a disorder and that there is a whole range of complex relations to cross-gendered life, some of them may involve dressing in another gender, some of them may involve living in another gender, some of them may involve hormones, and surgery, and most of them involve one or more of the above. Sometimes this implies a change in so-called object choice, but sometimes not. One can become a transman and want boys (and become a male homosexual), or one can become a transman and want girls (and become a heterosexual), or one can become a transman and undergo a set of shifts in sexual orientation that constitute a very specific life history and narrative. That narrative is not capturable by a category, or it may only be capturable by a category for a time. Life histories are histories of becoming, and categories can sometimes act to freeze that process of becoming. Shifts in sexual persuasion can be in response to particular partners, so that lives, trans or no, don't always emerge as coherently heterosexual or homosexual, and the very meaning and lived experience of bisexuality can also shift through time, forming a particular history that reflects certain kinds of experiences rather than others.

The diagnosis of gender dysphoria requires that a life takes on a more or less definite shape over time; a gender can only be diagnosed if it meets the test of time.[4] You have to show that you have wanted for a long time to live life as the other gender; it also requires that you prove that you have a practical and livable plan to live life for a long time as the other gender. The diagnosis, in this way, wants to establish that gender is a relatively permanent phenomenon. It won't do, for instance, to walk into a clinic and say that it was only after you read a book by Kate Bornstein that you realized what you wanted to do, but that it wasn't really conscious for you until that time. It can't be that cultural life changed, that words were written and exchanged, that you went to events and to clubs, and saw that certain ways of living were really possible and desirable, and that something about your own possibilities became clear to you in ways that they had not been before. You would be ill-advised to say that you believe that the norms that govern what is a recognizable and livable life are changeable, and that within your lifetime, new cultural efforts were made to broaden those norms, so that people like yourself might well live within supportive communities as a transsexual, and that it was precisely this shift in the public norms, and the presence of a supportive community, that allowed you to feel that transitioning had become possible and desirable. In this sense, you cannot explicitly subscribe to a view that changes in gendered experience follow upon changes in social norms, since that would not suffice to satisfy the Harry Benjamin standard rules for the care of gender identity disorder. Indeed, those rules presume, as does the GID diagnosis, that we all more or less "know" already what the norms for gender—"masculine" and "feminine"—are and that all we really need to do is figure out whether they are being embodied in this instance or some other. But what if those terms no longer do the descriptive work that we need them to do? What if they only operate in unwieldy ways to describe the experience of gender that someone has? And if the norms for care and the measures for the diagnosis assume that we are permanently constituted in one way or another, what happens to gender as a mode of becoming? Are we stopped in time, made more regular and coherent than we necessarily want to be, when we submit to the norms in order to achieve the entitlements one needs, and the status one desires?

Although there are strong criticisms to be made of the diagnosis—and I will detail some of them below when I turn to the text itself—it would be wrong to call for its eradication without first putting into place a set of structures through which transitioning can be paid for and legal status attained. In other words, if the diagnosis is now the instrument through which benefits and status can be achieved, it cannot be simply disposed of without finding other, durable ways to achieve those same results.

One obvious response to this dilemma is to argue that one should approach the diagnosis *strategically*. One could then reject the truth claims that the diagnosis makes, that is, reject the description it offers of transsexuality but nevertheless make use of the diagnosis as a pure instrument, a vehicle for achieving one's goals. One would, then, ironically or facetiously or half-heartedly submit to the diagnosis, even as one inwardly maintains that there is nothing "pathological" about the desire to transition or the resolve to realize that desire. But here we have to ask whether submitting to the diagnosis does not involve, more or less consciously, a certain subjection to the diagnosis such that one does end up internalizing some aspect of the diagnosis, conceiving of oneself as mentally ill or "failing" in normality, or both, even as one seeks to take a purely instrumental attitude toward these terms.

The more important point in support of this last argument has to do with children and young adults, since when we ask who it is who would be able to sustain a purely instrumental relation to the diagnosis, it tends to be shrewd and savvy adults, ones who have other discourses available for understanding who they are and want to be. But are children and teens always capable of effecting the distance necessary to sustain a purely instrumental approach to being subjected to a diagnosis?

Dr. Richard Isay gives as the primary reason to get rid of the diagnosis altogether its effect on children. The diagnosis itself, he writes, "may cause emotional damage by injuring the self-esteem of a child who has no mental disorder."[5] Isay accepts the claim that many young gay boys prefer so-called feminine behavior as children, playing with their mother's clothes, refusing rough and tumble activities, but he argues that the problem here is not with the traits but with "parental admonitions . . . aimed at modifying this behavior [which] deleteriously affect[s] these boys' self-regard." His solution is for parents to learn to be supportive of what he calls "gender atypical traits." Isay's contribution is important in many respects, but one clear contribution it makes is that it calls for a reconceptualization of the phenomenon that refuses pathologizing language: he refuses to elevate typical gender attributes to a standard of psychological normality or to relegate atypical traits to abnormality. Instead, he substitutes the language of typicality for normality altogether. Physicians who argue against Isay not only insist that the disorder *is* a disorder, and that the presentation of persistently atypical gender traits in children is a "psychopathology,"[6] but they couple this insistence on pathologization with a paternalistic concern for the afflicted, citing how the diagnosis is necessary for insurance benefits and other entitlements. Indeed, they exploit the clear and indisputable need that poor, working class, and middle class trans-aspirants have for medical insurance and legal support to argue not only in favor of keeping the diagnosis on the books but in favor of their view that this is a pathology that must be corrected. So even if the diagnosis is approached as an instrument or vehicle for accomplishing the end goal of transitioning, the diagnosis can still (a) instill a sense of mental disorder on those whom it diagnoses, (b) entrench the power of the diagnosis to conceptualize transsexuality as a pathology, and (c) be used as a rationale by those who are in well-funded research institutes whose aim is to keep transsexuality within the sphere of mental pathology.

Some other solutions have been proposed that seek to ameliorate the pathological effects of the diagnosis by taking it out of the hands of the mental health profession altogether. Jacob Hale argues that this matter should not be mediated by psychologists and psychiatrists; the question of whether and how to gain access to medical and technological resources should be a matter between client and medical doctor exclusively.[7] His view is that one goes to the doctor for other kinds of reconstructive surgeries or on other occasions where taking hormones may prove felicitous, and no one asks you a host of questions about your earliest fantasies or childhood practices of play. The certification of stable mental health is not required for breast reduction or menopausal ingestion of estrogen. The required intervention of a mental health professional on the occasion in which one wants to transition inserts a paternalistic structure into the process and undermines the very autonomy that is the basis for the claim of entitlement to begin with. A therapist is asked to worry about whether you will be able, psychologically, to integrate into an established social world characterized by large-scale conformity to accepted gender norms, but the therapist is not asked to say whether you are brave enough or have enough community support to live a transgendered life when the threat of violence and discrimination against you will be heightened. The therapist is not asked whether your way of living gender will help to produce a world of fewer constrictions on gender, or whether you are up to that important task. The therapist is asked to predict whether your choice will lead to postoperative regret, and here your desire is examined for its persistence and tenacity, but little attention is given to what happens to one's persistent and tenacious desires when the social world, and the diagnosis itself, demeans them as psychic disorders.[8]

I began this essay by suggesting that the view one takes on keeping or opposing the diagnosis depends in part on how one conceives the conditions for autonomy. In the arguments of Isay, we see an argument that claims that the diagnosis not only undermines the autonomy of children but mistakes their autonomy for pathology. In the argument that Hale offers, we see that the diagnosis itself takes on a different meaning if it is no longer used by mental health professionals. The question remains, though, whether medical practitioners with no particular background in mental health will nevertheless use mental health criteria to make decisions that could be no less favorable than those made by mental health practitioners. If Hale is arguing, though, that it ought to be shifted to medical doctors as part of a drive to redefine the diagnosis so that it no longer contains mental health criteria in it, then he is also proposing a new diagnosis or no diagnosis, since the DSM-IV rendition cannot be voided of its mental health criteria. To answer the question of whether the shift to medical doctors would be propitious, we would have to ask whether the inclinations of medical practitioners are generally to be trusted with this responsibility, or whether the world of progressive therapists offers a better chance for humane and successful passage through the process of diagnosis. Although I do not have a sociologically grounded answer to this question, I consider that it has to be pursued before one can judge the appropriateness of Hale's recommendation. The great benefit of his view is that it treats the patient as a client who is exercising consumer autonomy within the medical domain. That autonomy is assumed, and it is also posited as the ultimate goal and meaning of the process of transitioning itself.

But this raises the question of how autonomy ought to be conceived in this debate, and whether revisions in the diagnosis itself might provide a way around the apparent stand-off between those who wish to have the diagnosis deleted and those who wish to keep it for the instrumental value it provides, especially for those in financial need. There are two different conceptions of autonomy at work in this debate. The view that opposes the diagnosis altogether tends to be individualist, if not libertarian, and the views that argue in favor of keeping the diagnosis tend to acknowledge that there are material conditions for the exercise of liberty. The view which worries that the diagnosis may well be internalized or damaging suggests that the psychological conditions for autonomy can be undermined, and have been undermined, and that youth are at higher risk for this compromised and damaged sense of self.

Autonomy, liberty, and freedom are all related terms, and they also imply certain kinds of legal protections and entitlements. After all, the U.S. Constitution guarantees the pursuit of liberty. It could be argued that restrictive conditions imposed upon transsexual and transgendered individuals to exercise a liberty proper to that identity and practice is discriminatory. Paradoxically, the insurance companies demean the notion of liberty when they distinguish, say, between mastectomies that are "medically necessitated" and those that constitute "elective surgery." The former are conceived as operations that no one readily chooses, that are imposed upon individuals by medical circumstance, usually cancer. But even that conceptualization misrepresents the kinds of choices that informed patients can make about how to approach cancer, when possible treatments include radiation, chemotherapy, Arimidex, lumpectomy, partial and full mastectomy. Women will make different choices about treatment depending on how they feel about their breasts and the prospects of further cancer, and the range of choices made is significantly broad. Some women will struggle to keep their breasts no matter what, and others let them go without much difficulty. Some will choose reconstruction and make some choices about prospective breasts, and others choose not to.

A rather butch lesbian in San Francisco recently had cancer in one breast, and decided, in consultation with her doctor, to have a full mastectomy. She thought it was a good idea to have the other breast removed as well, since she wanted to minimize the chances of a recurrence. This choice was made easier for her because she had no strong emotional attachment to her breasts: they did not form an important part of her gendered or sexual self-understanding. Whereas her insurance company agreed to pay for the first mastectomy, they worried that the second breast was "elective surgery" and that, if they paid for that, it would be setting a precedent for covering elective transsexual surgery. The insurance company thus wanted to limit both consumer autonomy in medical decision making (understanding the woman as someone who wanted for medical reasons to have the second breast removed), and to dismiss autonomy as the basis for a transsexual operation (understanding the woman as a possible transitioner). At the same time, a friend of mine recovering from a mastectomy sought to understand what possibilities existed for her for reconstructive surgery. She was referred by her doctor to transsexual clients who could introduce her to various technologies and the relative aesthetic merits of those options. Although I'm not aware of coalitions of breast-cancer survivors and transsexuals, I can see how a movement could easily emerge whose main demand would be to petition insurance companies to recognize the role of autonomy in producing and maintaining primary and secondary sex characteristics. All this seems less strange, I would suggest, when we understand cosmetic surgery on a continuum with all the other practices that humans engage in order to maintain and cultivate primary and secondary sex characteristics for cultural and social reasons. I gather that men who want penile augmentation or women who want breast augmentation and reduction are not sent to psychiatrists for certification. It is, of course, interesting to consider in light of current gender norms why a woman who wants breast reduction requires no psychological certification, but a man who wants penile reduction may well. There is no presumption of mental malfunctioning for women who take estrogen or men who take Viagra. This is, I presume, because they are operating within the norm to the extent that they are seeking to enhance the "natural," making readjustments within acceptable norms, and sometimes even confirming and strengthening traditional gender norms.

The butch, nearly trans, person who wanted both her cancerous and noncancerous breasts removed understood that the only way she could gain the benefits of a mastectomy was to get cancer in her other breast or to subject her own gender desires to medical and psychiatric review. Although she didn't consider herself trans, she understood that she could present as trans in order to qualify for the GID and insurance benefits. Sometimes reconstructive breast surgery is covered by medical insurance, even if done for elective reasons, but mastectomy is not included as elective surgeries covered by insurance. In the world of insurance, it appears to make sense that a woman might want less breast, but no sense that she would want no breast. Wanting no breast puts into question whether she still wants to be a woman. It is as if the butch's desire to have the breast removed is not quite plausible as a healthy option unless it is the sign of a gender disorder or some other medical urgency.

But why is it that we do accept these other choices as choices, regardless of what we take their social meaning to be? Society doesn't consider itself to have a right to stop a woman from enlarging or diminishing her breasts, and we don't consider penile enhancement to be a problem, unless it is being done by an illegitimate doctor who botches the results. No one gets sent to a psychiatrist for announcing a plan to cut or grow his or her hair or to go on a diet, unless one is at risk for anorexia. Yet these practices are part of the daily habits of cultivating secondary sex characteristics, if that category is taken to mean all the various bodily indicators of sex. If the bodily traits "indicate" sex, then sex is not quite the same as the means by which it is indicated. Sex is made understandable through the signs that indicate how it should be read or understood. These bodily indicators are the cultural means by which the sexed body is read. They are themselves bodily, and they operate as signs, so there is no easy way to distinguish between what is "materially" true, and what is "culturally" true about a sexed body. I don't mean to suggest that purely cultural signs produce a material body, but only that the body does not become sexually readable without those signs, and that those signs are irreducibly cultural and material at once.

So what are the versions of autonomy at work in these various approaches to the *DSM* diagnosis of Gender Identity Disorder? And how might we conceive of autonomy in such a way that we might find a way of thinking through the very reasonable disagreements that have emerged regarding whether to preserve or eradicate the diagnosis? Although it is obvious that not all individuals diagnosed with GID are or wish to become transsexual, they are nevertheless affected by the use of the diagnosis to further the aims of transsexuals, since to use the diagnosis is to strengthen its status as a useful instrument. This is no reason not to use it, but it does imply a certain risk, and certain implications. A strengthened diagnosis can have effects that its users do not intend or condone. And though it may well serve an individual's important needs to secure status and funding for a transition, it may well be used by the medical and psychiatric establishments to extend its pathologizing influence on populations of transsexuals, trans youth, and lesbian, bi-, and gay youth as well. From the point of view of the individual, the diagnosis can be regarded as an instrument by which to further one's self-expression and self-determination. Indeed, it can be counted among the very fundamental instruments one needs in order to make a transition that makes life livable, and that provides the grounds for one's flourishing as an embodied subject. On the other hand, the instrument takes on a life of its own, and it can work to make life harder for those who suffer by being pathologized, and who lose certain rights and liberties, including child custody, employment, and housing, by virtue of the stigma attached to the diagnosis or, more precisely, by virtue of the stigma that the diagnosis strengthens and furthers. Whereas it would no doubt be best to live in a world in which there was no such stigma, and no such diagnosis, we do no yet live in such a world. Moreover, the profound suspicion about the mental health of those who transgress gender norms structures the majority of psychological discourses and institutions, medical approaches to gender, and legal and financial institutions that regulate questions of status and possibilities for financial assistance and medical benefits.

There is an important argument to be made from the perspective of freedom, however. It is important to remember that the specific forms which freedom takes depend upon the social conditions and social institutions that govern human options at this time. Those who claim that transsexuality is, and should be, a matter of choice, an exercise of freedom, are surely right, and they are right as well to point out that the various obstacles posed by the psychological and psychiatric professions are paternalistic forms of power by which a basic human freedom is being suppressed. Underlying some of these positions is a libertarian approach to sex transformation. Richard Green, president of the Harry Benjamin International Gender Dysphoria Association, and a strong advocate for transsexual rights, including the rights of transsexual parents, argues on behalf of this issue as a matter of personal freedom and of privacy. He cites John Stuart Mill, writing that he "argued forcefully that adults should be able to do with their bodies as they wish providing that it did not bring harm to another. Therefore, if the third gender, the transsexual, or the would-be limb amputee can continue to shoulder social responsibilities post-surgery, then the surgical requests are not society's business."[9] Although Green makes this claim, one he himself calls "philosophical," he notes that it comes into conflict with the question of who will pay, and whether society has an obligation to pay for a procedure which is being defended as a matter of personal liberty.

I don't find many people writing in this area, except from within the discourse of the Christian Right, whose response to the GID is to embrace it wholeheartedly and say, "Don't take this diagnosis away from me! Pathologize me, please!" There are, surely, many psychiatrists and psychologists who insist upon gender identity disorder as a pathology. And there is a well-funded and impossibly prolific professor of neuropsychiatry and behavioral science at the University of South Carolina, George Rekers, who combines a polemical political conservatism with an effort to intensify and extend the use of this diagnosis.[10] His main concern seems to be about boys, boys becoming men, and men becoming strong fathers in the context of heterosexual marriage. He also traces the rise of GID to the breakdown of the family, the loss of strong father figures for boys, and the subsequent "disturbance" that it is said to cause. His manifest concern about the emergence of homosexuality in boys is clear from his discussion as well, citing as he does the 1994 *DSM* conclusion that 75 percent of GID youth turn out to be homosexual as adults. Rekers has published loads of studies strewn with "data" presented within the context of empirical research protocols. Although intensely polemical, he understands himself as a scientist and an empiricist, and he attributes ideological bias to his opponents. He writes that "in a generation confused by radical ideologies on male and female roles, we need solid research on men and women who are well-adjusted examples of a secure male identity and a secure female identity."[11] His "solid research" is intended to show the benefits of distinguishing clearly between gender norms and their pathologies "for family life and the larger culture." In this vein, Rekers also notes that "preliminary findings have been published in the literature which report on the positive therapeutic effects of religious conversion for curing transsexualism . . . and on the positive therapeutic effect of a church ministry to repentant homosexuals."[12] He seems to be relatively unconcerned with girls, which impresses me as entirely symptomatic of his preoccupation with patriarchal authority, and his inability to see the threat that women of all kinds might pose to the presumptions he makes about male power. The fate of masculinity absorbs this study because masculinity, a fragile and fallible construct, needs the social support of marriage and stable family life in order to find its right path. Indeed, masculinity by itself tends to falter, in his view, and needs to be housed and propped up by various social supports, suggesting that masculinity is itself a function of these social organizations, and has no intrinsic meaning outside of them. In any case, there are people like Rekers who make an adamant and highly polemical case, not only for retaining the diagnosis, but for strengthening it, and they give highly conservative political reasons for strengthening the diagnosis so that the structures that support normalcy can be strengthened.

Ironically, it is these very structures that support normalcy that compel the need for the diagnosis to begin with, including its benefits for those who need it in order to effect a transition.

It is with some irony, then, that those who suffer under the diagnosis also find that there is not much hope for doing without it. The fact is that under current conditions a number of people have reason to worry about the consequences of having their diagnosis taken away or failing to establish eligibility for the diagnosis. Perhaps the rich will be able to shell out the tens of thousands of dollars that an FTM transformation entails, including double mastectomy and a very good phalloplasty, but most people, especially poor and working-class transsexuals, will not be able to foot the bill. At least in the United States where socialized medicine is largely understood as a communist plot, it won't be an option to have the state or insurance companies pay for these procedures without first establishing that there are serious and enduring medical and psychiatric reasons for doing so. A conflict has to be established; there has to be enormous suffering; there has to be persistent ideation of oneself in the other gender; there has to be a trial period of cross-dressing throughout the day to see if adaptation can be predicted; and there have to be therapy sessions and letters attesting to the balanced state of the person's mind. In other words, one must be subjected to a regulatory apparatus, as Foucault would have called it, in order to get to the point where something like an exercise in freedom becomes possible. One has to submit to labels and names, to incursions, to invasions; one has to be gauged against measures of normalcy; and one has to pass the test. Sometimes what this means is that one needs to become very savvy about these standards, and know how to present oneself in such a way that one comes across as a plausible candidate. Sometimes therapists find themselves in a bind, being asked to supply a letter for someone they want to help but abhorring the very fact that they have to write this letter, in the language of diagnosis, in order to help produce the life that their client wants to have.

In a sense, the regulatory discourse surrounding the diagnosis takes on a life of its own: it may not actually describe the patient who uses the language to get what he or she wants; it may not reflect the beliefs of the therapist who nevertheless signs her name to the diagnosis and passes it along. Approaching the diagnosis strategically involves a series of individuals not quite believing what they say, signing on to language that does not represent what the reality is or should be. The price of using the diagnosis to get what one wants is that one cannot use language to say what one really thinks is true. One pays for one's freedom, as it were, by sacrificing one's claim to use language truthfully. In other words, one purchases one sort of freedom only by giving up another.

Perhaps this brings us closer to understanding the quandary of autonomy that the diagnosis introduces and the specific problem of how freedom is to be understood as conditioned and articulated through specific social means. The only way to secure the means by which to start this transformation is by learning how to present yourself in a discourse that is not yours, a discourse that effaces you in the act of representing you, a discourse that denies the language you might want to use to describe who you are, how you got here, and what you want from this life. Such a discourse denies all this at the same time that it holds out the promise, if not the blackmail, that you stand a chance of getting your life, the body and the gender you want, if you agree to falsify yourself, and in so doing support and ratify the power of this diagnosis over many more people in the future. If one comes out in favor of choice, and against diagnosis, it would seem that one has to deal with the enormous financial consequences of this decision for those who cannot pay for the resources at hand, and whose insurance, if there is insurance, will not honor this choice as one that is to be included as a covered elective treatment. And even when local laws are passed, offering insurance to city workers who seek such treatments, as is the case now in San Francisco, there are still diagnostic tests to pass, so choice is clearly bought at a price, sometimes at the price of truth itself.

The way things are set up, if we want to support the poor and the uninsured in this area, it would seem that we have to support efforts to extend insurance coverage and to work within the diagnostic categories accepted by the AMA and the APA, codified in the *DSM-IV*. The call to have matters of gender identity depathologized and for elective surgery and hormone treatment to be covered as a legitimate set of elective procedures seems bound to fail, only because most medical, insurance, and legal practitioners are only committed to supporting access to sex change technologies if we are talking about a disorder. Arguments to the effect that there is an overwhelming and legitimate human demand here are bound to prove inadequate. Examples of the kinds of justifications that ideally would make sense and should have a claim on insurance companies include: this transition will allow someone to realize certain human possibilities that will help this life to flourish, or this will allow someone to emerge from fear and shame and paralysis into a situation of enhanced self-esteem and the ability to form close ties with others, or that this transition will help to alleviate a source of enormous suffering, or give reality to a fundamental human desire to assume a bodily form that expresses a fundamental sense of selfhood. However, some gender identity clinics, like the one at the University of Minnesota run by Dr. Walter Bockting, do make such arguments and do provide supportive therapeutic contexts for people disposed to make a choice on this issue, whether it be to live as transgendered or transsexual, whether to be third sex, whether to consider the process as one of a becoming whose end is not in sight, and may never be.[13] But even that clinic has to supply materials to insurance companies that comply with *DSM-IV*.[14]

The exercise of freedom that is performed through a strategic approach to the diagnosis involves one in a measure of unfreedom, since the diagnosis itself demeans the self-determining capacities of those it diagnoses, but whose self-determination, paradoxically, it sometimes furthers. When the diagnosis can be used strategically, and when it undermines its own presumption that the individual diagnosed is afflicted with a condition over which no choice can be exercised, the use of the diagnosis can subvert the aims of the diagnosis. On the other

hand, in order to pass the test, one must submit to the language of
the diagnosis. Although the stated aim of the diagnosis is that it wants
to know whether an individual can successfully conform to living
according to the norms of another gender, it seems that the real test
that the GID poses is whether one can conform to the language of the
diagnosis. In other words, it may not be a matter of whether you can
conform to the norms that govern life as another gender, but whether
you can conform to the *psychological discourse* that stipulates what
these norms are.

Let's take a look at that language. The GID section of the *DSM*
starts by making clear that there are two parts of this diagnosis. The
first is that "there must be strong and persistent cross-gender identification." This would be difficult to ascertain, I would think, since identifications do not always appear as such: they can remain aspects of
hidden fantasy, or parts of dreams, or inchoate structures of behavior.
But the *DSM* asks us to be a bit more positivist in our approach to
identification, assuming that we can read from behavior what identifications are at work in any given person's psychic life. Cross-gender
identification is defined as "the desire to be" the other sex, "or the
insistence that one is." The "or" in this phrase is significant, since it
implies that one might desire to be the other sex—we have to suspend
for the moment what "the other sex" is and, by the way, in my mind,
it is not quite clear—without necessarily insisting upon it. These are
two separate criteria. They do not have to emerge in tandem. So if
there is a way to determine that someone has this "desire to be" even
though he or she does not insist upon it, that would seem to be sa-
tisfactory grounds for concluding that cross-gender identification is
happening. And if there is "an insistence that one is" the other sex,
then that would function as a separate criterion which, if fulfilled,
would warrant the conclusion that cross-gender identification is happening. In the second instance, an act of speech is required in which
someone insists that one *is* the other sex; this insistence is understood
as a way of laying claim to the other sex in one's own speech and of
attributing that other sex to oneself. So certain expressions of this
"desire to be" and "insistence that I am" are precluded as viable evidence for the claim. "This must not merely be a desire for any perceived
cultural advantages of being the other sex." Now, this is a moment for
pause, since the diagnosis assumes that we can have an experience of sex

without considering what the cultural advantages of being a given sex are. Is this, in fact, possible? If sex is experienced by us within a cultural matrix of meanings, if it comes to have its significance and meaning in reference to a wider social world, then can we separate the experience of "sex" from its social meanings, including the way in which power functions throughout those meanings? "Sex" is a term that applies to people across the board, so that it is difficult to refer to my "sex" as if it were radically singular. If it is, generally speaking, then, never only "my sex" or "your sex" that is at issue but a way in which the category of "sex" exceeds the personal appropriations of it, then it would seem to be impossible to perceive sex outside of this cultural matrix and to understand this cultural matrix outside of the possible advantages it may afford. Indeed, when we think about cultural advantages, whether we are doing something—anything—for the cultural advantage it affords, we have to ask whether what we do is advantageous for me, that is, whether it furthers or satisfies my desires and my aspirations.

There are crude analyses that suggest that FTM happens only because it is easier to be a man in society than a woman. But those analyses don't ask whether it is easier to be *trans* than to be in a perceived bio-gender, that is, a gender that seems to "follow" from natal sex. If social advantage were ruling all these decisions unilaterally, then the forces in favor of social conformity would probably win the day. On the other hand, there are arguments that could be made that it is more advantageous to be a woman if you want to wear fabulous red scarves and tight skirts on the street at night. In some places in the world, that is obviously true, although bio-women, those in drag, transgendered, and transwomen, all share certain risks on the street, especially if any of them are perceived as prostitutes. Similarly, one might say, it is generally more culturally advantageous to be a man if you want to be taken seriously in a philosophy seminar. But some men are at no advantage at all, if they cannot talk the talk; being a man is not a sufficient condition for being able to talk that talk. So I wonder whether it is possible to consider becoming one sex or the other without considering the cultural advantage it might afford, since the cultural advantage it might afford will be the advantage it affords to someone who has certain kinds of desires and who wants to be in a position to take advantage of certain cultural opportunities.

If the GID insists that the desire to be another sex or the insistence that one is the other sex has to be evaluated without reference to cultural advantage, it may be that the GID misundertands some of the cultural forces that go into making and sustaining certain desires of this sort. And then the GID would also have to respond to the epistemological question of whether sex can be perceived *at all* outside the cultural matrix of power relations in which relative advantage and disadvantage would be part and parcel of that matrix.

The diagnosis also requires that there be "persistent discomfort" about one's assigned sex or "inappropriateness," and here is where the discourse of "not getting it right" comes in. The assumption is that there is an appropriate sense that people can and do have, a sense that this gender is appropriate for me, to me. And that there is a comfort that I would have, could have, and that it could be had if it were the right norm. In an important sense, the diagnosis assumes that gender norms are relatively fixed, and that the problem is making sure that you find the right one, the one that will allow you to feel appropriate where you are, comfortable in the gender that you are. There must be evidence of "distress"—yes, certainly, distress. And if there is not "distress," then there should be "impairment." Here it makes sense to ask where all this comes from: the distress and the impairment, the not being able to function well at the workplace or in handling certain daily chores. The diagnosis presumes that one feels distress and discomfort and inappropriateness because one is in the wrong gender, and that conforming to a different gender norm, if viable for the person in question, will make one feel much better. But the diagnosis does not ask whether there is a problem with the gender norms that it takes as fixed and intransigent, whether these norms produce distress and discomfort, whether they impede one's ability to function, or whether they generate sources of suffering for some people or for many people. Nor do they ask what the conditions are in which they provide a sense of comfort, or belonging, or even become the site for the realization for certain human possibilities that let a person feel futurity, life, and well-being.

The diagnosis seeks to establish criteria by which a cross-gendered person might be identified, but the diagnosis, in articulating criteria, articulates a very rigid version of gender norms. It offers the following account of gender norms (the emphases are mine) in the language of simple description: "In boys, cross-gendered identification is manifested by a marked preoccupation with traditionally feminine activities. They may have a preference for dressing in girls' or women's clothes *or may improvise such items from available materials* when genuine materials are unavailable. Towels, aprons, and scarves are often used to represent long hair or skirts." The description seems to be based on a history of collected and summarized observations; someone has seen boys doing this, and reported it, and others have done the same, and those reports are collected, and generalizations are derived from the observable data. But who is observing, and through what grid of observation? This we do not know. And though we are told that in boys this identification is "marked" by a preoccupation with "traditionally feminine activities," we are not told what this mark consists of. But it seems important, since the "mark" will be what selects the observation as evidence for the thesis at hand.

In fact, what follows from this claim seems to undermine the claim itself, since what the boys are said to do is to engage in a series of substitutions and improvisations. We are told that they may have a preference for dressing in girls' or women's clothes, but we're not told whether the preference manifests itself in actually dressing in them. We are left with a vague notion of "preference" that could simply describe a supposed mental state, or internal disposition, or it may be inferred by practice. This last seems open to interpretation. We are told that one practice they do engage in is improvisation, taking items that are available and making them work as feminine clothing. Feminine clothing is called "genuine clothing," which leaves us to conclude that the materials with which these boys are improvising is less than genuine, other than genuine, if not ungenuine and "false." "Towels, aprons, scarves are often used to represent long hair or skirts." So there is a certain imaginary play, and a capacity to transfigure one item into another through a process of improvisation and substitution. In other words, there is an art practice at work here, one that would be difficult to name, simply, as the simple act of conforming to a norm. Something is being made, something is being made from something else, something is being tried out. And if it is an improvisation, it is not fully scripted in advance.

Although the description goes on to insist on the fascination of these boys with "stereotypical female-type dolls"—"Barbie" is mentioned by name—as well as "female fantasy figures," we are not really given an account of the place that dolls and fantasy have in the formulation of gender identification. For a given gender to be a site of fascination, or indeed, for a so-called stereotype to be a source of fascination, may well involve several kinds of relations to the stereotype. It may be that the stereotype is fascinating because it is overdetermined, that it has become the site for a number of conflicting desires. The *DSM* assumes that the doll you play with is the one you want to be, but maybe you want to be her friend, her rival, her lover. Maybe you want all this at once. Maybe you do some switching with her. Maybe playing with the doll, too, is a scene of improvisation that articulates a complex set of dispositions. Maybe something else is going on in this play besides a simple act of conforming to a norm. Perhaps the norm itself is being played, explored, even busted. We would need to take play as a more complex phenomenon than does the *DSM* if we were to begin to pose and pursue these kinds of questions.

The way you can tell that girls are having cross-gendered identification according to the *DSM-IV* is that they argue with their parents about wearing certain kinds of clothes. They prefer boys clothing and short hair, apparently, and they have mainly boy friends, express a desire to become a boy, but also, oddly, "they are often misidentified by strangers as boys." I am trying to think through how it could be that evidence of one's cross-gendered identification is confirmed by being identified as a boy by a stranger. It would seem that random social assignment functions as evidence, as if the stranger *knows* something about the psychological make-up of that girl, or as if the girl has solicited that interpellation from the stranger. The *DSM* goes on to say that the girl "may ask to be called by a boy's name." But even there, it seems, she is first addressed as a boy, and only after being addressed, wants to take on a name that will confirm the rightness of the address itself. Here again, the very language that the *DSM* provides seems to undercut its own arguments, since it wants to be able to claim cross-gendered identification as part of gender identity disorder, and so as a psychological problem that can be addressed through treatment. It imagines that each individual has a relation to its "assigned sex" and that this relation is either one of discomfort and distress or a sense of comfort and being at peace. But even this notion of "assigned sex"— sex "assigned" at birth—implies that sex is socially produced and relayed, and that it comes to us not merely as a private reflection that each of us makes about ourselves but as a critical interrogation that each of us makes of a social category that is assigned to us that exceeds us in its generality and power, but that also, consequentially, instances itself at the site of our bodies. It is interesting that the *DSM* seeks to establish gender as a set of more or less fixed and conventional norms, even as it keeps giving us evidence to the contrary, almost as if it is at cross purposes with its own aims. Just as the boys who were improvising and substituting were doing something other than conforming to preestablished norms, so the girls seem to be understanding something about social assignment, about what might happen if someone starts to address them as a boy, and what that might make possible. I'm not sure that the girl who seizes upon this stray and felicitous interpellation is giving evidence to a preestablished "disorder" of any kind. Rather she is noting that the very means by which sex comes to be, through assignment, open up possibilities for reassignment that excite her sense of agency, play, and possibility. Just as the boys who are playing with scarves as if they were something else are already versing themselves in the world of props and improvisation, so the girls, seizing upon the possibility of being called by another name, are exploring the possibilities of naming themselves in the context of that social world. They are not simply giving evidence to internal states, but performing certain kinds of actions, and even engaging practices, practices that turn out to be essential to the making of gender itself.

The *DSM* offers a certain discourse of compassion, as many psychiatrists do, suggesting that life with such a disorder is a cause of distress and unhappiness. The *DSM* has its own antipoetry on this subject: "in young children, distress is manifested by the stated unhappiness about their assigned sex." And here it seems that the only unhappiness is one that is created by an internal desire, not by the fact that there is no social support for such children, that the adults to whom they express their unhappiness are diagnosing and pathologizing them, that the norm of gender frames the conversation in which the expression of unhappiness takes place. At the same time that the *DSM* understands itself as diagnosing a distress which then becomes a candidate for alleviation as a result of the diagnosis, it also understands that "social pressure" can lead to "extreme isolation for such a child." The *DSM* does not talk about suicide, even though we know that the cruelty of adolescent peer pressure on transgendered youth can lead to suicide. The *DSM* does not talk about risks of death, generally, or murder, something that happened only miles from my home in California in 2002 when transgendered Gwen Araujo arrived at a teen party in a dress, and her body was found dead from beating and strangulation in the Sierra foothills.

Apparently, the "distress" that comes from living in a world in which suicide and death by violence remain real issues is not part of the diagnosis of GID. Consider that the *DSM* remarks, after a brief discussion of the euphemistically called "peer teasing and rejection," that "children may refuse to attend school because of teasing or pressure to dress in attire stereotypical of their assigned sex." Here the language of the text seems to understand that there may be an impairment of ordinary functioning caused by the pressure of social norms. But then, in the next sentence, it domesticates the distress caused by social norms, by claiming that it is the person's own preoccupation with cross-gender wishes that often "interferes with ordinary activities" and ends up in situations of social isolation. In a way, the fact of social violence against transgendered youth is euphemized as teasing and pressure, and then the distress caused by that is recast as an internal problem, a sign of preoccupation, self-involvement, which seems to follow from the wishes themselves. Indeed, is the "isolation" noted here real, or are the communities of support eclipsed from the observation? And when there is isolation, is it, therefore, a sign of a pathology? Or is it, for some, the cost of expressing certain kinds of desires in public?

What is most worrisome, however, is how the diagnosis works as its own social pressure, causing distress, establishing wishes as pathological, intensifying the regulation and control of those who express them in institutional settings. Indeed, one has to ask whether the diagnosis of transgendered youth does not act precisely as peer pressure, as an elevated form of teasing, as a euphemized form of social violence. And if we conclude that it does act in such a way, standing for gender norms, seeking to produce adaptation to existing norms, then how do we return to the vexed issue of what the diagnosis also offers? If part of what the diagnosis offers is a form of social recognition, and if that is the form that social recognition takes, and if it is only through this kind of social recognition that third parties, including medical insurance, will be willing to pay for the medical and technological changes that are sometimes desired, is it really possible to do away with the diagnosis altogether? In a way, the dilemma with which we are faced in the end has to do with the terms by which social recognition is constrained. Since even if we are tempted by the civil libertarian position in which this is understood as a personal right, the fact is that personal rights are only protected and can only be exercised through social and political means. To assert a right is not the same as being empowered to exercise it, and in this case, the only recognizable right at hand is the "right to be treated for a disorder and to take advantage of medical and legal benefits that seek its rectification." One exercises this right only by submitting to a pathologizing discourse, and in submitting to the discourse, one also gains a certain power, a certain freedom.

It is possible to say, and necessary to say, that the diagnosis leads the way to the alleviation of suffering; and it is possible, and necessary, to say that the diagnosis intensifies the very suffering that requires alleviation. Under present and entrenched social conditions in which gender norms are still articulated in conventional ways, and departures from the norm regarded as suspect, autonomy remains a paradox.[15] Of course, it is possible to move to a country where the state will pay for sex reassignment surgery, to apply to a "transgender fund" that a broader community supplies to help those who cannot pay the high costs, or indeed to apply for a "grant" to individuals that cover "cosmetic surgery." The movement for trans people to become the therapists and diagnosticians has and will surely help matters. These are all ways around the bind, until the bind goes away. But if the bind is to go away for the long run, the norms that govern the way in which we understand the relation between gender identity and mental health would have to change radically, so that economic and legal institutions would recognize how essential becoming a gender is to one's very sense of personhood, one's sense of well-being, one's possibility to flourish as a bodily being. Not only does one need the social world to be a certain way in order to lay claim to what is one's own, but it turns out that what is one's own is always from the start dependent upon what is not one's own, the social conditions by which autonomy is, strangely, dispossessed and undone.

In this sense, we must be undone in order to do ourselves: we must be part of a larger social fabric of existence in order to create who we are. This is surely the paradox of autonomy, a paradox that is heightened when gender regulations work to paralyze gendered agency at various levels. Until those social conditions are radically changed, freedom will require unfreedom, and autonomy is implicated in subjection. If the social world—a sign of our constitutive heteronomy—must change for autonomy to become possible, then individual choice will prove to be dependent from the start on conditions that none of us author at will, and no individual will be able to choose outside the context of a radically altered social world. That alteration comes from an increment of acts, collective and diffuse, belonging to no single subject, and yet one effect of these alterations is to make acting like a subject possible.

5. Is Kinship Always Already Heterosexual?

The topic of gay marriage is not the same as that of gay kinship, but it seems that the two become confounded in U.S. popular opinion when we hear not only that marriage is and ought to remain a heterosexual institution and bond but also that kinship does not work, or does not qualify as kinship, unless it assumes a recognizable family form. There are several ways to link these views. One way is to claim that sexuality needs to be organized in the service of reproductive relations, and that marriage, which gives the legal status to the family form or, rather, is conceived as that which should secure the institution through conferring that legal status, *should* remain the fulcrum that keeps these institutions leveraging one another.

The challenges to this link are, of course, legion, and they take various forms domestically and internationally. On the one hand, there are various sociological ways of showing that in the United States a number of kinship relations exist and persist that do not conform to the nuclear family model and that draw on biological and nonbiological relations, exceeding the reach of current juridical conceptions, functioning according to nonformalizable rules. If we understand kinship as a set of practices that institutes relationships of various kinds which negotiate the reproduction of life and the demands of death, then kinship practices will be those that emerge to address fundamental forms of human dependency, which may include birth, child rearing, relations of emotional dependency and support, generational ties, illness, dying, and death (to name a few). Kinship is neither a fully autonomous sphere, proclaimed to be distinct from community and friendship—or the regulations of the state—through some definitional fiat, nor is it "over" or "dead" just because, as David Schneider has consequentially argued, it has lost the capacity to be formalized and tracked in the conventional ways that ethnologists in the past have attempted to do.[1]

In recent sociology, conceptions of kinship have become disjoined from the marriage assumption, so that for example, Carol Stack's now classic study of urban African-American kinship, *All Our Kin,* shows how kinship functions well through a network of women, some related through biological ties, and some not.[2] The enduring effect of the history of slavery on African-American kinship relations has become the focus of new studies by Nathaniel Mackey and Fred Moten, showing how the dispossession of kin relations by slavery offers a continuing legacy of "wounded kinship" within African-American life. If, as Saidiya Hartman maintains, "slavery is the ghost in the machine of kinship,"[3] it is because African-American kinship has been at once the site of intense state surveillance and pathologization, which has led to the double bind of being subject to normalizing pressures within the context of a continuing social and political delegitimation. As a result, it is not possible to separate questions of kinship from property relations (and conceiving persons as property), and from the fictions of "bloodline" as well as the national and racial interests by which these lines are sustained.

Kath Weston has supplied ethnographic descriptions of lesbian and gay nonmarital kinship relations that emerge outside of heterosexually based family ties and only partially approximate the family form in some instances.[4] In 2001, anthropologist Cai Hua offered a dramatic refutation of the Lévi-Straussian view of kinship as a negotiation of a patrilineal line through marriage ties in his study of the Na of China, in which neither husbands nor fathers figure prominently in determinations of kinship.[5]

Marriage has also been separated from questions of kinship to the extent that gay marriage legislative proposals often exclude rights to adoption or reproductive technologies as one of the assumed entitlements of marriage. These proposals have been offered in Germany and France; in the United States, successful gay marriage proposals do not always have a direct impact on family law, especially when they seek as their primary aim to establish "symbolic recognition" for dyadic relations by the state.[6]

The petition for marriage rights seeks to solicit state recognition for nonheterosexual unions, and so configures the state as withholding an entitlement that it really should distribute in a nondiscriminatory way, regardless of sexual orientation. That the state's offer might result in the intensification of normalization is not widely recognized as a problem within the mainstream lesbian and gay movement, typified by the Human Rights Campaign.[7] The normalizing powers of the state are made especially clear, however, when we consider how continuing quandaries about kinship both condition and limit the marriage debates. In some contexts, the symbolic allocation of marriage, or marriagelike arrangements, is preferable to altering the requirements for kinship and for individual or plural rights to bear or adopt children or, legally, to co-parent. Variations on kinship that depart from normative, dyadic heterosexually based family forms secured through the marriage vow are figured not only as dangerous for the child but perilous to the putative natural and cultural laws said to sustain human intelligibility.

It is important to know that the debates in France targeted certain U.S. views on the social construction and variability of gender relations as portending a perilous "Americanization" of kinship relations (*filiation*) in France.[8] As a result, this essay seeks to offer a response to this critique, outlined in the third section that follows, as an effort not to defend "Americanization" but to suggest instead that the kinship dilemmas of first-world nations often provide allegories for one another of their own worries about the disruptive effects of kinship variability on their own national projects. In turn, I seek here to query the French debate on kinship and marriage to show how the argument in favor of legal alliance can work in tandem with a state normalization of recognizable kinship relations, a condition that extends rights of contract while in no way disrupting the patrilineal assumptions of kinship or the project of the unified nation which it supports.

In what follows I consider at least two dimensions of this contemporary predicament in which the state is sought for the recognition it might confer on same-sex couples and countered for the regulatory control on normative kinship that it continues to exercise. The state is not the same state in each of these bids, for we ask for an intervention by the state in the one domain (marriage) only to suffer excessive regulation in another (kinship). Does the turn to marriage make it thus more difficult to argue in favor of the viability of alternative kinship arrangements, or for the well-being of the "child" in any number of social forms? Moreover, what happens to the radical project to articulate and support the proliferation of sexual practices outside of marriage and the obligations of kinship? Does the turn to the state signal the end of a radical sexual culture? Does such a prospect become eclipsed as we become increasingly preoccupied with landing the state's desire?

Gay Marriage: Desiring the State's Desire and the Eclipse of Sexuality

Gay marriage obviously draws upon profound and abiding investments not only in the heterosexual couple per se but also in the question of what forms of relationship ought to be legitimated by the state.[9] This crisis of legitimation can be considered from a number of perspectives, but let us consider for the moment the ambivalent gift that legitimation can become. To be legitimated by the state is to enter into the terms of legitimation offered there, and to find that one's public and recognizable sense of personhood is fundamentally dependent on the lexicon of that legitimation. It follows that the delimitation of legitimation will take place only through an exclusion of a certain sort, though not a patently dialectical one. The sphere of legitimate intimate alliance is established through the producing and intensifying regions of illegitimacy. There is, however, a more fundamental occlusion at work here. We misunderstand the sexual field if we consider that the legitimate and the illegitimate appear to exhaust its immanent possibilities. There is outside the struggle between the legitimate and the illegitimate—which has as its goal the conversion of the illegitimate into the legitimate—a field that is less thinkable, one not figured in light of its ultimate convertibility into legitimacy. This is a field outside the disjunction of illegitimate and legitimate; it is not yet thought as a domain, a sphere, a field; it is not yet either legitimate or illegitimate, has not yet been thought through in the explicit discourse of legitimacy.

Indeed, this would be a sexual field that does not have legitimacy as its point of reference, its ultimate desire. The debate over gay marriage takes place through such a logic, for we see the debate break down almost immediately into the question of whether marriage ought to be extended legitimately to homosexuals. This means that the sexual field is circumscribed in such a way that sexuality is already thought of in terms of marriage and marriage is already thought of as the purchase on legitimacy.

In the case of gay marriage or of affiliative legal alliances, we see how various sexual practices and relationships that fall outside the purview of the sanctifying law become illegible or, worse, untenable, and new hierarchies emerge in public discourse. These hierarchies not only enforce the distinction between legitimate and illegitimate queer lives, but they also produce tacit distinctions among forms of illegitimacy. The stable pair who would marry if only they could are cast as illegitimate but eligible for a future legitimacy, whereas the sexual agents who function outside the purview of the marriage bond and its recognized, if illegitimate, alternative form now constitute sexual possibilities that will never be eligible for a translation into legitimacy. These are possibilities that become increasingly disregarded in the sphere of politics as a consequence of the priority that the marriage debate has assumed. This is an illegitimacy whose temporal condition is to be foreclosed from any possible future transformation. It is not only *not yet* legitimate, but it is we might say the irrecoverable and irreversible past of legitimacy: *the never will be, the never was.*

Here a certain normative crisis ensues. On the one hand, it is important to mark how the field of intelligible and speakable sexuality is circumscribed, so that we can see how options outside of marriage are becoming foreclosed as the unthinkable, and how the terms of thinkability are enforced by the narrow debates over who and what will be included in the norm. On the other hand, there is always the possibility of savoring the status of unthinkability, if it is a status, as the most critical, the most radical, the most valuable. As the sexually unrepresentable, such sexual possibilities can figure the sublime within the contemporary field of sexuality, a site of pure resistance, a site unco-opted by normativity. But how does one think politics from such a site of unrepresentability? And lest I am misunderstood here, let me state an equally pressing question: How can one think politics without considering these sites of unrepresentability?

One may wish for another lexicon altogether. The history of sexual progressivism surely recurs time and again to the possibility of a new language and the promise of a new mode of being. And in the light of this quandary, one might find oneself wanting to opt out of this whole story, to operate somewhere that is neither legitimate nor illegitimate. But here is where the critical perspective, the one that operates at the limit of the intelligible, also risks being regarded as apolitical. For politics, as it is constituted through this discourse of intelligibility, demands that we take a stand, for or against gay marriage; but critical reflection, which is surely part of any seriously normative political philosophy and practice, demands that we ask why and how this has become the question, the question that defines what will and will not qualify as meaningful political discourse here. Why, under present conditions, does the very prospect of "becoming political" depend on our ability to operate within that discursively instituted binary and not to ask, and endeavor not to know, that the sexual field is forcibly constricted through accepting those terms? This dynamic of force is rendered all the more forceful because it grounds the contemporary field of the political, grounds it through the forcible exclusion of that sexual field from the political. And yet, the operation of this force of exclusion is set outside of the domain of contest, as if it were not part of power, as if it were not an item for political reflection. Thus, to become political, to act and speak in ways that are recognizably political, is to rely on a foreclosure of the very political field that is not subject to political scrutiny. Without the critical perspective, politics relies fundamentally on an unknowingness—and depoliticization—of the very relations of force by which its own field of operation is instituted.

Criticality is thus not a position per se, not a site or a place that might be located within an already delimitable field, although one must, in an obligatory catachresis, speak of sites, of fields, of domains. One critical function is to scrutinize the action of delimitation itself. By recommending that we become critical, that we risk criticality, in thinking about how the sexual field is constituted, I do not mean to suggest that we could or should occupy an atopical elsewhere, undelimited, radically free. The questioning of taken-for-granted conditions becomes possible on occasion; but one cannot get there through a thought experiment, an *epoché,* an act of will. One gets there, as it were, through suffering the dehiscence, the breakup, of the ground itself.

Even within the field of intelligible sexuality, one finds that the binaries that anchor its operations permit for middle zones and hybrid formations, suggesting that the binary relation does not exhaust the field in question. Indeed, there are middle regions, hybrid regions of legitimacy and illegitimacy that have no clear names, and where nomination itself falls into a crisis produced by the variable, sometimes violent boundaries of legitimating practices that come into uneasy and sometimes conflictual contact with one another. These are not precisely places where one can choose to hang out, subject positions one might opt to occupy. These are nonplaces in which one finds oneself in spite of oneself; indeed, these are nonplaces where recognition, including self-recognition, proves precarious if not elusive, in spite of one's best efforts to be a subject in some recognizable sense. They are not sites of enunciation, but shifts in the topography from which a questionably audible claim emerges: the claim of the not-yet-subject and the nearly recognizable.

That there are such regions, and they are not precisely options, suggests that what troubles the distinction between legitimacy and illegitimacy are social practices, specifically sexual practices, that do not appear immediately as coherent in the available lexicon of legitimation. These are sites of uncertain ontology, difficult nomination. If it seems that I am now going to argue that we should all be pursuing and celebrating sites of uncertain ontology and difficult nomination, I actually want to pursue a slightly different point, which is to attend to the foreclosure of the possible that takes place when, from the urgency to stake a political claim, one naturalizes the options that figure most legibly within the sexual field. Attending to this foreclosure, as an act of politics that we unwittingly perform, unwittingly perform time and again, offers the possibility for a different conception of politics, one that attends to its own foreclosures as an effect of its own conscious activism. Yet, one must maintain a double-edge in relation to this difficult terrain, for neither the violence of foreclosure that stabilizes the field of activism nor the path of critical paralysis that is entrenched at the level of fundamental reflection will suffice. On the topic of gay marriage, it becomes increasingly important to keep the tension alive between maintaining a critical perspective and making a politically legible claim.

My point here is not to suggest that one must, in relation to gay marriage and kinship debates, remain critical rather than political, as if such a distinction were finally possible or desirable, but only that a politics that incorporates a critical understanding is the only one that can maintain a claim to being self-reflective and nondogmatic. To be political does not merely mean to take a single and enduring "stand." For instance, to say that one is for or against gay marriage is not always easy to do, since it may be that one wants to secure the right for those who wish to make use of it even as one does not want it for oneself, or it may be that one wants to counter the homophobic discourses that have been marshaled against gay marriage, but one does not want to be, therefore, in favor of it. Or it may be that one believes very strongly that marriage is the best way for lesbian and gay people to go and would like to install it as a new norm, a norm for the future. Or it may be that one not only opposes it for oneself but for everybody, and that the task at end is to rework and revise the social organization of friendship, sexual contacts, and community to produce non-state-centered forms of support and alliance, because marriage, given its historical weight, becomes an "option" only by extending itself as a norm (and thus foreclosing options), one that also extends property relations and renders the social forms for sexuality more conservative. For a progressive sexual movement, even one that may want to produce marriage as an option for nonheterosexuals, the proposition that marriage should become the only way to sanction or legitimate sexuality is unacceptably conservative. Even if the question is not one of marriage but of legal contracts, augmenting domestic partnership arrangements as legal contracts, certain questions still follow: Why should it be that marriage or legal contracts become the basis on which health care benefits, for instance, are allocated? Why shouldn't there be ways of organizing health care entitlements such that everyone, regardless of marital status, has access to them? If one argues for marriage as a way of securing those entitlements, then does one not also affirm that entitlements as important as health care ought to remain allocated on the basis of marital status? What does this do to the community of the nonmarried, the single, the divorced, the uninterested, the non-monogamous, and how does the sexual field become reduced, in its very legibility, once we extend marriage as a norm?[10]

Regardless of one's view on gay marriage, there is clearly a demand upon those who work in sexuality studies to respond to many of the most homophobic arguments that have been marshaled against gay marriage proposals. Many of these arguments are not only fueled by homophobic sentiment but often focus on fears about reproductive relations, whether they are natural or "artificial." What happens to the child, the child, the poor child, the martyred figure of an ostensibly selfish or dogged social progressivism? Indeed, the debates on gay marriage and gay kinship, two issues that are often conflated, have become sites of intense displacement for other political fears, fears about technology, about new demographics, and also about the very unity and transmissability of the nation, and fears that feminism, in the insistence on childcare, has effectively opened up kinship outside the family, opened it to strangers. In the French debates on the PACS (the "pacts of civil solidarity" that constitute an alternative to marriage for any two individuals unrelated by blood, regardless of sexual orientation), the passage of the bill finally depended on proscribing the rights of non-heterosexual couples from adopting children and accessing reproductive technology. The same provision was recently proposed and adopted in Germany as well.[11] In both cases, one can see that the child figures in the debate as a dense site for the transfer and reproduction of culture, where "culture" carries with it implicit norms of racial purity and domination.[12] Indeed, one can see a conversion between the arguments in France that rail against the threat to "culture" posed by the prospect of legally allied gay people having children—and I will suspend for the purposes of this discussion the question of what it means to "have" in this instance—and those arguments concerning issues of immigration, of what Europe is. This last concern raises the question, implicitly and explicitly, of what is truly French, the basis of its culture, which becomes, through an imperial logic, the basis of culture itself, its universal and invariable conditions. The debates center not only on the questions of what culture is and who should be admitted but also on how the subjects of culture should be reproduced. They also concern the status of the state, and in particular its power to confer or withdraw recognition for forms of sexual alliance. Indeed, the argument against gay marriage is always, implicitly or explicitly, an argument about what the state should do, and what it should provide, as well as what kinds of intimate relations ought to be eligible

for state legitimation. What is this desire to keep the state from offering recognition to nonheterosexual partners, and what is the desire to
compel the state to offer such recognition? For both sides of the
debate, the question is not only which relations of desire ought to be
legitimated by the state but also who may desire the state, *who may
desire the state's desire.*

Indeed, the questions are even more complicated: Whose desire
might qualify as a desire for state legitimation? Whose desire might
qualify as the desire of the state? Who may desire the state? And whom
may the state desire? Whose desire will be the state's desire? Conversely, and this is just speculation—but perhaps academic work might
be regarded as a social site for such speculation—it seems that what
one is wanting when one wants "state recognition" for marriage, and
what one is not wanting when one wants to limit the scope of that
recognition for others, are complex wants. The state becomes the
means by which a fantasy becomes literalized: desire and sexuality are
ratified, justified, known, publicly instated, imagined as permanent,
durable. And, at that very moment, desire and sexuality are dispossessed
and displaced, so that what one "is," and what one's relationship "is,"
are no longer private matters. Indeed, ironically, one might say that
through marriage, personal desire acquires a certain anonymity and
interchangeability, becomes, as it were, publicly mediated and, in that
sense, a kind of legitimated public sex. But more than that, marriage
compels, at least logically, universal recognition: everyone must let you
into the door of the hospital; everyone must honor your claim to grief;
everyone will assume your natural rights to a child; everyone will
regard your relationship as elevated into eternity. In this way, the desire
for universal recognition is a desire to become universal, to become
interchangeable in one's universality, to vacate the lonely particularity
of the nonratified relation, and, perhaps above all, to gain both place
and sanctification in that imagined relation to the state. Place and sanctification: these are surely powerful fantasies, and they take on particular phantasmatic form when we consider the bid for gay marriage.
The state can become the site for the recirculation of religious desires,
for redemption, for belonging, for eternity. And we might well ask what
happens to sexuality when it runs through this particular circuit of fantasy: Is it alleviated of its guilt, its deviance, its discontinuity, its aso-
ciality, its spectrality? And if it is alleviated of all that, where precisely

do these negativities go? Do they not tend to be projected onto those who have not or will not enter this hallowed domain? And does the projection take the form of judging others morally, of enacting a social abjection, and, hence, of becoming the occasion to institute a new hierarchy of legitimate and illegitimate sexual arrangement?

The Poor Child and the Fate of the Nation

The proposal in France to institute civil unions (pacts of social solidarity) as an alternative to marriage sought at once to sidestep marriage and secure legal ties. It ran up against a limit, however, when questions of reproduction and adoption surfaced. Indeed, in France, concerns over reproduction work in tandem with concerns over the reproduction of an identifiably French culture. As suggested above, one can see a certain implicit identification of French culture with universalism, and this has its own consequences for the fantasy of the nation at stake. For understanding this debate, it is important to recognize how, in particular, the figure of the child of nonheterosexual parents becomes a cathected site for anxieties about cultural purity and cultural transmission. In the recent fracas over the PACS, the only way that the proposal could pass was by denying rights of joint adoption to individuals in such relations. Indeed, as Eric Fassin and others have argued, it is the alteration of rights of filiation that is most scandalous in the French context, not marriage per se.[13] The life of the contract can be, within a range, extended, but the rights of filiation cannot.

In some of the cultural commentary that accompanied this decision to deny adoptive rights to openly gay people, we heard from Sylviane Agacinski, a well-known French philosopher, that it goes against the "symbolic order" to let homosexuals form families.[14] Whatever social forms these are, they are not marriages, and they are not families; indeed, in her view, they are not properly "social" at all but private. The struggle is in part over words, over where and how they apply as well as about their plasticity and their equivocity. But it is more specifically a struggle over whether certain practices of nomination keep in place the presuppositions about the limits of what is humanly recognizable. The argument rests on a certain paradox, however, that would be hard to deny. Because if one does *not* want to recognize certain human relations as part of the humanly recognizable, then one has *already* recognized them, and one seeks to deny what it is one has already, in one way or another, understood. "Recognition" becomes an effort to deny what exists and, hence, becomes the instrument for the refusal of recognition. In this way, it becomes a way of shoring up a normative fantasy of the human over and against dissonant versions of itself. To defend the limits of what is recognizable against that which challenges it is to understand that the norms that govern recognizability have already been challenged. In the United States, we are used to hearing conservative and reactionary polemics against homosexuality as unnatural, but that is not precisely the discourse through which the French polemic proceeds. Agacinski, for instance, does not assume that the family takes a natural form. Rather, the state is constrained in recognizing marriage as heterosexual, in her view, not by nature or natural law, but by something called "the symbolic order" (which corresponds to and ratifies a natural law). It is according to the dictates of this order that the state is obligated to refuse to recognize such relations.

I will lay out Agacinski's view in a moment, not because she is the most vocal opponent to the transformations in kinship that gay marriage might imply, but because some time ago a colleague sent me an editorial Agacinski had written in *Le Monde,* a missive that in some way demanded a response.[15] In her editorial, she identifies a certain American strain of queer and gender theory as the monstrous future for France were these transformations to occur. So let us say, without going into details, that a certain interpellation occurred on the front page of *Le Monde* in which my name figured as a sign of the coming monstrosity. And consider that I am in a quandary here because my own views are used to caution against a monstrous future that will come to pass if lesbian and gay people are permitted to form state-ratified kinship arrangements. So on the one hand there is a demand to respond and to rebut these allegations; on the other hand, it seems crucial not to accept the terms in which one's opponent has framed the debate, a debate which, I fear, is no debate at all, but a highly publicized polemic and fear-mongering. My own quandary is not mine alone. Will I, in opposing her, occupy a position in which I argue for state legitimation? Is this what I desire?

On the one hand, it would be easy enough to argue that she is wrong, that the family forms in question are viable social forms, and that the current episteme of intelligibility might be usefully challenged and rearticulated in light of these social forms.[16] After all, her view matches and fortifies those that maintain that legitimate sexual relations take a heterosexual and state-sanctioned form, and who work to derealize viable and significant sexual alliances that fail to conform to that model. Of course, there are consequences to this kind of derealization that go beyond hurting someone's feelings or causing offense to a group of people. It means that when you arrive at the hospital to see your lover, you may not. It means that when your lover falls into a coma, you may not assume certain executorial rights. It means that when your lover dies, you may not be permitted to receive the body. It means that when your child is left with you, the nonbiological parent, you may not be able to counter the claims of biological relatives in court and may lose custody, and even access. It means you may not be able to provide health care benefits for one another. These are all very significant forms of disenfranchisement, which are made all the worse by the personal effacements that occur in daily life and invariably take a toll on a relationship. The sense of delegitimation can make it harder to sustain a bond, a bond that is not real anyway, a bond that does not "exist," that never had a chance to exist, that was never meant to exist. If you're not real, it can be hard to sustain yourselves over time. Here is where the absence of state legitimation can emerge within the psyche as a pervasive, if not fatal, sense of self-doubt. And if you've actually lost the lover who was never recognized to be your lover, did you really lose that person? Is this a loss, and can it be publicly grieved? Surely this is something that has become a pervasive problem in the queer community, given the losses from AIDS, the losses of lives and loves who are always in struggle to be recognized as such.

On the other hand, to pursue state legitimation in order to repair these injuries brings with it a host of new problems, if not new heartaches. The failure to secure state recognition for one's intimate arrangements can be experienced only as a form of derealization if the terms of state legitimation are those that maintain hegemonic control over the norms of recognition, in other words, if the state monopolizes the resources of recognition. Are there not other ways of feeling possible, intelligible, even real, apart from the sphere of state recognition? Should there not be other ways? It makes sense that the lesbian and gay movement would turn to the state, given the movement's history:

the current drive for gay marriage is in some ways a response to AIDS and, in particular, a shamed response, one in which a gay community seeks to disavow its so-called promiscuity, one in which we appear as healthy and normal and capable of sustaining monogamous relations over time. This, of course, brings me back to the question, a question posed poignantly by Michael Warner, of whether the drive to become recognizable within the existing norms of legitimacy requires that we subscribe to a practice that delegitimates those sexual lives structured outside of the bonds of marriage and the presumptions of monogamy.[17] Is this a disavowal that the queer community is willing to make? And with what social consequence? How is it that we give the power of recognition over to the state at the moment that we insist that we are unreal and illegitimate without it? Are there other resources by which we might become recognizable or mobilize to challenge the existing regimes within which the terms of recognizability take place?

One can see the terrain of the dilemma here: on the one hand, living without norms of recognition results in significant suffering and forms of disenfranchisement that confound the very distinctions among psychic, cultural, and material consequences. On the other hand, the demand to be recognized, which is a very powerful political demand, can lead to new and invidious forms of social hierarchy, to a precipitous foreclosure of the sexual field, and to new ways of supporting and extending state power, if it does not institute a critical challenge to the very norms of recognition supplied and required by state legitimation. Indeed, in making the bid to the state for recognition, we effectively restrict the domain of what will become recognizable as legitimate sexual arrangements, thus fortifying the state as the source for norms of recognition and eclipsing other possibilities in civil society and cultural life. To demand and receive recognition according to norms that legitimate marriage and delegitimate forms of sexual alliance outside of marriage, or to norms that are articulated in a critical relation to marriage, is to displace the site of delegitimation from one part of the queer community to another or, rather, to transform a collective delegitimation into a selective one. Such a practice is difficult, if not impossible, to reconcile with a radically democratic, sexually progressive movement. What would it mean to exclude from the field of potential legitimation those who are outside of marriage, those who live nonmonogamously, those who live alone, those who are in whatever arrangements they are in that are not the marriage form? I would add a caveat here: we do not always know what we mean by "the state" when we are referring to the kind of "state legitimation" that occurs in marriage. The state is not a simple unity and its parts and operations are not always coordinated with one another. The state is not reducible to law, and power is not reducible to state power. It would be wrong to understand the state as operating with a single set of interests or to gauge its effects as if they are unilaterally successful. I think the state can also be worked and exploited. Moreover, social policy, which involves the implementation of law to local instances, can very often be the site where law is challenged, thrown to a court to adjudicate, and where new kinship arrangements stand a chance of gaining new legitimacy. Of course, certain propositions remain highly controversial: interracial adoption, adoption by single men, by gay male couples, by parties who are unmarried, by kinship structures in which there are more than two adults. So there are reasons to worry about requesting state recognition for intimate alliances, and so becoming part of an extension of state power into the socius. But do these reasons outweigh those we might have for seeking recognition and entitlement through entering legal contract? Contracts work in different ways—and surely differently in the United States and French contexts—to garner state authority and to subject the individuals who enter into contracts to regulatory control. But even if we argue that in France, contracts are conceived as individual entitlements and so less tethered to state control, the very form of individuation is thus sustained by state legitimation, even if, or precisely when, the state appears to be relatively withdrawn from the contractual process itself.

In this way, the norms of the state work very differently in these disparate national contexts. In the United States, the norms of recognition supplied by the state not only often fail to describe or regulate existing social practice but become the site of articulation for a fantasy of normativity that projects and delineates an ideological account of kinship, at the moment when it is undergoing social challenge and dissemination. Thus, it seems that the appeal to the state is at once an appeal to a fantasy already institutionalized by the state and a leave-taking from existing social complexity in the hope of becoming "socially coherent" at last. What this means as well is that there is a site to which we can turn, understood as the state, which will finally render us coherent, a turn that commits us to the fantasy of state power. Jacqueline Rose persuasively argues that "if the state has meaning only 'partly as something existing,' if it rests on the belief of individuals that it 'exists or should exist,' then it starts to look uncannily like what psychoanalysis would call an 'as if' phenomenon."[18] Its regulations do not always seek to order what exists, but to figure social life in certain imaginary ways. The incommensurability between state stipulation and existing social life means that this gap must be covered over for the state to continue to exercise its authority and to exemplify the kind of coherence which it is expected to confer on its subjects. As Rose reminds us, "It is because the state has become so alien and distant from the people it is meant to represent that, according to Engels, it has to rely, more and more desperately, on the sacredness and inviolability of its own laws."[19]

So there are two sides to this coin; yet I do not mean to resolve this dilemma in favor of one or the other but to develop a critical practice that is mindful of both. I want to maintain that legitimation is double-edged: it is crucial that, politically, we lay claim to intelligibility and recognizability; and it is crucial, politically, that we maintain a critical and transformative relation to the norms that govern what will and will not count as an intelligible and recognizable alliance and kinship. This latter would also involve a critical relation to the desire for legitimation as such. It is also crucial that we question the assumption that the state furnish these norms, and that we come to think critically about what the state has become during these times or, indeed, how it has become a site for the articulation of a fantasy that seeks to deny or overturn what these times have brought us.

As we return to the French debate, then, it seems important to remember that the debate about laws is at once a debate about what kinds of sexual arrangements and forms of kinship can be admitted to exist or deemed to be possible, and what the limits of imaginability might be. For many who opposed the PACS, or who, minimally, voiced skeptical views about it, the very status of culture was called into question by the variability of legitimated sexual alliance. Immigration and gay parenting were figured as challenging the fundamentals of a culture that had already been transformed, but that sought to deny the transformation it had already undergone.[20]

To understand this we have to consider how the term "culture" operates, and how, in the French context, the term became invoked in these debates to designate not the culturally variable formations of human life, but the universal conditions for human intelligibility.

Natural, Cultural, State Law

Although Agacinski, the French philosopher, is not a Lacanian and, indeed, hardly a psychoanalyst, we do see in her commentary, which was prominent in the French debate, a certain anthropological belief that is shared by many Lacanian followers and other psychoanalytic practitioners in France and elsewhere.[21] The belief is that culture itself requires that a man and a woman produce a child, and that the child have this dual point of reference for its own initiation into the symbolic order, where the symbolic order consists of a set of rules that order and support our sense of reality and cultural intelligibility.

She writes that gay parenting is both unnatural and a threat to culture in the sense that sexual difference, which is, in her view, irrefutably biological, gains its significance in the cultural sphere as the foundation of life in procreation: "This foundation (of sexual difference) is generation; this is the difference between the paternal and maternal roles. There must be the masculine and the feminine to give life." Over and against this life-giving heterosexuality at the foundation of culture is the specter of homosexual parenting, a practice that not only departs from nature and from culture but also centers on the dangerous and artificial fabrication of the human and is figured as a kind of violence or destruction. She writes: "It takes a certain 'violence,' if one is homosexual, to want a child [*Il faut une certaine 'violence,' quand on est homosexuel, pour vouloir un enfant*] . . . . I think that there is no absolute right to a child, since the right implies an increasingly artificial fabrication of children. In the interests of the child, one cannot efface its double origin." The "double origin" is its invariable beginning with a man and woman, a man who occupies the place of the father, and a woman who occupies the place of the mother. "This mixed origin, which is natural," she writes, "is also a cultural and symbolic foundation."[22]

The argument that there must be a father and a mother as a double point of reference for the child's origin rests on a set of presumptions which resonate with the Lévi-Straussian position in *The Elementary*

Structures of Kinship in 1949. Although Agacinski is not a Lévi-Straussian, her framework nevertheless borrows from a set of structuralist premises about culture that have been revived and redeployed in the context of the present debate. My point is less to hold the views of Lévi-Strauss responsible for the terms of the present debate than to ask what purpose the reanimation of these views serves within the contemporary political horizon, considering that in anthropology, the Lévi-Straussian views promulgated in the late 1940s are generally considered surpassed and are no longer owned in the same form by Lévi-Strauss himself.[23]

For Lévi-Strauss, the Oedipal drama was not to be construed as a developmental moment or phase. It consists instead of a prohibition that is at work in the inception of language, one that works at all times to facilitate the transition from nature to culture for all emerging subjects. Indeed, the bar that prohibits the sexual union with the mother is not arrived at in time, but is, in some sense, *there* as a precondition of individuation, a presumption and support of cultural intelligibility itself. No subject emerges without this bar or prohibition as its condition, and no cultural intelligibility can be claimed without first passing through this founding structure. Indeed, the mother is disallowed because she belongs to the father, so if this prohibition is fundamental, and it is understood, then the father and the mother exist as logically necessary features of the prohibition itself. Now, psychoanalysis will explain that the father and the mother do not have to actually exist; they can be positions or imaginary figures, but that they have to figure structurally in some way. Agacinski's point is also ambiguous in this way, but she will insist that they must have existed, and that their existence has to be understood by the child as essential to his or her origin.

To understand how this prohibition becomes foundational to a conception of culture is to follow the way in which the Oedipal complex in Freud becomes recast as an inaugural structure of language and the subject in Lacan, something I cannot do in this context and probably have done too many times before.[24] What I want to underscore here is the use of Oedipus to establish a certain conception of culture that has rather narrow consequences for both formations of gender and sexual arrangements and that implicitly figures culture as a whole, a unity, one that has a stake in reproducing itself, and its singular wholeness through the reproduction of the child. When Agacinski argues, for instance, that for every child to emerge in nonpsychotic way, there must be a father and a mother, she appears at first not to be making the empirical point that a father and mother must be present and known through all phases of child rearing. She means something more ideal: that there must at least be a psychic point of reference for mother and father and a narrative effort to recuperate the male and female parent, even if one or the other is never present and never known. But if this were guaranteed without the social arrangement of heterosexuality, she would have no reason to oppose lesbian and gay adoption. So it would appear that social arrangements support and maintain the symbolic structure, even as the symbolic structure legitimates the social arrangement. For Agacinski, heterosexual coitus, regardless of the parent or parents who rear the child, is understood as the origin of the child, and that origin will have a symbolic importance.

This symbolic importance of the child's origin in heterosexuality is understood to be essential to culture for the following reason. If the child enters culture through the process of assuming a symbolic position, and if these symbolic positions are differentiated by virtue of Oedipalization, then the child presumably will become gendered on the occasion that the child takes up a position in relation to parental positions that are prohibited as overt sexual objects for the child. The boy will become a boy to the extent that he recognizes that he cannot have his mother, that he must find a substitute woman for her; the girl will become a girl to the extent that she recognizes she cannot have her mother, substitutes for that loss through identification with the mother, and then recognizes she cannot have the father and substitutes a male object for him. According to this fairly rigid schematic of Oedipalization, gender is achieved through the accomplishment of heterosexual desire. This structure, which is already much more rigidly put forward here, in the effort to reconstruct Agacinski's position, than one would find in Freud (i.e., in either *The Three Essays on the Theory of Sexuality* or *The Ego and the Id*), is then deprived of its status as a developmental phase and asserted as the very means by which an individuated subject within language is established. To become part of culture means to have passed through the gender-differentiating mechanism of this taboo and to accomplish both normative heterosexuality and discrete gender identity at once.

There are many reasons to reject this particular rendition of Oedipalization as the precondition of language and cultural intelligibility. And there are many versions of psychoanalysis that would reject this schema, allowing for various ways of rearticulating the Oedipal but also limiting its function in relation to the pre-Oedipal. Moreover, some forms of structural anthropology sought to elevate the exchange of women into a precondition of culture and to identify that mandate for exogamy with the incest taboo operating within the Oedipal drama. In the meantime, other theories of culture have come to take its place and call that structuralist account into question. Indeed, the failure of structuralism to take into account kinship systems that do not conform to its model was made clear by anthropologists such as David Schneider, Sylvia Yanagisako, Sarah Franklin, Clifford Geertz, and Marilyn Strathern.[25] These theories emphasize modes of exchange different from those presumed by structuralism, and they also call into question the universality of structuralism's claims. Sociologists of kinship such as Judith Stacey and Carol Stack, as well as anthropologist Kath Weston, have also underscored a variety of kin relations that work, and work according to rules that are not always or only traceable to the incest taboo.[26]

So why would the structuralist account of sexual difference, conceived according to the exchange of women, make a "comeback" in the context of the present debates in France? Why would various intellectuals, some of them feminist, proclaim that sexual difference is not only fundamental to culture but to its transmissibility, that reproduction must remain the prerogative of heterosexual marriage, and that limits must be set on viable and recognizable forms of nonheterosexual parenting arrangements?

To understand the resurgence of a largely anachronistic structuralism in this context, it is important to consider that the incest taboo functions in Lévi-Strauss not only to secure the exogamous reproduction of children but also to maintain a unity to the "clan" through compulsory exogamy, as it is articulated through compulsory heterosexuality. The woman from elsewhere makes sure that the men from here will reproduce their own kind. She secures the reproduction of cultural identity in this way. The ambiguous "clan" designates a "primitive" group for Lévi-Strauss in 1949, but it comes to function ideologically for the cultural unity of the nation in 1999–2000, in the context of a

Europe beset with opening borders and new immigrants. The incest taboo thus comes to function in tandem with a racialist project to reproduce culture and, in the French context, to reproduce the implicit identification of French culture with universality. It is a "law" that works in the service of the "as if," securing a fantasy of the nation that is already, and irreversibly, under siege. In this sense, the invocation of the symbolic law defends against the threat to French cultural purity that has taken place, and is taking place, through new patterns of immigration, increased instances of miscegenation, and the blurring of national boundaries. Indeed, even in Lévi-Strauss, whose earlier theory of clan formation is redescribed in his short text, *Race and History,* we see that the reproducibility of racial identity is linked to the reproduction of culture.[27] Is there a link between the account of the reproduction of culture in Lévi-Strauss's early work and his later reflections on cultural identity and the reproduction of race? Is there a connection between these texts that might help us read the cultural link that takes place in France now between fears about immigration and desires to regulate nonheterosexual kinship? The incest taboo might be seen as working in conjunction with the taboo against miscegenation, especially in the contemporary French context, insofar as the defense of culture that takes place through mandating the family as heterosexual is at once an extension of new forms of European racism.

We see something of this link prefigured in Lévi-Strauss, which explains in part why we see the resurrection of his theory in the context of the present debate. When Lévi-Strauss makes the argument that the incest taboo is the basis of culture and that it mandates exogamy, or marriage outside the clan, is "the clan" being read in terms of race or, more specifically, in terms of a racial presupposition of culture that maintains its purity through regulating its transmissibility? Marriage must take place outside the clan. There must be exogamy. But there must also be a limit to exogamy; that is, marriage must be outside the clan, but not outside a certain racial self-understanding or racial commonality. So the incest taboo mandates exogamy, but the taboo against miscegenation limits the exogamy that the incest taboo mandates. Cornered then between a compulsory heterosexuality and a prohibited miscegenation, something called culture, saturated with the anxiety and identity of dominant European whiteness, reproduces itself in and as universality itself.

There are, of course, many other ways of contesting the Lévi-Straussian model that have emerged in recent years, and its strange resurgence in the recent political debate will no doubt strike anthropologists as the spectral appearance of an anachronism. Arguments have been made that other kinds of kinship arrangements are possible in a culture. There are also other ways of explaining the ordering practices that kinship sometimes exemplified. These debates, however, remain internal to a study of kinship that assumes the primary place of kinship within a culture, and assumes for the most part that a culture is a unitary and discrete totality. Pierre Clastres made this point most polemically several years ago in the French context, arguing that it is not possible to treat the rules of kinship as supplying the rules of intelligibility for any society, and that culture is a not a self-standing notion but must be regarded as fundamentally imbued by power relations, power relations that are not reducible to rules.[28] But if we begin to understand that cultures are not self-standing entities or unities, that the exchanges between them, their very modes of delimiting themselves in distinction constitute their provisional ontology and are, as a result, fraught with power, then we are compelled to rethink the problem of exchange altogether: no longer as the gift of women, which assumes and produces the self-identity of the patrilineal clan, but as a set of potentially unpredictable and contested practices of self-definition that are not reducible to a primary and culture-founding heterosexuality. Indeed, if one were to elaborate on this point, the task would be to take up David Schneider's suggestion that kinship is a kind of *doing*, one that does not reflect a prior structure, but that can only be understood as an enacted practice. This would help us, I believe, move away from the situation in which a hypostatized structure of relations lurks behind any actual social arrangement and permit us to consider how modes of patterned and performative doing bring kinship categories into operation and become the means by which they undergo transformation and displacement.

The hypostatized heterosexuality, construed by some to be symbolic rather than social, and so to operate as a structure which founds the field of kinship itself—and informs social arrangements no matter how they appear, no matter what they do—has been the basis of the claim that kinship is always already heterosexual. According to its precept, those who enter kinship terms as nonheterosexual will only make sense if they assume the position of mother or father. The social variability of kinship has little or no efficacy in rewriting the founding and pervasive symbolic law. The postulate of a founding heterosexuality must also be read as part of the operation of power—and I would add fantasy—such that we can begin to ask how the invocation of such a foundation works in the building of a certain fantasy of state and nation. The relations of exchange that constitute culture as a series of transactions or translations are not only or primarily sexual, but they do take sexuality as their issue, as it were, when the question of cultural transmission and reproduction is at stake. I do not mean to say that cultural reproduction takes place solely or exclusively or fundamentally through the child. I mean only to suggest that the figure of the child is one eroticized site in the reproduction of culture, one that implicitly raises the question of whether there will be a sure transmission of culture through heterosexual procreation—not only whether heterosexuality will serve the purposes of transmitting culture faithfully, but whether culture will be defined, in part, as the prerogative of heterosexuality itself.

Indeed, to call this entire theoretical apparatus into question is not only to question the founding norms of heterosexuality but also to wonder whether "culture" can be talked about at all as a self-sufficient kind of field or terrain. Though I do it, manifesting or symptomatizing a struggle to work through this position in an act of public thinking, I am aware that I am using a term that no longer signifies in the way that it once could. It is a placeholder for a past position, one I must use to make that position and its limits clear, but one that I also suspend in the using. The relation between heterosexuality and the unity and, implicitly, the purity of culture, is not a functional one. Although we may be tempted to say that heterosexuality secures the reproduction of culture and that patrilineality secures the reproduction of culture in the form of a whole that is reproducible in its identity through time, it is equally true that the conceit of a culture as a self-sustaining and self-replicating totality supports the naturalization of heterosexuality, and that the entirety of the structuralist approach to sexual difference emblematizes this movement to secure heterosexuality through the thematics of culture. But is there a way to break out of this circle whereby heterosexuality institutes monolithic culture and monolithic culture reinstitutes and renaturalizes heterosexuality?

Efforts within anthropology no longer situate kinship as the basis of culture, but conceive it as one cultural phenomenon complexly inter-linked with other phenomena, cultural, social, political, and economic. Anthropologists Franklin and McKinnon write, for instance, that kin-ship has become linked to "the political formations of national and transnational identities, the economic movements of labor and capital, the cosmologies of religion, the hierarchies of race, gender, and species taxonomies, and the epistemologies of science, medicine, and technology." As a result, they argue, the very ethnographic study of kinship has changed such that it now "include[s] topics such as diasporic cultures, the dynamics of global political economy, or changes occurring in the contexts of biotechnology and biomedicine."[29] Indeed, in the French debate, Eric Fassin argues that one must understand the invocation of the "symbolic order" that links marriage to filiation in a necessary and foundational way as a compensatory response to the historical breakup of marriage as a hegemonic institution, the name for which in French is *démariage*.[30] In this sense, the opposition to the PACS is an effort to make the state sustain a certain fantasy of marriage and nation whose hegemony is already, and irreversibly, challenged at the level of social practice.

Similarly, Franklin and McKinnon understand kinship to be a site where certain displacements are already at work, where anxieties about biotechnology and transnational migrations become focused and dis-avowed. This seems clearly at work in Agacinski's position in at least two ways: the fear she bespeaks about the "Americanization" of sexual and gender relations in France attests to a desire to keep those relations organized in a specifically French form, and the appeal to the univer-sality of the symbolic order is, of course, a trope of the French effort to identify its own nationalist project with a universalist one. Similarly, her fear that lesbians and gay men will start to fabricate human beings, exaggerating the biotechnology of reproduction, suggests that these "unnatural" practices will eventuate in a wholesale social engineering of the human, linking, once again, homosexuality with the potential resurgence of fascism. One might well wonder what technological forces at work in the global economy, or indeed, what consequences of the human genome project raise these kinds of anxieties in con-temporary cultural life. But it seems a displacement, if not a halluci-nation, to identify the source of this social threat, if it is a threat, with lesbians who excavate sperm from dry ice on a cold winter day in Iowa when one of them is ovulating.

Franklin and McKinnon write that kinship is "no longer conceptualized as grounded in a singular and fixed idea of 'natural' relation, but is seen to be self-consciously assembled from a multiplicity of possible bits and pieces."[31] It would seem crucial, then, to understand the assembling operation they describe in light of the thesis that kinship is itself a kind of doing, a practice that enacts that assemblage of significations as it takes place. But with such a definition in place, can kinship be definitively separated from other communal and affiliative practices? Kinship loses its specificity as an object once it becomes characterized loosely as modes of enduring relationship. Obviously, not all kinship relations last, but whatever relations qualify for kinship enter into a norm or a convention that has some durability, and that norm acquires its durability through being reinstated time and again. Thus, a norm does not have to be static in order to last; in fact, it *cannot* be static if it is to last. These are relations that are prone to naturalization and disrupted repeatedly by the impossibility of settling the relation between nature and culture; moreover, in Franklin and McKinnon's terms, kinship is one way for signifying the origin of culture. I would put it this way: the story of kinship, as we have it from Lévi-Strauss, is an allegory for the origin of culture and a symptom of the process of naturalization itself, one that takes place, brilliantly, insidiously, in the name of culture itself. Thus, one might add that debates about the distinction between nature and culture, which are clearly heightened when the distinctions among animal, human, machine, hybrid, and cyborg are no longer settled, become figured at the site of kinship, for even a theory of kinship that is radically culturalist frames itself against a discredited "nature" and so remains in a constitutive and definitional relation to that which it claims to transcend.

One can see how quickly kinship loses its specificity in terms of the global economy, for instance, when one considers the politics of international adoption and donor insemination. For new "families" where relations of filiation are not based on biology are sometimes conditioned by innovations in biotechnology or international commodity relations and the trade in children. And now there is the question of control over genetic resources, conceived of as a new set of property relations to be negotiated by legislation and court decisions. But there are also clearly salutary consequences of the breakdown of the symbolic order, since kinship ties that bind persons to one another may well be no more or less than the intensification of community ties, may or may not be based on enduring or exclusive sexual relations, and may well consist of ex-lovers, nonlovers, friends, and community members. In this sense, then, the relations of kinship arrive at boundaries that call into question the distinguishability of kinship from community, or that call for a different conception of friendship. These constitute a "breakdown" of traditional kinship that not only displaces the central place of biological and sexual relations from its definition but gives sexuality a domain separate from that of kinship, which allows for the durable tie to be thought outside of the conjugal frame and thus opens kinship to a set of community ties that are irreducible to family.

Psychoanalytic Narrative, Normative Discourse, and Critique

Unfortunately, the important work in what might be called postkinship studies in anthropology has not been matched by similarly innovative work in psychoanalysis, and the latter sometimes still relies on presumptive heterosexual kinship to theorize the sexual formation of the subject although there is some important work there, for instance, that of Ken Corbett.[32] Whereas several scholars in anthropology have not only opened up the meaning and possible forms of kinship but have called into question whether kinship is always the defining moment of culture. Indeed, if we call into question the postulate by which Oedipalization, conceived in rigid terms, becomes the condition for culture itself, how do we then return to psychoanalysis once this delinkage has taken place? If Oedipus is not the sine qua non of culture, that does not mean there is no place for Oedipus. It simply means that the complex that goes by that name may take a variety of cultural forms, and that it will no longer be able to function as a normative condition of culture itself. Oedipus may or may not function universally, but even those who claim that it does would have to find out in what ways it figures and would not be able to maintain that it always figures in the same way. For it to be a universal—and I confess to being an agnostic on this point—in no way confirms the thesis that it is the condition of culture. Such a thesis purports to know that Oedipus always functions in the same way, namely, as a condition of culture itself. But if Oedipus is interpreted broadly, as a name for the triangularity of desire, then the salient questions become: What forms does that triangularity take? Must it presume heterosexuality? And what happens when we begin to understand Oedipus outside of the exchange of women and the presumption of heterosexual exchange?

Psychoanalysis does not need to be associated exclusively with the reactionary moment in which culture is understood to be based on an irrefutable heterosexuality. Indeed, there are so many questions that psychoanalysis might pursue in order to help understand the psychic life of those who live outside of normative kinship or in some mix of normative and "non-": What is the fantasy of homosexual love that the child unconsciously adopts in gay families? How do children who are displaced from original families or born through implantation or donor insemination understand their origins? What cultural narratives are at their disposal, and what particular interpretations do they give to these conditions? Must the story that the child tells about his or her origin, a story that will no doubt be subject to many retellings, conform to a single story about how the human comes into being? Or will we find the human emerging through narrative structures that are not reducible to one story, the story of a capitalized Culture itself? How must we revise our understanding of the need for a narrative understanding of self that a child may have that includes a consideration of how those narratives are revised and interrupted in time? And how do we begin to understand what forms of gender differentiation take place for the child when heterosexuality is not the presumption of Oedipalization?

Indeed, this is the occasion not only for psychoanalysis to rethink its own uncritically accepted notions of culture but for new kinship and sexual arrangements to compel a rethinking of culture itself. When the relations that bind are no longer traced to heterosexual procreation, the very homology between nature and culture that philosophers such as Agacinski support tends to become undermined. Indeed, they do not stay static in her own work, for if it is the symbolic order that mandates heterosexual origins, and the symbolic is understood to legitimate social relations, why would she worry about putatively illegitimate social relations? She assumes that the latter have the power to undermine the symbolic, suggesting that the symbolic does not precede the social and, finally, has no independence from it.

It seems clear that when psychoanalytic practitioners make public claims about the psychotic or dangerous status of gay families, they are wielding public discourse in ways that need to be strongly countered. The Lacanians do not have a monopoly on such claims. In an interview with Jacqueline Rose, the well-known Kleinian practitioner Hanna Segal reiterates her view that "homosexuality is an attack on the parental couple," and "a developmental arrest." She expresses outrage over a situation in which two lesbians raise a boy. She adds that she considers "the adult homosexual structure to be pathological."[33] When asked at a public presentation in October of 1998 whether she approved of two lesbians raising a boy, she answered flatly "No." To respond directly to Segal, as many people have, with an insistence on the normalcy of lesbian and gay families is to accept that the debate should center on the distinction between normal and pathological. But if we seek entrance to the halls of normalcy or, indeed, reverse the discourse, to applaud our "pathology" (i.e., as the only "sane" position within homophobic culture), we have not called the defining framework into question. And once we enter that framework, we are to some degree defined by its terms, which means that we are *as* defined by those terms when we seek to establish ourselves within the boundaries of normality as we are when we assume the impermeability of those boundaries and position ourselves as its permanent outside. After all, even Agacinski knows how to make use of the claim that lesbians and gays are "inherently" subversive when she claims that they should *not* be given the right to marry because homosexuality is, by definition, "outside institutions and fixed models."[34]

We may think that double-edged thinking will lead us only to political paralysis but consider the more serious consequences that follow from taking a single stand in such debates. If we engage the terms that these debates supply, then we ratify the frame at the moment in which we take our stand. This signals a certain paralysis in the face of exercising power to change the terms by which such topics are rendered thinkable. Indeed, a more radical social transformation is precisely at stake when we refuse, for instance, to allow kinship to become reducible to "family," or when we refuse to allow the field of sexuality to become gauged against the marriage form. For as surely as rights to adoption and, indeed, to reproductive technology ought to be secured for individuals and alliances outside the marriage frame, it would constitute a drastic curtailment of progressive sexual politics to allow marriage and family, or even kinship, to mark the exclusive parameters within which sexual life is thought. That the sexual field has become foreclosed through such debates about whether we might marry or conceive or raise children makes clear that any answer, that is, both the "yes" and the "no," works in the service of circumscribing reality in precipitous ways. If we decide that these are the decisive issues, and know which side we are on, then we have accepted an epistemological field structured by a fundamental loss, one that we can no longer name enough even to grieve. The life of sexuality, kinship, and community that becomes unthinkable within the terms of these norms constitutes the lost horizon of radical sexual politics, and we find our way "politically" in the wake of the ungrievable.

6. Longing for Recognition

Jessica Benjamin's recent work seeks to establish the possibility for intersubjective recognition, thereby setting a philosophical norm for a therapeutic discourse. Her work has always been distinctively defined by its groundedness in critical social theory and clinical practice. Whereas the Frankfurt School maintained a strong theoretical interest in psychoanalysis and spawned the important work of Alexander and Margarete Mitscherlich, *The Inability to Mourn,* among other texts, it has been rare since that time to find a critical theorist trained in that venue who actively practices psychoanalysis, and whose theoretical contributions combine critical reflection and clinical insight in the way that Benjamin's does. Central to her philosophical inheritance is the notion of recognition itself, a key concept that was developed in Hegel's *Phenomenology of Spirit* (111–19) and which has assumed new meanings in the work of Jürgen Habermas and Axel Honneth.[1] In some ways, Benjamin's work relies on the presumption that recognition is possible, and that it is the condition under which the human subject achieves psychic self-understanding and acceptance.

There are several passages in almost any text of hers that give a sense of what recognition is. It is not the simple presentation of a subject for another that facilitates the recognition of that self-presenting subject by the Other. It is, rather, a process that is engaged when subject and Other understand themselves to be reflected in one another, but where this reflection does not result in a collapse of the one into the Other (through an incorporative identification, for instance) or a projection that annihilates the alterity of the Other. In Benjamin's appropriation of the Hegelian notion of recognition, recognition is a normative ideal, an aspiration that guides clinical practice. Recognition implies that we see the Other as separate, but as structured psychically in ways that are shared. Of utmost importance for Benjamin, following Habermas in some ways, is the notion that communication itself becomes both the vehicle and example of recognition. Recognition is neither an act that one performs nor is it literalized as the event in which we each "see" one another and are "seen." It takes place through communication, primarily but not exclusively verbal, in which subjects are transformed by virtue of the communicative practice in which they are engaged. One can see how this model supplies a norm for both social theory and therapeutic practice. It is to Benjamin's credit that she has elaborated a theory that spans both domains as productively as it does.

One of the distinctive contributions of her theory is to insist that intersubjectivity is not the same as object relations, and that "intersubjectivity" adds to object relations the notion of an external Other, one who exceeds the psychic construction of the object in complementary terms. What this means is that whatever the psychic and fantasmatic relation to the object may be, it ought to be understood in terms of the larger dynamic of recognition. The relation to the object is not the same as the relation to the Other, but the relation to the Other provides a framework for understanding the relation to the object. The subject not only forms certain psychic relations to objects, but the subject is formed by and through those psychic relations. Moreover, these various forms are implicitly structured by a struggle for recognition in which the Other does and does not become dissociable from the object by which it is psychically represented. This struggle is one that is characterized by a desire to enter into a communicative practice with the Other in which recognition takes place neither as an event nor a set of events, but as an ongoing process, one that also poses the psychic risk of destruction. Whereas Hegel refers to "negation" as the risk that recognition always runs, Benjamin retains this term to describe the differentiated aspect of relationality: the Other is not me, and from this distinction, certain psychic consequences follow. There are problematic ways of handling the fact of negation, and these are, of course, explained in part through Freud's conception of aggression and Kleinian conceptions of destruction. For Benjamin, humans form psychic relations with Others on the basis of a necessary negation, but not all of those relations must be destructive. Whereas the psychic response that seeks to master and dispel that negation is destructive, that destruction is precisely what needs to be worked through in the process of recognition. Because human psychic life is characterized by desires both for omnipotence and for contact, it vacillates between "relating to the object and recognizing the outside [O]ther."[2]

In a sense, Benjamin tells us that this vacillation or tension is what constitutes human psychic life fundamentally or inevitably. And yet, it seems that we are also to operate under a norm that postulates the transformation of object-relations into modes of recognition, whereby our relations to objects are subsumed, as it were, under our relation to the Other. To the extent that we are successful in effecting this transformation, we seem to put this tension into play in the context of a more fluid notion of communicative practice mentioned above. Benjamin is insistent upon the "inherently problematic and conflictual make-up in the psyche,"[3] and she does not go back on her word. But what becomes difficult to understand is what meaning recognition can and must assume, given the conflictual character of the psyche. Recognition is at once the norm toward which we invariably strive, the norm that ought to govern therapeutic practice, and the ideal form that communication takes when it becomes a transformative process. Recognition is, however, also the name given to the process that constantly risks destruction and which, I would submit, could not be recognition without a defining or constitutive risk of destruction. Although Benjamin clearly makes the point that recognition risks falling into destruction, it seems to me that she still holds out for an ideal of recognition in which destruction is an occasional and lamentable occurrence, one that is reversed and overcome in the therapeutic situation, and which does not turn out to constitute recognition essentially.

My understanding of her project is that whereas the tension between omnipotence and contact, as she puts it, is necessary in psychic life, there are ways of living and handling that tension that do not involve "splitting," but which keep the tension both alive and productive. In her view, we must be prepared to overcome modes of splitting that entail disavowal where we either disparage the object to shore ourselves up, or project our own aggression onto the object to avoid the psychically unlivable consequences that follow when that aggression is recognized as our own. Aggression forms a break in the process of recognition, and we should expect such "break-downs," to use her words, but the task will be to work against them and to strive for the triumph of recognition over aggression. Even in this hopeful formulation, however, we get the sense that recognition is something other than aggression or that, minimally, recognition can do without aggression. What this means is that there will be times when the relation to the Other relapses into the relation to the object, but that the relation to the Other can and must be restored. It also means that misrecognition is occasional, but not a constitutive or insurpassable feature of psychic reality, as Lacan has argued, and that recognition, conceived as free of misrecognition, not only ought to triumph, but can.

In what follows, I hope to lay out what I take to be some of the consequences of this view and its component parts. For if it is the case that destructiveness can turn into recognition, then it follows that recognition can leave destructiveness behind. Is this true? Further, is the relationship assumed by recognition dyadic, given the qualification that the process of recognition now constitutes "the third" itself based upon a disavowal of others forms of triangulation? And is there a way to think triangulation apart from oedipalization? Does the dyadic model for recognition, moreover, help us to understand the particular convergences of straight, bisexual, and gay desire that invariably refer desire outside the dyad in which it only apparently occurs? Do we want to remain within the complementarity of gender as we seek to understand, for instance, the particular interplay of gender and desire in transgender? Finally, I'll return to Hegel to see the way in which he offers us another version of the self than the one emphasized by Benjamin in order to understand whether a certain division in the subject can become the occasion and impetus for another version of recognition.

From Complementarity to Postoedipal Triangularity

Over time, Benjamin's work has moved from an emphasis on complementarity, which assumes a dyadic relation, to one that accommodates a triadic relation. What is the third term in relation to which the dyad is constituted? As one might expect from her earlier contributions, the triad will not be reducible to oedipalization. It will not be the case that the dyad is tacitly and finally structured in relation to a third, the tabooed parental object of love. The third emerges, however, in a different way for Benjamin, indeed, in a way that focuses not on prohibition and its consequences but on "both partners [in a] pattern of excitement." This pattern is the third, and it is "cocreated": "outside the mental control of either partner we find a site of mediation, the music of the third to which both attune."[4] Indeed, the third constitutes an ideal of transcendence for Benjamin, a reference point for reciprocal desire that exceeds representation. The third is not the concrete Other who solicits desire, but the Other of the Other who (or which) engages, motivates, and exceeds a relation of desire at the same time that it constitutes it essentially.

Benjamin is careful in *The Shadow of the Other* to distinguish her position from that of Drucilla Cornell or any position inspired by the Levinasian notion that the Other is transcendent or ineffable (93). But in her most recent writing, she admits this Other as external to the psychic object, nearing the Levinasian position and so perhaps enacting for us the expansive possibilities of the critic who makes an identification with formerly repudiated possibilities.

This way of approaching the triadic relation is a very happy one, and I'll confess that I am not sure it is finally credible or, indeed, desirable. It is indisputably impressive, though, as an act of faith in relationships and, specifically, in the therapeutic relationship itself. But as an act of faith, it is difficult to "argue" with. So what I hope to do in what follows is less to counter this exemplar of happiness than to offer a few rejoinders from the ranks of ambivalence where some of us continue to dwell. Further, I think that some less jubilant reflections on triangulation and the triadic relation (to be distinguished from one another) may be possible and will not return us to the prison house of Oedipus with its heterosexist implications for gender. Finally, I'd like to suggest that a triadic structure for thinking about desire has implications for thinking gender beyond complementarity and reducing the risk of heterosexist bias implied by the doctrine of complementarity.

I'm no great fan of the phallus, and have made my own views known on this subject before,[5] so I do not propose a return to a notion of the phallus as the third term in any and all relations of desire.

Nor do I accept the view that would posit the phallus as the primary or originary moment of desire, such that all desire either extends through identification or mimetic reflection of the paternal signifier. I understand that progressive Lacanians are quick to distinguish between the phallus and the penis and claim that the "paternal" is a metaphor only. What they do not explain is the way the very distinction that is said to make "phallus" and "paternal" safe for use continues to rely upon and reinstitute the correspondences, penis/phallus and paternal/maternal that the distinctions are said to overcome. I believe in the power of subversive resignification to an extent and applaud efforts to disseminate the phallus and to cultivate, for instance, dyke dads and the like. But it would be a mistake, I believe, to privilege either the penis or paternity as the terms to be most widely and radically resignified. Why those terms rather than some others? The "other" to these terms is, of course, the question interrogated here, and Benjamin has helped us to imagine, theoretically, a psychic landscape in which the phallus does not control the circuit of psychic effects. But are we equipped to rethink the problem of triangulation now that we understand the risks of phallic reduction?

The turn to the preoedipal has been, of course, to rethink desire in relation to the maternal, but such a turn engages us, unwittingly, in the resurrection of the dyad: not the phallus, but the maternal, for the two options available are "dad" and "mom." But are there other kinds of descriptions that might complicate what happens at the level of desire and, indeed, at the level of gender and kinship? Benjamin clearly asks these questions, and her critique of the Lacanian feminist insistence on the primacy of the phallus is, in large part, a critique of both its presumptive heterosexuality and the mutually exclusive logic through which gender is thought. Benjamin's use of the notion of "overinclusiveness" implies that there can be, and ought to be, a postoedipal recuperation of overinclusive identifications characteristic of the preoedipal phase, where identifications with one gender do not entail repudiations of another.[6] Benjamin is careful in this context to allow for several coexisting identifications and even to promote as an ideal for therapeutic practice the notion that we might live such apparently inconsistent identifications in a state of creative tension. She shows as well how the oedipal framework cannot account for the apparent paradox of a feminine man loving a woman, a masculine man loving a man. To the extent that gender identification is always considered to be at the expense of desire, coherent genders might be said to correspond without fail to heterosexual orientations.

I am in great sympathy with these moves, especially as they are argued in Chapter 2, "Constructions of Uncertain Content," in *Shadow of the Other*. Although I continue to have some questions about the doctrine of "overinclusiveness," in spite of liking its consequences, I believe that Benjamin is working toward a nonheterosexist psychoanalysis in this book (45–49). I do think, however, that (a) triangulation might be profitably rethought beyond oedipalization or, indeed, as part of the very postoedipal displacement of the oedipal; (b) certain assumptions about the primacy of gender dimorphism limit the radicalism of Benjamin's critique; and (c) that the model of overinclusiveness cannot quite become the condition for recognizing difference that Benjamin maintains because it resists the notion of a self that is ek-statically[7] involved in the Other, decentered through its identifications which neither excludes nor includes the Other in question.

Let us first consider the possibilities of postoedipal triangulation. I suggest we take as a point of departure the Lacanian formulation that suggests that desire is never merely dyadic in its structure. I would like to see not only whether this formulation can be read apart from any reference to the phallus, but whether it might also lead in directions that would exceed the Lacanian purview. When Jean Hyppolite introduces the notion of "the desire of desire" in his commentary on Hegel's *Phenomenology of Spirit*, he means to suggest not only that desire seeks its own renewal (a Spinozistic claim), but that it also seeks to be the object of desire for the Other.[8] When Lacan rephrases this formulation of Hyppolite, he enters the genitive in order to produce an equivocation: "desire is the desire *of* the Other" (my emphasis).[9] What does desire desire? It clearly still continues to desire itself; indeed, it is not clear that the desire which desires is different from the desire that is desired. They are homonymically linked, at a minimum, but what this means is that desire redoubles itself; it seeks its own renewal, but in order to achieve its own renewal, it must reduplicate itself and so become something other to what it has been. It does not stay in place as a single desire, but becomes other to itself, taking a form that is outside of itself. Moreover, what desire wants is the Other, where the Other is understood as its generalized object. What desire also wants is the Other's desire, where the Other is conceived as a subject of desire. This last formulation involves the grammar of the genitive, and it suggests that the Other's desire becomes the model for the subject's desire.[10] It is not that I want the Other to want me, but I want to the extent that I have taken on the desire of the Other and modeled my desire after the Other's desire. This is, of course, only one perspective within what is arguably a kaleidoscope of perspectives. Indeed, there are other readings of this formulation, including the oedipal one: I desire what the Other desires (a third object), but that object belongs to the Other, and not to me; this lack, instituted through prohibition, is the foundation of my desire. Another oedipal reading is the following: I want the Other to want me rather than the sanctioned object of its desire; I want no longer to be the prohibited object of desire. The inverse of the latter formulation is: I want to be free to desire the one who is prohibited to me and, so, to take the Other away from the Other and, in this sense, *have* the Other's desire.

Lacan's way of formulating this position is, of course, derived in part from Lévi-Strauss's theory of the exchange of women. Male clan members exchange women in order to establish a symbolic relation with other male clan members. The women are "wanted" precisely because they are wanted by the Other. Their value is thus constituted as an exchange value, though one that is not reducible to Marx's understanding of that term. Queer theorist Eve Sedgwick came along in *Between Men* and asked who was, in fact, desiring whom in such a scene. Her point was to show that what first appears to be a relation of a man who desires a woman turns out to be implicitly a homosocial bond between two men. Her argument was not to claim, in line with the "phallus" affiliates, that the homosocial bond comes at the expense of the heterosexual, but that the homosocial (distinct from the homosexual) is articulated precisely through the heterosexual. This argument has had far-reaching consequences for the thinking of both heterosexuality and homosexuality, as well as for thinking the symbolic nature of the homosocial bond (and, hence, by implication, all of the Lacanian symbolic). The point is not that the phallus is had by one and not by another, but that it is circulated along a heterosexual and homosexual circuit at once, thus confounding the identificatory positions for every "actor" in the scene. The man who seeks to send the woman to another man sends some aspect of himself, and the man who receives her, receives him as well. She circuits, but is she finally wanted, or does she merely exemplify a value by becoming the representative of both men's desire, the place where those desires meet, and where they fail to meet, a place where that potentially homosexual encounter is relayed, suspended, and contained?

I raise this issue because it seems to me that it is not possible to read the profound and perhaps inescapable ways that heterosexuality and homosexuality are defined through one another. For instance, to what extent is heterosexual jealousy often compounded by an inability to avow same-sex desire?[11] A man's woman lover wants another man, and even "has" him, which is experienced by the first man at his own expense. What is the price that the first man has to pay? When, in this scene, he desires the desire of the Other, is it his lover's desire (let us imagine that it is)? Or is it also the prerogative that his lover has to take another *man* as her lover (let us imagine that it also is)? When he rages against her for her infidelity, does he rage because she refuses to make the sacrifice that he has already made? And even though such a reading might suggest that he identifies with her in the scene, it is unclear how he identifies, or whether it is, finally, a "feminine" identification. He may want her imagined position in the scene, but what does he imagine her position to be? It cannot be presumed that he takes her position to be feminine, even if he imagines her in a receptive response to the other man. If that is his receptivity that he finds relocated there at the heart of his own jealous fantasy, then perhaps it is more appropriate to claim that he imagines her in a position of passive male homosexuality. Is it, finally, really possible to distinguish in such a case between a heterosexual and a homosexual passion? After all, he has lost her, and that enrages him, and she has acted the aim he cannot or will not act, and that enrages him.

Benjamin's insistence that we do not have to understand desire and identification in a relation of mutual exclusion clearly makes room for such simultaneous passions. But does she give us a way to describe how heterosexuality becomes a venue for homosexual passion or how homosexuality becomes the conduit for heterosexual passion? It seems that the dyadic structure, when it is imposed upon gender, comes to assume a gender complementarity that fails to see the rigors at work to keep the "dyadic" relation reassuringly just between those two. To claim, as Benjamin does, that the third comes in as the intersubjective process itself, as the "surviving" of destruction as a more livable and creative "negation," is already to make the scene definitionally happier than it can be. Of course, she lets us know that incorporation and destruction are risks that every relation runs, but these are to be worked through in order to reach the possibility of a recognition in which the "two" selves in relation are transformed by virtue of their dynamic relation with one another.

But what are they to do with the other third? Note here that the queer theoretical redescription of the "exchange of women" does not return to the Lacanian feminist insistence on the primacy of the phallus. It is not that one wants the desire of the Other, because that desire will mimetically reflect one's own position as having the phallus. Nor does one want what other men want in order more fully to identify as a man. Indeed, as the triangulation begins in which heterosexuality is transmuted into homosociality, the identifications proliferate with precisely the complexity that the usual Lacanian positions either rule out or describe as pathology. Where desire and identification are played out as mutually exclusive possibilities against the inescapable background of a (presumptively heterosexual) sexual difference, the actors in the scene I describe can be understood only as trying to occupy positions in vain, warring with a symbolic that has already arranged in advance for their defeat. Thus, the man is trying to "refuse" sexual difference in imagining himself in his lover's position with another man, and so the moralizing relegation of desire to pathology takes place once again within the preorchestrated drama of sexual difference. I believe that both Benjamin and I agree on the untenability of such an approach.

But where precisely do we differ? In the first place, as I've suggested above, the relationship cannot be understood apart from its reference to the third, and the third cannot be easily described as the "process" of the relationship itself. I do not mean to suggest either that the third is "excluded" from the dyad or that the dyad must exclude the third for the dyad to take place. No the third is both inside the relationship, as a constituting passion, and "outside" as the partially unrealized and prohibited object of desire.

So let's complicate the scene again by rethinking it from the woman's point of view. Let's imagine that she is bisexual and has sought to have a relationship with "man number 1," putting off for a while her desires for women, which tend to be desires to be a bottom. But instead of finding a woman as the "third," she finds a man (man number 2), and "tops" him. Let's say, for argument's sake, that man number 1 would rather die than be "topped" by his girlfriend, since that would be too "queer" for him. So he knows that she is topping another man, possibly penetrating him anally, and he is furious for several reasons. But what is she after? If she is bisexual, she is a bisexual who happens to be "doing" a few men right now. But perhaps she is also staging a scene in which the outbreak of jealousy puts the relation at risk. Perhaps she does this in order to break from the relationship in order to be free to pursue "none of the above." Would it be possible to see her intensification of heterosexual activity at this moment as a way of (a) seeing her first lover's jealousy and goading him toward greater possessiveness; (b) topping her second lover and gratifying the desire that is off limits to her with the first; and (c) setting the two men against one another in order to make room for the possibility of a lesbian relationship in which she is not a top at all; and (d) intensifying her heterosexuality in order to ward off the psychic dangers she associates with being a lesbian bottom? Note that it may be that the one desire is not in the service of another, such that we might be able to say which one is the real and authentic one, and which is simply a camouflage or deflection. Indeed, it may be that this particular character can't find a "real" desire that supersedes the sequence that she undergoes, and that what is real is the sequence itself. But it may be that the affair with man number 2 becomes, indirectly, the venue for the convergence of these passions, their momentary constellation, and that to understand her one must accept something of their simultaneous and dissonant claims on truth. Surely, the pattern in which a man and woman heterosexually involved both amicably break their relationship in order to pursue homosexual desires is not uncommon in urban centers. I don't claim to know what happens here, or what happens when a gay male and a lesbian who are friends start to sleep with one another. But it seems fair to assume that a certain crossing of homosexual and heterosexual passions takes place such that these are not two distinct strands of a braid, but simultaneous vehicles for one another.

I think that this comes out most distinctly in discussions of trans-gender. It becomes difficult to say whether the sexuality of the trans-gendered person is homosexual or heterosexual. The term "queer" gained currency precisely to address such moments of productive unde-cidability, but we have not yet seen a psychoanalytic attempt to take account of these cultural formations in which certain vacillating notions of sexual orientation are constitutive. This becomes most clear when we think about transsexuals who are in transition, where iden-tity is in the process of being achieved, but is not yet there. Or, most emphatically, for those transsexuals who understand transition to be a permanent process. If we cannot refer unambiguously to gender in such cases, do we have the point of reference for making claims about sex-uality? In the case of transgender, where transsexualism does not come into play, there are various ways of crossing that cannot be understood as stable achievements, where the gender crossing constitutes, in part, the condition of eroticization itself. In the film *Boys Don't Cry*,[12] it seems that transgender is both about identifying as a boy and want-ing a girl, so it is a crossing over from being a girl to being a hetero-sexual boy. Brandon Teena identifies as a heterosexual boy, but we see several moments of disidentification as well, where the fantasy breaks down and a tampon has to be located, used, and then discarded with no trace. His identification thus recommences, has to be reorchestrated in a daily way as a credible fantasy, one that compels belief. The girl lover seems not to know, but this is the not-knowing of fetishism, an uncertain ground of eroticization. It remains unclear whether the girl-friend does not know, even when she claims that she does not, and it is unclear whether she knows even when she claims to know. Indeed, one of the most thrilling moments of the film is when the girlfriend, knowing, fully reengages the fantasy. And one of the most brittle moments takes place when the girlfriend, knowing, seems no longer to be able to enter the fantasy fully. The disavowal not only makes the fantasy possible, but strengthens it, and on occasion strengthens it to the point of being able to survive avowal.

Similarly, it would not be possible to say that Brandon's body stays out of the picture, and that this occlusion makes the fantasy possible, since it does enter the picture but only through the terms that the fan-tasy instates. This is not a simple "denial" of anatomy, but the erotic deployment of the body, its covering, its prosthetic extension for the purposes of a reciprocal erotic fantasy. There are lips and hands and eyes, the strength of Brandon's body on and in Lana, his/her girlfriend, arms, weight, and thrust. So it is hardly a simple picture of "disembodiment," and hardly "sad." When s/he desires his/her girlfriend's desire, what is it that s/he wants? Brandon occupies the place of the subject of desire, but s/he does not roll on his/her back in the light and ask his/her girl to suck off his/her dildo. Perhaps that would be too "queer," but perhaps as well it would kill the very conditions that make the fantasy possible for both of them. S/he works the dildo in the dark so that the fantasy can emerge in full force, so that its condition of disavowal is fulfilled. S/he occupies that place, to be sure, and suffers the persecution and the rape from the boys in the film precisely because s/he has occupied it too well. Is Brandon a lesbian or a boy? Surely, the question itself defines Brandon's predicament in some way, even as Brandon consistently answers the predicament by doing himself as a boy. It will not work to say that because Brandon must do himself as a boy that this is a sign that Brandon is lesbian. For boys surely do themselves as boys, and no anatomy enters gender without being "done" in some way.

Would it be any easier for us if we were to ask whether the lesbian who only makes love using her dildo to penetrate her girlfriend, whose sexuality is so fully scripted by apparent heterosexuality that no other relation is possible, is a boy or a "boy"? If she says that she can only make love as a "boy," she is, we might say, transgendered in bed, if not in the street. Brandon's crossing involves a constant dare posed to the public norms of the culture, and so occupies a more public site on the continuum of transgender. It is not simply about being able to have sex a certain way, but also about appearing as a masculine gender. So, in this sense, Brandon is no lesbian, despite the fact that the film, caving in, wants to return him to that status after the rape, implying that the return to (achievement of?) lesbianism is somehow facilitated by that rape, returning Brandon, as the rapists sought to do, to a "true" feminine identity that "comes to terms" with anatomy. This "coming to terms" means only that anatomy is instrumentalized according to acceptable cultural norms, producing a "woman" as the effect of that instrumentalization and normalizing gender even as it allows for desire to be queer. One could conjecture that Brandon only wants to be a public boy in order to gain the legitimate right to have sexual relations as he does, but such an explanation assumes that gender is merely instrumental to sexuality. But gender has its own pleasures for Brandon, and serves its own purposes. These pleasures of identification exceed those of desire, and, in that sense, Brandon is not only or easily a lesbian.

Recognition and the Limits of Complementarity

Can gender complementarity help us here? Benjamin writes, "the critique of gender complementarity results in a necessary paradox: It at once upsets the oppositional categories of femininity and masculinity while recognizing that these positions inescapably organize experience."[13] And right before this statement, she asks, "if we do not begin with the opposition between woman and man, with woman's negative position in that binary, we seem to dissolve the very basis for our having questioned gender categories in the first place." But what were those questions, and were they really posed in the right way? Were we right to presume the binary of man and woman when so many gendered lives cannot assume that binary? Were we right to see the relation as a binary when the reference to the tertiary is what permitted us to see the homosexual aims that run through heterosexual relationality? Should we have asked these questions of gender instead? At what psychic price does normative gender become established? How is it that presuming complementarity presumes a self-referential heterosexual that is not definitionally crossed by homosexual aims? If we could not ask these questions in the past, do they not now form part of the theoretical challenge for a psychoanalysis concerned with the politics of gender and sexuality, at once feminist and queer?

It is important to ask these questions in this way if what we want to do is offer recognition, if we believe that recognition is a reciprocal process that moves selves beyond their incorporative and destructive dispositions toward an understanding of another self whose difference from us is ethically imperative to mark. As I hope is clear, I do not have a problem with the norm of recognition as it functions in Benjamin's work, and think, in fact, that it is an appropriate norm for psychoanalysis. But I do wonder whether an untenable hopefulness has entered into her descriptions of what is possible under the rubric of recognition. Moreover, as I indicated above, I question specifically whether overinclusiveness as she describes it can become the condition for the recognition of a separate Other, neither repudiated nor incorporated.

Let us turn first to the question of whether negation can be clearly separated from destruction, as Benjamin suggests. And then let us reconsider the Hegelian notion of recognition, emphasizing its ek-static structure and ask whether that is compatible with the model of over-inclusiveness. How do such different models fare regarding the ethical question of whether they facilitate recognition, and in what form? Finally, what are the implications of these different notions of recognition for thinking about the self in relation to identity.

Benjamin clearly states that it has been her position since the publication of *The Bonds of Love* that "negation is an equally vital moment in the movement of recognition. Nor can any appeal to the acceptance of otherness afford to leave out the inevitable breakdown of recognition into domination."[14] This represents her position published in 1998. And yet, since then she has moved away from this "inevitable breakdown." Whereas the earlier position seemed to claim that recognition presupposes negativity, her present one seems to imply that negativity is an occasional and contingent event that befalls recognition, but which in no sense defines it. She writes, for instance, that "we should expect breakdowns in recognition," but that "destruction" can be surmounted: "destruction continues until survival becomes possible at a more authentic level." Recognition is the name given to this authentic level, defined as the transcendence of the destructive itself. It is subsequently described as a "dialogic" process" in which externality is recognized. The analyst in such a situation is not an idealization, for that is still a failure to release the analyst from internality. It is the Other as he or she breaks through either the ideal or the persecutory image that marks the "authentic" emergence of a dialogic encounter and the creation of what Benjamin refers to as "intersubjective space."

My question is whether intersubjective space, in its "authentic" mode, is really ever free of destruction? And if it is free of destruction, utterly, is it also beyond the psyche in a way that is no longer of use for psychoanalysis? If the "third" is redefined as the music or harmony of dialogic encounter, what happens to the other "thirds?" The child who interrupts the encounter, the former lover at the door or on the phone, the past that cannot be reversed, the future that cannot be contained, the unconscious itself as it rides the emergence of unanticipated circumstance? Surely, these are all negativities, even sources of "destruction" that cannot be fully overcome, sublated, resolved in the harmonious music of dialogue. What discord does that music drown out? What does it disavow in order to be? What if the music turns out to be Mahler? If we accept that the problem in relationship is not just a function of complementarity, of projecting onto another what belongs to the self, of incorporating another who ought properly to be regarded as separate, it will be hard to sustain the model of recognition that remains finally dyadic in structure. But if we accept that desire for the Other might be desire for the Other's desire, and accept as well the myriad equivocal formulations of that position, then it seems to me that recognizing the Other requires assuming that the dyad is rarely, if ever, what it seems. If relations are primarily dyadic, then I remain at the center of the Other's desire, and narcissism is, by definition, satisfied. But if desire works through relays that are not always easy to trace, then who I am for the Other will be, by definition, at risk of displacement. Can one find the Other whom one loves apart from all the Others who have come to lodge at the site of that Other? Can one free the Other, as it were, from the entire history of psychic condensation and displacement or, indeed, from the precipitate of abandoned object-relations that form the ego itself? Or is part of what it means to "recognize" the Other to recognize that he or she comes, of necessity, with a history which does not have oneself as its center? Is this not part of the humility necessary in all recognition, and part of the recognition that is involved in love?

I believe that Benjamin might say that when one recognizes that one is not at the center of the Other's history, one is recognizing difference. And if one does not respond to that recognition with aggression, with omnipotent destruction, then one is in a position to recognize difference as such and to understand this distinguishing feature of the Other as a relation of "negation" (not-me) that does not resolve into destruction. Negation is destruction that is survived. But if this is her response, it seems to me to entail a further recognition of the necessary breakdown of the dyadic into something that cannot be contained or suppressed within that limited structure. The dyad is an achievement, not a presupposition. Part of the difficulty of making it work is precisely caused by the fact that it is achieved within a psychic horizon that is fundamentally indifferent to it. If negation is destruction that is survived, in what does "survival" consist? Certainly, the formulation implies that "destruction" is somehow overcome, even overcome once and for all. But is this ever really possible—for humans, that is? And would we trust those who claimed to have overcome destructiveness for the harmonious dyad once and for all? I, for one, would be wary.

We do not need to accept a drive theory that claims that aggression is there for all times, constitutive of who we are, in order to accept that destructiveness poses itself continually as a risk. That risk is a perennial and irresolvable aspect of human psychic life. As a result, any therapeutic norm that seeks to overcome destructiveness seems to be basing itself on an impossible premise. Now, it may be that the ethical imperative that Benjamin wishes to derive from her distinction between destruction and negation is that the former must continually be survived as negation, that this is an incessant task. But the temporal dynamism she invokes is not that of a struggle that repeats itself, a laboring with destructiveness that must continually be restaged, a relationship where forms of breakdown are expected and inevitable; it is, rather, a dialogue that sustains tension as a "goal in itself," a teleological movement, in other words, where the overcoming of destruction is the final end.

When Hegel introduces the notion of recognition in the section on lordship and bondage in *The Phenomenology of Spirit*, he narrates the primary encounter with the Other in terms of self-loss. "Self-consciousness . . . has *come out of itself.* . . . it has lost itself, for it finds itself as an *other* being" (111). One might understand Hegel to be describing merely a pathological state in which a fantasy of absorption by the Other constitutes an early or primitive experience. But he is saying something more. He is suggesting that whatever consciousness is, whatever the self is, will find itself only though a reflection of itself in another. To be itself, it must pass through self-loss, and when it passes through, it will never be "returned" to what it was. To be reflected in or as another will have a double significance for consciousness, however, since consciousness will, through the reflection, regain itself in some way. But it will, by virtue of the external status of the reflection, regain itself as external to itself and, hence, continue to lose itself. Thus, the relationship to the Other will be, invariably, ambivalent. The

price of self-knowledge will be self-loss, and the Other poses the possibility of both securing and undermining self-knowledge. What becomes
clear, though, is that the self never returns to itself free of the Other,
that its "relationality" becomes constitutive of who the self is.

On this last point Benjamin and I agree. Where we differ, I believe,
is how we understand this relationality. In my view, Hegel has given
us an ek-static notion of the self, one which is, of necessity, outside
itself, not self-identical, differentiated from the start. It is the self over
here who considers its reflection over there, but it is equally over there,
reflected, and reflecting. Its ontology is precisely to be divided and
spanned in irrecoverable ways. Indeed, whatever self emerges in the
course of the *Phenomenology of the Spirit* is always at a temporal
remove from its former appearance; it is transformed through its
encounter with alterity, not in order to return to itself, but to become
a self it never was. Difference casts it forth into an irreversible future.
To be a self is, on these terms, to be at a distance from who one is, not
to enjoy the prerogative of self-identity (what Hegel calls self-certainty),
but to be cast, always, outside oneself, Other to oneself. I believe that
this conception of the self emphasizes a different Hegel from the one
found in Benjamin's work. It is surely one for which the metaphor of
"inclusion," as in "the inclusive self" would not quite work. I'll try to
explain why.

In the chapter titled "The Shadow of the Other Subject," Benjamin
offers a sustained discussion, possibly the most important published
discussion that exists, on the volume *Feminist Contentions*, which I
co-wrote with four other feminist philosophers. She worries that I subscribe to a notion of the self that requires exclusion (102), and that I
lack a complementary term for "inclusion." She suggests that if I object
to certain ways in which the subject is formed through exclusion, it
would make sense that I embrace a normative ideal in which exclusion
would be overcome: "only inclusion, the avowal of what was disavowed, in short *owning*, could allow that otherness a place outside
the self in the realm of externality, could grant it recognition separate
from self" (103). A metaphorical problem emerges, of course, insofar as
"inclusion" names the process by which the "external" is recognized. But
is this more than a metaphorical difficulty or, rather, does the metaphorical difficulty trace the outlines for us of a more problematic theoretical
question at hand? Benjamin offers "inclusion" as the complementary

opposite to the negative form of exclusion or abjection that I discuss in *Bodies that Matter*, but she also reserves the term "external" for the aspect of the Other that appears under conditions of authentic dialogue. So, exclusion, in the sense of expulsion or abjection or disavowal, remains within the orbit of a complementary form of splitting, in her view, one that fully eclipses the Other with a disavowed projection. The Other emerges as "external," then, only when it is no longer "excluded." But is the Other "owned" at such a moment, or is there a certain dispossession that takes place that allows the Other to appear to begin with? This would be Laplanche's point, and it would certainly be that of Levinas and Drucilla Cornell as well.[15] It is precisely the movement beyond the logic of owning and disowning that takes the Other out of the narcissistic circuit of the subject. Indeed, for Laplanche, alterity emerges, one might say, beyond any question of owning.[16]

I would suggest that the ek-static notion of the self in Hegel resonates in some ways with this notion of the self that invariably loses itself in the Other who secures that self's existence. The "self" here is not the same as the subject, which is a conceit of autonomous self-determination. The self in Hegel is marked by a primary enthrallment with the Other, one in which that self is put at risk. The moment in "Lordship and Bondage" when the two self-consciousnesses come to recognize one another is, accordingly, in the "life and death struggle," the moment in which they each see the shared power they have to annihilate the Other and, thereby, destroy the condition of their own self-reflection. Thus, it is at a moment of fundamental vulnerability that recognition becomes possible, and need becomes self-conscious. What recognition does at such a moment is, to be sure, to hold destruction in check. But what it also means is that the self is not its own, that it is given over to the Other in advance of any further relation, but in such a way that the Other does not own it either. And the ethical content of its relationship to the Other is to be found in this fundamental and reciprocal state of being "given over." In Hegel, it would only be partially true to say that the self comes to "include" the Other. (Benjamin would distinguish here between "inclusion" and "incorporation" and, indeed, pose them as opposites.) For the self is always other to itself, and so not a "container" or unity that might "include" Others within its scope. On the contrary, the self is always finding itself as the Other, becoming Other to itself, and this is another way of marking the opposite of "incorporation." It does not take the Other in; it finds itself transported outside of itself in an irreversible relation of alterity. In a sense, the self "is" this relation to alterity.

Although Benjamin sometimes refers to "postmodern" conceptions of the self that presume its "split" and "decentered" character, we do not come to know what precisely is meant by these terms. It will not do to say that there is first a self and then it engages in splitting, since the self as I am outlining it here is beyond itself from the start, and defined by this ontological ek-stasis, this fundamental relation to the Other in which it finds itself ambiguously installed outside itself. This model is, I would suggest, one way of disputing any claim concerning the self-sufficiency of the subject or, indeed, the incorporative character of all identification. And in this sense, it is not so far from Benjamin's position. This may not be "splitting" in the precise psychoanalytic sense, but it may be an ontological dividedness that the psychoanalytic notion of splitting relies upon and elaborates. If we assume that the self exists and then it splits, we assume that the ontological status of the self is self-sufficient before it undergoes its splitting (an Aristophanic myth, we might say, resurrected within the metapsychology of ego psychology). But this is not to understand the ontological primacy of relationality itself and its consequences for thinking the self in its necessary (and ethically consequential) disunity.

Once we think the self this way, one can begin to see how verb forms come closest to expressing this fundamental relationality. Although common sense would have us ask: Is there not a self who identifies? A self who mourns? Don't we all know that such a self exists? But here it seems that the conventional and precritical needs of grammar trump the demands of critical reflection. For it makes good sense to talk about a self, but are we sure it is intact prior to the act of splitting, and what does it mean to insist upon a subject who "performs" its splitting? Is there nothing from which a subject is split off at the outset that occasions the formation of the subject itself? Is there no production of the unconscious that happens concomitantly with the formation of the subject, understood as a self-determining activity? And if it is a self who is already at a distance who splits itself, how are we to understand what splitting means for such a self? Yes, it is possible and necessary to say that the subject splits, but it does not follow from that formulation that the subject was a single whole or autonomous. For if the subject is both split and splitting, it will be necessary to know what kind of split was inaugurative, what kind is undergone as a contingent psychic event, and how those different levels of splitting relate to one another, if at all.

It is, then, one perspective on relationality derived from Hegel which claims that the self seeks and offers recognition to another, but it is another which claims that the very process of recognition reveals that the self is always already positioned outside itself. This is not a particularly "postmodern" insight, since it is derived from German Idealism and earlier medieval ecstatic traditions. It simply avows that that "we" who are relational do not stand apart from those relations and cannot think of ourselves outside of the decentering effects that that relationality entails. Moreover, when we consider that the relations by which we are defined are not dyadic, but always refer to a historical legacy and futural horizon that is not contained by the Other, but which constitutes something like the Other of the Other, then it seems to follow that who we "are" fundamentally is a subject in a temporal chain of desire that only occasionally and provisionally assumes the form of the dyad. I want to reiterate that displacing the binary model for thinking about relationality will also help us appreciate the triangulating echoes in heterosexual, homosexual, and bisexual desire, and complicate our understanding of the relation between sexuality and gender.

We have Jessica Benjamin to thank for beginning the most important dialogue on gender and sexuality that we have at the interstices of philosophy and psychoanalysis. Let us now begin to think again on what it might mean to recognize one another when it is a question of so much more than the two of us.

7. Quandaries of the Incest Taboo

I would like to address two issues that have not only caused some discontent for psychoanalysis, but that emerge as internal to psychoanalysis as its own proper sphere of discontent: incest and normative kinship. They are related, most prominently through the incest taboo, what the taboo forecloses on the one hand, what it inaugurates and legitimates on the other. I would like to make two separate remarks about incest and kinship: one having to do with contemporary debates on incest and how, and whether, it can be conceptualized; and the other, concerning the relation between the prohibition against incest and the institution of normative kinship arrangements that take a presumptively heterosexual form. What I hope to suggest is that psychoanalysis as a theory and a practice might well be rejuvenated by returning to the questions of incest and kinship, as well as to their interrelation. On the one hand, psychoanalytic theory has assumed that the Oedipal drama in which the son's incestuous love for the mother is fantasized and feared is followed by an interdiction that forces the son to love a woman other than his mother. The daughter's incestuous passion is less fully explored in the Freudian corpus, but her renunciation for her desire for her father culminates in an identification with her mother and a turn to the child as a fetish or penis substitute. In the context of structuralist linguistics, this primary incest taboo becomes the way in which sexual positions are occupied, masculine and feminine are differentiated, and heterosexuality is secured. Even as psychoanalysis has charted for us this path through the normalization of gender and sexuality, it has also insisted from the start that the "development" which is described is in no sense secure. As a result, psychoanalysis gives us, and perhaps enacts for us, something of this drama of sexual normalization as well as its inevitable deviations.

In the developmental story, incest is generally described as a punishable fantasy. And one of the main questions that emerges within the context of the contemporary social discussion of incest is whether it is real or whether it is fantasized, and how one might be able to determine epistemologically the difference between the two. For some, the answer to the epistemological quandary lies in whether there can be false memories, and what respect is to be given to first-person narrative accounts of experiences that are often attributed to early childhood. For others, the question of the "reality" of incest links up with broader questions in the historiography of memory, whether historical "events" can be confirmed apart from the interpretive field in which they appear and, whether, accordingly, something like the nondeniability of traumatic events, usually typified by the destruction of European Jewry, can be confidently asserted against revisionist historians.

These matters are complicated all the more now that trauma studies has emerged (Caruth, Felman, Laub) in which the argument prevails that trauma is, by definition, not capturable through representation or, indeed, recollection; it is precisely that which renders all memory false, we might say, and which is known through the gap that disrupts all efforts at narrative reconstruction.

With regard to incest, the question thus turns on the relations among memory, event, and desire: is it an event that *precedes* a memory? is it a memory that retroactively posits an event? is it a wish that takes the form of a memory? Those who want to underscore the prevalence of incest as an abusive family practice tend to insist that it is an event, and that insofar as it is a memory, it is a memory of an event. And sometimes this takes the form of a dogmatic premise: for it to be traumatic and real, incest must be understood as an event. This view is confounded, however, precisely by the trauma studies position mentioned above in which the sign of the trauma and its proof is precisely its resistance to the narrative structure of the event.

Those who worry about false allegations, and believe we are in the midst of a public rash of such false allegations, can speak against a psychoanalytic perspective or for one. They can, for instance, insist that incest is either a memory induced by therapy or, less often, a wish transmuted into false memory. One psychoanalytic approach asks whether incest is merely a wish or, derivatively, a wish transmuted into memory. This view suggests that the narrative report of incest correlates with a psychic event, but not an historical one, and that the two orders of event are clearly dissociable. A third position, however, is possible within psychoanalysis; it insists that trauma takes its toll on narrativity; that is, insofar as incest takes traumatic form, it is not recoverable as an event; as trauma, it cannot take the form of a remembered or narratable event. Thus, the claim on historical veracity is not secured through establishing the event-structure of incest. On the contrary, when and where incest is *not* figurable as an event, is where its very unfigurability testifies to its traumatic character. This would, of course, be "testimony" difficult to prove in a court of law that labors under standards that determine the empirical status of an event. Trauma, on the contrary, takes its toll on empiricism as well.

Incestuous trauma, then, is variously figured as a brute imposition on the child's body, as the exploitative incitation of the child's desire, as the radically unrepresentable in the child's experience or in the adult's memory whose childhood is at issue. Moreover, to the extent that psychoanalysis attributes incestuous fantasy and its prohibition to the process by which gendered differentiation takes place (as well as the sexual ordering of gender), it remains difficult to distinguish between incest as a traumatic fantasy essential to sexual differentiation in the psyche, and incest as a trauma that ought clearly to be marked as abusive practice and in no sense essential to psychic and sexual development.

The opportunities for divisive debate are rife here. From a psychoanalytic view (which is, emphatically, not a unified and harmonious set of perspectives), the urgent questions seem to be these: how do we account for the more or less general persistence of the incest taboo and its traumatic consequences as part of the differentiation process that paves the way toward adult sexuality without demeaning the claims made about incestuous practice that clearly are traumatic in nonnecessary and unacceptable ways? The effort to reduce all claims about the reality of incest to the symptoms of disavowed fantasy is no more acceptable than the effort to presume the veracity of all incest claims. The task will be to find out how the incestuous passions that are part of emerging childhood sexuality are exploited precisely through the practice of incest which overrides prohibitive boundaries that ought to be kept firmly in place. Moreover, to understand the trauma of that practice, it will be important not to dismiss the psychic register of pain, nor to read the absence of empirical evidence or narratable history as a sign that this trauma exists purely at the level of fantasy. If trauma theory is right to assert that trauma often leads to the impossibility of representation, then there is no way to decide questions of the psychic and social status of traumatic incest through direct recourse to its representation. One will have to become a reader of the ellipsis, the gap, the absence, and this means that psychoanalysis will have to relearn the skill of reading broken narratives.

There are two brief points I would like to recapitulate in relation to this epistemological set of quandaries that have emerged. The first is simply to remind us that the distinction between event and wish is not as clear as it is sometimes held to be. It is not necessary to figure parent-child incest as a unilateral impingement on the child by the parent, since whatever impingement takes place will also be registered within the sphere of fantasy. In fact, to understand the violation that incest can be—and also to distinguish between those occasions of incest that are violation and those that are not—it is unnecessary to figure the body of the child exclusively as a surface imposed upon from the outside. The fear, of course, is that if it emerges that the child's desire has been exploited or incited by incest, this will somehow detract from our understanding of parent-child incest as a violation. The reification of the child's body as passive surface would thus constitute, at a theoretical level, a further deprivation of the child: the deprivation of psychic life. It may also be said to perpetrate a deprivation of another order. After all, when we try to think of what kind of exploitation incest can be, it is often precisely the child's love that is exploited in the scene of incest. By refusing to consider what happens to the child's love and desire in the traumatic incestuous relation with an adult, we fail to describe the depth and psychic consequence of that trauma.

One might be tempted to conclude that the event is always psychically registered and as a result not, strictly speaking, separable from the psychic staging of the event: what is narrated, if it can be narrated, is precisely the mix of the two. But this solution does not address the nonnarratable, that for which there is no story, no report, no linguistic representation. For the trauma that is neither event nor memory, its relation to wish is not readily legible. To avow the seriousness of the violation, which is ethically imperative, it is not necessary to compel the subject to prove the historical veracity of the "event." For it may be that the very sign of trauma is the loss of access to the terms that establish historical veracity, that is, where what is historical and what is true become unknowable or unthinkable.

It is always possible, from a clinical perspective, to claim that it does not matter whether trauma happened or did not, since the point is to interrogate the psychic meaning of a report without judging the question of its reality. But can we really dissociate the question of psychic meaning from that of the "event" if a certain fuzziness about the event having taken place is precisely part of its traumatic effect? It may be that what is unthinkable is precisely a fantasy that is disavowed, or it may be that what is unthinkable is the act that a parent performed (was willing to perform), or it may be that what is unthinkable is precisely their convergence in the event.

What constitutes the limit of the thinkable, the narratable, the intelligible? What constitutes *the limit of what can be thought as true?* These are, I believe, questions that psychoanalysis has always interrogated precisely because it relies on a form of analytic listening and a form or "reading" which takes for granted that what is constituted as the thinkable realm is predicated on the exclusion (repression or foreclosure) of what remains difficult or impossible to think.

This is, of course, not to say that nothing is thought, that no story is told, and no representation made, but only to say that whatever story and representation emerge to account for this event, which is no event, will be subject to this same catachresis that I perform when I speak about it improperly as an event; it will be one that must be read for what it indicates, but cannot say, or for the unsayable in what is said. What remains crucial is a form of reading that does not try to find the truth of what happened, but, rather, asks, what has this non-happening done to the question of truth? For part of the effect of that violation, when it is one, is precisely to make the knowing of truth into an infinitely remote prospect; this is its epistemic violence. To insist, then, on verifying the truth is precisely to miss the effect of the violation in question, which is to put the knowability of truth into enduring crisis.

So I keep adding this qualification: "when incest is a violation," suggesting that I think that there may be occasions in which it is not. Why would I talk that way? Well, I do think that there are probably forms of incest that are not necessarily traumatic or which gain their traumatic character by virtue of the consciousness of social shame that they produce. But what concerns me most is that the term "incest" is overinclusive; that the departure from sexual normalcy it signifies blurs too easily with other kinds of departures. Incest is considered shameful, which is one reason it is so difficult to articulate, but to what extent does it become stigmatized as a sexual irregularity that is terrifying, repulsive, unthinkable in the ways that other departures from normative exogamic heterosexuality are? The prohibitions that work to prohibit nonnormative sexual exchange also work to institute and patrol the norms of presumptively heterosexual kinship. Interestingly, although incest is considered a departure from the norm, some theorists, Linda Alcoff among them, argue that it is a practice that generally supports the patriarchalism of the family. But within psychoanalysis, and structuralist psychoanalysis in particular, positions such as mother and father are differential effects of the incest taboo. Although the very existence of a taboo against incest presumes that a family structure is already there, for how else would one understand the prohibition on sexual relations with members of one's own family without a prior conception of family? Within structuralism, however, the symbolic positions of Mother and Father are only secured through the prohibition, so that the prohibition produces both the positions of Mother and Father in terms of a set of proscribed endogamic sexual relations. Some Lacanian analysts treat these positions as if they were timeless and necessary, psychic placeholders that every child has or acquires through the entry into language.

Although this is a complicated question that I pursue elsewhere, it is important to note that the symbolic status of this position is not considered to be equivalent to its social position, and that the social variability of parenting and family structure is not reflected in the enduring binarism of Mother/Father installed at the symbolic level. To insist that kinship is inaugurated through linguistic and symbolic means which are emphatically not social is, I believe, to miss the point that kinship is a contingent social practice. In my view, there is no symbolic position of Mother and Father that is not precisely the idealization and ossification of contingent cultural norms. To treat these variable norms as presuppositions of culture and of psychic health is thus to divorce the psychoanalysis of sexual difference fully from its sociological context. It is also to restrict available notions of normativity to those which are always already encoded in a universal law of culture.

Thus, the law that would secure the incest taboo as the foundation of symbolic family structure states the universality of the incest taboo as well as its necessary symbolic consequences. One of the symbolic consequences of the law so formulated is precisely the derealization of lesbian and gay forms of parenting, single-mother households, blended family arrangements in which there may be more than one mother or father, where the symbolic position is itself dispersed and rearticulated in new social formations.

If one holds to the enduring symbolic efficacy of this law, then it seems to me that it becomes difficult, if not impossible, to conceive of incestuous practice as taking place. It also becomes difficult, if not impossible, to conceive of the psychic place of the parent or parents in ways that challenge heterosexual normativity. Whether it is a challenge to the universality of exogamic heterosexuality from within (through incest) or from rival social organizations of sexuality (lesbian, gay, bisexual, as well as nonmonogamous), each of these departures from the norm becomes difficult to acknowledge within the scheme that claims that the efficacious incest taboo determines the field of sexual intelligibility. In a sense, incest is disavowed by the law on incest, and the forms of sexuality that emerge at a distance from the norm become unintelligible (sometimes, for instance, even psychosis-inducing, as when analysts argue in the structuralist vein that same-sex parenting risks psychosis in the children who are raised under such conditions).

One argument that psychoanalysts sometimes make is that although the incest taboo is supposed to facilitate heterosexual exogamy, it never quite works, and that the array of perversion and fetishism that populates regular human sexuality testifies to the failure of the symbolic law fully to order our sexual lives. By this argument we are supposed to be persuaded that no one really occupies that norm, and that psychoanalysis makes perverts and fetishists of us all. The problem with this response is that the form of the norm, however uninhabitable, remains unchanged, and though this formulation would have us all be equally deviant, it does not break through the conceptual structure that posits a singular and unchanging norm and its deviant departures. In other words, there is no way that gay parenting or bisexuality might be acknowledged as a perfectly intelligible cultural formation and, thus, to escape its place as deviance. Similarly, there is no way to distinguish, as there must be, between deviations from the norm such as lesbian sexuality and incestuous practice.

To the extent that there are forms of love that are prohibited or, at least, derealized by the norms established by the incest taboo, both homosexuality and incest qualify as such forms. In the former case, this derealization leads to a lack of recognition for a legitimate love; in the latter case, it leads to a lack of recognition for what might have been a traumatic set of encounters, although it is important to note that not all forms of incest are necessarily traumatic (brother/sister incest in eighteenth-century literature, for instance, sometimes appears as idyllic). But whether the point is to legitimate or delegitimate a non-normative form of sexuality, it seems crucial that we have a theoretical framework that does not foreclose vital descriptions in advance. For if we say that, by definition, certain forms of sexuality are not intelligible or that they could not have existed, we risk duplicating in the very theoretical language we use the kinds of disavowals that it is the task of psychoanalysis to bring to light.

For those within structuralist psychoanalysis who take Lévi-Strauss's analysis as foundational, the incest taboo produces heterosexually normative kinship and forecloses from the realm of love and desire forms of love that cross and confound that set of kinship relations. In the case of incest, the child whose love is exploited may no longer be able to recover or avow that love as love. These are forms of suffering that are at once disturbances of avowal. And not to be able to avow one's love, however painful it may be, produces its own melancholia, the suppressed and ambivalent alternative to mourning. What, then, of the other ways in which kinship, which forms the conditions of cultural intelligibility for the structuralist position, is abrogated by a love that breaks the boundaries of what will and should be livable social relations, and yet continues to live? There another sort of catachresis or improper speech comes into operation. For if the incest taboo is also what is supposed to install the subject in heterosexual normativity, and if, as some argue, this installation is the condition of possibility for a symbolically or culturally intelligible life, then homosexual love emerges as the unintelligible within the intelligible: a love that has no place in the name of love, a position within kinship that is no position.

When the incest taboo works in this sense to foreclose a love that is not incestuous, what is produced is a shadowy realm of love, a love that persists in spite of its foreclosure in an ontologically suspended mode. What emerges is a melancholia that attends living and loving outside the livable and outside the field of love.

It might, then, be necessary to rethink the prohibition on incest as that which sometimes protects against a violation, and sometimes becomes the very instrument of a violation. What counters the incest taboo offends not only because it often involves the exploitation of those whose capacity for consent is questionable, but because it exposes the aberration in normative kinship, an aberration that might also, importantly, be worked against the strictures of kinship to force a revision and expansion of those very terms. If psychoanalysis, in its theory and practice, retains heterosexual norms of kinship as the basis of its theorization, if it accepts these norms as coextensive with cultural intelligibility, then it, too, becomes the instrument by which this melancholia is produced at a cultural level. Or if it insists that incest is under taboo and, therefore, could not exist, what forfeiture of analytic responsibility toward psychic suffering is thereby performed? These are both surely discontents with which we do not need to live.

8. Bodily Confessions

I propose to consider the relation between language, the body, and psychoanalysis in this essay by focusing on a particular act, the act of confession.[1] This act is not a simple one, as you probably know, but it does have a central relationship to the clinical setting, as I understand it. In popular culture, the therapist's office is very often figured as the place one goes in order to make a confession. In the first volume of Michel Foucault's *History of Sexuality*, psychoanalysis is described as the historical descendant of the confessional, a view that constitutes something of an accepted version of psychoanalysis among his followers.[2]

The organization of modern political power maintains and recirculates some elements from Christian institutions, and so something Foucault names "pastoral power" survives into late modern institutions. By this, he means to suggest that a certain class of people emerges who care for and minister to the souls of others and whose task is to cultivate them ethically and to know and direct the conscience of others. Implicit within the Christian notion of the pastor, according to Foucault, is that such a person has sure knowledge of the person to whom he ministers, and that application of this knowledge to the person is the means by which that person is administered and controlled. Pastoral power is thus that form of power by which the administration of the soul takes place. The claim to really know the soul of the other, and to be in the position to direct that soul toward good conscience and salvation is a powerful one, and only certain well-trained individuals are in a position to make it. By accepting the knowledge about themselves that is offered, those whose souls are administered in this way come to accept that the pastor has an authoritative discourse of truth about who they are, and come to speak about themselves through the same discourse of truth.

For the Foucault of *The History of Sexuality: Volume I*, the way in which we come to be controlled by such authoritative discourses is by confession. We say what it is we have thought or done, and that information then becomes the material by which we are interpreted. It lays us open, as it were, to the authoritative discourse of the one who wields pastoral power. In confession we show that we are not truly repressed, since we bring the hidden content out into the open. The postulate that "sex is repressed" is actually in the service of a plan that would have you disclose sex. The imposed compulsion to disclose relies upon and exploits the conjectured thesis that sex is repressed. In Foucault's view the only reason we say that sex is repressed is so that we might force it out into the open. The idea that sex is repressed thus prepares the way for our confession, and it is our confession that we apparently savor most.[3]

Why? Why would it be that we arrange everything so that we might, with difficulty and courage, speak our desire before another human being, and await the words they will speak in return? Foucault imagines the analyst as a dispassionate judge and an "expert" who will pass judgment and seek to exercise control, who will solicit confession in order to subject the analysand to a normalizing judgment. It turns out that Foucault recanted his account of pastoral power, and that in his later work he returned to the history of the confessional in late antiquity only to find that it was not administered exclusively in the service of regulation and control. In "About the Beginning of the Hermeneutics of the Self" (1980),[4] he offers an "autocritique" (161) of his earlier position in which he reconsiders the role of confession in Seneca's writings. Foucault claims to have found there an account of confession that is not about the revelation of "profound desires" (167), but an effort, through speech, to "transform pure knowledge and simple consciousness in a real way of living" (167). In this instance, according to Foucault, "truth . . . is not defined by a correspondence to reality but as a force inherent to principles and which has to be developed in a discourse" (167). Confession here works without the repressive hypothesis, elaborated by Foucault in the first volume of *The History of Sexuality*. There are no desires that are muted by repressive rules, but, rather, only an operation by which the self constitutes itself in discourse with the assistance of another's presence and speech. He writes, "the self is not something that has to be discovered or deciphered as a very obscure part of our selves. The self has, on the contrary, not to be discovered but to be constituted through the force of truth. The force lies in the rhetorical quality of the master's discourse, and this rhetorical quality depends for a part on the exposé of the disciple, who has to explain how far he is in his way of living from the true principles that he knows" (168).

In his consideration of John Cassian, one of the church fathers, Foucault considers how confession is constructed as a "permanent verbalization" (178). The aim of this verbalization is to convert the attachment that the human being has to himself to an attachment to something beyond the human, to God. In this sense, Foucault writes, "verbalization is self-sacrific" (179). For Cassian, according to Foucault, the sacrifice involved in confession is a giving up of desire and the body. He writes, "we have to understand this sacrifice not only as a radical change in the way of life but as a consequence of a formula like this: you will become the manifestation of truth when and only when you disappear or you destroy yourself as a real body and a real existence" (179). This version of confession involves a full repudiation of the subject of will, one that is, nevertheless, performed through verbalization and, hence, understood as a form of verbalization that suspends the will itself.

In this version of confession, then, it would appear that Foucault's earlier claim that pastoral power is defined by the aims of domination and control proves to be off the mark in certain ways. We could read self-sacrifice as compelled by power, as a strategy of containment, but that would be to misread its desire and its achievement. The point is not to ferret out desires and expose their truth in public, but rather to constitute a truth of oneself through the act of verbalization itself. The first relies on a repressive hypothesis; the second emphasizes instead the performative force of spoken utterance. The role of the confessor is also slightly different in this later account: "the role of the interpreter is assumed by the work of a continuous verbalization of the most imperceptible movements of thought," since the interpreter will attend to those "imperceptible movements" not to discern a preexisting truth but to facilitate a detachment of the self from itself. In this sense, the aim of sacrifice or, indeed, of reconstituting the self in a divine light, implies "the opening of the self as a field of indefinite interpretation" (180).

If Foucault's early account of pastoral power turns out to be partial or mistaken, and if psychoanalysis continues to be identified as an inheritor of pastoral power, how are we to understand the way in which pastoral power survives in psychoanalysis? The role of the confessor within pastoral power is no longer understood primarily as governed by the desire to enhance his own power but to facilitate a transition or conversion through the process of verbalization, one that opens the self to interpretation and, in effect, to a different kind of self-making in the wake of sacrifice.

But if Foucault is wrong that psychoanalysis, as the inheritor of pastoral power, seeks to use the confession to augment its own control and power, then what would be the reason for someone listening so hard to desires that are so difficult for the other person to bring forth? If it is not a simple sadism that motivates those who bear witness to other people's confessions, how do we account for the purpose of that kind of listening? And if the point is not to find out the "truth of what happened" and to treat the language of the analysand as corresponding to a set of internal or external events, then what is language doing in this exchange?

Of course, it is not only desire to which psychoanalysis listens. And it seems fair to say that most therapists and analysts do not pronounce upon the truth of what is said in the context of their offices. Indeed, it may be that finding meanings is very different from finding truths, and that one way to get to meanings is to suspend the kinds of judgments that might block communication. The confession strikes me as an important moment to consider because not only does it constitute, within the psychoanalytic setting, a communication of what one's desire or deed has been, but the very speaking constitutes another act, one that within the field of the analytic setting confers a certain reality on the deed, if it is a deed in question, and that also implicates the analyst as listener in the scene of desire.[5] If it is one desire that the analysand seeks to speak to the analyst, it is another desire that takes hold in the speaking. For by the time the speech is made, the analysand desires for the analyst to know and expects or fears some kind of reaction to what is said. In this way, the confession does not simply bring an already existing desire or an already accomplished deed before the analyst, but alters the desire and the deed so that neither was what they become once they are stated for the analyst.

Let us make the confession perhaps more dramatic. Foucault imagined in his earlier work that what happens in the analytic scene is that everyone gets to speak about their surreptitious desires, that license is given to talk about sex. He also makes a psychoanalytic point, perhaps in spite of himself, by claiming that what is enjoyed most is this very speaking about sex: verbalization becomes the scene for sexuality. My question follows from here: is the enjoyment in speaking about sex an enjoyment about the sex or the speaking? And if these are two different forms of enjoyment, are they perchance related to one another? What is the content of confession? Is it a deed, a desire, an anxiety, and abiding guilt for which the confessional form serves as a balm? As the confession begins, it usually centers on a deed, but it may be that the deed conceals the source of the desire for confession. But let us begin with the initial presumption of the confessor that there is a deed that awaits revelation in speech. By imagining the content of the confession as a deed, a deed of desire, a sexual act, the analysand speaks, but that speaking becomes the new vehicle; for the act becomes, indeed, a new act or a new life for the old act. Now not only has one done the deed, but one has spoken of it as well, and something in the speaking, a speaking that is *before* another and, obliquely, *to* another, a speaking that presumes and solicits recognition and constitutes the first act as public, as known, as having truly happened. Thus the speaking of the confession in the psychoanalytic setting becomes a different bodily act than the one that is being confessed, but what remains continuous between the two acts? The body that is on the couch is the same body that did the deed, but on the couch, the deed is relayed verbally; the body acts again, but this time through the bodily act of speaking itself. Does the speaking of the deed bring the deed into play between the analyst and the analysand? And what about the body? It is the referent of the deed; it is that whose activities are reported, relayed, communicated. But in the confession, the body acts again, displaying its capacity for doing a deed, and announces, apart from what is actually said, that it is, actively, sexually there. Its speech becomes the present life of the body, and though the deed is made more real by virtue of its being spoken, it also, at the moment it is uttered, becomes strangely past, completed, over. This is why perhaps confessions almost always come after the fact, and why they are postponed until the time in which the speaker is ready for the sacrifice of the object that speaking the words sometimes implies.

Of course, to have a confession to make is also to have speech that has been withheld for some time. To have a confession to make means that it is not yet made, that it is there, almost in words, but that the speaking remains in check, and that the speaker has withdrawn from the relationship in some way. But it also means that these words have not yet been performed for the analyst, the words have not yet been offered up as material. The words, the deeds they convey, have not yet been made vulnerable to another perspective, one that might subject the words and the deeds to a reinterpretation, so that the originally highly cathected meaning invested in the deeds is not yet made into an event whose meaning is intersubjectively constituted. The secret erodes the intersubjective presumption of the analytic scene, but it also can become a new event, an event that becomes material for analysis only on the condition that the confession forces the secret into view. And it may be that by the time the confession is made, the delay in making it becomes a new cause for guilt and remorse.

Let me offer another view by making use of the moment in Sophocles' play, *Antigone*, in which Antigone confesses before Creon that she has broken his law and buried her brother, Polyneices.[6] Her crime is not exactly a sexual one, although her relation to Polyneices is intense, if not overdetermined by incestuous meaning. She is guilty for disobeying the edict that Creon has delivered, the one that sentences anyone to death who buries her brother, Polyneices. But is she guilty for other reasons as well, reasons that are covered over by her large and public crime? And when she makes her confessions, does she add to her guilt, becoming guilty for more than what she possibly did? Does her confession, in fact, exacerbate her guilt?

Antigone is introduced to us, you will remember, by the act by which she defies Creon's sovereignty, contesting the power of his edict, which is delivered as an imperative, explicitly forbidding anyone to bury that body.[7] Antigone thus mocks Creon's authority; she contests him verbally, refusing to deny that she was the one who performed the crime: "I say that I did it and I do not deny it" (43), "Yes, I confess it," or "I say I did it"—thus she answers a question that is posed to her from another authority, and thus she concedes the authority that this other has over her. "I will not deny my deed"—"I do not deny," I will not be forced into a denial, I will refuse to be forced into a denial by the other's language, and what I will not deny is my deed—a deed that becomes her possession, one that makes sense only within the context of the scene in which a forced confession is refused by her. In other words, to claim, "I will not deny my deed" is to refuse to perform a denial, but it is not precisely to claim the act. To say, "Yes, *I say* I did it," is to claim the act, but it is also to commit another deed in the very claiming, the act of publishing one's deed, a new criminal venture that redoubles and takes the place of the old.

Antigone's deed is, in fact, ambiguous from the start, not only the defiant act in which she buries her brother, but the verbal act in which she answers Creon's question; thus, hers is an act in language. To publish one's act in language is in some sense the completion of the act; it is the moment that implicates her in the masculine excess called hubris. Interestingly, at this moment in which she is understood to oppose Creon fiercely, there are at least two troubling problems. One, she begins to resemble him. They both seek to display their deeds in public, and to gain public recognition for their acts. Two, she speaks to him and in front of him, so he becomes the intended audience of her confession, the one to whom it is intended, the one who must receive it. Thus, she requires his presence even as she opposes him bitterly. Is she like him? Is she, through her confession, binding herself to him more tightly?

The first deed was bad enough. She broke the law and buried her brother. She did it in the name of a higher law, a different ground of justification, but she is not able to make clear what precisely that law is. But as she begins to confess and, so, to act in language, her motivations appear to shift. Her speech is supposed to underscore her own sovereignty, but something else is revealed. Although she uses language to claim her deed, to assert a "manly" and defiant autonomy, she can perform that act only through embodying the norms of the power she opposes. Indeed, what gives these verbal acts their power is the normative operation of power that they embody without quite becoming.

Antigone comes, then, to act in ways that are called manly not only because she acts in defiance of the law, but she also assumes the voice of the law in committing the act against the law. She not only does the deed, refusing to obey the edict, but she also does it again by refusing to deny that she has done it, thus appropriating the rhetoric of agency from Creon himself. Her agency emerges precisely through her refusal to honor his command, and yet the language of this refusal assimilates the very terms of sovereignty—he is, after all, the model of sovereignty—that she refuses. He expects that his word will govern her deeds, and she speaks back to him, countering his sovereign speech act with an assertion of her own sovereignty. The claiming becomes an act that reiterates the act it affirms, extending the act of insubordination by performing its avowal in language. But this avowal, paradoxically, requires a sacrifice of autonomy at the very moment in which it is performed: she asserts herself through appropriating the voice of the other, the one to whom she is opposed; thus, her autonomy is gained through the appropriation of the authoritative voice of the one she resists, an appropriation that has within it traces of a simultaneous refusal and assimilation of that very authority.

In her open defiance of the state, we see something else about her motivations. At the moment in which she defies Creon, she becomes like the brother that she buried. She repeats the defiant act of her brother, thus offering a repetition of defiance that in affirming her loyalty to her brother, situates her as the one who may substitute for him and, hence, replaces and perhaps territorializes him, taking over his place in a violent substitution of herself for him, vanquishing him, perhaps, in the name of fidelity to him. She assumes manhood through vanquishing manhood, but she vanquishes it only by idealizing it. At one point her act appears to establish her rivalry and superiority to Polyneices. She asks, "And yet how could I have gained greater glory [*kleos*] than by placing my brother in his grave?"

So if we thought that it was her abiding love for her brother that drove her to act as she did, her own words put into question the manifest purpose of her deed. The deed might be said to begin with the burial, but to escalate with the confession. And it is with the confession, an apparently guiltless one, that Antigone both assumes her power and secures her death. She seems to defy the law, but she is also giving herself over to its death sentence. Why would she pursue this course of action that is certain to lead to death? Why does she solicit this most fatal of punishments through her deed and her word?

In Freud's essay, "Criminals From a Sense of Guilt," he reports on patients who commit misdeeds because they were forbidden, and and "their execution was accompanied by mental relief for their doer."[8] The patient seems to be relieved by the act because now "his sense of guilt was at least attached to something." Freud maintains that "the sense of guilt was present before the misdeed, that it did not arise from it, but conversely—the misdeed arose from the sense of guilt." He then goes on to remark that this "obscure sense of guilt," a guilt that does not know its reason for being, can be "derived from the Oedipus complex and was a reaction to the two great criminal intentions of killing the father and having sexual relations with the mother." And he goes on to conjecture that "the conscience of mankind, which now appears as an inherited mental force, was acquired in connection with the Oedipus complex." In a rare moment, Freud here refers to Nietzsche who classified those who committed misdeeds from a sense of guilt as "pale criminals," but this is surely a connection to pursue on another occasion.

What seems of interest here, however, is that Freud assumes that the two great criminal intentions—killing the father, sleeping with the mother—are derived from Oedipus; but Antigone, who is also derived from Oedipus, has perhaps another sort of criminal intention at work, producing an obscure guilt for which death itself appears as the fitting punishment. Antigone, as we know, is in a bind when she cries out that she has performed her crime for her "most precious brother," since her brother is not only Polyneices, but Eteocles, also slain, and Oedipus, son of her mother and his wife, Jocasta. She loves her brother, and so she buries him. But who is this brother? And is Polyneices, as her brother, overdetermined by the brother who is also dead, denied a proper burial, Oedipus himself? She loves her brother, says, in fact, she wants to "lie with him," and so pursues death, which she also calls her "bridal chamber" in order to be with him forever. She is the child of incest, but how does incest run through her own desire? And how is that criminal intention, as it were, occluded precisely by the crime that she does commit? Is there another crime, a specter of a crime, a premonition of a crime, a crime uncommitted, attested to by an obscure guilt? And does this guilt not make itself known at the same time that it continues to hide itself as she commits the criminal deed of burying Polyneices and then redoubles the deed by producing a confession that brings on her the death sentence she knew was waiting in store for her? Is it her own guilt for which she becomes punishable by death, or the guilt of her father? And is there any way finally to distinguish between them since they are both cursed in apparently similar ways? And is the punishment a way of atoning for the sin, or does it produce the possibility of a fantasmatic scenario in which she is, finally, freed from cultural taboo, free to lie with her brothers in eternity?

Although I began this chapter by focusing on the confession as an act that shifts the desire that it reports, especially when it takes place within the scene of analysis, I want to end the paper by remarking that the confession not only "changes the subject" from the misdeed in question, but can work as well to occlude and rationalize a sense of guilt that is derivable from no deed of one's own. Antigone's confession makes plain what she has done, but it does not transparently reveal her desire. And her confession is the means by which she submits to the punishment that Creon has laid out for her, thus hastening her own movement toward death. Although it reads as guiltless defiance, it seems in fact to be a suicidal act propelled by an obscure sense of guilt. The confession thus produces a set of consequences that in retrospect illuminate a desire for punishment, a final relief from guilt. How important then it must be for the analyst to know that the confession might well expect or solicit Creon.

Foucault was doubtless mistaken to think that the confession is only and always the occasion for the analyst to assume control and authority over the truth of one's soul. But perhaps Foucault was articulating something about the fear of analysis, in which the analyst is projected as a pastor and judge, and the activity of the analysand, a confession that leads to inevitable and recurrent punishment. Of course, it is this very fantasy of analysis that must be brought into the analytic scene, read for its investments, especially its defensive one. The analyst is not Creon, but it probably remains true that the expectation of Creon's punishment may well structure the desire for confession, at least, the desire for confession that Foucault imagines. The very speaking of the crime is thus another act, a new deed, one that either defies or submits to a punishing law, but which does not yet know how to subject that fantasy of the law to reflections. For the one for whom self-expression appears as confession, there may be, as there was with Antigone, an expectation that the punishment of guilt will be literalized and externalized. Guilt functions as a form of psychic punishment that preexists its deed and its confession, and it becomes writ large as the projected threat of judgment posed by the analyst. What seems clear, though, is that insofar as speech is structured as confession, it poses the question of whether the body will be condemned. Confession borne of that obscure guilt will be that form of speech that fears and solicits its own denunciation. All the more reason that the analyst who finds him or herself as confessor or, indeed, as Creon, must decline the honor, and take that speech as a solicitation to help undo the curse whose fatal consequences sometimes seem so sure.

Postscript on Speech Acts and the Transference

Analytic speech tends to be rhetorical, and by that I mean that what is said in analysis is not always or only considered for what it purports to say, but also for what the saying says, what the very mode or speech says, what the very choice of words does. Of course, this is always a tricky business, since the analysand wants at some level to have his or her intentions honored, and yet a certain respectful dishonoring of intention takes place when the analyst calls attention to the mode of the speech act, the consequence of the speech act, its timing, or its tenor. By focusing on the rhetorical aspects of speech, the analyst finds meanings that exceed and sometimes confound intention, and I gather that the response to such speech runs the risk of doing something it does not mean to do, of exercising effects that exceed and sometimes confound the intentions of the analyst.

A speech act in the context of the transference thus might be said to attempt to communicate a content, but also to display or enact another set of meanings that may or may not have a relation to the content that is said. Of course, there are differences of opinions about how to deal with "content" or with the surface meaning of the utterance. But one thing seems clear, which is that the content, the intended meaning, cannot be fully overcome or transcended, since how one utters that content, or what the uttering of that content does, will probably comment on the content, will probably comment on the intention that bears the content along. So, in this sense, it is the constellation of intended meaning, mode of delivery, and unintended effect that must be considered as a particular kind of unity, even when each of these aspects of the speech act diverge in different relations.

One aspect of the speech act that becomes especially important in this context is the fact that speaking is a bodily act. It is a vocalization; it requires the larynx, the lungs, the lips, and the mouth. Whatever is said not only passes through the body but constitutes a certain presentation of the body. I am not talking about what the mouth looks like, though I can imagine that in some therapeutic sessions that may be relevant, especially if the client faces the therapist. But the speaking is a sounding forth of the body, its simple assertion, a stylized assertion of its presence. I am saying what I mean: but there is a body here, and there can be no saying without that body—a potentially humiliating and productive fact of life. Of course, there are ways of using speech that occlude the body as its condition, which act as if the meanings that are conveyed emanate from a disembodied mind and are addressed toward another disembodied mind. But that is, as it were, still a way of doing the body, a way of doing the body as disembodied.

In the case of sexual confession, the speaker is usually saying something about what the body has done, or what the body has undergone. The saying becomes implicated in the act that it relays since saying is, of course, another way in which the body does something. Saying is, one might say, another bodily deed. And the body that speaks its deed is the same body that did its deed, which means that there is, in the saying, a presentation of that body, a bodying forth of the guilt, perhaps, in the saying itself. The speaker may be relaying a set of events in the past, but the speaker is doing something more: the speaker, in speaking, is presenting the body that did the deed, and is doing another deed at the same time, presenting the body in its action. And there is an implicit rhetorical question posed in such an instance, a question of whether that speech will be received, but since speech is an action of the body, there is an added question: will that body be received as well.

Transference is thus clearly a question of how language is exchanged, but because it is spoken, it is always a question of how bodies orchestrate an exchange, even when they are sitting or lying still. Spoken words are, strangely, bodily offerings: tentative or forceful, seductive or withholding, or both at once. The couch does not put the body out of play, but it does enforce a certain passivity of the body, an exposure and a receptivity, that implies that whatever act the body will be able to sustain in that position will be through speech itself.

If transference is a form of love or, minimally, an enactment of a certain relation to love, then we might say further that it is a love that takes place in language. This is not to say that language substitutes for the body, since that is not quite true. The spoken word is a bodily act at the same time that it forms a certain synecdoche of the body. The vocalizing larynx and mouth become the part of the body that stages the drama of the whole; what the body gives and receives is not a touch, but the psychic contours of a bodily exchange, a psychic contour that engages the body that it represents. Without this moment of exposure, a moment in which one displays something more than one intends, there is no transference. And of course, this display cannot be intentionally performed, since it is always at some critical distance from intention itself. We might see this as the confession at the core of psychoanalytic practice: the fact that we always show something more or different than what we mean, and that we hand this unknowing part of ourselves to another to return to us in ways that we cannot anticipate in advance. If this moment of confession is in psychoanalysis itself, then it is not the moment in which we necessarily become vulnerable to another's control, as Foucault suggested in his earlier work. As Foucault realized in his account of Cassian, verbalization entails a certain dispossession, a severing of an attachment to the self, but not for that reason a sacrifice of attachment altogether. The "relational" moment comes to structure the speaking, so that one is speaking to, in the presence of, sometimes in spite of, another. Moreover, the self in its priority is not being discovered at such a moment, but becoming elaborated, through speaking, in a new way, in the course of conversation. In these scenes of speech, both interlocutors find that what they say is to some extent beyond their control but not, for that reason, out of control. If saying is a form of doing, and part of what is getting done is the self, then conversation is a mode of doing something together and becoming otherwise; something will be accomplished in the course of this exchange, but no one will know what or who is being made until it is done.

9. The End of Sexual Difference?

I am not sure that the millennium is a significant way to mark time or, indeed, to mark the time of feminism. But it is always important to take stock of where feminism is, even as that effort at reflection is necessarily marred. No one stands in the perspective that might afford a global view of feminism. No one stands within a definition of feminism that would remain uncontested. I think it is fair to say that feminists everywhere seek a more substantial equality for women, and that they seek a more just arrangement of social and political institutions. But as we enter any room to consider what we mean, and how we might act, we are confronted quite quickly with the difficulty of the terms that we need to use. Differences emerge over whether equality means that men and women ought to be treated interchangeably. The Parity movement in France has argued that that is not an appropriate notion of equality, given the social disadvantages that women suffer under current political circumstances. We will surely argue as well over justice, and by what means it ought to be achieved. Is it the same as "fair treatment"? Is it distinct from the conception of equality? What is its relation to freedom? And which freedoms are desired, how are they valued, and what do we make of serious disagreements among women on the question of how sexual freedom is to be defined, and whether it can receive a meaningful international formulation?

Add to these zones of contestation continuing questions about what a woman is, how we are to say "we," who is to say it and in the name of whom? It seems that feminism is in a mess, unable to stabilize the terms that facilitate a meaningful agenda. Criticisms of feminism as inattentive to questions of race and to the conditions of global inequality that condition its Euro-American articulation continue to put into doubt the broad coalitional power of the movement. In the United States, the abuse of sexual harassment doctrine by the conservative Right in its persecutorial inquiries into sex in the workplace present a serious public-relations problem for feminists on the Left. Indeed, the relation between feminism *and* the Left is another thorny matter, since there are now pro-business forms of feminism that focus on actualizing women's entrepreneurial potential, hijacking models of self-expression from an earlier, progressive period of the movement.

One might be tempted to despair, but I believe that these are among the most interesting and productive unsolved issues at the beginning of this century. The program of feminism is not one in which we might assume a common set of premises and then proceed to build in logical fashion a program from those premises. Instead, this is a movement that moves forward precisely by bringing critical attention to bear on its premises in an effort to become more clear about what it means and to begin to negotiate the conflicting interpretations, the irrepressible democratic cacophony of its identity. As a democratic enterprise, feminism has had to forfeit the presumption that at base we can all agree about some things or, equivalently, to embrace the notion that each of our most treasured values are under contestation and that they will remain contested zones of politics. This may sound as if I am saying that feminism can never build from anything, that it will be lost to reflection upon itself, that it will never move beyond this self-reflective moment toward an active engagement with the world. On the contrary, it is precisely in the course of engaged political practices that these forms of internal dissension emerge. And I would argue emphatically that resisting the desire to resolve this dissension into unity is precisely what keeps the movement alive.

Feminist theory is never fully distinct from feminism as a social movement. Feminist theory would have no content were there no movement, and the movement, in its various directions and forms, has always been involved in the act of theory. Theory is an activity that does not remain restricted to the academy. It takes place every time a possibility is imagined, a collective self-reflection takes place, a dispute over values, priorities, and language emerges. I believe that there is an important value in overcoming the fear of immanent critique and to maintaining the democratic value of producing a movement that can contain, without domesticating, conflicting interpretations on fundamental issues. As a latecomer to the second wave, I approach feminism with the presumption that no undisputed premises are to be agreed upon in the global context. And so, for practical and political reasons, there is no value to be derived in silencing disputes. The questions are: how best to have them, how most productively to stage them, and how to act in ways that acknowledge the irreversible complexity of who we are?

I propose to consider a set of terms in this essay that have come into conflict with one another: sexual difference, gender, and sexuality. My title suggests perhaps that I am announcing the end to "sexual difference" in its presumed facticity or as a useful theoretical entry into questions of feminism. My title is intended as a citation of a skeptical question, one that is often posed to theorists who work on gender or sexuality, a challenge I wish both to understand and to which I propose a response. My purpose is not to win a debate, but to try to understand why the terms are considered so important to those who use them, and how we might reconcile this set of felt necessities as they come into conflict with one another. I am here as interested in the theoretical reasons proffered for using one framework at the expense of another as the institutional possibilities that the terms alternately open and foreclose in varying contexts.

I do not ask the question about the end of sexual difference in order to make a plea for that end. I do not even propose to enumerate reasons why I think that framework, or that "reality," depending on your take, is no longer worth pursuing. For many, I think, the structuring reality of sexual difference is not one that one can wish away or argue against, or even make claims about in any reasonable way. It is more like a necessary background to the possibility of thinking, of language, of being a body in the world. And those who seek to take issue with it are arguing with the very structure that makes their argument possible. There is sometimes a laughing and dismissive response to the problem:

you think that you might do away with sexual difference, but your very desire to do away with it is only further evidence of its enduring force and efficacy. Defenders of sexual difference make dismissive reference to the famous feminine "protest" elaborated by psychoanalysis, and in this way the protest is defeated before it is articulated. To challenge the notion of femininity is the consummately feminine act, a protest that can be read as evidence for that which it seeks to contest. Sexual difference—is it to be thought of as a framework by which we are defeated in advance? Anything that might be said against it is oblique proof that it structures what we say. Is it there in a primary sense, haunting the primary differentiations or structural fate by which all signification proceeds?

Irigaray makes clear that sexual difference is not a fact, not a bedrock of any sorts, and not the recalcitrant "real" of Lacanian parlance. On the contrary, it is a question, a question for our times. As a question, it remains unsettled and unresolved, that which is not yet or not ever formulated in terms of an assertion. Its presence does not assume the form of facts and structures but persists as that which makes us wonder, which remains not fully explained and not fully explicable. If it is the question for our time, as she insists in *The Ethics of Sexual Difference*,[1] then it is not one question among others, but, rather, a particularly dense moment of irresolution within language, one that marks the contemporary horizon of language as our own. Like Drucilla Cornell, Irigaray has in mind an ethics which is not one that follows *from* sexual difference but is a question that is posed by the very terms of sexual difference itself: how to cross this otherness? How to cross it without crossing it, without domesticating its terms? How to remain attuned to what remains permanently unsettled about the question?

Irigaray then would not argue for or against sexual difference but, rather, offer a way to think about the question that sexual difference poses, or the question that sexual difference *is*, a question whose irresolution forms a certain historical trajectory for us, those who find ourselves asking this question, those of whom this question is posed. The arguments in favor and against would be so many indications of the persistence of this question, a persistence whose status is not eternal, but one, she claims, that belongs to *these times*. It is a question that

Irigaray poses of modernity, a question that marks modernity for her. Thus, it is a question that inaugurates a certain problematic of time, a question whose answer is not forthcoming, a question that opens up a time of irresolution and marks that time of irresolution as our own.

I think for many of us it is a sad time for feminism, perhaps even a defeated time. A friend asked what I would teach in a feminist theory course right now, and I found myself suggesting that feminist theory has no other work than in responding to the places where feminism is under challenge. And by responding to those challenges, I do not mean a defensive shoring up of terms and commitments, a reminding of ourselves of what we already know, but something quite different, something like a submission to the demand for rearticulation, a demand that emerges from crisis. It makes no sense, I would argue, to hold fast to theoretical paradigms and preferred terminologies, to make the case for feminism on the basis of sexual difference, or to defend that notion against the claims of gender, the claims of sexuality, of race, or the umbrella claims of cultural studies. I begin with Irigaray because I think her invocation of sexual difference is something other than foundational. Sexual difference is not a given, not a premise, not a basis on which to build a feminism; it is not that which we have already encountered and come to know; rather, as *a question* that prompts a feminist inquiry, it is something that cannot quite be stated, that troubles the grammar of the statement, and that remains, more or less permanently, to interrogate.

When Irigaray refers to the question of sexual difference as a question for our times, she appears to refer to modernity. I confess to not knowing what modernity is, but I do know that many intellectuals are very worked up about the term, defending it or decrying it. Those who are considered at odds with modernity, or are considered postmodern, get characterized in the following way: one who "calls into question or debunks terms like reason, the subject, authenticity, universality, the progressive view of history." What always strikes me about these kinds of generalizations is that "calling into question" is assumed to mean "debunk" (rather than, say, "revitalize") and the status of the question itself is never given much intellectual play. If one calls such terms into question, does that mean that they cannot be used anymore? Does it mean that one is now prohibited from such a term by the superego of theoretical postmodernism or that they are proclaimed as exhausted and finished? Or is it simply that the terms do not function in quite the same way as they once did?

A few years ago, I had the occasion to discuss Leo Bersani's book, *Homos*. I realized that he was no longer sure whether he could say that lesbians were women, and I found myself reassuring him that no one had issued a prohibition on the use of the word. I certainly have no qualms about using such terms and will reflect later in this essay on how one might continue *at the same time* to interrogate and to use the terms of universality. If the notion of the subject, for instance, is no longer given, no longer presumed, that does not mean that it has no meaning for us, that it ought no longer to be uttered. On the contrary, it means only that the term is not simply a building block on which we rely, an uninterrogated premise for political argument. On the contrary, the term has become an object of theoretical attention, something for which we are compelled to give an account. I suppose that this places me on the divide of the modern/postmodern in which such terms remain in play, but no longer in a foundational mode.

Others have argued that all the key terms of modernity are premised on the exclusion of women, of people of color, that they are wrought along class lines and with strong colonial interests. But it would also be important to add, following Paul Gilroy in *The Black Atlantic: Modernity and Double-Consciousness*, that the struggle against those exclusions very often ends up reappropriating those very terms from modernity, appropriating them precisely to initiate an entrance into modernity as well as the transformation of modernity's parameters. Freedom comes to signify what it never signified before; justice comes to embrace precisely what could not be contained under its prior description.[2]

In the same way that the terms of an exclusionary modernity have been appropriated for progressive uses, progressive terms can be appropriated for regressive aims. The terms that we use in the course of political movements which have been appropriated by the Right or for misogynist purposes are not, for that reason, strategically out of bounds. These terms are never finally and fully tethered to a single use. The task of reappropriation is to illustrate the vulnerability of these often compromised terms to an unexpected progressive possibility; such terms belong to no one in particular; they assume a life and a purpose that exceed the uses to which they have been consciously put.

They are not to be seen as merely tainted goods, too bound up with the history of oppression, but neither are they to be regarded as having a pure meaning that might be distilled from their various usages in political contexts. The task, it seems, is to compel the terms of modernity to embrace those they have traditionally excluded, where the embrace does not work to domesticate and neutralize the newly avowed term; such terms should remain problematic for the existing notion of the polity, should expose the limits of its claim to universality, and compel a radical rethinking of its parameters. For a term to be made part of a polity that has been conventionally excluded is for it to emerge as a threat to the coherence of the polity, and for the polity to survive that threat without annihilating the term. The term would then open up a different temporality for the polity, establishing for that polity an unknown future, provoking anxiety in those who seek to patrol its conventional boundaries. If there can be a modernity without foundationalism, then it will be one in which the key terms of its operation are not fully secured in advance, one that assumes a futural form for politics that cannot be fully anticipated, a politics of hope and anxiety.

The desire to foreclose an open future can be a strong one, threatening one with loss, loss of a sense of certainty about how things are (and must be). It is important, however, not to underestimate the force of the desire to foreclose futurity and the political potential of anxiety.[3] This is one reason that asking certain questions is considered dangerous. Imagine the situation of reading a book and thinking, I cannot ask the questions that are posed here because to ask them is to introduce doubt into my political convictions, and to introduce doubt into my political convictions could lead to the dissolution of those convictions. At such a moment, the fear of thinking, indeed, the fear of the question, becomes moralized as the defense of politics. And politics becomes that which requires a certain anti-intellectualism. To remain unwilling to rethink one's politics on the basis of questions posed is to opt for a dogmatic stand at the cost of both life and thought.

To question a term, a term like feminism, is to ask how it plays, what investments it bears, what aims it achieves, what alterations it undergoes. The changeable life of that term does not preclude its use. If a term becomes questionable, does that mean it cannot be used any longer, and that we can only use terms that we *already know how to master*? Why is it that posing a question about a term is considered the same as effecting a prohibition against its use? Why is it that we sometimes feel that if a term is dislodged from its foundational place, we will not be able to live, to survive, to use language, to speak for ourselves? What kind of guarantee does the foundational fix exercise, and what sort of terror does it forestall? Is it that in the foundational mode, terms are assumed, terms like the subject and universality, and the sense in which they "must" be assumed is a *moral* one, taking the form of an imperative, and like some moral interdictions, a defense against what terrifies us most? Are we not paralyzed by a kind of moral compulsion that keeps us from interrogating the terms, taking the risk of living the terms that we keep in question?[4]

As a way of showing how passions for foundations and methods sometimes get in the way of an analysis of contemporary political culture, I propose to consider the way in which the efforts to secure a theoretical basis for political struggle often read precisely in opposition to the travels of certain key political signifiers within contemporary public culture. The most confusing for me has to do with the status of the term "gender" in relation to feminism, on the one hand, and lesbian and gay studies, on the other. I was surprised, perhaps naively, to understand from my queer studies friends that a proposed methodology for gay and lesbian studies accepts the notion that whereas feminism is said to have *gender* as its object of inquiry, lesbian and gay studies is said to have *sex and sexuality* as its "proper" object. Gender, we are told, is not to be mistaken for sexuality, which seems right in a certain way, but imagine then my shock when the Vatican announced that gender ought to be stricken from the United Nations Non-Governmental Organizations (NGO) platform on the status of women because it is nothing other than a code for homosexuality![5] Added to my worries is that some of my closest associates within feminist theory scorn the notion of gender. They claim that sexual difference is the preferred term to gender, that "sexual difference" indicates a fundamental difference, and that gender indicates a merely constructed or variable effect.

The United Nations Meeting on the Status of Women in Beijing in 1995 exhibited yet another challenge to academic commitments. In particular, what is the status of universal claims within the domain of international human rights work? Although many feminists have come to the conclusion that the universal is always a cover for a certain epistemological imperialism, insensitive to cultural texture and difference, the rhetorical power of claiming universality for rights of sexual autonomy and related rights of sexual orientation within the international human rights domain appears indisputable.

Consider first the surprising use of gender in the UN context. The Vatican not only denounced the term gender as a code for homosexuality but insisted that the platform language return to the notion of sex, in an apparent effort to secure a link between femininity and maternity as a naturally and divinely ordained necessity. In late April 1995, in preparation for the NGO meetings in Beijing—called the prepcom—several member states, under the guidance of the Catholic Church, sought to expunge the word "gender" from the Platform for Action and to replace it with the word "sex." This was called by some on the prepcom committee an "insulting and demeaning attempt to reverse the gains made by women, to intimidate us and to block further progress."[6] They wrote further: "We will not be forced back into the 'biology is destiny' concept that seeks to define, confine, and reduce women and girls to their physical sexual characteristics. We will not let this happen—not in our homes, our workplaces, our communities, our countries and certainly not at the United Nations, to which women around the world look for human rights, justice, and leadership." The statement notes:

> The meaning of the word "gender" has evolved as differentiated from the word "sex" to express the reality that women's and men's roles and status are socially constructed and subject to change. In the present context, "gender" recognizes the multiple roles that females fill through our life cycles, the diversity of our needs, concerns, abilities, life experiences and aspirations . . . the concept of "gender" is embedded in contemporary social, political and legal discourse. It has been integrated into the conceptual planning, language, documents and programmes of the UN system. The infusion of gender perspectives into all aspects of UN activities is a major commitment approved at past conferences and it must [be] reaffirmed and strengthened at the 4th world conference.[7]

This debate led Russell Baker in the *New York Times* to wonder if the term gender hasn't so supplanted the notion of sex that we will soon find ourselves in relation to our erotic lives confessing to having had "gender" with someone.

As gender became intensified at the UN discussion as a code for homosexuality, the local fields of queer theory and feminism were taking quite a different direction, at least apparently. The analogy offered by methodologically minded queer theorists in which feminism is said to be concerned with gender and lesbian and gay studies with sex and sexuality seems far afield from the above debate. But it is surprising to see that in the one case gender appears to stand for homosexuality, and in the other, it seems to be its opposite.

My point is not simply that academic debate seems woefully out of synch with the contemporary political usage of such terms, but that the effort to take distance from gender marks two political movements that are in many ways opposed to one another. In the international debate, the Vatican denounces the use of the term "gender" because it either (1) is a code for homosexuality, or (2) offers a way for homosexuality to be understood as one gender among others, threatening to take its place among masculine, feminine, bisexual, and transsexual, or, more likely, threatening to take the place of male and female altogether. The Vatican's fear—and they cite Anne Fausto-Sterling[8] on this matter—that homosexuality implies the proliferation of genders. (*La Repubblica* claims that in the United States the number of genders has leaped to five: masculine, feminine, lesbian, homosexual, and transsexual.) This view of homosexuality as proliferating gender seems to be based on the notions that homosexuals have in some sense departed from their sex, that in becoming homosexuals, they cease to be men or women, and that gender as we know it is radically incompatible with homosexuality; indeed, it is so incompatible that homosexuality must become its own gender, thus displacing the binary opposition between masculine and feminine altogether.

Interestingly, the Vatican seems to share a certain presupposition with those who would make queer studies into a methodology distinct from feminism: whereas the Vatican fears that sexuality threatens to displace sex as the reproductive aim and necessity of heterosexuality, those who accept the methodological division between queer theory and feminism hold out the promise that sexuality might exceed and displace gender. Homosexuality in particular leaves gender behind. The two are not only separable but persist in a mutually exclusive tension in which queer sexualities aspire to a utopian life beyond gender, as Biddy Martin has so ably suggested.[9] The Vatican seeks to undo gender in an effort to rehabilitate sex, but method-oriented queer theory seeks to undo gender in an effort to foreground sexuality. The Vatican fears the separation of sexuality from sex, for that introduces a notion of sexual practice that is not constrained by putatively natural reproductive ends. And in this sense it appears that the Vatican, in fearing gender, fears the separation of sexuality from sex, and so fears queer theory. Queer methodology, however, insists on sexuality, and even in *The Lesbian and Gay Studies Reader*, on "sexuality and sex." Such understandings evacuate gender as well, but only because gender stands for feminism and its presumptive heterosexuality.[10]

In both contexts, the debates were about terminology and whether the term "gender" could be allowed into the platform language for the NGO meetings, and whether the term "sexual orientation" would be part of the final language of the UN conference resolutions. (The answer to the first is yes; to the second, no, but language regarding sexual autonomy was deemed acceptable.) Terms such as gender, sexual orientation, and even universality, were contested publicly precisely on the question of what they will mean, and a special UN meeting was convened in July of 1995 to come up with an understanding of what "gender" means.

My view is that no simple definition of gender will suffice, and that more important than coming up with a strict and applicable definition is the ability to track the travels of the term through public culture. The term "gender" has become a site of contest for various interests. Consider the domestic U.S. example in which gender is often perceived as a way to defuse the political dimension of feminism, in which gender becomes a merely discursive marking of masculine and feminine, understood as constructions that might be studied outside a feminist framework or as simple self-productions, manufactured cultural effects of some kind. Consider also the introduction of gender studies programs as ways to legitimate an academic domain by refusing to engage polemics against feminism, as well as the introduction of gender studies programs and centers in Eastern Europe where the overcoming of "feminism" is tied to the overcoming of Marxist state ideology in which feminist aims were understood to be achievable only on the condition of the realization of Communist aims.

As if that struggle internal to the gender arena were not enough, the challenge of an Anglo-European theoretical perspective within the academy casts doubt on the value of the overly sociological construal of the term. Gender is thus opposed in the name of sexual difference precisely because gender endorses a socially constructivist view of masculinity and femininity, displacing or devaluing the *symbolic* status of sexual difference and the political specificity of the feminine. Here I am thinking of criticisms that have been leveled against the term by Naomi Schor, Rosi Braidotti, Elizabeth Grosz, and others.

In the meantime, sexual difference is clearly out of favor within some reigning paradigms in queer theory. Indeed, even when queer theory is seeking to establish the anachronism of feminism, feminism is described as a project unambiguously committed to gender. Within critical race studies one finds, I believe, very little reference to sexual difference as a term.[11]

But what is this sexual difference? It is not a simple facticity, but neither is it simply an effect of facticity. If it is psychic, it is also social, in a sense that is not yet elaborated. Much recent scholarship seeks to understand how psychic structure becomes implicated in dynamics of social power. How are we to understand this conjuncture or disjuncture, and what has it to do with the theorization of sexual difference?

I want to suggest that the debates concerning the theoretical priority of sexual difference to gender, of gender to sexuality, of sexuality to gender, are all crosscut by another kind of problem, a problem that sexual differences poses, namely, the permanent difficulty of determining where the biological, the psychic, the discursive, the social begin and end. If the Vatican seeks to replace the language of gender with the language of sex, it is because the Vatican wishes to rebiologize sexual difference, that is, to reestablish a biologically narrow notion of reproduction as women's social fate. And yet, when Rosi Braidotti, for instance, insists that we return to sexual difference, it is rather different from the Vatican's call for such a return; if for her sexual difference is a difference that is irreducible to biology and irreducible to culture or to social construction, then how are we to understand the ontological register of sexual difference? Perhaps it is precisely that sexual difference registers ontologically in a way that is permanently difficult to determine.[12] Sexual difference is neither fully given nor fully constructed, but partially both. That sense of "partially" resists any clear sense of "partition"; sexual difference then operates as a chiasm, but the terms that overlap and blur are perhaps less importantly masculine or feminine than the problematic of construction itself; that what is constructed is of necessity prior to construction, even as there appears no access to this prior moment except through construction.

As I understand it, sexual difference is the site where a question concerning the relation of the biological to the cultural is posed and reposed, where it must and can be posed, but where it cannot, strictly speaking, be answered. Understood as a border concept, sexual difference has psychic, somatic, and social dimensions that are never quite collapsible into one another but are not for that reason ultimately distinct. Does sexual difference vacillate there, as a vacillating border, demanding a rearticulation of those terms without any sense of finality? Is it, therefore, not a thing, not a fact, not a presupposition, but rather a demand for rearticulation that never quite vanishes—but also never quite appears?

What does this way of thinking sexual difference do to our understanding of gender? Is what we mean by gender that part of sexual difference that *does* appear as the social (gender is thus the extreme of sociality in sexual difference), as the negotiable, as the constructed—precisely what the Vatican seeks to restore to "sex"—to the site of the natural, where the natural itself is figured as fixed and non-negotiable? Is the Vatican's project as unrealizable as the project to produce gender *ex nihilo* either from the resources of culture or from some fabulous will? Is the queer effort to override gender, or to relegate it to the superseded past as the proper object of some other inquiry, feminist, for example, that is not its own? Is this not an effort to still sexual difference as that which is radically separable from sexuality? The regulation of gender has always been part of the work of heterosexist normativity and to insist upon a radical separation of gender and sexuality is to miss the opportunity to analyze that particular operation of homophobic power.[13]

From quite separate quarters, the effort to associate gender with nefarious feminist aims continues along other lines. In a disturbing cooptation of antiimperialist discourse, the Vatican went so far as to suggest that gender was an import from decadent strains within Western feminism, one imposed on "Third World countries," often used interchangeably with the term "developing countries."

Although it is clear that gender did become a rallying point for some feminist organizing at the 1995 UN conference, it became most tense as an issue that emerged when a Honduran women's group objected to the appointment of an ultraconservative Christian delegation to represent the Honduran government at the September conference. Led by Oscar Rodriguez, the president of the Latin American Episcopal conference, the attempt to oppose a kind of feminism labeled as "Western" was opposed by grassroots movements within the country, including the vocal Women's Rights Centre in Honduras.[14] The state apparatus thus in conjunction with the church appropriates an anticultural imperialist language in order to disempower women in its own country. Apart from claiming that Beijing was going to represent a feminism that was "a culture of death" and one that viewed "motherhood as slavery," this still unnamed form of feminism also claimed that the concerns of the Beijing conference represent a false feminism. (The Vatican as well in its letter of apology for its own patriarchalism sought to distinguish between a feminism that remained committed to the essence of the dignity of women, and a feminism that would destroy maternity and destroy sexual difference.) Both Rodriguez and the Vatican took aim at "unnatural genders" as well, homosexuals and transsexuals. The Women's Rights Centre (CDM) responded by pointing out that it was not interested in destroying maternity but was fighting for mothers to be free of abuse, and that the focus of the Beijing conference was not "unnatural genders," but "the effects of structural adjustment plans on women's economic status, and violence against women." Significantly, the Christian group representing Honduras was also vocally anti-abortiion, drawing clear lines among so-called unnatural genders, the destruction of maternity, and the promotion of abortion rights.

In the platform language, gender was finally allowed to stay, but lesbian had to remain "in brackets." Indeed, I saw some delegates in San Francisco preparing for the meetings by wearing tee shirts with "lesbian" in brackets. The brackets are, of course, supposed to signal that this is disputed language, that there is no agreement on the appropriate use of this term. Though they are supposed to relieve the word of its power, calling into question its admissability, they offer up the term as a diacritically compounded phrase, one which achieves a kind of hypervisibility by virtue of its questionability.

The term "lesbian" went from this bracketed form to being dropped from the language altogether. But the success of this strategy seemed only to stoke the suspicion that the term was reappearing at other linguistic sites: through the word gender, through the discourse of motherhood, through references to sexual autonomy, and even to the phrase "other status"—understood as a basis on which rights could be violated; "other status"—a status that could not be named directly, but which designated lesbians through the obliquity of the phrase: the status that is "other," the one that is not speakable here, the one that has been rendered unspeakable here, the status that is not one.

Within the discursive frame of this international meeting, it seems crucial to ask what it is that occasions the linking of the inclusion of lesbian rights with the production of unnatural gender and the destruction of maternity as well as the introduction of a culture of death (presumably antilife, a familiar Rightist translation of what it is to be pro-choice). Clearly, those who would oppose lesbian rights on this basis (and there were others who oppose them on other bases), either assume that lesbians are not mothers or, if they are, they are nevertheless participating in the destruction of maternity. So be it.

Importantly, though, I think we see in this scene a number of issues simultaneously at play that are not easily separable from one another. The presumption that gender is a code for homosexuality, that the introduction of lesbian is the introduction of a new gender, an unnatural one that will result in the destruction of maternity, and that is linked with feminist struggles for reproductive rights, is irreducibly homophobic and misogynist at once. Moreover, the argument, advanced by a church-state alliance, one that was echoed by the U.S. delegation as well, is that sexual rights are a western imposition was used most forcefully to debunk and contain the claims of the grassroots women's movement in Latin America to represent women at the conference. Hence, we see an augmentation of church–state ideological power over the women's movement precisely through the appropriation of an antiimperialist discourse from such movements.

Over and against a church-state alliance that sought to rehabilitate and defend traditional ethnic purities in an effort to impede claims of sexual autonomy, an alliance emerged at the meetings between feminists seeking language supporting reproductive rights, rights to be free of abuse within marriage, and lesbian rights.

Significantly, the organizing at both conferences on the issue of sexual orientation did not, as the Vatican presumed it would, take cover behind the term "gender"; "sexual orientation," for all its legal and medical strangeness as a term, and "lesbian" became the language that the International Gay and Lesbian Human Rights Commission sought to have included among the bases on which human rights violations against women can take place.

What does seem noteworthy, though, is that the UN conference did achieve consensus on language. The language is rhetorically important because it represents the prevailing international consensus on the issue and can be used by both governmental and nongovernmental agencies in various countries to advance policies that are consistent with the wording of paragraph 96 of the conference's Platform for Action:

> The human rights of women include their right to have control over and decide freely and responsibly on matters related to their sexuality, including sexual and reproductive health, free of coercion, discrimination, and violence. Equal relationships between women and men in matters of sexual relations and reproduction, including full respect for the integrity of the person, require mutual respect, consent and shared responsibility for sexual behavior and its consequences.

Lastly, it seems important to ask after the status of the UN language itself, a language that is supposed to be wrought of international consensus, not unanimity, one that is supposed to represent the consensus on what are universally acceptable claims, universally presumed rights. That what is permitted within the term "universal" is understood to be dependent on a "consensus" appears to undercut some of the force of universality itself, but perhaps not. The process presumes that what will and will not be included within the language of universal entitlement is not settled once and for all, that its future shape cannot be fully anticipated at this time. The UN deliberations became the site for the public ritual that articulates and rearticulates this consensus on what will be the limits of universality.

The meaning of "the universal" proves to be culturally variable, and the specific cultural articulations of "the universal" work against its claim to a transcultural status. This is not to say that there ought to be no reference to the universal or that it has become, for us, an impossibility. The bracketing of the universal only means that there are cultural conditions for its articulation that are not always the same, and that the term gains its meaning for us precisely through the decidedly less than universal cultural conditions of its articulation. This is a paradox that any injunction to adopt a universal attitude will encounter. For it may be that in one culture a set of rights are considered to be universally endowed, and that in another those very rights mark the limit to universalizability, that is, "if we grant those rights to those people we will be undercutting the foundations of the universal as we know it." This has become especially clear to me in the field of lesbian and gay human rights where "the universal" is a contested term, and where various governments and various mainstream human rights groups voice doubt over whether lesbian and gay humans ought properly to be included in "the human," and whether their putative rights fit within the existing conventions governing the scope of rights considered universal.

It is for me no surprise that the Vatican refers to the possible inclusion of lesbian rights as "anti-human." Perhaps that is true. To admit the lesbian into the realm of the universal might be to undo the human, at least in its present form, but it might also be to imagine the human beyond its conventional limits.

Here the notion of universality is not a foundation upon which to build nor is it a presumption that allows us to proceed; it is a term that has become scandalous, threatening to include in the human the very "other" against which the human was defined. In this sense, in this more radical usage, "universality" works against and destroys the foundations that have become conventionally accepted as foundations. "Universality" becomes an antifoundationalism. To claim a set of rights as universal even when existing conventions governing the scope of universality preclude precisely such a claim is both to destroy a concept of the universal and to admit what has been its "constitutive outside," in so doing performing the reverse of any act of assimilation to an *existing* norm. I would insist that such a claim runs the productive risk of provoking and demanding a radical rearticulation of universality itself, forcing the universal into brackets, as it were, into an important sense of unknowingness about what it is and what it might include in a future not fully determined in advance.

To be excluded from the universal, and yet to make a claim within its terms, is to utter a performative contradiction of a certain kind. One might seem foolish and self-defeating, as if such a claim can only be met with derision; or the wager might work the other way, revising and elaborating historical standards of universality proper to the futural movement of democracy itself. To claim that the universal has not yet been articulated is to insist that the "not yet" is proper to an understanding of the universal itself: that which remains "unrealized" by the universal constitutes it essentially. The universal begins to become articulated precisely through challenges to its *existing* formulation, and this challenge emerges from those who are not covered by it, who have no entitlement to occupy the place of the "who," but who, nevertheless, demand that the universal as such ought to be inclusive of them. The excluded, in this sense, constitutes the contingent limit of universalization. This time around, the brackets fell from "lesbian" only to be consigned to "other status," the status of what remains other to language as we speak it. It is this otherness by which the speakable is instituted, that haunts its boundaries, and that threatens to enter the speakable through substitutions that cannot always be detected. Although gender was not the means by which homosexuality entered the official UN language, sexual freedom did become such a term, a rubric that brought lesbians and heterosexual women together for a time, one which gave value to autonomy and refused a return to any notion of fated biology. That the sexual freedom of the female subject challenged the humanism that underwrites universality suggests that we might consider the social forms, such as the patriarchal heterosexual family, that still underwrite our "formal" conceptions of universality. The human, it seems, must become strange to itself, even monstrous, to reachieve the human on another plane. This human will not be "one," indeed, will have no ultimate form, but it will be one that is constantly negotiating sexual difference in a way that has no natural or necessary consequences for the social organization of sexuality. By insisting that this will be a persistent and open question, I mean to suggest that we make no decision on what sexual difference is but leave that question open, troubling, unresolved, propitious.

Response to Rosi Braidotti's *Metamorphoses*

Metamorphoses is Braidotti's third large book in feminist theory, following *Patterns of Dissonance* and *Nomadic Subjects*. It is the first of two volumes, the second of which is forthcoming from Polity Press. Before we enter the details of the book, let us consider what this work seeks to accomplish. It essays to bring together a Deleuzian perspective on the body and becoming, with a feminist perspective on sexual difference and the becoming of Woman; it undertakes a sustained work in the philosophical and cultural criticism of film and, in particular, the ways in which bodies, machines, and animals become intermixed under specific social conditions of production and consumption. It is, as well, not only a sustained defense of Irigaray, but a pedagogical effort to get readers of Irigaray to read her otherwise. The text also makes use, despite some Deleuzian protestations against a psychoanalytic perspective, of a psychoanalytic account of the subject that emphasizes the noncoincidence of the subject to its own psychic constitution, the persistence of the unconscious wish, and the cultural and social structuring of unconscious aims. The text also bespeaks a faith in the continuing use of psychoanalysis as a cure for certain orders of psychic suffering. If we thought before reading this text that bringing Deleuze and Lacan together would be difficult, or that subjecting both authors to a feminist reading that insists upon the primacy of sexual difference might be taxing, or that all this high theory would be difficult to bring together with a culturally savvy analysis of a number of popular films, we were doubtless right. But the text does achieve a certain syncretism of views, and this syncretic accomplishment is mobilized in the service of a theory of affirmation, one that not only seeks to counter the logics of negativity associated with Hegel, but that implies the possibility of an activism that does not rely upon a liberal ontology for the subject.

The text also offers a complex and knowing critique of technology, refusing recourse to a pretechnological past. Braidotti believes instead that a philosophical approach to the origin of life in sexual difference has concrete ethical implications for technological interventions in bodily and reproductive life. While embracing the breakdown among distinctions that humanism has supported among animal, human, and machine, Braidotti cautions us against thinking that we might produce and transform the body in *any and all* directions. Whereas transformation is the stated task of her text, and we might say that it is the event of this text, it would be wrong to think that nomadology, as Braidotti conceives it, or that the work of metamorphosis, of literally changing shape, is an infinite task, one that can take place without any limits. There are modes of transformation that work with and through the body, but there are others, in her view, that seek to overcome bodily life or exceed the parameters of bodily difference. These latter Braidotti opposes on ethical and political grounds. It suits the aims of phallogocentrism, for instance, to construe "transformation" as the overcoming of sexual difference, to use it as the occasion to reinstall masculinist forms of mastery and autonomy, and so to obliterate sexual difference and the specific symbolic domain—the specific symbolic future—of the feminine. Similarly, she opposes any capitulation to a technological remaking of the body that colludes with somatophobia, an effort to escape from bodily life altogether. (Difference and the body remain, for Braidotti, not only conditions of transformation, but the very vehicle and instrument of transformation, that without which transformation in the normative sense cannot take place.)

Braidotti's view of transformation not only establishes a relation to a certain philosophical inheritance but also constitutes one of the most significant dimensions of her own philosophical contribution. At once a theory of activism, or an activist theory, her account of embodiment works philosophically and politically at once, construing transformation in both of these ways at once. Whereas some critics of poststructuralism have maintained that there can be no "agency" without a located and unitary subject, Braidotti shows that activity, affirmation, and the very capacity to transform conditions are derived from a subject multiply constituted and moving in several directions. The line from Spinoza through Deleuze that Braidotti follows, which includes a certain reading of psychoanalysis and might also share some affinities with Nietzsche, argues that the will to live, the affirmation of life takes place through the play of multiplicity. The dynamic interaction of multiple effects brings forth transformation itself. For those who claim that a multiply constituted agent is diffuse or scattered, it should be said that for Braidotti multiplicity is a way of understanding the play of forces that work upon one another and that generate new possibilities of life. Multiplicity is not the death of agency, but its very condition. We misconstrue where action comes from if we fail to understand how multiple forces interact and produce the very dynamism of life.

Transformation is produced by the play of forces, some of which are importantly unconscious, working through bodily means, so that when creativity takes place and something new is inaugurated, it is the result of an activity that precedes the knowing subject, but is not, for that reason, fully external to the subject. Something that precedes me constitutes who I am, and this paradox gives articulation to a conception of the subject irreducible to consciousness. We are not referring to a master subject—a liberal individual who knows and decides on a course of action—as if the subject only inaugurates action and is not acted upon in various ways. That the subject is produced in sexual difference seems to mean, for Braidotti, that this is a body acted upon by other bodies, producing the possibility of a certain transformation. It is an induction into life, a seduction to life, where life itself cannot be understood apart from the dynamic transformation for which we seek to give an account.

This philosophical view has particular global and cultural relevance for those who seek to know what transformation might look like in the context of dynamic global networks. Whereas some would say, in a Marxist vein for instance, that the social world is a sum of totalizing and totalized effects, Braidotti would, I think, oppose this stasis, and seek to know how from various networks, technological and economic, possibilities of transformation are conditioned and produced. But here again, we have to understand that this transformation can only take place if we understand bodily processes as its condition and venue. For Braidotti, bodily processes have to be specified in terms of sexual difference. And sexual difference is the name for a future symbolic that comes to value the not-one as the condition of life itself.

In a way, and without my quite knowing it, I have produced some of the texts that Braidotti's position opposes. Like Braidotti, I have come to represent a version of feminist poststructuralism that has overlapping commitments with hers, but one that tends to work with different texts and different problematics. Poststructuralism is not a monolith; it is not a unitary event or set of texts, but a wide range of works that emerged in the aftermath of Ferdinand de Saussure, the French Hegel, existentialism, phenomenology, and various forms of linguistic formalism. My sense is that it would be right to say, as Braidotti does, that I sometimes stay within the theology of lack, that I sometimes focus on the labor of the negative in the Hegelian sense, and that this involves me in considerations of melancholy, mourning, conscience, guilt, terror, and the like. I tend to think that this is simply what happens when a Jewish girl with a Holocaustal psychic inheritance sits down to read philosophy at an early age, especially when she turns to philosophy from violent circumstances. It may be also that I am concerned very often with questions of survival since I wasn't sure that either my own gender or my own sexuality—whatever those terms finally mean—were going to allow me to be immune from social violence of various forms. Survival is not the same as affirmation, but there is no affirmation without survival (unless we read certain suicidal acts as affirmative). Survival, however, is not enough, even as nothing more can happen for a subject without survival.[15] When Braidotti considers pain and suffering and limitation, she is moved to find the way through and beyond them, to engage a certain activism that overcomes passivity without taking the form of mastery or control. This is a fine art form that is crafted through a certain insistence on finding the possibilities for both affirmation and transformation in what might be difficult, if not potentially dangerous: new technologies of the body, global communication networks, and patterns of transnational immigration and displacement.

I suppose the questions I would be compelled to ask about forced emigration would include the following: What forms of loss do those who are compelled to emigrate undergo? What kind of dissonance is experienced by those who no longer have a home in one country, and do not yet have a home in a new country, but live in a suspended zone of citizenship? What forms do the pains and sufferings of continued colonization take? What is it to be displaced at home, which is surely the case for Palestinians under occupation at the present time?

My wager is that Braidotti would not dismiss these scenes of suffering *as* suffering, but that, methodologically, she would seek to identify these sites of fracture and mobility as conditions for new possibility. In this sense, her critical mode of reading seeks to identify possible sites of transformation, seeking to open up what might otherwise seem like a trap or a dead end, and finding there a new social condition for affirmation. That there is a fractured state, or a state of displacement, can surely be a site of suffering, but it can also be the site for a new possibility of agency. We might lament the loss of proximity and privacy as conditions for human communication but also consider the possibilities for transformation by global networks and the possibilities for global alliance.

There is, I think, not so much a program for transformation in this text that is a detailed agenda about what should be transformed and how. Rather, the work of transformation is exemplified by the text, in its practice of reading, in its relentless search for what is mobile and generative. Braidotti counters, on the one hand, the pessimistic predictions of a Left that thinks that social processes have already done all their dirty work, and that we live as the lifeless effects of their prior efficacy. On the other hand, she counters forms of agency—usually modeled as phallogocentric mastery—that either deny the body or refuse sexual difference, thereby, in her terms, fail to understand how life itself requires the play of multiplicity.

There are, of course, some unsettled questions between Braidotti's position and mine. I'll try to formulate them in question form with the hope that this text, like others, will be taken up as part of an ongoing critical conversation.

Sexual Difference

Braidotti argues that sexual difference is often rejected by theorists because femininity is itself associated with a pejorative understanding of its meaning. She dislikes this pejorative use of the term, but thinks that the term itself can be released into a different future. This may well be true. But is it fair to say that those who oppose this framework therefore demean or debase femininity, or believe that femininity can only have a debased meaning? Is it fair to say that those who do not subscribe to this framework are therefore against the feminine, or even misogynist? It seems to me that the future symbolic will be one in which femininity has multiple possibilities, where it is, as Braidotti herself claims, released from the demand to be one thing, or to comply with a singular norm, the norm devised for it by phallogocentric means. But must the framework for thinking about sexual difference be binary for this feminine multiplicity to emerge? Why can't the framework for sexual difference itself move beyond binarity into multiplicity?

Butch Desire

As a coda to the above remark, consider the following: There may be women who love women, who even love what we might call "femininity," but who cannot find a way to understand their own love through the category of women or as a permutation of femininity.[16] Butch desire may, as some say, be experienced as part of "women's desire," but it can also be experienced, that is, named and interpreted, as a kind of masculinity, one that is not to be found in men. There are many ways of approaching this issue of desire and gender. We could immediately blame the butch community, and say that they/we are simply antifeminine or that we have disavowed a primary femininity, but then we would be left with the quandary that for the most part (but not exclusively) butches are deeply, if not fatally, attracted to the feminine and, in this sense, love the feminine.

We could say, extending Braidotti's frame of reference, that this negative judgment of butch desire is an example of what happens when the feminine is defined too narrowly as an instrument of phallogocentrism, namely, that the full range of possible femininity is not encompassed within its terms, and that butch desire ought properly to be described as another permutation of feminine desire. This last view seeks a more open account of femininity, one that goes against the grain of the phallogocentric version. The view improves upon the first position, which simply attributes a psychological disposition of self-loathing or misogyny to the desiring subject at hand. But if there is masculinity at work in butch desire, that is, if that is the name through which that desire comes to make sense, then why shy away from the fact that there may be ways that masculinity emerges in women, and that feminine and masculine do not belong to differently sexed bodies? Why shouldn't it be that we are at an edge of sexual difference for which the language of sexual difference might not suffice, and that this follows, in a way, from an understanding of the body as constituted by, and constituting, multiple forces? If this particular construction of desire exceeds the binary frame, or confounds its terms, why could it not be an instance of the multiple play of forces that Braidotti accepts on other occasions?

Deleuze

Although Braidotti refers to my 1987 book, *Subjects of Desire*, to support the claim that I reject Deleuze, she needs to know that every year I receive several essays and comments from people who insist that I am Deleuzian. I think this might be a terrible thought for her, but I would ask that she consider that the Spinozan *conatus* remains at the core of my own work. Like her, I am in favor of a deinstitionalized philosophy (a "minority" philosophy), and that I am also looking for the new, for possibilities that emerge from failed dialectics and that exceed the dialectic itself. I confess, however, that I am not a very good materialist. Every time I try to write about the body, the writing ends up being about language. This is not because I think that the body is reducible to language; it is not. Language emerges from the body, constituting an emission of sorts. The body is that upon which language falters, and the body carries its own signs, its own signifiers, in ways that remain largely unconscious. Although Deleuze opposed psychoanalysis, Braidotti does not. Psychoanalysis seems centered on the problem of the lack for Deleuze, but I tend to center on the problem of negativity. One reason I have opposed Deleuze is that I find no registration of the negative in his work, and I feared that he was proposing a manic defense against negativity. Braidotti relinks Deleuze with psychoanalysis in a new way and thus makes him readable in a new way. But how does she reconcile the Deleuze who rejects the unconscious with a psychoanalysis that insists, rightly, upon it?

Speech, Bodies, and Performativity

In my view, performativity is not just about speech acts. It is also about bodily acts. The relation between the two is complicated, and I called it a "chiasmus" in *Bodies that Matter*. There is always a dimension of bodily life that cannot be fully represented, even as it works as the condition and activating condition of language.

Generally, I follow Shoshana Felman's view in *The Scandal of the Speaking Body* in which she claims, following Lacan, that the body gives rise to language, and that language carries bodily aims, and performs bodily deeds that are not always understood by those who use language to accomplish certain conscious aims. I take it that this is the importance of the transference not only for the therapeutic situation but for the theorization of language that it occasions. We say something, and mean something by what we say, but we also do something with our speech, and what we do, how we act upon another with our language, is not the same as the meaning we consciously convey. It is in this sense that the significations of the body exceed the intentions of the subject.

Heterosexuality

It would be a mistake to say that I am against it. I just think that heterosexuality doesn't belong exclusively to heterosexuals. Moreover, heterosexual practices are not the same as heterosexual norms; heterosexual normativity worries me and becomes the occasion of my critique. No doubt, practicing heterosexuals have all kinds of critical and comedic perspectives on heterosexual normativity. On the occasions where I have sought to elucidate a heterosexual melancholia, that is, a refusal of homosexual attachment that emerges within heterosexuality as the consolidation of gender norms ("I am a woman, therefore I do not want one"), I am trying to show how a prohibition on certain forms of love becomes installed as an ontological truth about the subject: The "am" of "I am a man" encodes the prohibition "I may not love a man," so that the ontological claim carries the force of prohibition itself. This only happens, however, under conditions of melancholia, and it does not mean that all heterosexuality is structured in this way or that there cannot be plain "indifference" to the question of homosexuality on the part of some heterosexuals rather than unconscious repudiation. (I take this point from Eve Kosofsky Sedgwick.) Neither do I mean to suggest that I support a developmental model in which first and foremost there is homosexual love, and then that love becomes repressed, and then heterosexuality emerges as a consequence. I do find it interesting, though, that this account would seem to follow from Freud's own postulates.

I fully support Braidotti's view, for instance, that a child is always in love with a mother whose desire is directed elsewhere, and that this triangulation makes sense as the condition of the desiring subject. If this is her formulation of oedipalization, then neither of us rejects oedipalization, although she will *not* read oedipalization through the lack, and I will incorporate prohibition in my account of compulsory heterosexuality. It is only according to the model that posits heterosexual disposition in the child as a given, that it makes sense to ask, as Freud asked in *The Three Essays on the Theory of Sexuality*, how heterosexuality is accomplished. In other words, only within the thesis of a primary heterosexuality does the question of a prior homosexuality emerge, since there will have to be some account given of how heterosexuality becomes established. My critical engagement with these developmental schemes has been to show how the theory of heterosexual dispositions presupposes what would defeat it, namely a preheterosexual erotic history from which it emerges. If there is a triangularity that we call oedipalization, it emerges only on the basis of a set of prohibitions or constraints. Although I accept that triangularity is no doubt a condition of desire, I also have trouble accepting it. That trouble is no doubt a sign of its working, since it is what introduces difficulty into desire, psychoanalytically considered. What interests me most, however, is disarticulating oedipalization from the thesis of a primary or universalized heterosexuality.

Mimesis

Braidotti reports her pleasure at finding at the Institute for Contemporary Art in London a work of art that contains the phrase, "ironic mimesis is not a critique." I wonder whether the statement is true. Is the kind of critical mimesis that Luce Irigaray performs in *The Speculum of the Other Woman* included under such a view? Does Braidotti want to dispense with the part of Irigaray that enters into the language of philosophy as its shadow, to infiltrate its terms, to manifest the occluded feminine, and to provide a disruptive writing that casts the self-grounding authority of masculinist philosophy into question? Why would not this kind of mimesis be critical? I think we make a mistake if we think that this kind of mimesis results only in a slave morality, accepting and fortifying the terms of authority. Irigaray does something else with those terms. She turns them; she derives a place for women when there was no place; she exposes the exclusions by which certain discourses proceed; and she shows that those sites of absence can be mobilized. The voice that emerges "echoes" the master discourse, but this echo nevertheless establishes that there is a voice, that some articulatory power has not been obliterated, and that it is mirroring the words by which its own obliteration was to have taken place. Something is persisting and surviving, and the words of the master sound different when they are spoken by one who is, in the speaking, in the recitation, undermining the obliterating effects of his claim.

Anglo-European Divide

Braidotti argues that feminist theory in Europe has been subject to the hegemony of U.S. feminism, and I presume she is referring to white women's theory as well. For her, it is important to defend a European feminism in order to engage with key issues, including immigration, new European racisms, the ethics of reproductive technology, and the politics of the environment, to name a few. It is notoriously difficult for U.S. feminists and theorists more generally to take account of their first-world privilege in ways that do not resolve into self-aggrandizing guilt or histrionic efforts at self-effacement. Theory emerges from location, and location itself is under crisis in Europe, since the boundaries of Europe are precisely what is being contested in quarrels over who belongs to the European Union and who does not, on rules regarding immigration (especially in Belgium, France, the Netherlands), the cultural effects of Islamic communities, of Arab and North African populations. I am an American, but I am trained in European philosophy. Only decades ago, I was part of a family that understood itself as European Jews, and I grew up with older adults speaking several languages I did not understand and English in heavy accents. When I went to Germany to study German Idealism, my grandmother considered that I was "returning" to where I belonged, and that this was a good and proper thing. Her brothers were schooled in Prague, and she knew there was a German-Jewish intellectual heritage. I still spend too many Sundays reading Benjamin and Scholem, and it may be that this inheritance (one that can be traced through Derrida) is more important to me than American sociology and anthropology. I listen to Braidotti speak in English, knowing that Italian was her first language (even though she lived in Australia for many years), and I am aware that her English is quicker than mine. When I reflect upon it, I would wager she has more friends in the American feminist community than I do.

My German is not too bad, and I spend more time arguing with Habermasians than most people would believe. There is a transatlantic exchange at work between us: we both cross over. Braidotti has helped to show us what this process is, and how the multiple locations that we inhabit produce new sites for transformation. Can we then return to the bipolar distinction between European and American with ease? The wars against Afghanistan and Iraq have clearly produced a longing for the European Left among many progressive Americans, even though this longing in its naïve form tends to forget the resurgence of national sovereignty and the pervasive institutional racism against new immigrants that mire Europe at this time. Doubtless, however, one needs the distinction between European and American in order to mark the hegemonic functioning of the American scene within feminism. But it is perhaps more important at this time to consider the feminisms that are left out of that picture, those that emerge from subaltern localities, from "developing" countries, the southern hemisphere, Asia, and from new immigrant communities within the United States and Europe alike.

If American feminism signals a preoccupation with gender, then it would seem that "American" is allied with the sociological, the theory of social construction, and that the doctrine of difference risks losing its salience. But perhaps the most important task is to think through the debates on the body, since it may or may not be true that cultural construction effaces both sexual difference and bodily process. If the "drive" is the convergence of culture and biology, then it would seem that the "drive" holds out the possibility for a productive exchange between those who speak in the name of the body and those who speak in the name of culture. And if difference is not code for heterosexual normativity, then surely it needs to be articulated so that difference is understood as that which disrupts the coherence of any postulation of identity. If the new gender politics argues against the idealization of dimorphism, then does it argue against the primacy of sexual difference itself? And if technologies of the body (surgical, hormonal, athletic) generate new forms of gender, is this precisely in the service of inhabiting a body more fully or does it constitute a perilous effacement? It seems crucial to keep these questions open so that we might work theoretically and politically in broad coalitions. The lines we draw are invitations to cross over and that crossing over, as any nomadic subject knows, constitutes who we are.

10. The Question of Social Transformation

Feminism is about the social transformation of gender relations. Probably we could all agree on that, even if "gender" is not the preferred word for some. And yet the question of the relationship between feminism and social transformation opens up onto a difficult terrain. It should be obvious, one would think, but something makes it obscure. Those of us to whom this question is posed are asked to make clear what we already assume, but which is not at all to be taken for granted. We may imagine social transformation differently. We may have an idea of the world as it would be, or should be, transformed by feminism. We may have very different ideas of what social transformation is, or what qualifies as a transformative exercise. But we must also have an idea of how theory relates to the process of transformation, whether theory is itself transformative work that has transformation as one of its effects.

In what follows, I will argue that theory is itself transformative, so I will state that in advance. But one must also understand that I do not think theory is sufficient for social and political transformation. Something besides theory must take place, such as interventions at social and political levels that involve actions, sustained labor, and institutionalized practice, which are not quite the same as the exercise of theory. I would add, however, that in all of these practices, theory is presupposed. We are all, in the very act of social transformation, lay philosophers, presupposing a vision of the world, of what is right, of what is just, of what is abhorrent, of what human action is and can be, of what constitutes the necessary and sufficient conditions of life.

There are many questions that form the various foci of feminist research, and I would not want to identify any one of them as the essential or defining focus. I would say, however, that the question of life is in some ways at the center of much feminist theory and, in particular, feminist philosophy. The question about life might be posed in various ways: What is the good life? How has the good life been conceived such that women's lives have not been included in its conceptualization? What would the good life be for women? But perhaps there is, prior to these questions, all of which are important questions, another question: the question of survival itself. When we consider what feminist thought might be in relation to survival, a different set of questions emerges: Whose life is counted as a life? Whose prerogative is it to live? How do we decide when life begins and ends, and how do we think life against life? Under what conditions should life come into being, and through what means? Who cares for life as it emerges? Who tends for the life of the child? Who cares for life as it wanes? Who cares for the life of the mother, and of what value is it ultimately? And to what extent does gender, coherent gender, secure a life as livable? What threat of death is delivered to those who do not live gender according to its accepted norms?

That feminism has always thought about questions of life and death means that feminism has always, to some extent and in some way, been philosophical. That it asks how we organize life, how we accord it value, how we safeguard it against violence, how we compel the world, and its institutions, to inhabit new values, means that its philosophical pursuits are in some sense at one with the aim of social transformation.

It would be easier if I could lay out what I think the ideal relation between genders should be, what gender, as a norm and as an experience, should be like, in what equality and justice would consist. It would be easier. You would then know the norms that guide my thinking, and you could judge whether or not I have achieved the aims that I have set out for myself. But matters are not so easy for me. My difficulty will emerge not out of stubbornness or a will to be obscure. It emerges simply out of the doubled truth that although we need norms in order to live, and to live well, and to know in what direction to transform our social world, we are also constrained by norms in ways that sometimes do violence to us and which, for reasons of social justice, we must oppose. There is perhaps a confusion here, since many will say that the opposition to violence must take place *in the name of the norm*, a norm of nonviolence, a norm of respect, a norm that governs or compels the respect for life itself. But consider that normativity has this double meaning. On the one hand, it refers to the aims and aspirations that guide us, the precepts by which we are compelled to act or speak to one another, the commonly held presuppositions by which we are oriented, and which give direction to our actions. On the other hand, normativity refers to the process of normalization, the way that certain norms, ideas and ideals hold sway over embodied life, provide coercive criteria for normal "men" and "women." And in this second sense, we see that norms are what govern "intelligible" life, "real" men and "real" women. And that when we defy these norms, it is unclear whether we are still living, or ought to be, whether our lives are valuable, or can be made to be, whether our genders are real, or ever can be regarded as such.

A good Enlightenment thinker will simply shake her head and say that if one objects to normalization, it is in the name of a different norm that one objects. But that critic would also have to consider what the relationship is between normalization and normativity. Since it may be that when we talk about what binds us humans, and what forms of speech or thinking we seek in an effort to find a common bond, that we are, inevitably, seeking recourse to socially instituted relations, ones that have been formed over time, and which give us a sense of the "common" only by excluding those lives which do not fit the norm. In this sense, we see the "norm" as that which binds us, but we also see that the "norm" creates unity only through a strategy of exclusion. It will be necessary for us to think through this problem, this doubleness of the norm. But in this essay, I would like to start first by asking about the kind of norms that govern gender, and to ask, in particular, how they constrain and enable life, how they designate in advance what will and will not be a livable existence.

I would like to proceed with this first task through a review of *Gender Trouble*, the text in which I originally offered my theory of gender. I would like to consider this theory of gender explicitly in terms of the questions of violence, and the possible transformation of the scene of gender violence into a future of social survival. Second, I would like to consider this double nature of the norms, showing how we cannot do without them, and how we do not have to assume that their form is given or fixed. Indeed, even if we cannot do without them, it will be seen that we also cannot accept them as they are. I would like to pursue this paradox toward the end of my remarks in order to elucidate what I take to be the political stakes of feminist theory.

Gender Trouble and the Question of Survival

When I wrote this text, I was several years younger than I am today, and I was without a secure position in the academy. I wrote it for a few friends of mine, and I imagined maybe one or two hundred people might read it. I had two aims at the time: the first was to expose what I took to be a pervasive heterosexism in feminist theory; the second was to try to imagine a world in which those who live at some distance from gender norms, who live in the confusion of gender norms, might still understand themselves not only as living livable lives, but as deserving a certain kind of recognition. But let me be more honest than that. I wanted something of gender trouble to be understood and accorded dignity, according to some humanist ideal, but I also wanted it to disturb—fundamentally—the way in which feminist and social theory think gender, and to find it exciting, to understand something of the desire that gender trouble is, the desire it solicits, the desire it conveys.

So let me consider these two points again, since they have both changed in my mind, and as a result, they compel me to rethink the question of change.

In the first instance: feminist theory. What did I understand its heterosexism to be, and how do I now understand it? At the time, I understood the theory of sexual difference to be a theory of heterosexuality. And I also understood French feminism, with the exception of Monique Wittig, to understand cultural intelligibility not only to assume the fundamental difference between masculine and feminine, but to reproduce it. The theory was derived from Lévi-Strauss, from Lacan, from Saussure, and there were various breaks with those masters that one could trace. After all, it was Julia Kristeva who said that Lacan made no room for the semiotic and insisted on offering that domain not only as a supplement to the symbolic, but as a way of undoing it. And it was Cixous, for instance, who saw feminine writing as a way of making the sign travel in ways that Lévi-Strauss could not imagine at the end of *The Elementary Structures of Kinship*. And it was Irigaray who imagined the goods getting together, and even implicitly theorized a certain kind of homoerotic love between women when those lips were entangled to the extent that one couldn't tell the difference between the one and the other (and where not being able to tell the difference was not equivalent to "being the same"). The "high" at the time was to see that these French feminists had entered into a region considered fundamental to language and to culture to make an assertion that language came into being through sexual difference. The speaking subject was, accordingly, one who emerged in relation to the duality of the sexes, and that culture, as outlined by Lévi-Strauss, was defined through the exchange of women, and that the difference between men and women was instituted at the level of elementary exchange, an exchange which forms the possibility of communication itself.

To understand the exhilaration of this theory for those who were working within it, and for those who still do, one has to understand the sea-change that took place when feminist studies turned from being the analysis of "images" of women in this or that discipline or sphere of life to being an analysis of sexual difference at the foundation of cultural and human communicability. Suddenly, we were fundamental. Suddenly, no human science could proceed without us.

And not only were we fundamental, we were changing that foundation. There was a new writing, a new form of communicability, a challenge to the kinds of communicability that were fully constrained by a patriarchal symbolic. And there were also new ways for women as the gifts to be getting together, new modes, poetic modes, of alliance and cultural production. We had as it were the outlines of the theory of patriarchy before us, and we were also intervening in it, to produce new forms of intimacy, alliance, and communicability that were outside of its terms, but were also contesting its inevitability, its totalizing claim.

So it sounded rather good, but it did produce some problems for many of us. In the first place, it seemed that the model of culture, both in its patriarchal and feminist mode, assumed the constancy of sexual difference, and there were those of us for whom gender trouble was the contestation of sexual difference itself. There were many who asked whether they were women, and some asked it in order to become included in the category, and some asked it in order to find out whether there were alternatives to being in the category. In *"Am I That Name?"* Denise Riley wrote that she did not want to be exhausted by the category, but Cherríe Moraga and others were also beginning to theorize butch–femme categories, which called into question whether the kinds of masculinities at stake for a butch were always determined by an already operative sexual difference, or whether they were calling sexual difference into question.[1]

Femmes posed an important question: was this a femininity defined in relation to a masculinity already operative in the culture, part of a normative structure that could not be changed, or was this the challenge to that normative structure, a challenge from within its most cherished terms? What happens when terms such as butch and femme emerge not as simple copies of heterosexual masculinity and heterosexuality femininity, but as expropriations that expose the nonnecessary status of their assumed meanings? Indeed, the widely cited point that *Gender Trouble* made was the following: that categories like butch and femme were not copies of a more originary heterosexuality, but they showed how the so-called originals, men and women within the heterosexual frame, are similarly constructed, performatively established. So the ostensible copy is not explained through reference to an origin, but the origin is understood to be as performative as the copy. Through performativity, dominant and nondominant gender norms are equalized. But some of those performative accomplishments claim the place of nature or claim the place of symbolic necessity, and they do this only by occluding the ways in which they are performatively established.

I'll return to the theory of performativity, but for now, let me explain how my account of this particular rift between high structuralist feminist theory and poststructuralist gender trouble has become reformulated for me.

In the first instance, at work in my exposition of this transition from sexual difference to gender trouble, or indeed, from sexual difference to queer theory (which is not the same, since "gender trouble" is but a moment of queer theory), there is a slippage between sexual difference as a category that conditions the emergence into language and culture, and gender as a sociological concept, figured as a norm. Sexual difference is not the same as the categories of women and men. Women and men exist, we might say, as social norms, and they are, according to the perspective of sexual difference, ways in which sexual difference has assumed content. Many Lacanians, for instance, argued with me that sexual difference has only a formal character, that nothing follows about the social roles or meanings that gender might have from the concept of sexual difference itself. Indeed, some of them evacuate sexual difference of every possible semantic meaning, allying it with the structural possibility for semantics, but having no proper or necessary semantic content. Indeed, they even argue that the possibility of critique emerges when one comes to understand how sexual difference has not only become concretized in certain cultural and social instances, but how it has become reduced to its instance, since this constitutes a fundamental mistake, a way of foreclosing the fundamental openness of the distinction itself.

So this is one way of answering me, and it comes from the formalist Lacanians: Joan Copjec and Charles Shepherdson, but also Slavoj Žižek. But there is a stronger feminist argument that implicitly or explicitly takes issue with the trajectory I have laid out. It is articulated most buoyantly, most persuasively, perhaps by Rosi Braidotti whose most recent work I consider as part of the chapter, "The End of Sexual Difference?" in this book.[2] I think the argument goes something like this: we must maintain the framework of sexual difference because it brings to the fore the continuing cultural and political reality of patriarchal domination, because it reminds us that whatever permutations of gender take place, they do not fully challenge the framework within which they take place, for that framework persists at a symbolic level that is more difficult to intervene upon. Critics such as Carol Anne Tyler argued, for instance, that it will always be different for a woman to enter into transgressive gender norms than it will be for a man, and that *Gender Trouble* does not distinguish strongly enough between these very different positions of power within society.

Others suggest that the problem has to do with psychoanalysis, and with the place and meaning of oedipalization. The child enters desire through triangulation, and whether or not there is a heterosexual pair who are functioning as the parents, the child will still locate a paternal and maternal point of departure. This heterosexual dyad will have symbolic significance for the child and become the structure through which desire is given form.

In a sense, there are important alternatives to be thought together here. I am not suggesting that they can or should be reconciled. It may be that they stand in a necessary tension to one another, and that this necessary tension now structures the field of feminist and queer theory, producing their inevitable tension and necessitating the contentious dialogue between them. It is important to distinguish among theorists of sexual difference who argue on biological grounds that the distinction between the sexes is necessary (Barbara Duden, the German feminist, tends to do this[3]), and those who argue that sexual difference is a fundamental nexus through which language and culture emerge (the structuralists and the non-gender-troubled poststructuralists do this). But then there is a further distinction. There are those who only find the structuralist paradigm useful because it charts the continuing power differential between men and women in language and society and gives us a way of understanding how deeply it functions in establishing the symbolic order in which we live. Among the latter, I think, there is a difference still between those who consider that symbolic order inevitable, and so ratify patriarchy as an inevitable structure of culture, and those who think that sexual difference is inevitable and fundamental, but that its form as patriarchal is contestable. Rosi Braidotti belongs to the latter. One can see why I have had such useful conversations with her.

The problem arises when we try to understand whether sexual difference is necessarily heterosexist. Is it? Again, it depends on which version you accept. If you claim that oedipalization presupposes heterosexual parenting or a heterosexual symbolic that exceeds whatever parenting arrangement—if there is one at work—then the matter is pretty much closed. If you think that oedipalization produces heterosexual desire, and that sexual difference is a function of oedipalization, then it seems that the matter is closed again. And there are those, such as Juliet Mitchell, who are presently troubled by this issue, even though she is the one who, in *Psycho-analysis and Feminism*, declared the patriarchal symbolic order not to be a changeable set of rules but to be "primordial law" (370).

I take the point that the sociological concepts of gender, understood as women and men, cannot be reducible to sexual difference. But I worry still, actively, about understanding sexual difference as operating as a symbolic order. What does it mean for such an order to be symbolic rather than social?[4] And what happens to the task of feminist theory to think social transformation if we accept that sexual difference is orchestrated and constrained at a symbolic level? If it is symbolic, is it changeable? I ask Lacanians this question, and they usually tell me that changes in the symbolic take a long, long time. I wonder how long I will have to wait. Or they show me a few passages in what is called the Rome Discourse, and I wonder if these passages are the ones to which we are supposed to cling for hope that things might eventually change. Moreover, I'm compelled to ask, is it really true that sexual difference at the symbolic level is without semantic content? Can it ever be? And what if we have indeed done nothing more than abstracted the social meaning of sexual difference and exalted it as a symbolic and, hence, presocial structure? Is that a way of making sure that sexual difference is beyond social contestation?

One might wonder after all of this why I want to contest sexual difference at all, but the abiding assumption of my earlier gender theory was that gender is complexly produced through identificatory and performative practices, and that gender is not as clear or as univocal as we are sometimes led to believe. My effort was to combat forms of essentialism which claimed that gender is a truth that is somehow there, interior to the body, as a core or as an internal essence, something that we cannot deny, something which, natural or not, is treated as given. The theory of sexual difference makes none of the claims that natural essentialism does. At least one version of sexual difference argued that it was the "difference" in every identity that precludes the possibility of a unified category of identity. There were, in this regard, at least two different kinds of challenges that *Gender Trouble* needed to meet, and I see now that I needed to separate the issues and hope that I have begun to do that in my subsequent work. Nevertheless, I still worry that the frameworks we commit ourselves to because they describe patriarchal domination well and may well recommit us to seeing that very domination as inevitable or as primary, more primary in fact than other operations of differential power. Is the symbolic eligible for social intervention? Does sexual difference really remain other to its instituted form, the dominant one being heterosexuality itself?

What was it I imagined? And how has the question of social transformation and politics changed in the interim?

Gender Trouble ends with a discussion of drag, and the final chapter is in fact called "From Parody to Politics." A number of critics have scrutinized that chapter in order to resolve the transition: how do we get from parody to politics? There are those who think that the text has belittled politics and reduced politics to parody; some claim that drag becomes a model for resistance or for political intervention and participation more generally. So let us reconsider this controversial closure, a text I probably wrote too quickly, a text whose future I did not anticipate at the time.

Why drag? Well, there are biographical reasons, and you might as well know that in the United States the only way to describe me in my younger years was as a bar dyke who spent her days reading Hegel and her evenings, well, at the gay bar, which occasionally became a drag bar. And I had some relatives who were, as it were, in the life, and there was some important identification with those "boys." So I was there, undergoing a cultural moment in the midst of a social and political struggle. But I also experienced in that moment a certain implicit theorization of gender: it quickly dawned on me that some of these so-called men could do femininity much better than I ever could, ever wanted to, ever would. And so I was confronted by what can only be called the transferability of the attribute. Femininity, which I understood never to have belonged to me anyway, was clearing belonging elsewhere, and I was happier to be the audience to it, have always been very happier to be its audience than I ever was or would be being the embodiment of it. (This does not mean, by the way, that I am therefore disembodied, as some rather mean-spirited critics have said or implied.) Indeed, whether we follow the framework of sexual difference or that of gender trouble, I would hope that we would all remain committed to the ideal that no one should be forcibly compelled to occupy a gender norm that is undergone, experientially, as an unlivable violation. We might argue theoretically about whether social categories, imposed from elsewhere, are always "violations" in the sense that they are, at first and by necessity, unchosen. But that does not mean that we have lost the capacity to distinction between enabling violations and disabling ones. When gender norms operate as violations, they function as an interpellation that one refuses only by agreeing to pay the consequences: losing one's job, home, the prospects for desire, or for life. There is also a set of laws, criminal and psychiatric codes for which, still, imprisonment and incarcertion are possible consequences. Gender dysphoria can be used in many countries still to deny employment or to take away one's child. The consequences can be severe. It won't do to call this merely play or fun, even if those constitute significant moments. I don't mean to say that gender is not sometimes play, pleasure, fun, and fantasy; it surely is. I only mean to say that we continue to live in a world in which one can risk serious disenfranchisement and physical violence for the pleasure one seeks, the fantasy one embodies, the gender one performs.

Let me continue, then, by offering a few propositions to consider:

(A) What operates at the level of cultural fantasy is not finally dissociable from the ways in which material life is organized.

(B) When one performance of gender is considered real and another false, or when one presentation of gender is considered authentic, and another fake, then we can conclude that a certain ontology of gender is conditioning these judgments, an ontology (an account of what gender *is*) that is also put into crisis by the performance of gender in such a way that these judgments are undermined or become impossible to make.

(C) The point to emphasize here is not that drag is subversive of gender norms, but that we live, more or less implicitly, with received notions of reality, implicit accounts of ontology, which determine what kinds of bodies and sexualities will be considered real and true, and which kind will not.

(D) This differential effect of ontological presuppositions on the embodied life of individuals has consequential effects. And what drag can point out is that (1) this set of ontological presuppositions is at work, and (2) that it is open to rearticulation.

The question of who and what is considered real and true is apparently a question of knowledge. But it is also, as Foucault makes plain, a question of power. Having or bearing "truth" and "reality" is an enormously powerful prerogative within the social world, one way in which power dissimulates as ontology. According to Foucault, one of the first tasks of critique is to discern the relation "between mechanisms of coercion and elements of knowledge."[5] Here we are confronted with the limits of what is knowable, limits that exercise a certain force but are not grounded in any necessity, limits that one interrogates only at a risk to one's secure and available ontology: "[N]othing can exist as an element of knowledge if, on the one hand, it . . . does not conform to a set of rules and constraints characteristic, for example, of a given type of scientific discourse in a given period, and if, on the other hand, it does not possess the effects of coercion or simply the incentives peculiar to what is scientifically validated or simply rational or simply generally accepted, etc."(52).

Knowledge and power are not finally separable but work together to establish a set of subtle and explicit criteria for thinking the world: "It is therefore not a matter of describing what knowledge is and what power is and how one would repress the other or how the other would abuse the one, but rather, a nexus of knowledge-power has to be described so that we can grasp what constitutes the acceptability of a system" (52–53).

If we consider this relation of knowledge and power in relation to gender, we are compelled to ask how the organization of gender comes to function as a presupposition about how the world is structured. There is no merely epistemological approach to gender, no simple way to ask what are women's ways of knowing, or what might it mean to know women. On the contrary, the ways in which women are said to "know" or to "be known" are already orchestrated by power precisely at that moment in which the terms of "acceptable" categorization are instituted.

In Foucault's view, the critic thus has a double task: to show how knowledge and power work to constitute a more or less systematic way of ordering the world with its own "conditions of acceptability of a system," and "to follow the breaking points which indicate its emergence."[6] So it will not be enough to isolate and identify the peculiar nexus of power and knowledge that gives rise to the field of intelligible things. Rather, it is necessary to track the way in which that field meets its breaking point, the moments of its discontinuities, and the sites where it fails to constitute the intelligibility it promises. What this means is that one looks for the conditions by which the object field is constituted as well as the limits of those conditions, the moment where they point up their contingency and their transformability. In Foucault's terms, "schematically speaking, we have perpetual mobility, essential fragility or rather the complex interplay between what replicates the same process and what transforms it" (58).

What this means for gender, then, is that it is important not only to understand how the terms of gender are instituted, naturalized, and established as presuppositional but to trace the moments where the binary system of gender is disputed and challenged, where the coherence of the categories are put into question, and where the very social life of gender turns out to be malleable and transformable.

The turn to drag performance was, in part, a way to think not only about how gender is performed, but how it is resignified through collective terms. Drag performers, for instance, tend to live in communities, and there are strong ritual bonds, such as those we see in the film *Paris is Burning*,[7] which make us aware of the resignification of social bonds that gender minorities within communities of color can and do forge. Thus, we are talking about a cultural life of fantasy that not only organizes the material conditions of life, but which also produces sustaining bonds of community where recognition becomes possible, and which works as well to ward off violence, racism, homophobia, and transphobia. This threat of violence tells us something about what is fundamental to the culture in which they live, a culture that is not radically distinct from what many of us live, even as it is not the same as what any of us probably live. But there is a reason we understand it, if we do; this film travels, because of its beauty, its tragedy, its pathos, and its bravery. Its pleasure crosses cultural boundaries in a way, because what also crosses those boundaries, and not always in the same way, is the threat of violence, the threat of poverty, and the struggle to survive—all of which are more difficult for people of color. It is important to note that the struggle to survive is not really separable from the cultural life of fantasy. It is part of it. Fantasy is what allows us to imagine ourselves and others otherwise.

Fantasy is what establishes the possible in excess of the real; it points, it points elsewhere, and when it is embodied, it brings the elsewhere home.

This brings me back to the question of politics. How is it that drag or, indeed, much more than drag, transgender itself enters into the political field? It does this, I would suggest, by not only making us question what is real, and what has to be, but by showing us how contemporary notions of reality can be questioned, and new modes of reality instituted. Fantasy is not simply a cognitive exercise, an internal film that we project inside the interior theater of the mind. Fantasy structures relationality, and it comes into play in the stylization of embodiment itself. Bodies are not inhabited as spatial givens. They are, in their spatiality, also underway in time: aging, altering shape, altering signification—depending on their interactions—and the web of visual, discursive, and tactile relations that become part of their historicity, their constitutive past, present, and future.

As a consequence of being in the mode of becoming, and in always living with the constitutive possibility of becoming otherwise, the body is that which can occupy the norm in myriad ways, exceed the norm, rework the norm, and expose realities to which we thought we were confined as open to transformation. These corporeal realities are actively inhabited, and this "activity" is not fully constrained by the norm. Sometimes the very conditions for conforming to the norm are the same as the conditions for resisting it. When the norm appears at once to guarantee and threaten social survival (it is what you need to live; it is that which, if you live it, will threaten to efface you), then conforming and resisting become a compounded and paradoxical relation to the norm, a form of suffering and a potential site for politicization. The question of how to embody the norm is thus very often linked to the question of survival, of whether life itself will be possible. I think we should not underestimate what the thought of the possible does for those who experience survival itself as a burning issue.

This is one way in which the matter is and continues to be political. But there is something more, since what the example of drag sought to do was to make us question the means by which reality is made and to consider the way in which being called real or being called unreal can be not only a means of social control but a form of dehumanizing violence. Indeed, I would put it this way: to be called unreal, and to have that call, as it were, institutionalized as a form of differential treatment, is to become the other against which the human is made. It is the inhuman, the beyond the human, the less than human, the border that secures the human in its ostensible reality. To be called a copy, to be called unreal, is thus one way in which one can be oppressed. But consider that it is more fundamental than that. For to be oppressed means that you already exist as a subject of some kind, you are there as the visible and oppressed other for the master subject as a possible or potential subject. But to be unreal is something else again. For to be oppressed one must first become intelligible. To find that one is fundamentally unintelligible (indeed, that the laws of culture and of language find one to be an impossibility) is to find that one has not yet achieved access to the human. It is to find oneself speaking only and always as if one were human, but with the sense that one is not. It is to find that one's language is hollow, and that no recognition is forthcoming because the norms by which recognition takes place are not in one's favor.

If gender is performative, then it follows that the reality of gender is itself produced as an effect of the performance. Although there are norms that govern what will and will not be real, and what will and will not be intelligible, they are called into question and reiterated at the moment in which performativity begins its citational practice. One surely cites norms that already exist, but these norms can be significantly deterritorialized through the citation. They can also be exposed as nonnatural and nonnecessary when they take place in a context and through a form of embodying that defies normative expectation. What this means is that through the practice of gender performativity, we not only see how the norms that govern reality are cited but grasp one of the mechanisms by which reality is reproduced *and* altered in the course of that reproduction. The point about drag is not simply to produce a pleasurable and subversive spectacle but to allegorize the spectacular and consequential ways in which reality is both reproduced and contested.

The derealization of gendered violence has implications for understanding how and why certain gender presentations are criminalized and pathologized, how subjects who cross gender risk internment and imprisonment, why violence against transgendered subjects is not recognized as violence, and why it is sometimes inflicted by the very states who should be offering such subjects protection from violence.

So what if new forms of gender are possible, how does this affect the ways that we live and the concrete needs of the human community? How are we to distinguish between forms of gender possibility that are valuable and those that are not? These are questions that have been understandably posed to my arguments. I would respond that it is not a question merely of producing a new future for genders that do not yet exist. The genders I have in mind have been existing for a long time, but they have not been admitted into the terms that govern reality. It is a question of developing, within law, within psychiatry, within social and literary theory, a new legitimating lexicon for the gender complexity that we have always been living. Because the norms governing reality have not admitted these forms to be real, we will, of necessity, call them new. But I hope we will laugh knowingly when and if we do. The conception of politics at work here is centrally concerned with the question of survival, of how to create a world in which those who understand their gender and their desire to be nonnormative can live and thrive not only without the threat of violence from the outside but without the pervasive sense of their own unreality, which can lead to suicide or a suicidal life. Lastly, I would ask what place the thinking of the possible has within political theorizing. One can object and say, ah, but you are trying only to make gender complexity possible. But that does not tell us which forms are good or bad; it does not supply the measure, the gauge, the norm. But there is a normative aspiration here, and it has to do with the ability to live and breathe and move and would no doubt belong somewhere in what is called a philosophy of freedom. The thought of a possible life is only an indulgence for those who already know themselves to be possible. For those who are still looking to become possible, possibility is a necessity.

From Norms to Politics

In the essay, "Gender Regulations," I argue that the sense of what a norm is and what, finally, is "normative" depends on the kind of social theory from which these terms emerge. On the one hand, norms seem to signal the regulatory or normalizing function of power, but from another perspective, norms are precisely what binds individuals together, forming the basis of their ethical and political claims. When, in the analysis above, I oppose violence done by restrictive norms, I appear to appeal to a norm of nonviolence. It would seem to follow that norms can operate both as unacceptable restrictions and as part of any critical analysis that seeks to show what is unacceptable in that restrictive operation. This second sense of norms is associated with the work of Jürgen Habermas who identifies norms as the basis for the possibility of community or, indeed, any understanding that humans might hold in common. If we cannot accept that there is this possibility of commonness in the sense that he holds out, are we still precluded from making strong political claims, for instance, against gendered violence?

If we consider Habermas's argument in *Between Facts and Norms*, it is clear that he relies on norms to supply a common understanding for social actors and speakers: "Participants, in claiming validity for their utterances, strive to reach an understanding with one another about something in the world . . . the everyday use of language does not turn exclusively or even primarily on its representational (or fact-stating) functions: here all the functions of language and language-world relations come into play, so that the spectrum of validity claims takes in more than truth claims" (16). He further explains that "in explicating the meaning of linguistic expressions and the validity of statements, we touch on idealizations that are connected with the medium of language" (17). He makes clear that without these idealizations at the heart of language, we would not have the resources by which to orient ourselves to disparate kinds of claims made by any number of social actors. Indeed, the presumption of a common set of idealizations is what gives our action order and what orders it in advance, as well as what we take account of as we seek to order ourselves in relation to one another and a common future "With the concept of communicative action, which brings in mutual understanding as a mechanism of action coordination, the counterfactual presuppositions of actors who orient their action to validity claims also acquire *immediate relevance for the construction and preservation of social orders; for these orders exist through the recognition of normative validity claims*" (17, my emphasis).

Here we can see that norms, which orient action toward the common good, and which belong to an "ideal" sphere, are not precisely social in Ewald's sense. They do not belong to variable social orders, and they are not, in Foucault's sense, a set of "regulatory ideals" and, hence, part of the ideal life of social power. On the contrary, they function as part of a reasoning process that conditions any and every social order, and which gives that order its coherence. We know, though, that Habermas would not accept the "ordered" characteristic of any social order as a necessary good. Some orders clearly ought to be disrupted, and for good reason. Indeed, the order of gender intelligibility may well qualify as one such order. But do we have a way to distinguish here between the function of the norm as socially integrative and the value of "integration" under oppressive social conditions? In other words, is there not an inherently conservative function of the norm when it is said to preserve order? What if the very order is exclusionary or violent? We might respond, with Habermas, and say that violence goes against the normative idealizations found functioning, implicitly, in everyday language. But if the norm is socially integrative, then how will the norm actually work to break up a social order whose "order" is purchased and maintained through violent means? Is the norm part of such a social order, or is it "social" only in a hypothetical sense, part of an "order" that is not instantiated in the social world as it is lived and negotiated?

If the Habermasian point is that we cannot hope to live in consensus or in common orientation without assuming such norms, is the "common" in this instance then not instituted precisely through the production of what is uncommon, through what is outside the common, or what disrupts it from within, or what poses a challenge to its integrity? What is the value of the "common"? Do we need to know that, despite our differences, we are all oriented toward the same conception of rational deliberation and justification? Or do we need precisely to know that the "common" is no longer there for us, if it ever was, and that the capacious and self-limiting approach to difference is not only the task of cultural translation in this day of multiculturalism but the most important way to nonviolence?

The point is not to apply social norms to lived social instances or to order and define them (as Foucault has criticized) nor is it to find justificatory mechanisms for the grounding of social norms that are extrasocial (even as they operate under the name of the "social"). There are times when both of these activities do and must take place We level judgments against criminals for illegal acts and so subject them to a normalizing procedure; we consider our grounds for action in collective contexts and try to find modes of deliberation and reflection about which we can agree. But neither of these is all we do with norms. Through recourse to norms, the sphere of the humanly intelligible is circumscribed, and this circumscription is consequential for any ethics and any conception of social transformation. We might say, "we must know the fundamentals of the human in order to act in such a way that we preserve and promote human life as we know it." But what if the very categories of the human have excluded those who should be operating within its terms, who do not accept the modes of reasoning and justifying "validity claims" that have been proffered by western forms of rationalism? Have we ever yet known the "human"? What might it take to approach that knowing? Should we be wary of knowing it too soon? Should we be wary of any final or definitive knowing? If we take the field of the human for granted, then we fail to think critically—and ethically—about the consequential ways that the human is being produced, reproduced, deproduced. This latter inquiry does not exhaust the field of ethics, but I cannot imagine a "responsible" ethics or theory of social transformation operating without it.

Let me suggest here as a way of offering a closing discussion to this essay that the necessity of keeping our notion of the "human" open to a future articulation is essential to the project of a critical international human rights discourse and politics. We see this time and again when the very notion of the "human" is presupposed; it is defined in advance, and in terms that are distinctively western, very often American, and therefore parochial. The paradox emerges that the "human" at issue in human rights is already known, already defined, and yet it is supposed to be the ground for a set of rights and obligations that are international. How we move from the local to the international is a major question for international politics, but it takes a specific form for international feminism. And I would suggest to you that an anti-imperialist or, minimally, nonimperialist conception of international human rights must call into question what is meant by the human, and learn from the various ways and means by which it is defined across cultural venues. This means that local conceptions of what is "human" or, indeed, of what the basic conditions and needs of human life are, must be subjected to reinterpretation, since there are historical and cultural circumstances in which the "human" is defined differently or resignified, and its basic needs and, hence, basic entitlements are also defined differently.

Resignification as Politics

Does "resignification" constitute a political practice, or does it constitute one part of political transformation? One might well say that politicians on the Right and the Left can use these strategies. We can surely see how "multiculturalism" has its right-wing and left-wing variants, how "globalization" has its right-wing and left-wing variants. In the United States, the word "compassionate" has been linked to "conservative" and this struck many of us as an abomination of "resignification." One can point out, with full justification, that National Socialism was a resignification of "socialism." And that would be right. So it seems clear that resignification alone is not a politics, is not sufficient for a politics, is not enough. One can argue that the Nazis appropriated power by taking the language and concerns of democracy against itself, or that Haitian revolutionaries appropriated power by using the terms of democracy against those who would deny it. And so appropriation can be used by the Right and the Left, and there are no necessarily salutary ethical consequences for "appropriation." There is the queer appropriation of "queer" and, in the United States, a rap appropriation of racist discourse, and the left-wing appropriation of "no big government" and on and on. So appropriation by itself leads to myriad consequences, some of which we might embrace, and some of which we might abhor. But if it does work in the service of a radical democratic politics, how might it work?

Does resignification work as a politics? I want to suggest here that as we extend the realm of universality, become more knowing about what justice implies, provide for greater possibilities of life—and "life" itself is a contested term, one which has its reactionary and progressive followers—we need to assume that our already established conventions regarding what is human, what is universal, what the meaning and substance of international politics might be, are not sufficient. For the purposes of a radical democratic transformation, we need to know that our fundamental categories can and must be expanded to become more inclusive and more responsive to the full range of cultural populations. This does not mean that a social engineer plots at a distance how best to include everyone in his or her category. It means that the category itself must be subjected to a reworking from myriad directions, that it must emerge anew as a result of the cultural translations it undergoes. What moves me politically, and that for which I want to make room, is the moment in which a subject—a person, a collective—asserts a right or entitlement to a livable life when no such prior authorization exists, when no clearly enabling convention is in place.

One might hesitate and say, but there are fascists who invoke rights for which there are no prior entitlements. It cannot be a good thing to invoke rights or entitlements to what one considers a "livable life" if that very life is based on racism or misogyny or violence or exclusion. And I would, of course, agree with the latter. For example, prior to the overthrow of apartheid, some black South Africans arrived at the polling booths, ready to vote. There was at that time no prior authorization for their vote. They simply arrived. They performatively invoked the right to vote even when there was no prior authorization, no enabling convention in place. On the other hand, we might say that Hitler also invoked rights to a certain kind of life for which there was no constitutional or legal precedent, local or international. But there is a distinction between these two invocations, and it is crucial to my argument.

In both of these cases, the subjects in question invoked rights to which they were not entitled by existing law, though in both cases "existing law" had international and local versions that were not fully compatible with one another. Those who opposed apartheid were not restricted to existing convention (although they were, clearly, invoking and citing international convention against local convention in this case). The emergence of fascism in Germany, as well as the subsequent emergence of constitutional government in postwar Germany, was also not limited to existing convention. So both of those political phenomena involved innovation. But that does not answer the question: which action is right to pursue, which innovation has value, and which does not? The norms that we would consult to answer this question cannot themselves be derived from resignification. They have to be derived from a radical democratic theory and practice; thus, resignification has to be contextualized in that way. One must make substantive decisions about what will be a less violent future, what will be a more inclusive population, what will help to fulfill, in substantive terms, the claims of universality and justice that we seek to understand in their cultural specificity and social meaning. When we come to deciding right and wrong courses of action in that context, it is crucial to ask: what forms of community have been created, and through what violences and exclusions have they been created? Hitler sought to intensify the violence of exclusion; the anti-apartheid movement sought to counter the violence of racism and exclusion. That is the basis on which I would condemn the one, and condone the other. What resources must we have in order to bring into the human community those humans who have not been considered part of the recognizably human? That is the task of a radical democratic theory and practice that seeks to extend the norms that sustain viable life to previously disenfranchised communities.

So I have concluded it seems with a call to extend the norms that sustain viable life; so let me consider the relation between norms and life, since that has been crucial to my inquiry thus far. The question of life is a political one, although perhaps not exclusively political. The question of the "right to life" has affected the debates on the legalization of abortion. Feminists who are in favor of such rights have been called "anti-life," and they have responded by asking, "whose life?" And when does "life" begin? I think that if you were to canvas feminists internationally on the question of what life is or, perhaps more simply, when does life begin, you would have many different views. And that is why, considered internationally, not all women's movements are united on this question. There is the question of when "life" begins, and then the question of when "human" life begins, when the "human" begins; who knows, who is equipped or entitled to know, whose knowledge holds sway here, whose knowledge functions as power here? Feminists have argued that the life of the mother should be equally important. Thus, it is a question of one life versus another. Feminists have argued that every child should be wanted, should have a chance at a livable life, and that there are conditions for life, which must first be met. The mother must be well; there must be a good chance of feeding the child; there must be some chance of a future, a viable and enduring future, since a human life with no futurity loses its humanness and stands a chance of losing its life as well.

We see the term "life" functioning within feminism, and between feminism and its opponents, as a site of contest, an unsettled term, one whose meanings are being proliferated and debated in different ways in the context of different nation-states with different religious and philosophical conceptions of the problem. Indeed, some of my opponents may well argue that if one takes as a paramount value the "extension of norms that support viable life," it might follow, depending on your definitions, that the "unborn child" should be valued above all. This is not my view, and not my conclusion.

My argument against this conclusion has to do with the very use of "life" as if we know what it means, what it requires, what it demands. When we ask what makes a life livable, we are asking about certain normative conditions that must be fulfilled for life to become life. And so there are at least two senses of life, the one, which refers to the minimum biological form of living, and another, which intervenes at the start, which establishes minimum conditions for a livable life with regard to human life.[8] And this does not imply that we can disregard the merely living in favor of the "livable life," but that we must ask, as we asked about gender violence, what humans require in order to maintain and reproduce the conditions of their own livability. And what are our politics such that we are in whatever way possible, both conceptualizing the possibility of the livable life and arranging for its institutional support? There will always be disagreement about what this means, and those who claim that a single political direction is necessitated by virtue of this commitment will be mistaken. But this is only because to live is to live a life politically, in relation to power, in relation to others, in the act of assuming responsibility for a collective future. But to assume responsibility for a future is not to know its direction fully in advance, since the future, especially the future with and for others, requires a certain openness and unknowingness. It also implies that a certain agonism and contestation will and must be in play. They must be in play for politics to become democratic.

Democracy does not speak in unison; its tunes are dissonant, and necessarily so. It is not a predictable process; it must be undergone, as a passion must be undergone. It may also be that life itself becomes foreclosed when the right way is decided in advance, or when we impose what is right for everyone,without finding a way to enter into community and discover the "right" in the midst of cultural translation. It may be that what is "right" and what is "good" consist in staying open to the tensions that beset the most fundamental categories we require, to know unknowingness at the core of what we know, and what we need, and to recognize the sign of life—and its prospects.

Beyond the Subject with Anzaldúa and Spivak

In the United States, there were and are several different ways of questioning the foundational status of the category of the subject. To question the foundationalism of that category is not the same as doing away with the category altogether. Moreover, it is not to deny its usefulness, or even its necessity. To question the subject is to put at risk what we know, and to do it not for the thrill of the risk, but because we have already been put into question as subjects. We have already, as women, been severely doubted: do our words carry meaning? Are we capable of consent? Is our reasoning functioning like that of men? Are we part of the universal community of human kind?

Gloria Anzaldúa, in her work *Borderlands/La Frontera*, writes in both Spanish and English as well as native Indian dialects and compels her reader to read all of these languages as they attempt to read her book. She clearly crosses the border between academic and nonacademic writing, emphasizing the value of living on the border, living as the border in relation to an array of different cultural projects. She says that in order to have social transformation one must get beyond a "unitary" subject. She is in favor of social transformation, has struggled for it her whole life, has taught in the university, and has struggled in the movements. Do we say that she belongs to the group called "academic feminists"? Well, it would be ridiculous to exclude her from that group.[9] Her work is read in the academy. She sometimes teaches at the University of California. She struggles with different movements, especially for Latin American women, who suffer in the United States from lack of health care, exploitation within the labor market, and often with immigration issues as well. When she says, for instance, that she is no unitary subject, that she does not accept the binary oppositions of modernity, she is saying that she is defined by her very capacity to cross borders, as a Chicana. In other words, she is a woman who was compelled to cross the border from Mexico to the United States and for whom that border constitutes the geopolitical imaginary within which (across which) she writes her fiction. She struggles with the complex mix of cultural traditions and formations that constitute her for what she is: Chicana, Mexican, lesbian, American, academic, poor, writer, activist. Do all of these strands come together in a unified way, or does she live their incommensurability and simultaneity as the very meaning of her identity, an identity culturally staged and produced by the very complex historical circumstances of her life?

Anzaldúa asks us to consider that the source of our capacity for social transformation is to be found precisely in our capacity to mediate between worlds, to engage in cultural translation, and to undergo, through the experience of language and community, the diverse set of cultural connections that make us who we are. One could say that for her, the subject is "multiple" rather than unitary, and that would be to get the point in a way. But I think her point is more radical. She is asking us to stay at the edge of what we know, to put our own epistemological certainties into question, and through that risk and openness to another way of knowing and of living in the world to expand our capacity to imagine the human. She is asking us to be able to work in coalitions across differences that will make a more inclusive movement. What she is arguing, then, is that it is only through existing in the mode of translation, constant translation, that we stand a chance of producing a multicultural understanding of women or, indeed, of society. The unitary subject is the one who knows already what it is, who enters the conversation the same way as it exits, who fails to put its own epistemological certainties at risk in the encounter with the other, and so stays in place, guards its place, and becomes an emblem for property and territory, *refusing self-transformation, ironically, in the name of the subject.*

Gayatri Chakravorty Spivak has a similar view, although she would say, has said, that whereas Anzaldúa maintains a notion of a multiple subject, she has a notion of a fractured subject. Indeed, her view is that we cannot appreciate the oppression that women of color have experienced within the global political and economic framework of first world imperialism without realizing that "women" as a unitary category cannot hold, cannot describe, that this category must undergo crisis and expose its fractures to public discourse. She asks, time and again throughout her work, what does it mean not only to listen to the voices of the disenfranchised but also "to represent" those voices in one's work. On the one hand, it is possible to treat the disenfranchised as if they were voiceless and to appoint oneself as the voice of the disenfranchised. I think we saw this, quite problematically, when the American feminist Catharine MacKinnon announced at the Vienna Human Rights Forum several years ago that she "represented the women of Bosnia." Perhaps she thought that the women of Bosnia were voiceless, but she certainly learned otherwise when they made plain their clear public opposition to her effort to appropriate and colonize their position.

Given the history of the missionary, of colonial expansion that takes place in the name of "cultivation" and "modernity" and "progress" and "enlightenment," of "the white man's burden," feminists as well must ask whether the "representation" of the poor, the indigenous and the radically disenfranchised within the academy, is a patronizing and colonizing effort, or whether it seeks to avow the conditions of translation that make it possible, avow the power and privilege of the intellectual, avow the links in history and culture that make an encounter between poverty, for instance, and academic writing possible.

Spivak has translated the work of Mahasweta Devi, a fiction writer who is also an activist, whose work, thanks to Spivak, appears in the academy, at least the English speaking one. Devi writes as a tribal woman, for and about tribal women, but the "tribal" is precisely what becomes complex to identify in the course of her writing. Her voice arrives in the first world through a translation, a translation offered by Spivak, in which I, as reader, am asked to respond. Spivak insists that this writing, the tribal South Asian writing of Devi, cannot simply be called "tribal" or made to represent the "tribal" because in this writing there is also, and by way of the tribal, a vision of internationality at stake. In Devi's stories, women suffer in part because the land is exploited and ravished, because the traditional means of labor are systematically effaced or exploited by developers. In this sense, it is a local story. But those developers are also linked to broader currents in global capital. As Spivak puts it, "a strong connection, indeed a complicity, between the bourgeoisie of the Third World and migrants in the First cannot be ignored."[10]

If we read Devi closely, we see that she is making connections, living connections, between the tribal and the global, and that she is herself, as an author, a medium of transit between them. We should not think, however, that this transit is smooth, since it takes place via a rupture in representation itself. Devi comes to me through Spivak, which does not mean that Spivak authors her, but only that authorship is itself riven; what emerges from this translation, however, is a political vision that maintains that the possibilities of long-term global survival, of long-term radical environmental politics and nonviolence as a political practice depend *not* on a disembodied "reason" that goes under the name of universality but on elaborating the sense of the sacred. Spivak thus writes, "large-scale mind change is hardly ever possible on grounds of reason alone. In order to mobilize for non-violence, for example, one relies, however remotely, on building up a conviction of the 'sacredness' of human life" (199). Spivak also accords Devi the name of "philosopher" and offers the following advice for radical thinking and activism: "I have no doubt that we must *learn* to learn from the original ecological philosophers of the world, through the slow, attentive, mind-changing (on both sides), ethical singularity that deserves the name of 'love'—to supplement necessary collective efforts to change laws, modes of production, systems of education, and health care. This for me is the lesson of Mahasweta [Devi], activist/journalist and writer" (201).

For Spivak, the subaltern woman activist has been excluded from the parameters of the western subject and the historical trajectory of modernity. That means that for the most part, the tribal woman is a spectator to historical advance. Similarly, if we consider the traditions of Afro-Caribbean writings, we can ask as well whether these writings are inside the traditions of modernity, or whether they are, always, and in different ways, commenting on what it is to live "outside of history." So it should be clear that I think a critical relation to modernity is necessary.

We have witnessed the violence that is done in the name of the west and western values, as public skepticism in the United States and Europe has been stoked by questions such as: did Islam have its modernity? Has Islam yet achieved its modernity? From what point of view do such questions become possible, and in what framework are they sensible? Can the one who poses such questions know the conditions of his or her own asking? Without the Arabic translations of classical Greek texts, some of those texts would be lost forever. Without the libraries in Islamic cities throughout the world, the history of western values would not have been transmitted. It is telling that the preservative function of cultural translation is precisely what is forgotten here when we question whether Arabs have anything to do with modernity.

Clearly, we do not know our own modernity, the conditions of its own emergence and preservation, when any of us ask this question. Or rather, we are showing that what we call "modernity" is a form of forgetfulness and cultural erasure. Most importantly, we see the violence done in the name of preserving western values, and we have to ask whether this violence is one of the values that we seek to defend, that is, another mark of "western-ness" that we fear might be lost if we agree to live in a more culturally complex and hybrid world? Clearly, the west does not author all violence, but it does, upon suffering or anticipating injury, marshal violence to preserve its borders, real and imaginary.[11]

For those of us in the United States, there is some doubt whether there will ever be a significant public discourse outside of Left journalism and the countermedia, for instance, on the question of how a collective deals with its vulnerability to violence. Women know this question well, have known it in nearly all times, and nothing about the advent of capitalism made our exposure to violence any less clear. There is the possibility of appearing impermeable, of repudiating vulnerability itself. There is the possibility of becoming violent. But perhaps there is some other way to live in such a way that one is neither fearing death, becoming socially dead from fear of being killed, or becoming violent, and killing others, or subjecting them to live a life of social death predicated upon the fear of literal death. Perhaps this other way to live requires a world in which collective means are found to protect bodily vulnerability without precisely eradicating it. Surely, some norms will be useful for the building of such a world, but they will be norms that no one will own, norms that will have to work not through normalization or racial and ethnic assimilation, but through becoming collective sites of continuous political labor.

11. Can the "Other" of Philosophy Speak?

I write this essay as someone who was once trained in the history of philosophy, and yet I write now more often in interdisciplinary contexts in which that training, such as it was, appears only in refracted form. So for this and surely for other reasons as well what you will receive from me is not a "philosophy paper" or, indeed, a paper in philosophy, though it may be "on" philosophy but from a perspective that may or may not be recognizable as philosophical. For this I hope I will be forgiven. What I have to offer is not exactly an argument, and it is not exactly rigorous, and whether or not it conforms to standards of perspicacity that currently reign in the institution of philosophy is difficult for me to say. This may well have a certain importance, even philosophical importance, that I did not originally intend. I do not live or write or work in the institution of philosophy and have not for several years, and it has been almost as many years since I have asked myself the question: what would a philosopher make of what I have to offer?

I understand that this question is one that troubles those who work within that institution, especially doctoral candidates and junior faculty. We might pause to note that this is a perfectly reasonable worry, especially if one is trying to get a job within a department of philosophy, and needs to establish that the work one does is, indeed, properly philosophical. Philosophers in the profession must, in fact, make such judgments, and those of us outside philosophy departments hear those judgments from time to time. The judgment usually takes one of these forms: "I cannot understand this or I do not see the argument here, all very interesting . . . but certainly 'not' philosophy." These are all voiced by an authority who adjudicates what will and will not count as legitimate knowledge. These are voiced by one who seems to know, who acts with the full assurance of knowledge. It is surely impressive to be in such a situation and to be able to know, with clarity, what counts and what does not. Indeed, some might even say that it is one of the responsibilities of philosophers to make such decisions and abide by them.

Well and good, but I would like to suggest that a certain embarrassment has been introduced into this institution, into what Pierre Bourdieu has called the "ritualized institution of philosophy." That embarrassment consists of the fact that the term "philosophy" has ceased to be in control of those who would define and protect its institutional parameters. Surely, those who pay their dues to the American Philosophical Association and enter into that committee structure at various levels of power have been struck, surprised, perhaps even scandalized by the use of the word "philosophy" to designate kinds of scholarship that in no recognizable sense mirror the academic practice that they perform and which they understand as their duty and privilege to define and protect. Philosophy has, scandalously, doubled itself. It has, in Hegel's terms, found itself outside itself, has lost itself in the "Other," and wonders whether and how it might retrieve itself from the scandalous reflection of itself that it finds traveling under its own name. Philosophy, in its proper sense, if it has a proper sense, wonders whether it will ever return to itself from this scandalous appearance as the Other. It wonders, if not publicly, then surely in the hallways and bars of Hilton Hotels at every annual meeting, whether it is not besieged, expropriated, ruined by the improper use of its proper name, haunted by a spectral doubling of itself.

I don't mean to introduce myself as that spectral double, but it may be that my own essay, which is on philosophy but not of it, will seem somewhat ghostly as a result. Let me reassure you that the perspective from which I write is one that has been, from the start, at some distance from the institution of philosophy. Let me start, then, in the spirit of Edmund Husserl, who claimed that philosophy was, after all, a perpetual beginning, and refer to my own beginnings, humble and vexed as they surely were. When I was twelve, I was interviewed by a doctoral candidate in education and asked what I wanted to be when I grew up. I said that I wanted either to be a philosopher or a clown, and I understood then, I think, that much depended on whether or not I found the world worth philosophizing about, and what the price of seriousness might be. I was not sure I wanted to be a philosopher, and I confess that I have never quite overcome that doubt. Now it may be that having doubt about the value of a philosophical career is a sure sign that one should *not* be a philosopher. Indeed, if you have a student who contemplates that bleak job market and says as well that he or she is not sure of the value of a philosophical career or, put differently, of being a philosopher, then you would, as a faculty member, no doubt be very quick to direct this person to another corner of the market. If one is not absolutely sure about the value of being a philosopher, then one should surely go elsewhere. Unless, of course, we discern some *value* in not being sure about the value of becoming a philosopher, unless a resistance to its institutionalization has another kind of value, one that is not always marketable, but which nevertheless emerges, we might say, as a counterpoint to the current market values of philosophy. Could it be that not knowing for sure what should and should not be acknowledged as philosophy has itself a certain philosophical value? And is this a value we might name and discuss without it thereby becoming a new criterion by which the philosophical is rigorously demarcated from the nonphilosophical?

In what follows, I hope to show how I was introduced to philosophy in a fairly deinstitutionalized way and to show how this distance from the institutionalized life of philosophy has in some ways become a vocation for me and, indeed, for many contemporary scholars who work in the humanities on philosophical topics. I want to argue that there is a distinctive value to this situation. Much of the philosophical work that takes place outside of philosophy is free to consider the rhetorical and literary aspects of philosophical texts and to ask, specifically, what particular philosophical value is carried or enacted by those rhetorical and linguistic features. The rhetorical aspects of a philosophical text include its genre, which can be varied, the way of making the arguments that it does, and how its mode of presentation informs the argument itself, sometimes enacting that argument implicitly, sometimes enacting an argument that is quite to the contrary of what the philosophical text explicitly declares. A substantial amount of the work done in the continental philosophical tradition is done outside of philosophy departments at the current time, and it is sometimes done in especially rich and provocative ways in conjunction with literary readings. Paradoxically, philosophy has received a new life in contemporary studies of culture and the cultural study of politics, where philosophical notions both inform social and literary texts that are not, generically speaking, philosophical, but which nevertheless establish the site of cultural study as a vital one for philosophical thinking within the humanities. I hope to make this clear by narrating my own engagement with philosophy and my turn to Hegel. Toward the end of my remarks, I will discuss the place of Hegel in contemporary scholarship on the question of the struggle for recognition within the project of modernity.

My first introduction to philosophy was a radically deinstitutionalized one, autodidactic and premature. This scene might best be summed up by the picture of the young teenager hiding out from painful family dynamics in the basement of the house where her mother's college books were stored, where Spinoza's *Ethics* (the 1934 Elwes translation) was to be found. My emotions were surely rioting, and I turned to Spinoza to find out whether knowing what they were and what purpose they served would help me learn how to live them in some more manageable way. What I found in the second and third chapters of that text was rich indeed. The extrapolation of emotional states from the primary persistence of the *conatus* in human beings impressed me as the most profound, pure, and clarifying exposition of human passions. A thing endeavors to persist in its being. I suppose this signaled to me a form of vitalism that persists even in despair.

In Spinoza I found the notion that a conscious and persistent being responds to reflections of itself in emotional ways according to whether that reflection signifies a diminution or augmentation of its own possibility of future persistence and life. This being desires not only to persist in its own being but to live in a world of representations that reflect the possibility of that persistence, and finally to live in a world in which it both reflects the value of others' lives as well as its own.

In the chapter titled "On Human Bondage, or the Strength of the Emotions," Spinoza writes, "No one can desire to be blessed, to act rightly and to live rightly, without at the same time wishing to be, to act, and to live—in other words, to actually exist" (Prop. XXI, p. 206). And then again, he writes, "Desire is the essence of a man, that is, the endeavor whereby a man endeavors to persist in his own being."

I did not know at the time that this doctrine of Spinoza would prove essential for my subsequent scholarly work on Hegel, but this is the early modern precedent for Hegel's contention that desire is always the desire for recognition, and that recognition is the condition for a continuing and viable life. Spinoza's insistence that the desire for life can be found nascent in the emotions of despair led to the more dramatic Hegelian claim that "tarrying with the negative" can produce a conversion of the negative into being, that something affirmative can actually come of the experiences of individual and collective devastation even in their indisputable irreversibility.

I came upon the Spinoza at the same time that I came upon the first English publication of Kierkegaard's *Either/Or*, skirting Hegel until I arrived at college. I tried to read in Kierkegaard a written voice that was not exactly saying what it meant; in fact, this voice kept saying that what it had to say was not communicable in language. Thus, one of my first confrontations with a philosophical text posed the question of reading, and drew attention to its rhetorical structure as a text. As pseudonymous, the author was unforthcoming, never saying who it was who was speaking, nor letting me escape the difficulty of interpretation. This extraordinary stylistic feat was compounded by the fact that *Either/Or* is two books, each written in a perspective that wars with the other perspective, so whoever this author was, he surely was not one. On the contrary, the two volumes of this book stage a scene of psychic splitting that seemed, by definition, to elude exposition through direct discourse. There was no way to begin to understand this work without understanding the rhetorical and generic dimensions of Kierkegaard's writing. It was not that one must first consider the literary form and rhetorical situation of the text and then one might cull from those its philosophical truth. On the contrary, there was no way to extricate the philosophical point, a point that has to do with the insuperability of silence when it comes to matters of faith, without being brought through the language to the moment of its own foundering, where language shows its own limitation, and where this "showing" is not the same as a simple declaration of its limits. For Kierkegaard, the direct declaration of the limits of language is not to be believed; nothing less than the undoing of the declarative mode itself will do.

Kierkegaard and Spinoza were, for me, philosophy, and they were, interestingly, my mother's books, books bought and perhaps read for some undergraduate course at Vassar in the early 1950s. The third I found was Schopenhauer's *The World as Will and Representation*, and that belonged to my father. It appeared to have traveled with him to Korea where he worked on the dental staff of the army during that strange and suspended state of war. The book was given to him apparently by a lover who preceded my mother and her name was engraved on the first page, and I have no way of knowing how she came upon this book, why she gave it to my father, or what having it or reading it might have meant to him. But I assume that my father's lover took a class, or perhaps a friend of hers did, and that the institution of philosophy made the book available, and that I found it in my adolescent suffering at a time that allowed me to think of the world as having a structure and meaning that was larger than my own, that placed the problem of desire and will in a philosophical light, and exemplified a certain passionate clarity in thought.

So these books came to me, we might say, as by-products of the institution of philosophy, but in a deinstitutionalized form. Someone decided they should be translated and disseminated, and they were ordered by someone for courses that my parents took or that their intimates took, and then they were shelved, and emerged again as part of that visual horizon that graced the smoke-filled basement of the suburban home that was mine. I sat in that basement, sullen and despondent, having locked the door so that no one else could enter, having listened to enough music. And somehow I looked up through the smoke of my cigarette in that darkened and airless room and saw a title that aroused in me the desire to read, to read philosophy.

The second route by which philosophy arrived for me was the synagogue, and if the first route arose from adolescent agony, the second arose from collective Jewish ethical dilemmas. I was supposed to stop taking classes at the synagogue before high school, but I somehow decided to continue. The classes tended to focus on moral dilemmas, and questions of human responsibility, on the tension between individual decisions and collective responsibilities, and on God, whether God existed, and what use "he" might finally be, especially in light of the concentration camps. I was considered a disciplinary problem of sorts and given, as a sort of punishment, the task of taking a tutorial with the rabbi that focused on an array of Jewish philosophical writings. I found several instances of writing that reminded me of Kierkegaard's, where a certain silence informed the writing that was offered, where writing could not quite deliver or convey what it sought to communicate, but where the mark of its own foundering illuminated a reality that language could not directly represent. Thus, philosophy was not only a rhetorical problem, but it was tied in rather direct ways to questions of individual and collective suffering and what transformations were possible.

I began my institutionalized philosophical career within the context of a Jewish education, one that took the ethical dilemmas posed by the mass extermination of the Jews during World War II, including members of my own family, to set the scene for the thinking of ethicality as such. It was thus with difficulty that, upon arriving at college, I agreed to read Nietzsche, and I generally disdained him through most of my undergraduate years at Yale. A friend of mine brought me to Paul de Man's class on *Beyond Good and Evil* and I found myself at once compelled and repelled. Indeed, as I left his class for the first time, I felt myself quite literally lose a sense of groundedness. I leaned against a railing to recover some sense of balance. I proclaimed, with alarm, that he did not believe in the concept, that de Man was destroying the very presumption of philosophy, unraveling concepts unto metaphors, and stripping philosophy of its powers of consolation. I did not return to that particular class, though I occasionally listened in on others. At that time, I arrogantly decided that those who attended his seminars were not really philosophers, thereby enacting the very gesture that I am thinking about today. I resolved that they did not know the materials, that they were not asking the serious questions, and I returned to the more conservative wing of continental philosophy about 30 yards away, in Connecticut Hall, acting for the moment as if the distance that divided comparative literature from philosophy was much greater than it could possibly be. I refused and rejected de Man, but I did sometimes sit in the back of his class. The deconstructionists from that time sometimes still look at me askance: why wasn't I there in his classes? I wasn't there, but I was not too far away, and sometimes I was there without appearing to be. And sometimes I left very early on.

Moving from high school to Bennington College and then to Yale was not easy, and in some ways I never became acclimatized to the profession of philosophy. As a young person, I came upon philosophy as a way of posing the question of how to live, and took seriously the notion that reading philosophical texts and thinking philosophically might give me necessary guidance on matters of life. I was scandalized the first time I read Kierkegaard's remark that one could make out of philosophy a queer comedy if it were actually to occur to a person to act according to its teachings. How could there be this ironic and inevitable distance between knowing a thing to be true and acting in accordance with that knowledge? And then I was scandalized again when I heard the story about Max Scheler, pressed by his audience on how he could have led such an unethical life at the same time that he pursued the study of ethics, who responded by saying that the sign that points the way to Berlin does not need to go there to offer the right direction. That philosophy might be divorced from life, that life might not be fully ordered by philosophy, struck me as a perilous possibility. And it wasn't until several years later that I came to understand that philosophical conceptualization cannot fully relieve a life of its difficulty, and it was with some sadness and loss that I came to reconcile myself to this post-idealist insight.

But whether or not my belief about the relation of philosophy to life was right, it was still a belief that referred philosophy to existential and political dilemmas, and my disillusioned idealism was not as shocking finally as my entrance into the disciplinary definitions of philosophy. That happened in high school when I attended an introduction to philosophy class at Case Western Reserve University in 1977. My teacher was Ruth Macklin who is now a bioethicist at the Albert Einstein College of Medicine. She taught us Plato and Mill and an early essay on justice by John Rawls; the approach was distinctively analytic, something I did not understand or even know how to name at the time. I stumbled through that first course and then, determined, took another one with her on moral philosophy in which I read mainly British analytic thinkers from Russell and Moore through Stevenson and Phillipa Foot, interrogating the various senses of the word "good" as it is employed in ethical argument and expression. Although I triumphed finally by the end of that year, my senior year, I knew as I entered college that I might not find my version of philosophy mirrored for me in any institutional form.

After I traveled to Germany on a Fulbright to work with Hans Georg Gadamer and study German Idealism, I returned to Yale as a graduate student and began to become politically active within the university, to read books by someone named Foucault, to ask after the relation between philosophy and politics, and to inquire publicly whether something interesting and important might be made of feminist philosophy and, in particular, a philosophical approach to the question of gender. At the same time, the question of alterity became important to me in the context of continental philosophy. And I was interested in the problem of desire and recognition: under what conditions can a desire seek and find recognition for itself? This became for me an abiding question, as I moved into the area of gay and lesbian studies. This and the question of the "Other" seemed to me, as it did for Simone de Beauvoir, to be the point of departure for thinking politically about subordination and exclusion: I felt myself to occupy the term that I interrogated—as I do today in asking about the Other to philosophy—and so I turned to the modern source of the understanding of Otherness: Hegel himself.

My dissertation work on desire and recognition in Hegel's *Phenomenology of Spirit* took up some of the same issues that had preoccupied me at a much earlier age. In *The Phenomenology*, desire (paragraph 168) is essential to self-reflection, and there is no self-reflection except through the drama of reciprocal recognition. Thus the desire for recognition is one in which desire seeks its reflection in the Other. This is at once a desire that seeks to negate the alterity of the Other (it is, after all, by virtue of its structural similarity to me, in my place, threatening my unitary existence) and a desire that finds itself in the bind of requiring that very Other whom one fears to be and to be captured by; indeed, without this constituting passionate bind, there can be no recognition. One's consciousness finds that it is lost, lost in the Other, that it has come outside itself, that it finds itself as the other or, indeed, *in* the Other. Thus, recognition begins with the insight that one is lost in the other, appropriated in and by an alterity that is and is not oneself.

Recognition is motivated by the desire to find oneself reflected there, where the reflection is not a final expropriation. Indeed, consciousness seeks a retrieval of itself, a restoration to an earlier time, only to come to see that there is no return from alterity to a former self, but only a future transfiguration premised on the impossibility of any such return.

Thus, in "Lordship and Bondage," recognition is motivated by the desire for recognition, and recognition is itself a cultivated form of desire, no longer the simple consumption or negation of alterity, but the uneasy dynamic in which one seeks to find oneself in the Other only to find that that reflection is the sign of one's expropriation and self-loss.

It may be that institutionalized philosophy finds itself in this strange bind at the moment, though I know that I cannot speak from its perspective. It has before it something called "philosophy," which is emphatically "not philosophy," that does not follow the protocols of that discipline, that does not measure up to apparently transparent standards of logical rigor and clarity. I say "apparently transparent" only because I sit on several committees that review grant applications from the humanities, and the practice of clarity that many philosophers espouse and enact is one that often leaves other humanities scholars quite confused. Indeed, when standards of clarity become part of a hermetic discipline, they no longer become communicable, and what one gets as a result is, paradoxically, a noncommunicable clarity.

This institutionalized "philosophy," which is not itself, produces another paradox as well: it proliferates a second philosophy outside the boundary that philosophy itself has set, and so it seems that philosophy has unwittingly produced this spectral double of itself. Further, it may be that what is practiced as philosophy in most of the language and literature departments in this country has come to constitute the meaning of "philosophy," and so the discipline of philosophy must find itself strangely expropriated by a double. And the more it seeks to dissociate itself from this redoubled notion of itself, the more effective it is in securing the dominance of this other philosophy outside the boundary that was meant to contain it. Philosophy can no longer return to itself, for the boundary that might mark that return is precisely the condition by which philosophy is spawned outside of its institutional place.

There are, of course, more than two versions of philosophy, and here the Hegelian language no doubt forces me to restrict my characterizations to a false binary. Institutionalized philosophy has not been at one with itself for some time, if ever it was, and its life outside the borders of philosophy takes various forms. And yet, there is some way that each is haunted, if not stalked, by the other.

At the point where I started lecturing for the Department of Philosophy at Yale on feminist philosophy, I noticed a few rather disturbed figures at the back of the hall, adults pacing back and forth, listening to what I had to say and then abruptly leaving, only to return again after a week or two to repeat the same disturbed ritual. They were acting in the ways that I had acted when I tentatively attended de Man's seminars. They turned out to be political theorists who were enraged that what I was teaching took place under the rubric of philosophy. They couldn't quite come in and take a seat, but neither could they leave. They needed to know what I was saying, but they couldn't allow themselves to get close enough to hear. It was not a question of whether I was teaching bad philosophy, or not teaching philosophy well, but whether my classes were philosophy at all.

I don't propose today to answer the question of what philosophy should be, and I think that to be quite honest I no longer have definite views on this matter. This is not because I have left philosophy, but because I think that philosophy has, in a very significant way, departed from itself, become Other to itself, and found itself scandalized by the wandering of its name beyond its official confines. This became clear to me when I practiced feminist philosophy. I was appalled to learn that a few years ago graduate students at the New School for Social Research held a conference titled: "Is Feminist Philosophy Philosophy?" That was the question posed by the skeptics of feminist thought, and it was now being quoted by the young practitioners of feminism in earnest. Some may want to argue that, yes, feminist philosophy is philosophy, and proceed to show all the ways that feminist philosophy poses the most traditional of philosophical problems. But my own view is that such a question should be refused because it is the wrong question. The right question, as it were, has to do with how this redoubling of the term "philosophy" became possible such that we might find ourselves in this strange tautology in which we ask whether philosophy is philosophy. Perhaps we should simply say that philosophy, as we understand the institutional and discursive trajectory of that term, is no longer self-identical, if it ever was, and that its reduplication plagues it now as an insuperable problem.

For a while I thought I didn't have to deal with this issue because once I published on gender theory, I received many invitations from literature departments to speak, and to speak about something called "theory." It turned out that I had become something called a "theorist," and though I was glad to accept the kind invitations that came my way, I was somewhat bewildered and began trying to understand what kind of practice this enterprise called "theory" was supposed to be. Ah, yes, "the state of theory," I would say at the dinner table on such occasions, sipping my Chardonnay, and then look around anxiously to see whether there might be a kind soul there who might tell me precisely what this "theory" was supposed to be. I read literary theory and found my own work lodged on shelves under that rubric. I understood from my earlier days that there was such a practice (I thought of Wellek, Fletcher, Frye, Bloom, de Man, Iser, Felman), but it wasn't clear to me that what I was doing was "theory" and that that term could and should take the place of philosophy. At this point, it no longer bothered me that I wasn't doing philosophy, because the world of literature allowed me to read for rhetorical structure, ellipsis, metaphorical condensation, and to speculate on possible conjunctions between literary readings and political quandaries. I continued to suffer bouts of anxiety every time that word "theory" was used, and I still feel something of an uneasiness about it, even as I now know that I am part of it, that I am perhaps indissociable from that term.

I have come to see, however, that this confusion is not mine alone. It is now with some surprise that I pick up the catalogs of various publishers and see under the name "philosophy" several writers whose work is not taught in philosophy departments. This not only includes large numbers of continental philosophers and essayists, but literary theorists and scholars of art and media studies, scholars in ethnic and feminist studies. I note with some interest the number of dissertations on Hegel and Kant that emerge from the Humanities Center at Johns Hopkins or the Department of English at Cornell or German Studies at Northwestern; the number of young scholars in humanities departments who have traveled to France in the last ten years to work with Derrida, Levinas, Agamben, Balibar, Kofman, Irigaray, Cixous, or those who continue to travel to Germany to learn the tradition of German Idealism and the Frankfurt School. The most interesting work on Schelling and the Schlegels is being done by cultural and literary theorists at the moment, and the extraordinary work by a scholar like Peter Fenves on Kant and on Kierkegaard emerges from comparative literature and German studies. And some of the most philosophically important work on Foucault is produced by scholars such as Paul Rabinow, the philosopher of anthropology.

Consider the extraordinary interdisciplinary life of a figure such as Walter Benjamin, who in many ways epitomizes the excessive travels of philosophy outside the gates of its containment. One might expect to find him taught under the rubric of the "Frankfurt School" in philosophy departments that offer such courses (I would imagine there are about a dozen such departments at this point), but the difficulty of his language and his aesthetic preoccupations often lead to the excision of his work from philosophy courses and its reemergence in English, comparative literature, French, and German departments. I noted a few years ago with some interest that *New Formations*, the leftist British journal, published a volume on his work at the same time as the ostensibly postideological *Diacritics*, and now the most recent issue of *Critical Inquiry* joins the fray. Is it that his writing is not philosophical? The philosopher Jay Bernstein has argued passionately to the contrary. Or is it that philosophy appears here in a contentious and scattered form, through cultural analysis, through the consideration of material culture, or in light of failed or inverted theological structures, in language that moves from the aphoristic to the densely referential, or in the wake of Marxism, in the form of literary readings and theory. The multidisciplinary trajectory of this work makes a presumption about where one might look to find the question of the meaning of history, the referentiality of language, the broken promises of poetry and theology intrinsic to aesthetic forms, and the conditions of community and communication.

These are all clearly philosophical concerns, but they are pursued through a variety of means, forms of analysis, reading, and writing irreducible to argumentative form and which rarely follow a linear style of exposition. There are those who will say that Benjamin can become philosophical if one writes a book that transmutes his writing into that linear exposition of arguments. And there are others who claim that the very challenge to linear argumentation carries its own philosophical meaning, one that calls into question the power and appearance of reason, the forward motion of temporality. Unfortunately, most of the people willing to make the second sort of argument belong to humanities departments outside of the field of philosophy.

If one looks at the work of Luce Irigaray, for instance, we read a feminist interrogation of the problem of alterity that draws upon Hegel, Beauvoir, and Freud, but also Merleau-Ponty and Levinas, one that is profoundly immersed in the history of philosophy even as it counters its exclusion of the feminine and forces a rearticulation of its most basic terms. This work cannot be read without philosophy, for that is its text, and yet including it in the canon of the philosophy is not possible for most philosophy departments.

The question of what belongs to philosophy and what does not sometimes centers on this question of the rhetoricity of the philosophical text, whether it has any, and whether those rhetorical dimensions must or should be read as essential to the philosophical character of the text. We can see as well that certain ways of extending the philosophical tradition to touch upon questions of contemporary cultural politics and questions of political justice as they emerge in the vernacular or contemporary social movements also pave the way for an exit from institutional philosophy into a wider cultural conversation.

What do we make of the enormously influential philosophical work of Cornel West, for instance, whose utopian pragmatism and commitment to the DuBoisian vision has brought philosophical concerns to the forefront of African American politics in this country? He finds his home in a divinity school and in religion. Does it say something about the limitations of institutional philosophy that he finds no home there? In some ways, his work shows the continuing relevance of the tradition of American pragmatism for contemporary struggles for racial equality and dignity. Is it the transposition of that tradition onto the context of race relations that renders the philosophical dimension of that work impure? And if so, is there any hope left for philosophy unless it actively engages precisely such an impurity?

In a similar vein, nearly every feminist philosopher I know is no longer working in a philosophy department. When I look at the roster of the first anthologies of feminist philosophy in which I published (*Feminism as Critique, Feminism/Postmodernism*), the names were

Drucilla Cornell, Seyla Benhabib, Nancy Fraser, Linda Nicholson, Iris Marion Young, all students of scholars like Alasdair MacIntyre and Peter Caws and Jürgen Habermas. At one point or another in the last ten years, they were not primarily housed in philosophy departments; some of them remain sheltered elsewhere, as do I. We have all found auspicious homes in other disciplines: law, political science, education, comparative literature, English. And now this is true of Elizabeth Grosz as well, perhaps the most important Australian feminist philosopher of our time, who has moved through comparative literature and women's studies departments in recent years. This has been remarkably true as well of the many feminist philosophers of science who work in women's studies or science studies or education departments without an affiliation with philosophy. Some, if not many, of the most influential people in these fields are no longer grounded in philosophy as their primary or exclusive institutional home. The problem here is not simply that philosophy as practiced by these individuals remains to some extent outside the discipline of philosophy, creating once again the specter of "philosophy outside of philosophy." Awkwardly, these are the philosophical contributions that are constantly in contact with other fields and that establish the routes by which interdisciplinary travel of philosophy into the other humanities takes place. These are the philosophers who are in the conversations across disciplines, who are producing interest in philosophical work in French and German departments, in English and comparative literature, in science studies and women's studies.

Of course, philosophy has pursued interdisciplinary contacts in cognitive science and computer science, as well as in those areas of medical ethics, law, and public policy that are so essential to the field of applied ethics. But with respect to the humanities, it has been for the most part a loner, territorial, protective, increasingly hermetic. There are clearly as well exceptions to this rule, and one sees, for instance, in the work of Rorty, Cavell, Nehamas, Nussbaum, Appiah, and Braidotti, active ways of engaging with the arts, with literature, with cultural questions that form a common set of concerns across the disciplines. Moreover, I would suggest to you that none of these individuals has crossed the border into the wider conversation without paying some sort of price within his or her own discipline.

The presence of philosophy in the humanities disciplines is not simply the effect of trained philosophers having, as it were, been derailed. In some ways, the most culturally important discussions of philosophy are taking place by scholars who have always worked outside the institutional walls of philosophy. Indeed, one might say that what emerged after the days of high literary theory, what John Guillory understands to be literary formalism, was not the dissolution of theory but the movement of theory into the concrete study of culture, so that what one now confronts is the emergence of theoretical texts in the study of broader cultural and social phenomena. This is not the historicist displacement of theory; on the contrary, it is the historicizing of theory itself, which has become, we might say, the site of its new life. I've made that theory/philosophy conflation again, but consider that philosophical texts have a central place in many of the most trenchant of cultural analyses. Indeed, I would suggest that as philosophy has lost its purity, it has accordingly gained its vitality throughout the humanities.

Take the work of Paul Gilroy, a British sociologist and cultural studies practitioner, whose book *The Black Atlantic* has made a profound impact on both African American and diasporic studies in the last five years. The first ninety pages of that book are concerned with the Hegelian notion of modernity. He argues there that the exclusion of people of African descent from European modernity is not a sufficient reason to reject modernity, for the terms of modernity have been and still can be appropriated from their exclusionary Eurocentrism and made to operate in the service of a more inclusive democracy. At stake in his subtle historiography is the question of whether the conditions of reciprocal recognition by which the "human" comes into being can be extended beyond the geopolitical sphere presumed by the discourse of equality and reciprocity. And though Hegel gives us the strange scene of the lord and bondsman, a scene that vacillates between a description of serfdom and slavery, it is not until the work of W. E. B. DuBois, Orlando Patterson, and Paul Gilroy that we start to understand how the Hegelian project of reciprocal recognition might be renarrated from the history of slavery and its diasporic effects.

Gilroy argues that the perspective of slavery "requires a discrete view not just of the dynamics of power and domination in plantation societies dedicated to the pursuit of commercial profit but of such central categories of the Enlightenment project as the idea of universality, the fixity of meaning, the coherence of the subject, and, of course, the foundational ethnocentrism in which these have all tended to be anchored" (55). Less predictably, Gilroy then argues that it would be a great mistake to dismiss the project of modernity. Citing Habermas, he notes that even those who have been most radically excluded from the European project of modernity have been able to appropriate essential concepts from the theoretical arsenal of modernity to fight for their rightful inclusion in the process. "A concept of modernity worth its salt," he writes, "ought, for example, to have something to contribute to an analysis of how the particular varieties of radicalism articulated through the revolts of enslaved people made selective use of the ideologies of the western Age of Revolution and then flowed into social movements of an anti-colonial and decidedly anti-capitalist type" (44).

Gilroy takes issues with what he calls postmodern forms of skepticism that lead to a full-scale rejection of the key terms of modernity and, in his view, a paralysis of political will. But he then also takes his distance from Habermas, noting that Habermas fails to take into account the relationship between slavery and modernity. Habermas's failure, he notes, can be attributed to his preference for Kant over Hegel. Gilroy writes, "Habermas does not follow Hegel in arguing that slavery is itself a modernising force in that it leads both master and servant first to self-consciousness and then to disillusion, forcing both to confront the unhappy realisation that the true, the good, and the beautiful do not have a shared origin" (50).

Gilroy proceeds to read Frederick Douglass, for instance, as "lord and bondsman in a black idiom" and then to read the contemporary black feminist theorist, Patricia Hill Collins, as seeking to extend the Hegelian project into that of a racialized standpoint epistemology. In these and other instances, he insists that the Eurocentric discourse has been taken up usefully by those who were traditionally excluded from its terms, and that the subsequent revision carries radical consequences for the rethinking of modernity in nonethnocentric terms. Gilroy's fierce opposition to forms of black essentialism, most specifically, Afrocentrism, makes this point from another angle.

One of the most interesting philosophical consequences of Gilroy's work is that he provides a cultural and historical perspective on current debates in philosophy that threaten to displace its terms. Whereas he rejects the hyperrationalism of the Habermasian project, even as he preserves certain key features of its description of the Enlightenment project, he also rejects forms of skepticism that reduce all political positioning to rhetorical gesture. The form of cultural reading he provides attends to the rhetorical dimension of all sorts of cultural texts and labors under the aegis of a more radically democratic modernity. Thus, his position, I would suggest, is a position that is worth considering as one rehearses the debates between the defenders and detractors of the Enlightenment project.

But how often do we see job advertisements that emanate jointly from philosophy and sociology departments that seek to find someone who is versed in the philosophical and cultural problem of modernity in the context of slavery and its aftermath? Now, my example will not be compelling to most philosophers since Hegel is, in many departments throughout this country, not taught as part of any listed course; and, in some instances, he is explicitly excluded from the history of philosophy sequence. The resistances to Hegel are, of course, notorious: his language is ostensibly impenetrable, he rejects the law of noncontradiction, his speculations are unfounded and, in principle, unverifiable. So it is not within the walls of philosophy that we hear the question: according to what protocols that govern the readability of philosophy does Hegel's writing become unreadable? How is it that so many have, in fact, read him, and that he continues to inform so much contemporary scholarship? What is the argument that he offers against the law of noncontradiction, and what rhetorical form does that argument take? How are we to read that argument once we understand the rhetorical form by which it is structured? And what is the critique of verifiability that emerges in the course of his work? Because the standards that these questions seek to interrogate are *taken for granted* by those philosophers who invoke those standards in dismissing Hegel, we find the questions pursued elsewhere, in the humanities, in German and history and sociology departments, in English and comparative literature departments, and in American studies and ethnic studies.

Similarly, when was the last time you heard of a philosophy department joining with a German department in a search, looking for someone who works in German romanticism, including Kant, Hegel, Goethe, Hölderlin? Or when did you hear of a philosophy department joining with a French department to hire someone in twentieth-century

French philosophical thought? Perhaps we have seen a few instances of philosophy departments joining with African American studies or ethnic studies, but not often, and surely not often enough.

This is but one way that philosophy enters the humanities, redoubling itself there, making the very notion of philosophy strange to itself. We should, I suppose, be very thankful to live in this rich region that the institutional foreclosures of the philosophic have produced: such good company and better wine, and so many more unexpected conversations across disciplines, such extraordinary movements of thought that surpass the barriers of departmentalization, posing a vital problem for those who remain behind. The bondsman scandalizes the lord, you will remember, by looking back at him, evincing a consciousness he or she is not supposed to have had, and so showing the lord that he has become Other to himself. The lord is perhaps out of his own control, but for Hegel this self-loss is the beginning of community, and it may be that our current predicament threatens to do no more than to bring philosophy closer to its place as one strand among many in the fabric of culture.

Notes

Introduction: Acting in Concert

1. The Human Rights Campaign, situated in Washington, D.C., is the main lob-bying organization for lesbian and gay rights in the United States. It has maintained that gay marriage is the number one priority of lesbian and gay politics in the U.S. See www.hrc.org. See also the The Intersex Society of North America at www.isna.org.

2. Brandon Teena was killed on December 30, 1993, in Falls City, Nebraska after being raped and assaulted a week earlier for being transgendered. Mathew Shephard was killed (beaten and tied to a post) in Laramie Wyoming on October 12, 1998, for being a "feminine" gay man. Gwen Araujo, a transgendered woman, was found dead in the foothills of the Sierra mountains after being assaulted at a party in Newark, California, on October 2, 2002.

3. See Kate Bornstein, *Gender Outlaw.*

4. Frantz Fanon, *Black Skin, White Masks*, 8.

5. Sylvia Wynter, "Disenchanting Discourse: 'Minority' Literary Criticism and Beyond," in Abdul JanMohammed and David Lloyd, *The Nature and Context of Minority Discourse.*

6. See Sigmund Freud, "Instincts and their Vicissitudes."

7. See Maurice Merleau-Ponty, "The Body in its Sexual Being," in *The Phenomenology of Perception*, 154–73.

1. Beside Oneself: On the Limits of Sexual Autonomy

1. The Human Rights Campaign is the main lobbying organization for lesbian and gay rights in the United States. Situated in Washington, D.C. it has maintained that gay marriage is the number one priority of lesbian and gay politics in the U.S. See www.hrc.org.

2. Michel Foucault, "What is Critique?" in *The Politics of Truth*, 50. This essay is reprinted with an essay by me entitled "Critique as Virtue" in David Ingram, *The Political.*

3. "What is Critique?" 52

4. Ibid., 52–3

5. Ibid., 58.

6. Maurice Merleau-Ponty, *The Phenomenology of Perception*.

7. See *www.iglhrc.org* for more information on the mission and accomplishments of this organization.

8. See Adriana Cavarero, *Relating Narratives*, 20–29 and 87–92.

9. See Giorgio Agamben, *Homo Sacer: Sovereign Power and Bare Life*, 1–12.

2. Gender Regulations

1. See Carol Smart, ed., *Regulating Womanhood*.

2. See François Ewald, "Norms, Discipline, and the Law"; "A Concept of Social Law"; "A Power Without an Exterior"; and Charles Taylor, "To Follow a Rule . . . ."

3. See, for instance, the scholarship of Randolph Trumbach and Anne Fausto-Sterling.

4. See Luce Irigaray, *This Sex Which Is Not One*.

5. See Kate Bornstein, *Gender Outlaw*.

6. Dylan Evans, *An Introductory Dictionary of Lacanian Psychoanalysis*, 202, my emphasis.

7. See Vikki Bell, *Interrogating Incest*.

8. Juliet Mitchell, *Psychoanalysis and Feminism: A Radical Reassessment of Freudian Psychoanalysis*, 370.

9. On the relation between the social and the symbolic in relation to kinship, see Michel Tort, "Artifices du père"; "Le Différend" (on file with author); and *Le nom du père incertain*.

10. Jean Laplanche and J.-B. Pontalis write under the entry, "Symbolique" in *Vocabulaire de la Psychanalyse* (439–441) that, "The idea of a symbolic order structuring intersubjective reality was introduced into the social sciences most notably by Claude Lévi-Strauss who based his view on the model of structural linguistics taught by F. de Saussure. The thesis of *The Course in General Linguistics* (1955) is that the linguistic signified does not take place internally to the signifier; it produces a signification because it is part of a system of signifieds characterized by differential oppositions."

They cite Lévi-Strauss: "[E]very culture may be considered as an ensemble of symbolic systems which in the first instance regulate the taking place of language, matrimonial rules, economic relations, art, science, and religion." Lacan makes use of the symbolic, according to the above authors, to establish that the unconscious is structured like a language and to show the linguistic fecundity of the unconscious. The second use to which it is put, however, bears more directly on our inquiry: "to show that the human subject is inserted in a pre-established order which is itself a symbolic nature, in the sense that Lévi-Strauss describes."

In this view, one which is distinguished from other Lacanian expositeurs such as Malcolm Bowie, the sense of the symbolic as a preestablished order is in tension with Lacan's insistence that there be an arbitrary relation between signifier and signified. On some occasions, it seems, Lacan uses "the symbolic" to describe the discrete elements that function as signifieds, but other times he appears to use the term to describe the more general register in which those elements function. In addition, Laplanche and Pontalis argue that Lacan uses "the symbolic" "to designate the law (*la loi*) that founds this order." The foreclosure of the "symbolic father" or "the Name of the Father" is such an instance of founding that is irreducible to an imaginary or real father, and which enforces the law. Of course, no one inhabits the position of the symbolic father, and it is that "absence" that paradoxically gives the law its power.

Although Malcolm Bowie maintains that the symbolic is governed by the symbolic law (*Lacan*, 108), he also maintains that "the symbolic is often spoken of admiringly . . . it is the realm of movement rather than fixity, and of heterogeneity rather than similarity . . . the Symbolic is inveterately social and intersubjective . . . ." (92–93). The question remains, though, whether the "social" sphere designated by the symbolic is not governed by "the Name of the Father," a symbolic place for the father, which, if lost (the place, and not the father), leads to psychosis. What presocial constraint is thereby imposed upon the intelligibility of any social order?

11. See note 2 above.

12. It is perhaps useful to note the important historical work that Georges Canguilhem has done on the history of the normal in *The Normal and the Pathological*. Ewald remarks that the etymology links the norm with mathematical and architectural prototypes. Norm is, literally, the Latin word for a T-square; and *normalis* means perpendicular. Vitruvius used the word to indicate the instrument used to draw right angles, and Cicero used the term to describe the architectural regularity of nature; nature, he claimed, is the norm of the law.

13. See Cheryl Chase, "Hermaphrodites with Attitude."

14. This is a position put forward by Gayle Rubin in her essay "Thinking Sex: Towards a Political Economy of 'Sex'," which is elaborated upon by Eve Kosofsky Sedgwick in *Epistemology of the Closet*.

15. I believe my own work runs in this direction and is closely allied with that of Biddy Martin, Joan W. Scott, Katherine Franke, and the emergence of transgender theory.

16. See Jacqui Alexander's important essay, "Redrafting Morality."

3. Doing Justice to Someone: Sex Reassignment and Allegories of Transsexuality

1. This essay appeared in a slightly different version in *GLQ*. I have incorporated suggestions made by Vernon Rosario and Cheryl Chase and am grateful to them both for the important perspectives they provided.

2. See John Colapinto, "The True Story of John/Joan," and *As Nature Made Him*; Suzanne Kessler, *Lessons from the Intersexed*; John Money and Richard Green, *Transsexualism and Sex Reassignment*; Natalie Angier, "Sexual Identity Not Pliable After All, Report Says"; Milton Diamond and Keith Sigmundsen, "Sex Reassignment at Birth." See also the videotape "Redefining Sex" published by the Intersex Society of North America (http://www.isna.org/) for important perspectives on the ethics of sex reassignment. For an excellent overview of this controversy, see Anne Fausto-Sterling, *Sexing the Body*, 45–77.

3. *But I'm a Cheerleader!* (1999, Universal Studios, Director, Jamie Babbit).

4. Undiagnosing Gender

1. See Richard Friedman, "Gender Identity." This viewpoint, however, maintains that the diagnosis describes a pathology; so in his view the diagnosis should not be kept only for instrumental reasons.

2. See Robert Pela, "Boys in the Dollhouse, Girls with Toy Trucks," 55. He argues that "the American Psychiatric Association has invented mental health categories—specifically, gender identity disorder—that are meant to pathologize homosexuality and to continue the abuse of gay youth." He also cites Shannon Minter to the effect that "GID is just another way to express homophobia." See also, Katherine Rachlin, "Transgender Individuals' Experiences of Psychotherapy." She notes that "individuals may resent having to spend time and money for psychological services in order to obtain medical services. They may also have fears concerning speaking to someone who holds the power to grant or deny them access to the interventions they feel they need. This fear and resentment creates a dynamic between therapist and client which may have an impact on the process and outcome of treatment." See also A. Vitale, "The Therapist Versus the Client."

3. It is important to note that transsexualism was first diagnosed in 1980 in *DSM-III*. In *DSM-IV*, published in 1994, transsexualism does not appear but is treated instead under the rubric of gender identity disorder (GID). The diagnosis as it currently stands requires that applicants for transsexual surgery and treatment show "evidence of a strong and persistent cross-gender identification, which is the desire to be, or the insistence that one is the other sex." Moreover, "this cross-identification must not be merely the desire for any perceived cultural advantages of being the other sex," but "there must also be evidence of persistent discomfort about one's assigned sex or a sense of inappropriateness in the gender role of that sex." The diagnosis "is not made if the individual has a concurrent physical intersex condition," and "to make the diagnosis, there must be evidence of clinically significant distress or impairment in social, occupational, or other important areas of functioning."

For more information, see http://trans-health.com, Issue 4, Volume 1, spring 2002; see the same journal on-line, Issue 1, Volume 1, summer 2001 for an important critique titled "The Medicalization of Transgenderism," a five-part work by Whitney Barnes (published in successive issues), which very thoroughly and trenchantly covers a range of pertinent issues related to the diagnostic category.

4. For a discussion on changes of nomenclature within the history of the diagnosis to differentiate those who are considered to be "gender dysphoric" from the start from those who arrive at this conclusion in time, see "The Development of a Nomenclature," in the Harry Benjamin International Gender Dysphoria Association's *The Standards of Care for Gender Identity Disorders*.

5. Richard Isay, "Remove Gender Identity Disorder from *DSM*."

6. See, for example, Friedman, "Gender Identity."

7. Jacob Hale, "Medical Ethics and Transsexuality." See also Richard Green: "Should sex change be available on demand?" That was hardly the issue in 1969, as the nearly insurmountable hurdle then was professionally endorsed reassignment. If gender patients can procure surgeons who do not require psychiatric or psychological referral, research should address outcome for those who are professionally referred versus the self-referred. Then an ethical issue could be, if success is less (or failure greater) among the self-referred, should otherwise competent adults have that autonomy of self-determination? Later he asks, "should there be a limit to a person's autonomy over body?" ("Transsexualism and Sex Reassignment, 1966–1999"). Green also applauds the fact that some transgendered individuals have now entered into the profession, so that they are the ones making the diagnosis and also electing the medical benefits.

8. For a discussion of the etiology of the diagnosis that covers recent psychological findings about postoperative regret and sex reassignment surgery's "success rates," see P. T. Cohen-Kettenis and L. J. G. Gooren, "Transsexualism: A Review of Etiology, Diagnosis, and Treatment."

9. Richard Green, "Transsexualism and Sex Reassignment."

10. See, for example, George A. Rekers, "Gender Identity Disorder," in *The Journal of Family and Culture*, later revised for the *Journal of Human Sexuality*, a Christian Leadership Ministries publication in 1996, www.leaderu.com\jhs\rekers. He proposes conversion to Christianity as a "cure" for transsexuality and provides a psychological guide for those "afflicted" with and "repentant" of this condition in his *Handbook of Child and Adolescent Sexual Problems*.

11. Rekers, "Gender Identity Disorder."

12. Ibid.

13. See Walter O. Bockting and Charles Cesaretti, "Spirituality, Transgender Identity, and Coming Out," and Walter O. Bockting, "From Construction to Context: Gender Through the Eyes of the Transgendered."

14. For an impressive account of how that clinic works to provide a supportive environment for its clients at the same time that it seeks to secure benefits through use of the diagnosis, see Walter O. Bockting, "The Assessment and Treatment of Gender Dysphoria." For another impressive account, see Richard Green, "Transsexualism and Sex Reassignment, 1966–1999."

15. Richard Green in the lecture cited above suggests that the paradox is not between autonomy and subjection but is implied by the fact that transsexualism is self-diagnosed. He writes, "it is difficult to find another psychiatric or medical condition in which the patient makes the diagnosis and prescribes the treatment."

5. Is Kinship Always Already Heterosexual?

1. See David Schneider's *A Critique of the Study of Kinship* for an important analysis of how the approach to studying kinship has been fatally undermined by inappropriate assumptions about heterosexuality and the marriage bond in ethnographic description. See also his *American Kinship*. For a continuation of this critique, especially as it relates to the presuppositional status of the marriage bond in kinship systems, see John Borneman's critical review of contemporary feminist kinship studies in "Until Death Do Us Part: Marriage/Death in Anthropological Discourse."

2. Carol Stack, *All Our Kin: Strategies for Survival in a Black Community*.

3. Saidiya Hartman, in conversation, spring 2001.

4. Kath Weston, *Families We Choose: Lesbians, Gays, Kinship*.

5. In a blurb for Cai Hua's *A Society Without Fathers or Husbands: The Na of China*, Lévi-Strauss notes that Cai Hua has discovered a society in which the role of fathers "is denied or belittled," thus suggesting that the role may still be at work, but disavowed by those who practice kinship there. This interpretation effectively diminishes the challenge of the text, which argues that kinship is organized along nonpaternal lines.

6. I gather that recent domestic partnership state legislation in California as well as in other states does offer explicit provisions for parental rights shared equally by the couple, though many proposals explicitly seek to separate the recognition of domestic partnerships from rights of joint parenting.

7. See Michael Warner, *The Trouble with Normal: Sex, Politics, and the Ethics of Queer Life.*

8. For a full consideration of Franco-American cultural relations with respect to gender and sexuality, see the following work by Eric Fassin, which, in many ways, has formed a background for my own views on this subject: "'Good Cop, Bad Cop': The American Model and Countermodel in French Liberal Rhetoric since the 1980s," unpublished essay; "'Good to Think': The American Reference in French Discourses of Immigration and Ethnicity," "Le savant, l'expert et le politique: la famille des sociologues," "Same Sex, Different Politics: Comparing and Contrasting 'Gay Marriage' Debates in France and the United States," unpublished essay; "The Purloined Gender: American Feminism in a French Mirror."

9. In 1999 the state of California passed the Knight initiative, which mandated that marriage be a contract entered into exclusively by a man and a woman. It passed with 63% of the vote.

10. See Sylviane Agacinski, "Questions autour de la filiation," interview with Eric Lamien and Michel Feher; for an excellent rejoinder, see Michel Feher, "Quelques Réflexions sur 'Politiques des Sexes'."

11. In Germany, the Eingetragene Lebenspartnerschaft legislation (August 2001) stipulates clearly that the two individuals entering into this alliance are gay, and that the law obligates them to a long-term relationship of support and responsibility. The law thus obligates two individuals, understood to be gay, to an approximation of the social form of marriage. Whereas the French PACS simply extends the right of contract to any two individuals who wish to enter it in order to share or bequeath property, the German arrangement requires, in neo-Hegelian fashion, that the contract reflect a specific way of life, recognizably marital, worthy of recognition by the state. See Deutscher Bundestag, 14. Wahlperiode, *Drücksache 14/5627*, March 20, 2001.

12. Lauren Berlant, *The Queen of America Goes to Washington City: Essays on Sex and Citizenship*, argues persuasively that "in the reactionary culture of imperiled privilege, the nation's value is figured not on behalf of an actually existing and laboring adult, but of a future American, both incipient and pre-historical: especially invested with this hope are the American fetus and the American child," 5.

13. Fassin, "Same Sex."

14. Agacinski, "Questions," 23.

15. Agacinski, "Contre l'effacement des sexes."

16. This argument forms the center of my objection to Lacanian arguments against the viability of same-sex marriages and in favor of heteronormative family in *Antigone's Claim: Kinship Between Life and Death* (see especially 68–73). For a further argument against Jacques-Alain Miller's and other forms of Lacanian skepticism toward same-sex unions, see my "Competing Universalities," 136–81.

17. Michael Warner, "Beyond Gay Marriage," in *Left Legalism/Left Critique.*

18. Jacqueline Rose, *States of Fantasy*, 8–9.

19. Ibid., 10.

20. See Catherine Raissiguier, "Bodily Metaphors, Material Exclusions: The Sexual and Racial Politics of Domestic Partnerships in France," in *Violence and the Body.*

21. The Lévi-Straussian position has been even more adamantly defended by Françoise Héritier. For her most vehement opposition to the PACS, see "Entretien," where she remarks that "aucune societé n'admet de parenté homosexuelle." See also *Masculin/Féminin: La pensée de la différence*, and *L'Exercise de la parenté.*

22. Agacinski, "Questions," 23; my translation.

23. Lévi-Strauss made his own contribution to the debate, making clear that his views of over fifty years ago do not coincide with his present positions and suggesting that the theory of exchange does not have to be tied to sexual difference but must always have a formal and specific expression. See Claude Lévi-Strauss, *The Elementary Structures of Kinship*, and "Postface," *L'Homme*.

24. See Judith Butler, "Competing Universalities."

25. Schneider, *Critique*, and *American Kinship*; Sylvia Yanagisako, *Gender and Kinship: Essays Toward a United Analysis*; Sarah Franklin and Susan McKinnon, "New Directions in Kinship Study: A Core Concept Revisited," *Current Anthropology*, and Sarah Franklin and Susan McKinnon, eds. *Relative Values: Reconfiguring Kinship Studies*; Marilyn Strathern, *The Gender of the Gift: Problems with Women and Problems with Society in Melanesia*, and *Reproducing the Future: Anthropology, Kinship, and the New Reproductive Technologies*; Clifford Geertz, *The Interpretation of Cultures*.

26. Judith Stacey, *In the Name of the Family: Rethinking Family Values in the Postmodern Age*, and *Brave New Families: Stories of Domestic Upheaval in Late 20th Century America*; Stack, *All Our Kin*; and Weston, *Families We Choose*.

27. See Lévi-Strauss's discussion of "ethnocentrism" in *Race et histoire*, 19–26.

28. See Pierre Clastres, *Society Against the State: Essays in Political Anthropology* and *Archeology of Violence*. For a consideration of anthropological approaches to kinship after Lévi-Strauss, see Janet Carsten and Stephen Hugh-Jones, eds., *About the House: Lévi-Strauss and Beyond*.

29. Franklin and McKinnon, "New Directions," 17. See also Franklin and McKinnon, *Relative Values*.

30. Fassin, "Same Sex."

31. Franklin and McKinnon, "New Directions," 14.

32. Ken Corbett, "Nontraditional Family Romance: Normative Logic, Family Reverie, and the Primal Scene," unpublished essay, June 11, 2000.

33. Hanna Segal, "Hanna Segal interviewed by Jacqueline Rose." Segal remarks, "An analyst, worth his salt, knows about illness from the *inside*. He doesn't feel 'you are a pervert unlike me'—he feels: 'I know a bit how you came to that point, I've been there, am partly there still.' If he believes in God, he would say: 'there but for the grace of God go I.'" And then a bit later: "You could argue rightly that heterosexual relationships can be as, or more, perverse or narcissistic. But it's not inbuilt in them. Heterosexuality can be more or less narcissistic, it can be very disturbed or not so. In homosexuality it's inbuilt," 212.

34. Agacinski, "Questions," 24.

6. Longing for Recognition

1. Axel Honneth, *The Struggle for Recognition*; Jürgen Habermas, *The Theory of Communicative Action*.

2. Jessica Benjamin, Afterword to "Recognition and Destruction."

3. Benjamin, *The Shadow of the Other*, 2–3.

4. Benjamin, "How was It for You?" 28.

5. Judith Butler, "The Lesbian Phallus" in *Bodies that Matter*, 57–92.

6. Benjamin, *Like Subjects, Love Objects*, 54.

7. I offer the etymological version of ecstacy as *ek-stasis* to point out, as Heidegger has done, the original meaning of the term as it implies a standing outside of oneself.

8. Jean Hyppolite, *Genesis and Structure of Hegel's "Phenomenology of Spirit,"* 66.

9. Jacques Lacan, *Écrits: A Selection,* 58.

10. For a critique and radicalization of the Lacanian formulation of this account of the mimetic formation of desire, see See Mikkel Borsch-Jacobsen, *The Freudian Subject.*

11. On jealousy and the displacement of homosexual desire, see Freud's "Certain Neurotic Mechanisms in Jealousy, Paranoia and Homosexuality."

12. *Boys Don't Cry* (1999, Twentieth Century Fox, Director, Kimberley Peirce).

13. Benjamin, *The Shadow of the Other,* 37.

14. Ibid., 83–84.

15. See Drucilla Cornell, *The Philosophy of the Limit;* Emanuel Levinas, *Otherwise Than Being.*

16. See Jean Laplanche, *Essays on Otherness.*

8. Bodily Confessions

1. This paper was given at the American Psychological Division Meetings, (Division 39) in San Francisco in the Spring of 1999.

2. A different approach to the relation between the body and language in psychoanalysis can be found in Shoshana Felman's *The Scandal of the Speaking Body.* See my preface to that volume for further reflections on this issue.

3. See Michel Foucault, "The Subject and Power," 208–28.

4. For a fuller account of Foucault's early views on confession and repression, see the first chapter of Michel Foucault, *History of Sexuality,* vol. 1.

5. Foucault, *Religion and Culture.*

6. For a very interesting treatment of what confession "does," see Peter Brooks, *Troubling Confessions: Speaking Guilt in Law and Literature.*

7. All citations from Sophocles' *Antigone* are from the Loeb Library Series. Parts of the following discussion are recapitulations of an argument I make in *Antigone's Claim: Kinship Between Life and Death.*

8. Sigmund Freud, "Criminals from a Sense of Guilt," 332.

9. The End of Sexual Difference?

1. Luce Irigaray, *An Ethics of Sexual Difference.* 3.

2. For a fuller discussion of Gilroy's work on this topic, see the chapter "Can the 'Other' of Philosophy Speak?" in this volume.

3. I thank Homi Bhabha for this point.

4. Part of this discussion appeared in "Implicit Censorship and Discursive Agency" in *Excitable Speech.*

5. "La Chiesa si prepara alle guerre dei 5 sessi," *La Repubblica,* May 20, 1995, 11.

6. "IPS: Honduras Feminists and Church," Interpress Service, May 25, 1995.

7. *Report of the Informal Contact Group on Gender*, July 7, 1995.

8. See Anne Fausto-Sterling, "The Five Sexes: Why Male and Female are Not Enough."

9. Biddy Martin, "Extraordinary Homosexuals and the Fear of Being Ordinary."

10. Henry Abelove, Michele Aina Barale, and David M. Halperin, eds. *The Lesbian and Gay Studies Reader*.

11. Whereas feminism is key, and the concepts of "women" and even "womanist" are often central, the emphasis—in the work of Kimberle Crenshaw and Mari Matsuda—is more pervasively on the epistemological vantage point of those who are structurally subordinated and marginalized through their racialization. The emphasis on the social character of this subordination is nearly absolute, except for some psychoanalytic efforts to delineate the psychic workings of racialization in which becoming "raced" is figured as an interpellation with resounding psychic effects. The salience of this last issue is found, I think, in what has become a veritable return to Fanon within contemporary race studies. And there, the emphasis is not social in a restricted sense but on a socially articulated imaginary, the specular production of racial expectations, and the visual estrangement and visceral workings of the racial signifier. Where sexual difference enters, as it does, say, in the work of Rey Chow, it is to underscore the misogynistic consequences of Fanon's resistance to racism. More recently, Homi Bhabha has suggested in a Fanonian analysis of the white male subject that the splitting is to be understood in terms of a homophobic paranoia, one in which the threatened and externalizing relation to alterity forecloses homosexuality and sexual difference at once.

12. This was a suggestion made to me by Debra Keates's entry on sexual difference in *Psychoanalysis and Feminism: A Critical Dictionary*.

13. I have laid out elsewhere my theoretical difficulties with this way of understanding the disjunctive relation between gender and sexuality. I will try, though, to recapitulate briefly the terms of that argument. Whereas "sex and sexuality" have been offered as the proper objects for lesbian and gay studies, and this has been analogized with feminism whose proper object is described as "gender," it seems to me that most feminist research would not fall under this description. Feminism for the most part insists that sexual and gender relations, although in no sense causally linked, are structurally linked in important ways. A characterization of feminism as an exclusive focus on gender also misrepresents the recent history of feminism in several significant ways.

The history of radical feminist sexual politics is erased from the proper characterization of feminism:

1. the various antiracist positions developed within feminist frameworks for which gender is no more central than race, or for which gender is no more central than colonial positionality, or class—the entire movements of socialist feminism, postcolonial feminism, Third World feminism—are no longer part of the central or proper focus of feminism;

2. MacKinnon's account of gender and sexuality is taken as paradigmatic of feminism. She understands gender as the categories "women" and "men" that reflect and institutionalize positions of subordination and domination within

a social arrangement of sexuality that is always presumed to be heterosexual; the strong feminist opposition to her work is excluded from the offered definition of feminism;

3. gender is reduced to sex (and sometimes to sex-assignment), rendered fixed or "given," and the contested history of the sex/gender distinction is displaced from view;
4. the normative operation of gender in the regulation of sexuality is denied;
5. the sexual contestation of gender norms is no longer an "object" of analysis within either frame, as it crosses and confounds the very domains of analysis that this methodological claim for lesbian and gay studies strains to keep apart.

The significant differences between feminists who make use of the category of gender, and those who remain within the framework of sexual difference, are erased from view by this intellectually untenable formulation of what feminism is. How would we understand the history of black feminism, the pervasive intersectionality of its project, were we to accept what is a white feminist concern with gender as an isolable category of analysis?

14. InterPress Third World News Agency, www.ips.org.

15. Primo Levi's text, *Moments of Reprieve*, repeatedly stages the difference between survival and affirmation.

16. See Judith Halberstam, *Female Masculinities*.

10. The Question of Social Transformation

1. See Hollibaugh Moraga, "What We're Rolling Around in Bed With."
2. See also my interview with Rosi Braidotti, "Feminism By Any Other Name."
3. See Barbara Duden, *The Woman Beneath the Skin*.
4. I consider this issue at greater length in *Antigone's Claim: Kinship Between Life and Death*.
5. Michel Foucault, "What is Critique?" 50.
6. Part of this discussion of Foucault is parallel with my essay, "Virtue as Critique."
7. *Paris Is Burning* (1990, Fox Lorber, Director, Jennie Livingston).
8. See Giorgio Agamben on "bare life," in *Homo Sacer*.
9. For an excellent discussion of Anzaldúa's critical discourse, see Norma Alarcon, "Anzaldúa's Frontera: Inscribing Gynetics."
10. See the Introduction to Mahasweta Devi, *Imaginary Maps: Three Stories*, 198.
11. For a fuller discussion of these topics, see my *Precarious Life: Powers of Violence, and Mourning*.

Works Cited

Abelove, Henry, Michele Aina Barale, and David Halperin, eds. *The Lesbian and Gay Studies Reader*. New York: Routledge, 1993.

Agacinski, Sylviane. "Contre l'effacement des sexes." *Le Monde*, February 6, 1999.

———. "Questions autour de la filiation." Interview with Eric Lamien and Michel Feher. *Ex æquo* (July 1998): 22–24.

Agamben, Giorgio. *Homo Sacer: Sovereign Power and Bare Life*. Translated by Daniel Heller-Roazen. Stanford: Stanford University Press, 1998.

Alarcon, Norma. "Anzaldua's Frontera: Inscribing Gynetics." In *Chicana Feminisms: A Critical Reader*, edited by Gabrielle Arredonda, Aida Hurtada, Norman Kahn, Olga Najera-Ramirez, and Patricia Zavella. Durham, N.C.: Duke University Press, 2003.

Alexander, Jacqui. "Redrafting Morality: The Postcolonial State and the Sexual Offences Bill of Trinidad and Tobago." In *Third World Women and the Politics of Feminism*, edited by Mohanty, Russo, and Torres. Bloomington: Indiana University Press, 1991.

American Psychiatric Association. *Diagnostic and Statistical Manual of Mental Disorders DSM-IV*. Rev. ed. Washington, D.C.: American Psychiatric Association, 2000.

Angier, Natalie. "Sexual Identity Not Pliable After All, Report Says." *New York Times*. May 3, 2000, section C.

Anzaldúa, Gloria. *Borderlands/La Frontera: The New Mestiza*. San Francisco: Spinsters/Aunt Lute, 1967.

Barnes, Whitney. "The Medicalization of Transgenderism." http://trans-health.com Serialized in five parts beginning issue 1, vol. 1 (Summer 2001).

Bell, Vikki. *Interrogating Incest: Feminism, Foucault, and the Law*. London: Routledge, 1993.

Benhabib, Seyla, and Drucilla Cornell, eds. *Feminism as Critique: Essays on the Politics of Gender in Late-Capitalist Societies*. Minneapolis: University of Minnesota Press, 1987.

Benhabib, Seyla, Judith Butler, Drucilla Cornell, and Nancy Fraser. *Feminist Contentions: A Philosophical Exchange*. New York: Routledge, 1997.

Benjamin, Jessica. *The Shadow of the Other: Intersubjectivity and Gender in Psychoanalysis*. New York: Routledge, 1998.

———. "'How Was It For You?' How Intersubjective is Sex?" Division 39 Keynote Address, American Psychological Association. Boston, April 1998. On file with author.

Benjamin, Jessica. *Like Subjects, Love Objects: Essays on Recognition and Sexual Difference.* New Haven: Yale University Press, 1995.

———. Afterword to "Recognition and Destruction: An Outline of Intersubjectivity." In *Relational Psychoanalysis: The Emergence of a Tradition.* Hillsdale, N.J.: Analytic Press, 1999.

———. *Bonds of Love.* New York: Random House, 1988.

Berlant, Lauren. *The Queen of America Goes to Washington City: Essays on Sex and Citizenship.* Durham, N.C.: Duke University Press, 1997.

Bersani, Leo. *Homos.* Cambridge: Harvard University Press, 1995.

Bockting, Walter O. "From Construction to Context: Gender through the Eyes of the Transgendered." *Siecus Report* (October/November 1999).

———. "The Assessment and Treatment of Gender Dysphoria." *Direction in Clinical and Counseling Psychology,* 7, lesson 11 (1997): 11.3–11.22.

Bockting, Walter O. and Charles Cesaretti. "Spirituality, Transgender Identity, and Coming Out." *Journal of Sex Education and Therapy,.* 26, no. 4 (2001): 291–300.

Borneman, John. "Until Death Do Us Part: Marriage/Death in Anthropological Discourse." *American Ethnologist* 23, no. 2 (May 1996): 215–235.

Bornstein, Kate. *Gender Outlaw.* New York: Routledge, 1994.

Borsch-Jacobsen, Mikkel. *The Freudian Subject.* Stanford: Stanford University Press, 1988.

Bowie, Malcolm. *Lacan.* Cambridge, MA: Harvard University Press, 1991.

Braidotti, Rosi. "Feminism By Any Other Name." Interview with Judith Butler. *differences.* Special issue on "More Gender Trouble: Feminism Meets Queer Theory." (Winter 1995).

———. *Metamorphoses: Towards a Materialist Theory of Becoming.* Cambridge, England: Polity Press, 2002.

———. *Nomadic Subjects.* New York: Columbia University Press, 1994.

———. *Patterns of Dissonance.* Cambridge, England: Polity Press, 1991.

Brooks, Peter. *Troubling Confessions: Speaking Guilt in Law and Literature.* Chicago: University of Chicago Press, 2000.

Butler, Judith. *Bodies That Matter: On the Discursive Limits of "Sex."* New York: Routledge, 1998.

———. *Excitable Speech: A Politics of the Performative.* New York: Routledge, 1997.

———. *Gender Trouble: Feminism and the Subversion of Identity.* New York: Routledge, 1990.

———. *Antigone's Claim: Kinship Between Life and Death.* The Wellek Library Lectures. New York: Columbia University Press, 2000.

———. "Virtue as Critique." In *The Political,* edited by David Ingram. Oxford: Basil Blackwell, 2002.

———. *Precarious Life: Powers of Violence, and Mourning.* New York: Verso, 2004.

Butler, Judith, Ernesto Laclau, and Slavoj Žižek, eds. *Contingency, Hegemony, and Universality: Contemporary Dialogues on the Left.* London: Verso, 2000.

Canguilhem, Georges. *The Normal and the Pathological*. Translated by Carolyn Fawcett and Robert S. Cohen. New York: Zone Books, 1989.

Caruth, Cathy, ed. *Trauma: Explorations in Memory*. Baltimore: Johns Hopkins University Press, 1995.

———. *Unclaimed Experience: Trauma, Narrative, and History*. Baltimore: Johns Hopkins University Press, 1996.

Carsten, Janet and Stephen Hugh-Jones, eds. *About the House: Lévi-Strauss and Beyond*. Cambridge, England: Cambridge University Press, 1995.

Cavarero, Adriana. *Relating Narratives: Storytelling and Selfhood*. Translated by Paul A. Kottman. London: Routledge, 2000.

Chase, Cheryl. "Hermaphrodites with Attitude: Mapping the Emergence of Intersex Political Activism." *GLQ: A Journal of Gay and Lesbian Studies* 4, no. 2 (Spring, 1998): 189–211.

Clastres, Pierre. *Archeology of Violence*. Translated by Jeanine Herman. New York: Semiotext(e), 1994.

———. *Society Against the State: Essays in Political Anthropology*. Translated by Robert Hurley. New York: Zone Books, 1987.

Cohen-Kettenis, P. T. and L. J. G. Gooren. "Transsexualism: A Review of Etiology, Diagnosis, and Treatment." *Journal of Psychosomatic Research* 46, no. 4 (April 1999). 315–33.

Colapinto, John. "The True Story of John/Joan." *Rolling Stone*. December 11, 1999: 55ff.

———. *As Nature Made Him: The Boy Who Was Raised as a Girl*. New York: Harper-Collins, 2000.

Corbett, Ken. "Nontraditional Family Romance: Normative Logic, Family Reverie, and the Primal Scene." *Psychoanalytic Quarterly* 70, no. 3 (2001): 599–624.

Cornell, Drucilla. *The Philosophy of the Limit*. New York: Routledge, 1992.

Devi, Mahasweta. *Imaginary Maps: Three Stories by Mahasweta Devi*. Translated by Gayatri Chakravorty Spivak. New York: Routledge, 1995.

Diamond, Milton and Keith Sigmundsen. "Sex Reassignment at Birth: A Long-Term Review and Clinical Implications." *Archives of Pediatrics and Adolescent Medicine* 151 (March 1997): 298–304.

Duden, Barbara. *The Woman Beneath the Skin: A Doctor's Patients in Eighteenth–Century Germany*. Translated by Thomas Dunlap. Cambridge, MA: Harvard University Press, 1991.

Evans, Dylan. *An Introductory Dictionary of Lacanian Psychoanalysis*. London: Routledge, 1996.

Ewald, François. "A Concept of Social Law." In *Dilemmas of Law in the Welfare State*, edited by Gunter Teubner. Berlin: Walter de Gruyter, 1986.

———. "A Power Without an Exterior." *Michel Foucault, Philosopher*, edited by Timothy Armstrong. New York: Routledge, 1992.

———. "Norms, Discipline, and the Law." *Law and the Order of Culture*, edited by Robert Post. Berkeley: University of California Press, 1991.

Fanon, Frantz. *Black Skin, White Masks*. New York: Grove, 1967.

Fassin, Eric. "'Good Cop, Bad Cop': The American Model and Countermodel in French Liberal Rhetoric since the 1980s." Unpublished essay.

———. "'Good to Think': The American Reference in French Discourses of Immigration and Ethnicity." *Multicultural Questions*, edited by Christian Joppke and Steven Lukes. London: Oxford University Press, 1999.

———. "Le savant, l'expert et le politique: la famille des sociologues." *Genèses* 32 (October 1998): 156–169.

———. "Same Sex, Different Politics: Comparing and Contrasting 'Gay Marriage' Debates in France and the United States." Unpublished essay.

———. "The Purloined Gender: American Feminism in a French Mirror." *French Historical Studies* 22, no. 1 (Winter 1999): 113–139.

Fausto-Sterling, Anne. "The Five Sexes: Why Male and Female Are Not Enough." *The Sciences* 33, no. 2 (July 2000): 20–25.

Fausto-Sterling, Anne. *Sexing the Body: Gender Politics and the Construction of Sexuality*. New York: Basic, 2000.

Feher, Michel. "Quelques Réflexions sur 'Politiques des Sexes'." *Ex Æquo* (July 1998): 24–25.

Felman, Shoshana. *The Scandal of the Speaking Body*. Stanford: Stanford University Press, 2002.

Felman, Shoshana and Dori Laub. *Testimony: Crisis of Witnessing in Literature, Psychoanalysis and History*. New York: Routledge, 1992.

Foucault, Michel. "What is Critique?" *The Politics of Truth*, edited by Sylvère Lotringer and Lysa Hochroth. New York: Semiotext(e), 1997. Originally a lecture given at the French Society of Philosophy on May 27, 1978, subsequently published in *Bulletin de la Société française de la philosophie* 84, no. 2 (1990).

———. *The History of Sexuality, Volume One*. Translated by Robert Hurley. New York: Pantheon, 1978.

———. *Religion and Culture*, edited by Jeremy Carrette. New York: Routledge, 1999.

———. "The Subject and Power." In *Michel Foucault: Beyond Structuralism and Hermeneutics*, edited by Hubert Dreyfus and Paul Rabinow. Chicago: University of Chicago Press, 1982.

Franke, Katherine. "What's Wrong with Sexual Harrassment?" *Stanford Law Review* 49 (1997): 691–772.

Franklin, Sarah and Susan McKinnon, eds. *Relative Values: Reconfiguring Kinship Studies*. Durham, N.C.: Duke University Press, 2002.

Franklin, Sarah and Susan McKinnon. "New Directions in Kinship Study: A Core Concept Revisited." *Current Anthropology* 41, no. 2 (April 2000): 275–279.

Freud, Sigmund. "Certain Neurotic Mechanisms in Jealousy, Paranoia, and Homosexuality." *The Standard Edition of the Complete Works of Sigmund Freud*. Vol. 18, edited by James Strachey et al. London: The Hogarth Press and the Institute of Psychoanalysis, 1953–1974.

———. "Criminals from a Sense of Guilt." *Standard Edition*. Vol. 14.

———. "The Ego and the Id." *Standard Edition*. Vol. 19.

———. "Instincts and their Vicissitudes." *Standard Edition*. Vol. 14.

———. "The Three Essays on the Theory of Sexuality." *Standard Edition*. Vol. 7.

Friedman, Richard. "Gender Identity." *Psychiatric News*, January 1, 1998.

Geertz, Clifford. *The Interpretation of Cultures*. New York: Basic Books, 1973.

Gilroy, Paul. *The Black Atlantic: Modernity and Double-Consciousness*, Cambridge, MA: Harvard University Press, 1993.

Green, Richard. "Transsexualism and Sex Reassignment, 1966–1999." Presidential Address to the Harry Benjamin International Gender Dysphoria Association. http://www.symposion.com/ijt/greenpresidential/green00.htm/

Habermas, Jürgen. *Between Facts and Norms: Contributions to a Discourse Theory of Law and Democracy.* Translated by William Rehg. Cambridge, MA: MIT Press, 1996.

Habermas, Jürgen. *The Theory of Communicative Action.* 2 vols. Translated by Thomas McCarthy. Boston: Beacon Press, 1982.

Hale, Jacob. "Medical Ethics and Transsexuality." Paper presented at the 2001 Harry Benjamin International Symposium on Gender Dysphoria.

Harry Benjamin International Gender Dysphoria Association. *The Standards of Care for Gender Identity Disorders,* 6th ed. Düsseldorf: Symposion Publishing, 2001.

Hegel, G. W. F. *The Phenomenology of Spirit.* Translated by A. V. Miller. Oxford: Oxford University Press, 1977.

Héritier, Françoise. "Entretien." *La Croix* (November 1998).

———. *L'Exercice de la parenté.* Paris: Gallimard, 1981.

———. *Masculin/Féminin: La pensée de la difference.* Paris: Odile Jacob, 1996.

Honneth, Axel. *The Struggle for Recognition: The Moral Grammar of Social Conflicts.* Translated by Joel Anderson. Cambridge, MA: Polity Press, 1995.

Hua, Cai. *A Society without Fathers or Husbands: The Na of China.* Translated by Asti Hustvedt. New York: Zone Books, 2001.

Hyppolite, Jean. *Genesis and Structure of Hegel's "Phenomenology of Spirit."* Translated by Samuel Cherniaak and John Heckman. Evanston, IL: Northwestern University Press, 1974.

Irigaray, Luce. *An Ethics of Sexual Difference.* Translated by Carolyn Burke and Gillian C. Gill. Ithaca, N.Y.: Cornell University Press, 1993.

———. *This Sex Which is Not One.* Translated by Catherine Porter with Carolyn Burke. Ithaca, N.Y.: Cornell University Press, 1985.

Isay, Richard. "Remove Gender Identity Disorder from DSM." *Psychiatric News.* November 21, 1997.

Kessler, Suzanne. *Lessons from the Intersexed.* New Brunswick, N.J.: Rutgers University Press, 2000.

Kierkegaard, Søren. *Either/Or.* Translated by Walter Lowrie. Princeton, N.J.: Princeton University Press, 1971.

Lacan, Jacques. *Écrits: A Selection.* Translated by Alan Sheridan. New York: Norton, 1977.

Laplanche, Jean. *Essays On Otherness.* Translated by John Fletcher. London: Routledge, 1999.

Laplanche, Jean and J.-B. Pontalis. *The Vocabulary of Psycho-analysis.* Translated by Donald Nicholson-Smith. New York: Norton, 1973.

Levi, Primo. *Moments of Reprieve.* New York: Penguin, 1995.

Levinas, Emmanuel. *Otherwise Than Being.* Translated by Alphonso Lingis. Boston: M. Nijhoff, 1981.

Lévi-Strauss, Claude. *The Elementary Structures of Kinship.* Rev. ed. edited by Rodney Needham. Translated by James Harle Bell, John Richard von Sturmer, and Rodney Needham. Boston: Beacon, 1969.

———. "Ethnocentrism." *Race et histoire.* Paris: Denoël, 1987.

————. "Postface." *L'Homme* 154–55. Special issue on "Question de Parenté." (April-September 2000): 713–20.

————. Claude. *Race et histoire*. Paris: Denoël, 1987.

Macheray, Pierre. "Towards a Natural History of Norms." In *Michel Foucault, Philosopher*, edited by Timothy Armstrong. New York: Routledge, 1992.

MacKinnon, Catharine. *Feminism Unmodified: Discourses on Life and Law*. New York: Routledge, 1987.

Martin, Biddy. "Extraordinary Homosexuals and the Fear of Being Ordinary." *differences* 6, nos. 2–3 (1994): 100–125.

Merleau-Ponty, Maurice. "The Body in its Sexual Being." In *The Phenomenology of Perception*. Translated by Colin Smith. New York: Routledge, 1967.

Mitchell, Juliet. *Psychoanalysis and Feminism: A Radical Reassessment of Freudian Psychoanalysis*. New York: Vintage, 1975.

Mitscherlich, Alexander and Margarete Mitscherlich. *The Inability to Mourn*. Translated by Beverley Placzek. New York: Grove Press, 1975.

Money, John and Richard Green. *Transsexualism and Sex Reassignment*. Baltimore: Johns Hopkins University Press, 1969.

Moraga, Hollibaugh. "What We're Rolling Around in Bed With." *Pleasure and Danger: Exploring Female Sexuality*, edited by Carole S. Vance. Boston: Routledge & Kegan Paul, 1984.

Nicholson, Linda, ed. *Feminism/Postmodernism*. New York: Routledge, 1990.

Pela, Robert. "Boys in the Dollhouse, Girls with Toy Trucks." *The Advocate*. November 11, 1997.

Poovey, Mary. *Making a Social Body: British Cultural Formation, 1830–1964*. Chicago: University of Chicago Press, 1995.

Rachlin, Katherine. "Transgender Individuals' Experience of Psychotherapy." Paper presented at the American Psychological Association meeting in August 2001. http://www.symposion.com/ijt/ijtvoo6noo1_03.htm/

Raissiguier, Catherine. "Bodily Metaphors, Material Exclusions: The Sexual and Racial Politics of Domestic Partnerships in France." In *Violence and the Body*, edited by Arturo Aldama. New York: New York University Press, 2002.

Rekers, George A. "Gender Identity Disorder." *The Journal of Family and Culture* 2, no. 3, 1986. Revised for the *Journal of Human Sexuality* 1, no. 1 (1996): 11–20.

————. *Handbook of Child and Adolescent Sexual Problems*. Lexington: Simon and Schuster, 1995.

Riley, Denise. *"Am I That Name?" Feminism and the Category of "Women" in History*. Minneapolis: University of Minnesota Press, 1998.

Rose, Jacqueline. *States of Fantasy*. Oxford: Clarendon Press, 1996.

Rubin, Gayle. "Thinking Sex: Towards a Political Economy of 'Sex'." In *Pleasure and Danger*, edited by Carol Vance. New York: Routledge, 1984.

Schneider, David. *A Critique of the Study of Kinship*. Ann Arbor: University of Michigan Press, 1984.

————. *American Kinship: A Cultural Account*, 2nd ed. Chicago: University of Chicago Press, 1980.

Schopenhauer, Arthur. *The World as Will and Representation*. Translated by E. F. J. Payne. 2 vols. New York: Dover, 1969.

Sedgwick, Eve Kosofsky. *Between Men: English Literature and Male Homosocial Desire*. New York: Columbia University Press, 1985.

———. *Epistemology of the Closet.* Berkeley: University of California Press, 1991.

Segal, Hanna. "Hanna Segal interviewed by Jacqueline Rose." *Women: A Cultural Review* 1, no. 2 (November 1990): 198–214.

Smart, Carol, ed. *Regulating Womanhood: Historical Essays on Marriage, Motherhood and Sexuality.* London: Routledge, 1992.

Sophocles. *Antigone.* Loeb Library Series. Cambridge, MA: Harvard University Press, 1994.

Spinoza, Benedict de. *On the Improvement of Understanding, The Ethics, Correspondence.* Translated by R. H. M. Elwes, New York: Dover, 1955.

Stacey, Judith. *In the Name of the Family: Rethinking Family Values in the Postmodern Age.* Boston: Beacon Press, 1996.

Stacey, Judith. *Brave New Families: Stories of Domestic Upheaval in Late 20th Century America.* Berkeley: University of California Press, 1998.

Stack, Carol. *All Our Kin: Strategies for Survival in a Black Community.* New York: Harper and Row, 1974.

Strathern, Marilyn. *The Gender of the Gift: Problems with Women and Problems with Society in Melanesia.* Berkeley: University of California Press, 1988.

Strathern, Marilyn. *Reproducing the Future: Anthropology, Kinship, and the New Reproductive Technologies.* New York: Routledge, 1992.

Taylor, Charles. "To Follow a Rule . . . ." *Bourdieu: Critical Perspectives*, edited by Craig Calhoun et al. Chicago: University of Chicago Press, 1993.

Tort, Michel. "Artifices du père." *Dialogue–recherches cliniques et sociologiques sur le couple et la famille.* No. 104 (1989): 46–59.

———. *Le nom du père incertain: la question de la transmission du nom et la psychanalyse.* Work carried out at the request of the Service of Coordination of Research, Ministry of Justice, Paris, 1983.

Vitale, A. "The Therapist Versus the Client: How the Conflict Started and Some Thoughts on How to Resolve It." In *Transgender Care*, edited by G. Israel and E. Tarver. Philadelphia: Temple University Press, 1997.

Warner, Michael. *The Trouble with Normal: Sex, Politics, and the Ethics of Queer Life.* New York: Free Press, 1999.

———. "Beyond Gay Marriage." *Left Legalism/Left Critique*, edited by Wendy Brown and Janet Halley. Durham, N.C.: Duke University Press, 2002.

Weston, Kath. *Families We Choose: Lesbians, Gays, Kinship.* New York: Columbia University Press, 1991.

Wright, Elizabeth, ed. *Feminism and Psychoanalysis: A Critical Dictionary.* Oxford: Blackwell, 1992.

Wynter, Sylvia. "Disenchanting Discourse: 'Minority' Literary Criticism and Beyond." In *The Nature and Context of Minority Discourse*, edited by Abdul JanMohammed and David Lloyd. Oxford: Oxford University Press, 1997.

Yanagisako, Sylvia. *Gender and Kinship: Essays Toward a United Analysis.* Stanford: Stanford University Press, 1987.

Index

THE HOUSE OF TOMORROW

THE HOUSE OF

Jean Thompson

TOMORROW

HARPER & ROW, PUBLISHERS
NEW YORK, EVANSTON, AND LONDON

The lines on page ix are reprinted from *The Prophet* by Kahlil Gibran with the permission of the publisher, Alfred A. Knopf, Inc. Copyright 1923 by Kahlil Gibran; Renewal Copyright 1951 by Administrators C.T.A. of Kahlil Gibran Estate and Mary G. Gibran.

LIBRARY OF CONGRESS CATALOG CARD NUMBER: 67–10491

F-T

*This book is gratefully dedicated
to the staff and volunteers
at the Booth Memorial Hospitals.*

THE HOUSE OF TOMORROW

Your children are not your children.
They are the sons and daughters of Life's longing for itself.
They come through you but not from you,
And though they are with you yet they belong not to you.

You may give them your love but not your thoughts,
For they have their own thoughts.
You may house their bodies but not their souls,
For their souls dwell in the house of tomorrow,
    which you cannot visit, not even in your dreams.
                        —From THE PROPHET, by Kahlil Gibran

PROLOGUE

For nearly six years I kept a large brown manila envelope hidden in the bottom of a chest in our storeroom. Sealed in that envelope was my diary for the better part of a year—nearly a hundred typewritten pages and eight notebooks scribbled full. Those notebooks were just small enough to fit into the pocket of my maternity smock.

I spent much of that year in a Salvation Army home for unwed mothers. We were sixty girls with a common secret, hiding from the outside world and from each other. We were called by our first names and only the first letter of our last name, and for most of us even that name was fictional.

That is one reason why I've waited this long before taking out that old diary. Our secret was a shared one, and even though I want to relate mine, I have no right to tell about theirs, so I have changed names, dates, places and physical descriptions. I've also added some background information and cut out some of the repetitions, but basically this is a true account of what I saw and felt.

Much of what I wrote then, particularly in the first part of the diary, seems sadly unrealistic and childish now. But that was the way I was, and I have tried not to change any of it.

July, 1966

SEPTEMBER

Wednesday the 2nd

A blank page in my typewriter—I can tell you, can't I? You won't give me away?

I've been holed up in this messy apartment for nearly two weeks, not even answering the phone. I'm sick and tired of my own voice talking to the walls and the books. Arguing with myself, getting nothing settled. How did I ever get into this mess? How do I get out of it? I can't even think straight anymore. I've slept more these last two weeks than ever before in my whole life. But then I wake up and there it is again, that horrible fact. I don't even want to put it on paper. I keep pretending it'll go away if I don't admit it.

I am pregnant. I am going to have a baby! So, there it is! Now talk back to me, you innocent piece of paper, just staring back at me with my own silly words.

I think I'm going crazy. I've got to talk to someone. But who? The gang is out of town still; they won't be back till school starts, and maybe that's just as well. If they know, next thing someone would tell Gene and I'd really be in trouble.

Maybe I ought to call Dorothy. I think she can keep a secret even if her husband is my teacher.

3

Later

God, I'm so confused. I wanted to call Dorothy, and hearing her voice was so wonderful it made me cry and she could hear I was upset. She sounded real worried and said, "Where have you been? I've called you several times and no one answered." I tried to make my voice carefree and light and I know I failed completely.

"What's wrong?" Dorothy sounded serious and very motherly all of a sudden, and I could have kicked myself for whimpering like a kid and telling her I wanted to see her.

"I'll be right over," she said, and hung up before I could say anything else. And now what do I do? Why did I have to use that stupid phone? Why did I think I could trust Dorothy? She'll write my mother, I'm sure. If she tells her husband I'll be kicked out of school. Not that it matters right now—I won't be able to attend this semester anyway.

But I've got to keep this from Mother and Dad. That's been just about the only stroke of luck in this whole mess, the fact that Daddy is spending this year as an exchange professor in Europe. And my kid brother is in the Air Force in Germany. I'll have to tell them before they come back in June, of course, but by then I'll be straightened out. The baby will be here and we'll be on our own someplace.

Right now I've got to keep it from them. I can just see Mother flying home from France all upset. I can't stand thinking of all those tears and all that "shame, shame" business. And Daddy— it would just kill him. Not that he's approved of anything else I've done for the last several years.

This whole thing is a perfect nightmare. Sometimes I manage to think it's all a giant hoax. But of course I know it's true. It's crazy but I've known it ever since that last night with Gene. Deep down I've known it all along. Of course, I played the role. I counted the days in spite of myself, and went to a doctor just so I could tell Gene I had and give him that lie about everything being O.K.

How confused can a person get? I went for long vigorous walks and swam straight out into the ocean to the point of exhaustion, and like a coward thought maybe a big wave would come or a strong current, taking it all out of my hands. . . . I even prayed for a miracle.

"Dear God, please let me start menstruating and I promise never to take another chance." Deep inside, something in me knew that prayer wasn't meant to be answered.

What if I were dead? I've thought about it and I'll probably think about it again. So simple, no more problems. Nobody embarrassed and ashamed. Just keep on swimming. That's how I would do it, I've thought. But I don't have the guts to do it. I keep thinking that even if I might have the right to choose death for myself I don't have the right to kill the baby. That would be murder. Just like abortion would be murder. That's already another human being there inside me, even if he or she is only about the size of a walnut.

Thursday the 3rd

I'm installed in Dorothy's house. She said I needed to get away from that dreary apartment. I can stay here for maybe two weeks till it's time to enroll for the fall semester. By then I'll have to have some concrete plans.

Of course, I told Dorothy everything yesterday when she came to my apartment. I think I had expected her to act shocked or hurt or something like that, but instead she listened very calmly and sipped my lousy coffee. I could see from the way her blue eyes looked all over me and my room that she was disgusted with the overflowing ash trays and the stacks of books and clothes everywhere and the dust so thick every surface looked gray. She'd never been there before and I should have cleaned it up before she came. It really didn't look too bad when I had candles burning in the Chianti bottles on the orange crate I used for a table, with the light flickering over the olive-green walls and the Toulouse-Lautrec print of the absinthe drinkers. But yesterday afternoon, with the light filtering in through those dark burlap curtains, the place looked pretty bad. I could see how someone could be alarmed.

It's funny, but I had never noticed just how much Dorothy looks like my mother. Yesterday it really hit me. They both have large blue eyes, a strong face with broad cheekbones, and light-brown hair graying and piled in a soft bun. They are just about the same age. But inside they are as different as day and night. Dorothy is always an easy listener, her house open to anyone who wants to drop by for a piece of homemade pie and a chat. You know she really cares because she'll let you know immediately if she doesn't agree with what you think and do. Not condemning or judging, just letting you know her opinion, take it or leave it.

My mother is a professor's wife too, but I don't think I've had a real talk with her for years. She is sweet and all that, but she's as narrow-minded as they come. You know—made up her mind years ago and nothing can change it. She talks a lot about helping people in need—like her church work and her charities. But I don't think she ever stopped to think that what people really want is just plain understanding.

Dorothy asked me what I was going to do with myself.

"Go away, I guess," I said, "to a big city in the Midwest, maybe. Stay there till the baby gets here and we can live there together." I could hear how silly it sounded, but I got mad when

Dorothy smiled and said very calmly, "All alone?" I felt she was deliberately forcing me into a corner.

"And why not?" I said. "I've had child-guidance courses and worked as a camp counselor." My voice was rising. "Lots of girls get married and have babies while they're still in high school—"

"They get married," Dorothy interrupted me. I got her point. But of course it's too late to think about that now. My situation isn't perfect—she doesn't need to remind me of that—but I think I'm more qualified to raise my child than some mothers I've seen. It wasn't much use trying to explain that to Dorothy. Besides, I had an awful headache and for some reason I couldn't keep from crying.

Dorothy let me cry and then she looked straight at me and said, "Do what is right for the two of you—but get out of this hole you've dug for yourself." She meant my messy apartment. "Get out and start functioning. Meet people, get a job, get ready for the baby. . . ."

I let her talk. It sounded so easy to hear her say those things, and one day I'll have to think about them. But not just yet. I'm just too tired now.

Dorothy's youngest son is in the Navy. I'm staying in his room.

Friday the 4th

I've been reading a book on the psychology of the unwed mother. I saw it downstairs and couldn't help picking it up. I guess the house of a sociology professor isn't the best place to stay, if you are expecting a baby out of wedlock and would rather not think about it for a while.

The book says such a pregnancy is rarely accidental. It says the girl nearly always wants it—as a crutch, an excuse to fail, a way to rebel or demonstrate against her parents or other authority she felt she never could free herself from. Also the book says unmarried mothers often keep their babies because they are emotionally immature and unable to face reality. Phew, that sounds like a mouthful, as if the author is really looking for symptoms where there aren't any. That couldn't possibly be all true. Of course, maybe in some instances, but not in mine.

I admit I was beginning to make bad grades. But I couldn't have been afraid of failure; my teachers always said I should apply myself, that I am bright enough. I made straight A's through my sophomore year but then school started making less and less sense to me. In a crazy way I'm almost glad I don't have to go to school next year. I need time to think things over, decide what I want to do with myself. I thought I might want to go on and get a master's degree in psychology and be a social worker. Do something about this mixed-up world we live in. The way things are—one little war after another, riots, and millions starving in India and all that—I don't know what there is to believe in.

I guess Daddy thinks I'm a lost cause. He thinks I don't know who I am and where I'm going. Hell, he's the one who wanted me to come here instead of going to college at home. For once we agreed. I don't think I could stand going to school where he is teaching. What used to bug me was the way his students used to tell me how lucky I was to have a father like him. They said he gave such good advice and always had time to listen. Little did they know that whenever we got into a discussion about anything at home it always turned into an argument. Daddy thought I ought to be number one in my class, and he thought I brought absolute disgrace on the family because my friends grew beards and wore sandals and played guitars.

I think my friends are real people. They are natural because they don't want to pretend. Why should we wear make-up to look like something we're not? Why should we cut our hair when obviously it keeps growing? So Daddy called it childish and immature—a failure to cope with realities. Because we don't make believe and pretend all is well with a phony world.

By that standard, maybe I am a failure the way the book says. But I didn't want to get pregnant. If I did, I'd be happy as a lark now, wouldn't I, instead of in a mess?

Sunday the 6th

I've written Mother and Dad about not going back to school. They probably knew it was coming. I said I needed time to think about my future and I didn't want to waste their money on tuition when I'm not serious about studying. That part is true. I've hated taking their money. They've still got my kid brother Tommy to put through school when he gets out of the Air Force two years from now. He'll be well worth their efforts, I'm sure. He's always been the conscientious one in the family.

Next week is registration for the fall semester. I've got to do something. Dorothy came in and turned off my favorite TV program this morning just to ask me what I've done about the baby. Of course she knows darn well I haven't done a thing. She called me a selfish, self-centered brat and for the first time I saw her really angry.

"You sit around brooding about yourself!" she said. "Can't you see how cruel and selfish it is to bring that baby into the world without getting a name for it?"

I've never seen her carry on like that. I didn't know what to say, but I knew she would calm down and be sorry about the whole thing later. I know she doesn't really think those things about me. She knows I've been nauseated, and after all I'm in a

pretty horrible situation. She can't really expect me to settle everything this soon. I told her I was sick to my stomach, and for a
second I thought she was going to slap me.

"So what!" she said. "I've had four kids and been a lot sicker
than you. Quit thinking about yourself and go get a job!"

Late evening

Dorothy came to my room and said she was sorry.

"You know I want to help you," she said, "but you've got to
help yourself first. The baby is your responsibility." She sat on
my bed and waited for me to say something, but I didn't.

"Why don't you want to marry Gene?" I had been waiting for
that question.

"You know he's married," I said, and I was a little angry with
her for even asking.

"You told me he was separated from his wife when you met
him," she said. "You said he wanted to marry you. I'm sure he
would if he knew you were going to have his baby. Why don't you
tell him?"

"I just don't want to mess up his life," I said, and she shrugged
her shoulders.

"O.K. That's your business," she said. "But if you're going to
keep that baby you should marry someone else—at least on paper.
Gene will probably put two and two together if he ever hears
about you living alone with a child." That caught me off guard
and my voice wasn't too steady when I told her I was going far
away and I'd never see Gene again.

"There is a right thing for you to do," Dorothy said softly,
"and I know you can find it. But you must start looking."

Yes, I've got to start looking. But where? To Gene? No, I've already burned that bridge and it wouldn't be fair to go back. I think he loves his wife. I know he loves his kids. He'd never be happy with me, or I with him, for that matter. That trite thing about living in two different worlds really holds for us.

He looked so miserable and lost the night he came into the café near Harvard Square where our gang usually hangs out. Gene looked completely misplaced there in his business suit, but he sat down at a table by himself and after a while the kids stopped staring at him.

Joe Farrari was reading some of his own poetry and I was making background music on the guitar. I felt the stranger looking at me. All the way through our program those eyes were there and I really felt them all through me. As if we were really close, as if we understood each other. When we were through I just went down and sat next to him. I knew he wanted to talk to me. It's funny, but when I look back on it I see that we were never again as close as we were those first couple of hours when we were talking with our eyes.

Gene walked me home that night, leaving his Cadillac parked near the square and carrying my guitar over his shoulder. He held my hand and we walked along the river talking. That is, he did most of the talking. I can be a good listener when I want to.

Now I think it didn't matter too much *who* listened—he just needed to tell someone. Someone different. So he talked about working his way through high school and going into the Navy, and then starting in business for himself and getting married when he was only eighteen, his wife working all the time. Now they own a chain of laundromats and a ski lodge in New Hampshire, and have a maid and go to Europe on their vacations.

"I've got all the things I worked so hard for," he said, squeezing my hand. "And now I'm thirty-five years old, and suddenly it isn't important anymore. Nothing is. I've got to find myself again."

In my apartment that night we made love by candlelight and listened to Joan Baez. Gene had never even heard of her!

That was in April, and the ice was breaking on the river. All spring we did things together. Gene was like a big kid on his first vacation. He'd never fed the ducks in the pond or gone on picnics in the woods or sat on the grass listening to symphony under the stars. He hadn't browsed through secondhand book-stores or little art galleries or sailed paper boats on the river. I thought I was really falling in love this time.

Till one day in June he proposed to me, and I didn't get happy. I got scared. He said he loved me because I was so honest and didn't pretend to be anything but myself. But I wasn't honest enough to tell him I didn't want to live in a nice house with two cars in the garage and four kids. I wasn't even honest enough to admit it to myself at first, but I was becoming more miserable all the time. I talked about his kids a lot because I knew how much he loved them, and getting a divorce to marry me would mean giving up those kids. I could tell he thought about that, too.

When I thought maybe I was pregnant I got frantic at the idea of being trapped with him for the rest of my life, so one day I told him he ought to go back to his wife and make a try of it— for the kids' sake, I said.

"How can you be this unselfish?" he said, and I felt like a heel and only smiled. When he kissed me good-bye I felt like someone who's just been saved from the rip tide.

So there it is. I've written it down now. I'm scared to death of marriage, marriage to anyone. I'm scared of being trapped. But I am going to have a baby and I'm going to keep it. I'm not scared of motherhood.

But what about a name for my baby? Dorothy is right about that. Married on paper—to whom? I can't just stop someone on the street and say, look, I want to raise a baby without a father, how about lending me your name?

Maybe if I tell someone I can trust, someone who can keep a secret, maybe he'd offer to help me? David might be the type, and I've known him all my life. Maybe I'll write him tomorrow.

Monday the 7th

I told Dorothy I've written to David in New York. She said fine.

"But remember at first you wanted to raise the baby without any legalities. Maybe you're still out to demonstrate."

"I've got nothing to demonstrate about," I said.

"Then maybe you want an excuse to drop out of school."

Dorothy makes me mad sometimes. She has the nerve to ask the strangest questions. She knows I can't hold down a job, raise a child and complete an education all at once. Why does she remind me of the things I've got to give up? My first duty is to that child. Any mother would agree.

Wednesday the 9th

David must have answered right away. The letter got here this morning, airmail. It scared me a little. I didn't want to open it. As long as it was sealed I could hold it in my hand and imagine what was in it.

I understand how you wanted to keep the child at first. I am confident you already see how impossible that solution is. You don't have what the baby needs most, a home and a husband.

Also, you are an intelligent girl with a fine career ahead of you.

This experience, I am sure, will give you maturity and greater under-standing. You will have much to offer when all this is over. . . .

This may not be the kind of letter you're looking for but, frankly, I'm a little stunned by the whole thing. You should have known better.

I'm glad you found me worthy of your confidence. Let me know what you will do; I am curious. Will you go to a home for unwed mothers? Use agency or independent adoption? After all, this is one experience I can't have at first hand.

Let me hear from you as time goes on. Good luck. I'm sure you can make the best of this.

Love,
David

I felt numb. There was a spot of grease on the stove and I cleaned it. The water was boiling and I made some tea. I counted the five cigarettes in my package and lit one of them. I kept my mind blank and only thought that I ought to iron a skirt to wear tomorrow. And then the tears came. Bits of thoughts whirled in my mind, and crying made sense. Dorothy walked in and I handed her the letter. She read it and said, "Well?"

"I feel so cheap," I cried. "I didn't mean it that way."

"I don't think he thought so either," said Dorothy. She had brought me a tiny white pill.

"This'll make you sleep awhile," she said. Thank God I didn't dream.

Thursday the 10th

This morning I almost fainted in the shower and Dorothy sent me back to bed.

"You'd better be careful. We don't want you to have a mis-carriage, do we?" For some reason that sounded so funny to both

of us that we laughed till our stomachs ached and we had tears
in our eyes.

Friday the 11th

Registration starts at school Monday, and Joe Farrari called me
today. He just got back in town and tried to reach me at the
apartment. The landlady told him where I was.

"How about making the town tonight?" he asked, and I had a
wild thought. Maybe Joe can help. He's always been a regular
guy.

"O.K.," I said. "Let's go to the beach."

I don't want to think about David's letter or marriage or having
a baby. Maybe I can just have fun tonight—the way I did in the
old days. And maybe I can tell Joe what's going and maybe he'll
say something. . . .

Late Friday

It was cool on the beach and dark clouds hid the stars. The
sound of the surf drowned our voices and the crests of the waves
gleamed frosty blue. I love the sea but breaking waves are scary
sometimes; they keep coming and you can't stop them.

"What's the matter?" Joe said. He slid his arm around my
shoulders. "You were never this quiet. Got troubles?" I felt my
throat tighten and I was getting hot, the way I do when I know
I'm going to say something I shouldn't.

"I'm pregnant." I watched his face fall into a stupid stare.

"I'll be damned," Joe said and slid back behind the wheel.
"Who's the guy—are you getting married?"

"No," I said. "And you never met him."

"I'll be damned," he said again and slid back toward me. The surf was breaking in my ears.

"I'm sorry, kid," Joe said, and then he kissed me. He'd never kissed me before and I closed my eyes, holding onto him, wanting to be near someone and not alone. And then his hands tore at my clothes and he was breathing heavily. Something had gone wrong. I tried pushing him away but he didn't even notice. Then I bit him hard and he sat up with a jerk.

"What the hell!"

"Please," I said. "Don't be like that."

"Geeze," he said. "You don't have to put on a show for an old friend."

"We're not that kind of friends." I wanted to cry.

"You're pregnant, aren't you?" He was angry. "So what's the worry, let's have some fun." I wanted to die, but he was right. I was getting what I deserved.

"Take me home!" I was sobbing, and I guess Joe hadn't expected me to cry. He didn't say a word all the way home.

Saturday the 12th

I'm leaving. There is no use putting it off anymore. I told Dorothy this morning and she said, "That stinker," meaning Joe. But his reaction was a normal one, and I can expect others to react the same way. I can't run around throwing my problem into other people's laps and expect them to solve it for me. I've got to face it alone.

"I'll go to California," I said. I've read that California is one of the states where they don't mention the mother's marital status on the birth certificate. Dorothy looked at me, and I remembered that afternoon in my apartment. It seemed ages ago and it's only a couple of weeks. I wanted to cry on her shoulder again.

"What will you do there?" she said.

"Find a home for unwed mothers," I said. "There's bound to be one or more in the big cities." I wanted to smile in spite of it all. "You know, California, land of opportunity, where you can win fame or get lost in a day."

"Why don't you call the Salvation Army?" Dorothy said. "They would have that kind of information." She looked at me in her most matter-of-fact way. "Let me know if you need help in finding adoptive parents for the baby."

"No," I said. "I don't know what I'll do, but I'm not giving up the baby."

Sunday the 13th

Dorothy helped me pack the few things I am taking along. We've stored most of my clothes and books in her attic. She'll receive my mail here and forward it. I've told Mother and Dad that I'll be staying here this year, that Dorothy has invited me since her children have all gone now. I think we have worked out the practical details pretty well. If any of my friends calls me here, Dorothy will tell them I'm out of town for a couple of days.

It's almost time to go. Dorothy will drive me to the station. She's been so wonderful, but I guess this is the point where I go on alone.

Sunday night

The train isn't very crowded. I've got a double seat to myself, by the window. Can't afford a Pullman, but then I don't think I'll sleep very much anyway. Outside the landscape flies by—dark clusters of trees and hills outlined against the evening sky—

houses with windows showing families around the supper table under the lamplight.

I am alone, but this kind of loneliness doesn't matter. I feel snug and safe inside the train. It moves me from one end of the country to another. The tracks stretch ahead, the engineer knows what he's doing and I don't have to worry about anything.

Across the aisle and a few seats ahead of me is a sailor asleep, with his white cap over his eyes. Maybe he's going home on leave.

I once wanted to be a boy. When I was little I played with the boys, and I could run as fast as they did and climb the tallest tree. I didn't like dolls and girls, and my father used to laugh and call me his little tomboy. I think maybe he wanted me to be a boy. I used to think boys could do things girls couldn't do. Maybe if I'd been a boy I might have been a sailor now, asleep in a train on my way to someplace. Instead, I've got a real little live human being growing inside me. In spite of everything, I'm glad I'm a girl!

Later

The sailor's name is Dean Kirkpatrick but his friends call him Patrick because of his red hair, he said. I met him in the diner— I was sitting there with my pot of coffee, staring at the big yellow moon, and almost felt sorry for myself. He was suddenly standing next to my table with a big friendly grin on his face, his white cap in his hand, asking if I would mind if he sat down. I thought, why not, he's a stranger, he'll never know where I'm going.

"Please do," I said, and turned to stare out the window again. Our reflection looked as if we were together. He was looking at the window too. He smiled and nodded, and said, "Nice-looking couple, aren't they?" And I couldn't help laughing.

"It's fun," he said, looking directly at me across the table. "A trainful of people going someplace from somewhere." He laughed and looked as if he was having a ball. "Some of them think they'll be happier where they're going, some think they left happiness behind—and some don't think at all. They just go." His face looked suddenly serious but his eyes were still full of fun.

"I'm not really nuts," he said. "I just happen to be a compulsive talker—especially on trains—and especially to pretty girls." The way he said it I couldn't feel embarrassed or anything, I couldn't keep from laughing with him.

"Meeting people on trains is like peeking in the middle of books," he said. "You don't know the beginning and you won't know the end. You know just enough to be interested and not enough to be disappointed." For a quick moment I wondered what he would say if I told him the end of my "book," but he kept on talking, chasing away that awful feeling of being an outsider and watching people talking and laughing and living normal non-secret lives. He is on his way home after three years in the Navy and he's got money saved to finish college.

"Isn't it great to be alive?" he said, and I nodded at him even though I felt something like envy. Yes, it must be great to be alive when you're on top of the world the way Patrick feels now, when you haven't got yourself into a great big mess. But I'm glad he's on the train. That smile of his is contagious. And he likes me, he really does. I can see it in his eyes and it feels good to have someone tell you silly, funny compliments. He's going to the Coast too. That'll make the three days go quicker.

Wednesday the 16th

We'll be there tomorrow—then what? But I still have a few more hours when I don't have to think about it. The trip has gone so fast, mostly because of Patrick. He is going to get a degree in psychology and be a counselor, he says. He'll be a good one, I'm sure. Today he "analyzed" me. He said I'm bright, warm and adventurous ("Or you wouldn't have listened to a stranger like me"), but also that I'm lonely and don't have enough confidence in myself.

"You've got a wonderful life waiting for you," he said. "But you've got to go out there and live it, not hide in a corner."

"Thank you doctor," I said, and we both laughed. I think that if I told him where I'm going he would understand, maybe even want to see me again sometime, but I don't dare. I've felt almost happy these last couple of days. I don't want to talk about what's ahead; it'll come soon enough.

Maybe it won't be so bad. This secrecy will only have to last a few months and then there will be a whole wonderful life ahead. And a baby to share it with.

Thursday the 17th

I said good-bye to Patrick at the station and explained why I can't see him again while I'm here. I said I would be visiting relatives for just a few days before going back to Boston. I gave him Dorothy's address, and hope he'll write me even if he's sore about not seeing me here.

Then I took a taxi to the Y.W.C.A. and registered as Jean Thompson from Chicago. I've never been in Chicago except for a stopover at the station or the airport. If I'm going to lie about it I might as well pick someplace I don't know a thing about. I like my new name. Jean Thompson sounds like a real person.

Saturday the 19th

This is the end of the line, no more stalling. I am broke. Now is the time to take the next step.

I woke up early this morning because the girl in the bed next to mine was crying. She looked a mess, blond hair tangled, eyes swollen red—poor thing. She's been in this country from England for only a month and she's already been involved with a smart guy from Hollywood, who took her for a two weeks' "honeymoon" without a wedding and left her here while he took off for Vegas with her last hundred dollars. She told me the whole story in between sobs, how wonderful that guy was, how she was afraid maybe he wouldn't get his divorce after all, and maybe she's pregnant. I promised I wouldn't tell a soul about that, of course.

"Now I can't afford to stay here any longer, and how is he going to find me? He promised to call." She looked at me as though I knew all the answers, and I said she could go get a job, and if she's pregnant, there is always the Salvation Army.

Then I walked down the hall to the pay phone and dialed the Salvation Army. A pleasant voice answered, "Can I help you?" And I've never meant it more than when I said, "You sure can! I'm going to have a baby and I'm not married and I'm nearly broke. I don't know what to do."

"What's your name?" said the voice at the other end, as if what I'd just said was the sort of thing the voice handled every day. I told her my new name and she said to come right over.

"Since you're broke you'll probably want to make an arrangement right away, won't you?" she said, and I realized suddenly just how frightened and lost I had felt. It was going to be all right now. I would have food and shelter and no questions asked.

I went back to the room and gave the English girl my last ten-dollar bill.

The social worker was young and pretty. A small overnight bag stood by her chair and I remembered it was Saturday. A long time ago I had gone away on week-end trips too. It seems like an eternity ago.

"I have called our Home for Unwed Mothers about you," she said. "We don't usually admit girls on Saturday, but there happens to be room. You may go right away if you want to." She smiled and tapped her pencil on the pad.

"There are some questions," she said. "I suppose Jean Thompson isn't your real name?" I must have looked surprised and she said, "That's quite common. Many girls don't give their real names. We'd like to know, of course, in case of an emergency. But it would be confidential."

"I'd rather not," I said.

"All right, then what shall I put down as your hometown?"

"Chicago." She asked my age and occupation.

"Twenty-one, college student."

"What field?"

"Sociology," I said, and she laughed.

"Doing it the hard way, aren't you?" It wasn't hard to laugh with her. She wasn't at all what I had been afraid of—someone like my mother, maybe, strict and disapproving, there to "save" me from the gutter.

We shook hands and she wished me luck. I walked to the bus depot and people with Saturday looks on their faces hurried around me. I wanted to laugh out loud. It seemed too fantastic to be true. I was on my way to a home for unwed mothers!

Saturday afternoon

The house stands on a hilltop surrounded by park-like gardens with large old trees and brilliant flower beds along winding paths. A sign at the entrance to the park says: BOOTH MEMORIAL HOSPITAL. It looks more like a school dormitory to me. There are bright-colored curtains behind the wide windows and the big two-story house looks friendly.

I climbed the steep flight of steps from the street and tried to open the big green front door; it was locked. The tight feeling in my stomach was just plain fear. I felt as if I was being watched, and when I looked up I saw the curtain move behind a window upstairs. I wondered if it was one of the girls, and what they would be like. I felt like running back down the stairs. Going through that green door would be so final. I thought: that's where it will happen, in that house—all the things I'm scared to think about, the baby, how I'll feel when it's over, what I'll do. Even as I rang the bell I wished somehow I could get out of it, go back and undo that mistake.

If the door hadn't been opened right away I might have run. But a woman with a tight, pinched face opened it as if she'd been waiting for me. Without a word, she held it open so I could walk in and then locked it behind me again, and I couldn't help feeling trapped.

"Miss Peterson at the welfare office called about you," she said, without answering my "How do you do."

"You know we don't usually admit girls on Saturday. You'll fill out your papers Monday." She marched into the office adjoining the hall and flicked the switch on the intercom. I heard a wave of noise from a room somewhere, girls' chatter and laughter; they didn't sound like desperate unwed mothers.

The frozen-faced lady called into the microphone: "Karen T. and Lucy S." And several voices answered, "Not here!" She flipped another switch and tried again: "Karen T. and Lucy S." And the voices came over the din in the room, "Coming!"

"They'll be here to get you in a moment," the woman said and turned her back on me to shuffle papers on a desk.

I sat on the olive-green plastic couch and tried to think of something pleasant. The foyer looked depressing and smelled of strong soap. Brown, slightly worn linoleum covered the floor, and the walls were green. The furniture was heavy and dark. Someone had hung bright new flower-print curtains in front of the tall narrow window and had put artificial roses in a vase on the table. I leafed through the magazines, old copies of *Life* and *The New Yorker,* and *War Cry,* of course, the Salvation Army magazine. The name always seemed silly to me.

The frozen-faced lady wasn't wearing a uniform. She couldn't be a Soldier of the Cross (not with that look on her face anyway, I thought). There was a cupboard with glass doors in the corner. On the shelves were embroidered pillowcases and baby clothes neatly folded and priced. Maybe the girls made them. I can't think of anything I'd rather do less. Two girls walked by in the hall and peeked at me through the door. They wore bright cotton smocks over their big stomachs and were laughing. How can they be so cheerful in this place? They are safe in here, of course.

New footsteps sounded through the hall and two girls came into the foyer, one a tall, chocolate-brown Negro, the other white with dark hair and sparkling blue eyes. They smiled hello and the frozen-faced lady came to introduce us.

"A new girl, Jean T. She'll be in your dorm. This is Karen T. and Lucy S. They'll show you around." I smiled and wanted to giggle. How funny, really, the way we're going to share something as real as having babies and we call each other by a phony first name and last initial only. Or maybe I ought to cry instead.

"Hi, Jean," Karen said, blue eyes smiling. "Hope you'll like it here." She caught my stare and laughed. "Really, it isn't bad. Wait and see, the girls are lots of fun." Karen and Lucy each took one of my bags. Down the hall, out of hearing range from the office, Lucy nodded over her shoulder and whispered, "Don't mind Mrs. Warren. She always scares the new ones, but she isn't bad once you get used to the fact that she never smiles. At least she's consistent."

The long hall was gloomy, brown floor, green walls, no windows. But now I could hear the sounds of the house all around us. They were busy, happy sounds—rattling of dishes somewhere, voices talking and laughing, someone whistling. A door banged, and I heard a piano and someone singing.

"We'll take you on the whole tour of the premises," Karen said with a smile.

"And don't worry if you don't remember all the names." Lucy chuckled and put a chocolate-brown finger over her full mouth. "In here we don't mind, if you know what I mean."

"The girls sleep in four dorms," Karen said. "Two downstairs and two upstairs. We're upstairs and if you don't mind we'll take your bags there first."

"Gee I'm sorry." I suddenly realized that Karen was breathing heavily and straining to carry my bag. "Let me carry it." I grabbed the bag and she let go at once, smiling gratefully.

"When you get a little more pregnant I'll show you all the respect a mother-to-be deserves," she said. "Now you don't even look as if you belong in here. When is your due-date?" I'd never heard that expression before and they both laughed at me.

"You might as well get prepared," said Lucy. "We ask two questions in here. When is your due-date and where are you from."

"That means we want to know when your baby is due and we hope you don't come from someplace we know," Karen explained.

"I'm due in March," I said, and they exchanged glances.

"It'll go fast," said Lucy quickly. "Christmas will be here before you know it."

"I guess so," I said, and the time stretched out ahead of me in months and weeks and days and minutes to be counted.

"And I'm from Chicago," I said, and Karen said, "Don't worry, we haven't got anyone claiming Chicago as a hometown right now. Lucy comes from near here and I'm from Missouri."

The steps leading upstairs are a dark green. Lucy and Karen had to stop to catch their breath several times. They looked at my flat stomach and I felt almost guilty for not being tired.

There are fifteen girls in each of the two dorms upstairs, with just one bathroom between them. I bet that gets crowded. Six lavatories, five toilets, two showers and a tub. The dorms are identical except for the color. Ours is green, the other one pink. Thank heavens—I can't stand pink. The beds feel comfortable enough. They stand, headboards against the walls, around the large square room. Fifteen narrow lockers and four large chests of drawers are lined up back to back down the center of the room. Everything is green except for the girls and the bright yellow and red curtains. I've slept in dorms like this in summer camp. You don't get much privacy, but then maybe I don't need that here. Maybe the noise and movement keep you from brooding too much.

The room was full of girls when we came in the door. They were resting on the beds, or sewing or writing letters. Two radios were playing different songs at the same time and the noise was chaotic. Lucy clapped her hands and yelled, "Quiet, girls! Meet a new one." Dead silence fell over the room at once and twelve pairs of eyes traveled up and down over my flat stomach.

"Sure you got the right address?" Several girls laughed and the redhead in the corner bed who had asked grinned proudly.

"Be good girls now and introduce yourselves," Lucy said. "This is Jean T. from Chicago."

"Hi, Jean. Welcome aboard. Nice to know you." The names and the greetings came from all sides at once and I found myself just standing there thinking that, whatever it was I had expected the girls to be like this certainly wasn't it. I mean they were just like any other girls I know, nice, friendly, open, like roommates in school.

The only difference was that everyone was obviously pregnant. Some of them had propped pillows under their big bellies to rest more comfortably, and when they got up they moved slowly and waddled when they walked. It turns out all of them except one are due long before March. The one is called Cecilie. She is due in April and looks as skinny and out of place as I do.

"Let's dump your stuff and take the tour." Karen pointed to the bed in the corner next to hers. "You'll sleep here. You've got one locker and one drawer. Monday you can put your empty bags in the storeroom downstairs." I felt very tired suddenly.

"Let's rest for a while and take the tour later," I said, and Karen flopped on her bed with a loud sigh.

"Best idea I've heard in a long time," she said. "Nobody needs to tell me twice to rest. I was born lazy."

I closed my eyes and the noises in the room didn't bother me. I thought: I'm here and that's what I've been wanting for a long time. The outside world can't touch me now. My pregnancy is the one thing I don't have to lie about in here. I've even cut my hair! I did it myself at the "Y" yesterday. I bought a lipstick too. No more longhair stuff and dungarees and sandals, not while I'm here anyway. My guitar is safely stored in Dorothy's attic. And Jean Thompson from Chicago is a sensible, average kind of girl.

Later Saturday

I slept till a bell rang. All the girls were jumping off their beds heading for the door.

"Chow time," said Karen. "The highlight of the day." We marched downstairs and through the long hall, more and more girls joining the line. The sound of our steps and our loud voices echoed in the bare hall. Then down another flight of stairs to the dining room in the basement. The line stopped in front of the closed door and Karen explained the system: first bell means we've got to hurry into line outside the dining room and then we wait till the second bell rings and march quietly to our places.

We waited in that drab hall where the heating pipes go along the ceiling. Karen told me the kitchen is down there too and the laundry room, the storage room, the beauty shop and a tiny little room where the girls are allowed to smoke. Then the bell rang and we filed in and I was glad to see that the dining room is painted white and the oilcloth on the small tables for six and eight is checkered a bright red and white. Through the windows high on the wall I could see green treetops and blue sky.

Karen steered me to a small table for four in a corner, far from the head table where a plump woman in a cook's uniform was already standing behind her chair, hands folded on the backrest. I saw Lucy heading our way with a small Oriental girl just behind her. I was glad to see a face I knew and Lucy, showing her bright teeth in the dark brown face, introduced us, "Mikki, due any time—Jean, due in March."

"Let's bow our heads, girls." The cook's voice was soft. The girls behind their chairs bent their heads, their hands folded under large and small tummies. I couldn't bend my head. I looked through the window at two birds resting on a telephone wire and hoped that God, if He was there, would understand.

"Lord, we ask Thy blessing," came that soft voice, and I felt like a hypocrite. "We are poor lost sinners and our only hope for life is through Thy Son, Jesus. In His name we ask Thy blessing on our meal. Amen."

"Amen," came a mumbling from the girls, and Karen grimaced as she sat down.

"Don't forget your pills, girls," she said. "Healthy mommies, healthy babies, you know." She flipped three pills from the little paper cup into her mouth and followed with a sip of water. Iron, vitamins, calcium, they were all there. I swallowed mine in one gulp and smiled at Karen. I think I'm going to like her, whoever she is. The food was excellent. Broiled liver (no onions) and baked potatoes. Rice pudding for dessert, my favorite. Lucy and Mikki, the Japanese girl, kept up a constant barrage of friendly kidding back and forth.

"Gonna put those crumbs in my bed?" Lucy asked when Mikki crumbled her cracker deliberately between slender fingers.

"Only because you short-sheeted me last night," said Mikki, sweetly.

"You two are going to chase each other into the delivery room one of these days," Karen said. Lucy and Mikki smiled. "That's where we're all heading," said Mikki. "We're just trying to speed the action a little."

After supper Mikki went back upstairs and I came along with Karen and Lucy for a smoke in what Lucy called the "sanctuary."

"It's the only place in the house we can smoke," she explained. "The staff can't stand to smell the stuff, so they don't come around. We can sort of be a little more free down here." The little room was crowded with girls and the stink of tobacco was almost too much, even for a regular smoker like me. There is only one small window high in the wall, looking straight out at the back steps. The window is so filthy that very little light can come through. The concrete walls look as if they've never been painted, but by now they are stained a dark gray by dirt and smoke.

A group of girls were playing poker around a rickety table under the window. Others were chatting or reading or even sewing, perched on old furniture of every style and color. Most of the chairs looked as if they needed paint and repair badly. The smoke was getting in my eyes and I had to cough. "Not much of a view you've got," I said, and Karen looked at me.

"Are you kidding?" she said. "It's a great view—we can see the doctor coming and going and we know when a girl delivers. We have sort of a worm's-eye view of the whole thing." I could see her point. Just then a car drove up to the back steps and one of the girls jumped up on her chair to see better.

"Who's in labor? It's Doctor Carlsen," she said, and one of the poker players answered, "It's Carol. She's been upstairs for several hours now." Everybody suddenly looked very cheerful and somebody yelled, "Hurrah, she made it!"

Karen explained it to me. "Carol's folks are coming to see her next week—they don't know she's having a baby."

"It often happens that way," said Lucy. "A girl gets in a really tight squeeze—but no one's been caught yet. I guess someone is watching over us." Several girls nodded. They suddenly looked quite serious. I had the odd feeling that those poker-playing girls, with their bellies full of what most churches would call babies conceived in sin, have faith!

Karen pulled my arm. "Our tour," she said. "We've got to hurry if you want to see the place before bedtime. Lights are out at ten." We looked in the door to the huge kitchen. There's a bakery, too, and a separate dining area for the housekeeping staff. Karen explained that the dining room for the Salvation Army officers and the social workers is on the first floor; directly above is the diet kitchen for the mothers' ward where the nurses and the girls on special diets eat. The food is carried upstairs from the kitchen on a special elevator.

The housekeeping staff and the social workers work here only during the day, Karen said. Two nurses are on duty on the hospital floor around the clock, and the Salvation Army officers who are in over-all charge live in staff quarters nearby. "They're very nice," Karen said. "They make you feel they really care and they don't act as if they think we're big sinners just because we're in trouble."

"What about the social workers?" I said.

"You'll be assigned to one. You can talk over your plans for the future, and she handles the adoption through the state agency."

"I'm keeping my baby," I said. Karen looked at me, then quickly turned away.

"Not many girls in here do," she said, and I was glad she let me go first up the stairs so she wouldn't see me blushing.

"On the main floor are the offices for the staff and social workers," she resumed. "We have two case workers and one group worker. She's in charge of arts and crafts, and you can pick your own hobby; paint, ceramics, sewing, leathercraft—you name it, we've got it."

"Do I *have* to do something?" I thought of the embroidered baby clothes for sale in that glass cabinet in the entrance hall.

"Of course not," Karen said. "You'll be assigned to a housekeeping job, you know, laundry, kitchen, cleaning. That's the only thing you *have* to do—except go to chapel every Sunday and Wednesday. No one gets out of that."

The chapel is just off the main hall; the door was open. The lights were off in the room and the light from a lamp outside shone through the stained-glass window. We could see the rows of pews and the large cross behind the small altar.

"It isn't bad," Karen whispered. "One of the girls can really play the organ and Cora in our dorm is the soloist. She's a tough kid—but she's got a beautiful voice."

"I thought maybe they'd try to 'save' us," I whispered. "I don't think I could take that."

Karen shook her head. "The Salvation Army officers won't do that," she said, "but watch out for the cooks and the housekeeper. They're plain soldiers in the Salvation Army and they give you the full treatment, Bible quotations and reminding you of your sins. You know, the 'holier-than-thou' attitude. Some of the girls lose their tempers and then they've really had it."

"What do you mean?"

"You know, the housekeeper picks on their work, makes them wait longer in line for their linens, gives them bad marks with the staff. Just don't act proud in front of them and you'll be all right." Karen smiled. "You look scared," she said. "It'll be O.K." We passed the foyer where I'd waited for Karen and Lucy earlier today. It seemed a small eternity ago.

The library is next to the large TV lounge. The big lounge, with comfortable couches and chairs and a soft carpet on the floor, was empty.

"No smoking." Karen shrugged her shoulders. "Most of us here are kind of on edge—you know we're not exactly on vacation—and we smoke more than we should, I'm sure. But we've got to have something to calm our nerves." She opened the door to the library—soft green carpet, deep chairs, walls lined with books. Mikki, the Japanese girl, was the only one there; she looked up from a stack of what looked like textbooks and smiled at us.

"How's the tour?"

"Fine." I wanted to stay and talk to her, but Karen pulled on my arm. "Half an hour till bedtime—see you later, Mikki." The Japanese girl waved a slender hand at us; her eyes were already on the book she was reading.

"You don't want to see the dorms down here, do you?" Karen was heading for the stairs. I shook my head.

"The gray dorm is exactly like the ones upstairs and the little one—well, it's just a room with five beds."

"What about Mikki?" I said. "What's she reading?"

"It isn't a secret," Karen said. "She's a medical student. She's got two more years to go before she's a doctor. Being here has made her decide to specialize in obstetrics, so she's got a way to go yet."

"What about her baby?" Somehow I knew the answer. Karen didn't look at me.

"She's arranged for a private adoption. A Japanese lawyer and his wife."

"Oh." There was nothing more to say. Karen walked quickly ahead of me. We had talked about the sort of things that I understand are taboo in here, and maybe I shouldn't have asked. But I didn't think Mikki would mind if she knew. I don't think she'd mind even if I talked to her about it.

"Second floor," said Karen. She was breathing heavily after the climb. "Our home, sweet home." The girls from our dorm and from the pink dorm across the hall were flocking to the bathroom in pajamas and robes carrying toothbrushes and towels. Every time the doors swung open we heard the sounds of water splashing and voices echoing.

"The hospital is at the other end of our floor," said Karen. "You just walk right down there and report to the nurse on duty when your time comes. It beats having a baby in a taxi." She laughed. "Married mothers have all sorts of worries we don't even have to think about, like packing a toothbrush." I could see down the long hall with the shining linoleum floor; at the other end was a door painted baby blue.

"That's the nursery," said Karen. "We've got two labor rooms, a delivery room, nurse's office, examination room and two mothers' wards. A big one for mothers who don't keep their babies, a little one for the ones who do. Isolation is in that end of the house, too—for girls who are sick or on special diets. I guess that ends the tour—except for the schoolroom. I almost forgot." She opened the door halfway down the hall, and I stared at the rows of desks, the blackboard and the maps on the walls.

"Eighteen girls attend high school here," Karen explained. "They get credit for the courses they take, and when they leave they can go back to their old school—they haven't lost any time." The idea somehow chilled me. I thought of little mothers-to-be studying history and math—and when they leave they've got to go back to studying history and forget that they are mothers.

"We don't have any classes for junior high-ers yet," Karen said. "We've got five girls in that age group here now, and the way things are going it looks as if they'll need a classroom and a teacher before many seasons have gone by."

What a day this has been! I guess I won't be so confused when I've been here for a while. By the time March comes around I'll probably know it so well I won't ever be able to forget.

Sunday the 20th

After lights out last night we had a cookies-and-Kool-Aid party on our dorm. One of the girls has an aunt living down the street who brought us the cookies. We sat on pillows on the floor around the goodies, while the pale moon shone in through the windows on our bulky figures huddling together. We were whispering and trying to suppress our giggles. The Major was on duty last night, and our lookout reported that she was safely out of hearing distance in the diet kitchen, having coffee with the night nurse. The party ended in a pillow fight. I crawled into bed early and watched the spectacle from a safe distance. At last only Lucy and Mikki were left on the floor, chasing each other around the island of lockers and chests of drawers. All you could see of Lucy was her bulky white nightgown—her chocolate-brown skin blended with the darkness. Their shadows danced in the moonlight, their movements grotesquely exaggerated. I saw them sit together on Mikki's bed whispering quietly. Then Lucy climbed into her own bed and all was quiet.

I stayed awake and to me the night was full of new noises. The breathing of fourteen girls came from all around me. Someone in the far corner snored lightly and I heard the sound of steps— dragging slippers—in the hall and then the banging of the bathroom door. It wasn't midnight yet and through the open windows came the far-off sounds of the city. Who goes to bed this early on Saturday night?

When I lay on my back and felt my stomach there was a hard bump where it used to be hollow. I'm a big-boned girl and I used to be proud of my flat stomach. Now that thing is growing in there and I can't stop it. All of us in here have that thing inside and we're here to wait till it comes out. We laugh and talk and have pillow fights, and all the time it is growing inside us. They —we—don't talk about what it's going to be like to be mothers, what it's going to be like to give birth to a new little human being. We don't talk about what he or she will look like or if it will be a boy or a girl. I tossed in bed and thoughts going round and round kept me from sleeping.

"Why did You do it, God?" I wanted to cry it out loud. "Why did You let me do it?" But I don't believe in a fate sealed by anything or anyone, I thought. I've got to believe we are free to choose our own destinies. But if I believe that, then I must believe that I chose to be pregnant—chose to come here? I remembered Dorothy's voice: "You want this baby for reasons of your own. . . ."

Around me was the deep even breathing of girls sleeping and I could see their bulky shapes under the blankets. Suddenly I thought I knew what Dorothy had been talking about. Inside me is a baby waiting to be born—the baby didn't choose me anymore than I chose my mother. I am responsible for that baby's start in life, and till now all I've been thinking about has been me, how *I* feel about it, how *my* life is changed. I was glad for the darkness around me. I could feel myself blushing.

A sudden movement on the other side of the room startled me. I saw Mikki sit up in bed, toss her blanket aside, and reach over to shake Lucy. They whispered together, too low for me to hear the words. Then they tiptoed out the door. They were holding hands, I noticed. I turned my head and saw Karen looking my way with wide-awake eyes.

"Mikki must be in labor," she whispered. "They are probably going downstairs to count the minutes between pains and smoke till it's time to go to the nurse. The girls do that a lot. It beats being alone in the labor room."

I looked through the window at the sky and noticed that the Big Dipper had moved into full view from my window, and I wondered if I'd still be awake when it had disappeared behind the tree. That's the last thought I can remember. The next thing I knew, girls were jumping all over the place getting ready for chapel, and my first full day at Booth was under way!

Sunday afternoon

When we got out of chapel the word came; Mikki had a little boy. Her labor had been easy for a first baby, they said.

The Captain led the service. She is a rotund little woman, with a girlish voice and bright blue eyes. Her text for the day was

:

Romans 6:23: "For the wages of sin is death; but the gift of God is eternal life through Jesus Christ our Lord."

"What a glorious promise, girls!" said the Captain. "Confess your sins and ask Christ into your hearts and eternal life in Him is yours." The Captain's baby-blue eyes smiled kindly at her pregnant congregation. I moved uneasily on the slick, hard, wooden bench of the pew. I wondered if she meant by confessing my sins that I must recognize what I've done wrong, and then I shall find the strength to walk the narrow path of righteousness. But what did I do wrong—and where goes that right path?

Sixteen-year-old Cora from our dorm stood next to the altar, her long blond hair framing her young face, her hands clasped over the protruding stomach. Her voice rose clear and rich: "My faith looks up to Thee, Thou Lamb of Calvary, Saviour Divine." I could close my eyes and forget about the words. Worship in music is something I can understand. I felt at peace for a little while.

Monday the 21st

Miss O'Connor has been assigned as my case worker, or I've been assigned to her, depending on how you look at it. She is quite young, maybe twenty-five, plumpish, blond. Mostly I noticed that she isn't pregnant! Her office is a tiny cubicle, almost like a cell. On the wall are two watercolors of Paris in the spring. Paris —Mother and Dad—I'd love to go there one day. I'd love to walk along the banks of the Seine in spring and sip wine at a sidewalk cafe and be in love. I wouldn't have a care in the world and my skirts wouldn't be getting too tight around my waist.

Miss O'Connor offered me a cigarette (I took it) and said she would help me fill out the standard form: my name, the baby's father's name, record of illnesses in both families, anything that might be important about the baby. I gave my phony name and said I didn't want to tell the father's name.

"That's all right," Miss O'Connor said. "Just tell me his age, race and occupation."

"He's thirty-five, white and in business for himself," I said, and the thought of Gene didn't seem to have any connection with the baby inside me.

"You may apply for aid from the state," said Miss O'Connor. "They will pay for your stay here and your delivery. They also give you eleven dollars a month in pocket money." A ward of the state, I thought. I got myself pregnant and somebody's tax money is going to pay for it!

"Oh, no!" I said. "Isn't there another way?"

"Of course," Miss O'Connor said, reassuringly. "The cost of your stay here is a hundred dollars a month, plus seventy-five dollars for your delivery and postnatal medical care for you and the baby. You can pay that yourself."

"That'll be six hundred and seventy-five dollars," I said. "I don't have that kind of money."

"You may pay it in installments whenever you can afford it," said Miss O'Connor. "We trust you to keep your word and pay us back when you can—and we don't give you any time limit."

"You mean I don't sign something and promise a certain sum every month?" It was hard to believe. Miss O'Connor shook her head. "The Salvation Army doesn't operate on a profit basis," she said. "They believe that they work for Christ in looking after his children—you. They ask you to pay later—only so that they can help others like you."

"You mean they've got that much faith in us?" I said. "In unwed mothers who don't even tell them their names?"

Miss O'Connor smiled. "I've been here for three years and have never heard of a girl who hasn't paid her debt. Several girls

pay more, just to show their gratitude." I sat back in my chair
and took another of her cigarettes. What I'd just heard didn't
sound like the good old U.S.A. in the mid-twentieth century.

"But that's still an awful lot of money," I said. "I may not be
able to pay it back even if I want to. I'm going to support myself
and the baby, you know." I thought she would say something
about the advantages of adoption, but she just looked at me and
said, "The decision is yours. I'm sure you'll choose what is best—
for both of you." I don't know why everybody keeps saying they
know I'll make the best decision. I sure as hell don't know that
myself. It seems as if whatever I choose will be wrong. I can't
imagine giving up my own baby, and I can't imagine how that
baby can get along with me as a mother.

"There is one way you can cut your expenses while you're waiting for the baby," Miss O'Connor said, interrupting my hopeless
train of thought.

"You can go to a wage home and stay here only for your last
month."

"What's a wage home?" The thought of leaving this safe place
scared me.

"They are family homes nearby where a girl gets room and
board and ten dollars a week for doing light housekeeping and
baby-sitting. You still 'belong' here, so to speak; you come in for
your medical checkups and get your supply of iron, calcium and
vitamin pills. You may take along and wear the maternity clothes
you need. And of course you may come back here to stay any
time you want to."

"Then I'd only owe you one hundred and seventy-five or maybe
two hundred dollars by the time I leave," I said, after doing some
arithmetic. "That sounds a lot better—but I hate to go outside
and be an unwed mother in hiding again. In here I'm just one of
the girls."

"You'll get all the privacy you want in a wage home," said

Miss O'Connor. "We screen the families carefully before sending any girls to them."

"I'll give it a try," I said. Miss O'Connor will call a wage-home mother and have her come here to meet me first before I decide to go there. I'll probably stay here for a week anyway, for medical checkups and all that.

Before I left her office, Miss O'Connor told me that if I change my mind about keeping the baby she'll be glad to make arrangements with an adoption agency. The Home works both with a state and a local agency. She said they would do everything to find exactly the kind of family I would want for the baby. I shook my head and said, "No, thanks," and she smiled.

"Drop in whenever you feel like talking, Jean." I said thank you, and I will. She's really O.K. Easy to talk to and no pressure.

I looked at those watercolors on her wall and Paris seemed an awfully long way off. I'm twenty-one now and I'll be thirty-nine before this baby is eighteen. Am I going to be alone with the responsibility for the two of us till then?

Monday night

I'm beat. What a day. After I talked to Miss O'Connor I went upstairs to take a nap. The nights are kind of noisy and I haven't gotten used to it yet, so I don't sleep much. The dorm was empty. Monday morning everybody is either working or going to school. No sooner had I flopped on my bed than my name was called over the intercom. I jumped three feet. It was the first time I'd heard my new name over that thing and it shook me. I was called twice before I had sense enough to answer "Coming."

Downstairs in the office the skinny, tall Major with black hair pinned in a severe bun was waiting for me. Karen had pointed her out earlier and told me her name is Laski and that she came to this country from Poland in 1937. She still speaks with a thick accent and the girls imitate her.

"What were you doing in your dorm, Jean?" she said in a stern voice.

"Taking a nap," I said, and watched how the sudden smile started in her dark eyes and made her face look soft and young.

"No girls are allowed in the dorms during working hours unless they are sick," she said slowly, but still smiling. "I guess you need a job."

"I'm going to a wage home next week," I said, hoping to get out of the working bit.

"To be idle is not good," said the Major. "You will work in the kitchen, set the table for the housekeeping staff. It is an easy job."

"Thank you," I said.

"Are you comfortable in your dorm? Have you met friends?"

"Yes, thank you." It was hard to stand still under the Major's kind eyes.

"I am the housemother," she explained, "but you work for the cook. She will tell you what to do."

"Thank you," I said again. "But what do I do with my suitcase? It's still in my dorm."

"Take it downstairs. The housekeeper will open the storeroom for you." I said thank you and ran upstairs. There in the dorm was the housekeeper standing by my bed holding my empty suitcase. She looked pretty mad.

"Don't you know you can't have personal luggage in the dorm?" she said. "What do you think would happen if all of you kept suitcases under your beds?"

"I'm sorry," I said, trying to make my voice sound like I meant it. "But I'm new. I haven't had time to take it downstairs—I was going there now."

"So let's go." She tossed the suitcase at me and I grabbed it before it fell. Mrs. Larsen marched ahead of me muttering something about "think they're so smart" and I walked behind her, thanking heaven that Major Laski had given me a job in the kitchen instead of in Mrs. Larsen's department. Before she locked my suitcase in the storeroom in the basement, she turned and said, "Sure you ain't got something in here you need before you leave? I got other things to do than run up and down stairs unlocking this room for scatterbrained girls." My blood was boiling, but I remembered Karen's warning. Keep your temper with the housekeeping staff or you're in trouble. I shook my head, forced a smile and said, "No, I'm sure I won't need it." Mrs. Larsen looked me up and down.

"You don't look pregnant now—but you'll need smocks later. Might as well pick 'em out now. Save me a trip." She waved toward the rack of maternity tops and skirts lining one wall in the storage room. "What's your size? Ten? You'll get bigger than that. Take twelves!"

The smocks were mostly bright cotton prints. I took a brown and a black skirt and three tops with big pockets. They didn't look too washed-out. I remembered Karen had a green two-piece corduroy maternity dress. If it belongs to the Home maybe I can get it when she delivers. Mrs. Larsen left me in the basement corridor with a friendly "Take your clothes to the dorm and don't waste any time about it. We don't allow girls in the dorms during working hours!" Thank goodness *she* didn't catch me taking a nap.

I got the clothes put away in my locker and found Karen in the smoking room downstairs. Her job is in the scrub room next to the kitchen, where they wash the big pots and pans. I told her about my run-in with Mrs. Larsen. "I hope the cook is better," I said. Karen smiled and shook her head.

"They're bosom buddies," she said. "The cook and the assistant cook are sisters, Mrs. Tebbits and Mrs. Coralis. Mrs. Tebbits is the youngest and she's the head cook. Mrs. Coralis is the sourest. When the three of them aren't working or praying, they're scolding us or gossiping about us."

"Is it all that bad?" I was getting worried.

"Nah," said Karen. "They don't really hurt us, and deep down they really mean well—I hope." She pulled on her cigarette. "You know they think we're really sinners and that we ought to repent and get punished. It gripes them when the Salvation Army officers aren't more strict with us."

I said, "How do you put up with it?"

"They're really doing an awful lot of good for us," said Karen. "Where would we go if we couldn't be here? So maybe they want us to eat humble pie and lick their boots and say 'Yes, Ma'am, I'm sorry, Ma'am!' You can't really blame them."

"Why not?" I said. "Can you talk to the officers about it?"

Karen shook her head. "No, they're more like supervisors and administrators. They don't work directly with us as much as the housekeeping staff does." She got up and stubbed out her cigarette. "Time for kitchen duty. Let's go."

Karen introduced me to Mrs. Tebbits, the head cook, who smiled and said she was glad to meet me. Mrs. Tebbits has false upper teeth, and they fall with a soft click against her lower plate every time she talks. It sort of distracts you from what she's saying. She didn't sound too bad to me. She was very friendly when she showed me where to get the plates and the silverware for the table.

Only six of them eat at "my" table in the kitchen. The two cooks, the housekeeper, the woman in charge of the laundry, the janitor and the gardener. The cooks take turns with the Lieutenant in presiding at the table in the girls' dining room. My job is to set the table and put the food out before I go to eat with the others. Then after the meal I clear off the table again and help the girl who runs the dishwasher. Once a week I am supposed to help wash down the walls in the kitchen and the pantry. In between mealtimes I can do as I please, except, of course, stay in the dorm. I can watch TV, use the library, work with ceramics or paint, or sew in the craft room or walk in the park. In the afternoon I can get one two-hour pass every day, and I can get an eight-hour pass once a week. Of course, if I break any rules—get caught in the dorm during the day, come home late from a pass, or conduct myself badly in the eyes of the staff—I can lose my pass privileges. I just hope I can keep my temper.

The girl who runs the dishwasher is thirty-five years old. Her name is Maggie and she told me she wants to keep her baby.

"I've got enough money saved and my boss promised to keep my job open for me. But, you know, it's hard on a kid not to have a father." She pushed the hair back from her forehead with a wet hand.

"I just don't know if I've got the right to keep my baby," she said in a low, weary voice, and you could tell she had thought about it over and over again. The girls don't talk much about their reasons for giving up or keeping their babies, and it's an unwritten rule never to say what you think about another girl's decision. We go through this pregnancy together—but each of us faces the future alone.

Monday afternoon is weight-time. We all line up wearing our lightest smocks. We're called in alphabetical order; some of us have to wait in line for over an hour for our turn. Karen, Lucy and I have last initials S. and T., and Lucy fumed about it. "I'd have picked myself a name starting with an A if I'd known," she said. "That 'S' isn't my name, anyway."

Some of the girls are compulsive candy eaters and starve themselves all day Monday to get by Nurse Simpson's sharp eye. Nurse Simpson is tall and white-haired and strict, but her blue eyes are warm. When she restricts an overweight girl on passes, or sends her upstairs to sleep in Isolation or to eat in the diet kitchen, it is to help her.

"You want an easy delivery, don't you? And you want to look as if you haven't had a baby when you leave, don't you?" she says in an icy voice, and the unhappy girl whispers "Yes" and heads for Isolation.

Most of us want to look as if we've never had any babies when we leave here, of course. Some of the girls manage to keep their total weight-gain down to five pounds or less and look fashionably slim when they leave. If we thought we could starve ourselves into *feeling* as if we'd never had a baby, I bet we'd quit eating all that junk between meals. But we know we can't do that, so most of us spend our few extra pennies on cookies and candy and Cokes at the corner drugstore. I already weigh ten pounds over my normal weight and Nurse Simpson said I'll have to watch out.

"You've got six more months to go and only five more pounds allowed," she said.

If I can only get over this restlessness. There are plenty of things I could do here, but most of the time I end up just sitting around doing nothing. Most of the girls seem to feel the same way. All we do is talk about our pregnancy symptoms.

We just had mail call. The Lieutenant's voice announced it over the intercom and we all ran for the television lounge. I haven't told Dorothy I'm here yet so no one can write to me, but I still ran to stand on the outskirts of the eager group of girls pressing around the Lieutenant. Karen told me a lot of the girls get their mail routed through other Salvation Army post-office boxes in other cities.

"You stay out of sight for months, and someone you know is bound to try to look you up," she said. The thought makes me shudder. I hope I've covered my tracks well enough.

Tuesday the 22nd

Tuesday is a confusing day. First we strip our beds and spend at least an hour in line to dump our dirty linen and to get handed our clean linen. Then we rush back to make our beds. Half of us head for the hospital floor for our medical examination while the other half go to their jobs. I had my first checkup today and Doctor Norwad said I am in "perfect physical health." I wish I could say the same for my mental state.

Karen didn't have a checkup today, so she cleaned off the breakfast dishes in the kitchen for me. I helped Maggie rinse the dishes and put them in the dishwasher. We had oatmeal for breakfast.

"We always do, it seems, when we have checkup," said Maggie, as she scraped away at the hardened leftovers. The stuff is almost impossible to get off if you don't do it right away. We had just finished, when it was time to start all over with lunch! We put the hot dishes straight on the table from the dishwasher—not even time for a smoke in between.

Dr. Norwad holds a motherhood class in the TV lounge after lunch. We're all required to attend and can ask any questions we like. He talked about how our bodies change to accommodate the growing fetus and what we can do to keep ourselves in physical shape during the pregnancy. The slim young Lieutenant demonstrated exercises to do to prepare for the delivery.

"What's the best exercise?" asked a girl from the pink dorm.

"Other than a mile's brisk walk daily—this one," said the doctor, and demonstrated by pushing himself away from the table. "Practice whenever you're tempted to overeat." Karen has attended the whole lecture series before. She says the doctors cover the entire development of the baby from conception to birth.

"The last lecture is on contraceptives," she said, and smiled. "I guess they don't want us in here twice."

Wednesday the 23rd

There's a new girl in Mikki's bed in our dorm. She was there when I came back from kitchen duty after lunch. Her bags were still packed and she wore street clothes, a beige cashmere sweater over a brown and beige wool skirt. She didn't look the least pregnant and her face was skinny below straight ash-blond bangs.

"Hi, there," I said and she looked up quickly as if she expected me to be someone who knew her. That scared look left her eyes and she smiled when she saw I was a stranger.

"I'm Jean T. from Chicago, due in March," I said. The new girl nodded slightly and said, "I'm Marian C. from Norfolk, Virginia." I recognized her New England accent and wondered if she was from Boston.

"I'm due in April," she said, and must have noticed my eyes on the letter she was writing. "For my boyfriend," she said, and I wondered if he was the father of her baby. Her gray eyes were serious; she didn't look like someone who would sleep with a guy she didn't love. But in here you never know. When a girl talks about a boyfriend she's going to marry when she leaves, he is never the father of the baby. Like Clara who left just before I came. Karen told me Clara's boyfriend had followed her across the country, and begged her to marry him and let him adopt the baby, but she refused. Her baby went out for adoption through the agency, and Clara married the boy. She said that if she'd kept the baby she would never have known for sure if she married him just so she wouldn't have to give it up.

"We're going to get married—later," Marian said, smiling in spite of a fresh flow of tears.

"And the baby?" The question popped out against my better judgment.

"We're giving it up for adoption," she said and went on rapidly. "He doesn't want it that way either. He wants his baby as much as I do."

"His?" I said, and Marian looked hurt. "Of course!" she said. "You don't think I'd have someone else's baby, do you?" I shook my head and wondered what on earth had brought her here. Major Laski's voice broke in over the intercom: "Marian C., Marian C." The new girl looked as if the name had nothing to do with her. The Major called again: "Marian C., Marian C."

"Coming!" several girls yelled in chorus and I nudged Marian. "You're wanted in the office, they're calling your name." She still looked dazed when she walked out the door.

"She's sweet," said Lucy. "Wonder how she got into this mess." Cora, the girl who sang in chapel last Sunday, looked up from the confession magazine she was reading and laughed out loud. "Just like the rest of us, sweetie—don't you know how babies are made?"

Several girls laughed, and Cora turned with a toss of her bleached blond hair to Lisa on the next bed.

"You know how babies are made, don't you, honey?"

The dorm was quiet, and I knew why Karen had called Cora "a bad one." Lisa is fourteen and seems to be mentally retarded. She was brought here from Juvenile Hall and no one knows for sure when her baby is due. Lisa's pale gray eyes blinked behind the thick lenses of her glasses and she stammered, "I . . . I don't know. I didn't do nothing wrong."

"You kissed a boy, didn't you, honey?" Cora's voice was mockingly sweet. Lisa nodded. "Didn't he tell you that's how babies are made?" Cora feigned surprise, and Lisa looked around helplessly.

"N-no!" she whispered. Cora jumped off her bed and put her arm around Lisa's shoulders. She was enjoying herself.

"But you know there's a real live baby inside your tummy, don't you?"

Lisa's smile was sudden and glowing. She nodded happily. "The doctor told me," she said proudly. "Pretty soon the baby will come out and I'll play with it." The smile left Lisa's face as suddenly as it had come and she looked intently at Cora.

"You're nice to me," she said. "How does the baby come out of my tummy?" She put her hand between her legs. "Does it come out here?"

Cora nodded. "It sure does, honey," she said. "Same place it came in." Lisa pulled away from Cora's grasp.

"You're just kidding me—you always do."

"That's enough, Cora," said Lucy, her voice sharp. She walked to Lisa's bed and took her hand gently. "No one will hurt you," she said softly. "The doctor will help the baby come out of your tummy while you're asleep." Lisa beamed at Lucy.

"You're nice. Will you play checkers with me?"

"Sure, Lisa. Let's play in the lounge." The door closed after them and Cora threw herself backward on Lisa's bed.

"God Almighty, that kid gives me the creeps," she said. "You're nice to her and she hangs on like a leech."

"Don't be nice then," one of the girls said.

"Leave Lisa alone," said Karen. "She doesn't hurt anyone."

"Blah, blah, blah." Cora grimaced. "She isn't very smart, her parents don't want her and poor, poor Lisa." She looked around at all of us. "You all make me want to puke. So who do you think you're kidding? We're all alike in here, and don't you try to say 'Poor Cora' or I'll beat the shit out of you. I never had any parents and I worked all my goddamned life. I was dumb enough to get into this mess, and it isn't gonna happen again. Lisa isn't smart enough to hit back and you can't save her. But I've learned *my* lesson. I know damn well nobody's gonna love me and pay for my living just because I'm nice and sweet. Everybody's too busy grabbing for themselves. And let me tell you something. Old Cora's gonna get right in there grabbing with all she's got." No one tried to answer, and Cora laughed to herself as she curled up on her bed with the magazine again.

So that's our little girl who sings like an angel!

Thursday the 24th

I'm leaving for a wage home this afternoon. Miss O'Connor called me to her office to have me meet the wage-home mother. Mrs. Duncan is young, pretty and expecting her third baby in April. She was on her way to a luncheon and didn't have much time to talk. That's just as well. I don't want to get to know her and I don't want her to know me. The Duncans live in the hills outside town and Mrs. Duncan said she hoped I didn't mind being far from neighbors.

My feelings are so mixed up. I don't want to meet people on the outside—but I'm scared of being all alone with my thoughts.

Later Thursday

I sneaked down to the corner and bought a cream puff for Mikki. Lucy told me she liked them and I wanted an excuse to go visit her in the mothers' ward. Her bed was by the window where she could see the park and the old Russian gardener caring for his flowers all day long. On her bedstand were two books, the Bible and a thin little volume I recognized, *The Prophet* by Kahlil Gibran. Mikki was looking out the window, her pale, slim hands folded over her flat stomach where there wasn't a baby anymore. I thought maybe she wanted to be left alone, but it was too late. She turned her head and smiled when she saw me.

"Hi, there, Jean. How nice of you to come."

I held out the white bakery bag. "I brought you a cream puff."

"I love them!" Her eyes sparkled when she smiled, and I smiled back. "So do I."

"Let's have a party then." Mikki sat up in bed and divided the cream puff carefully, brushing one half against the other to share the cream.

"Have some," she said, offering me the top half. She looked like an impish little girl sitting there cross-legged on the bed, licking powdered sugar off her fingers. I kept wishing that was all we were: two girls sharing a cream puff and laughing about it, with the sun shining in on us through the tall windows. But Mikki had gone the long road from the decision to give away her baby to this moment, when she was actually facing it. My road was ahead and I was scared. I sensed in her a strength and an awareness I know are lacking in me.

"You're going back to school now, aren't you?" I hoped she wouldn't mind talking about it. Mikki nodded. "I sure am. It's going to be great working for what I want after all this fooling around."

"You mean having a baby and all?"

"Oh, no!" Mikki's dark eyes were suddenly serious. "This was no fooling!" She lay back on her pillow and looked up at the ceiling. "I don't think I ever did anything real before this. I was doing pretty well in school and some people used to think I was bright for my age." She laughed, a funny little laugh. "What a mess my mind was. I was terribly self-centered, but I had a hard time finding a real me. People—I mean my Dad and my teachers—used to tell me I would turn into something great one day, that I had it in me. Maybe I even believed it myself sometimes, but I was really scared that I wouldn't measure up." Mikki turned her head and looked straight at me.

"And so I got pregnant." She smiled but her eyes were serious. "Hope you don't mind me talking like this, Jean. But we won't meet again and when I leave here I won't speak of these things again."

"I don't mind," I said. "I really came because I hoped you'd talk. . . . I wanted to ask you something."

"What?" said Mikki. "I'll answer if I can."

"Why are you giving up the baby?" The question hung between us. Mikki was sitting up in bed, her hands calm in her lap, and behind her I could see the trees in the park lifting their gold and red crowns toward the September sky.

"The baby was never mine to give up," Mikki said, slowly. "I bore him and he came through me, but he doesn't belong to me." She took the little book from her bedstand and leafed through the pages till she found what she was looking for.

"This is what *The Prophet* says," she said, "that our children are not our children but part of life's longing for itself. That they are as arrows and we, the parents, the bow. God is the archer." I knew the chapter she was talking about. "I *did* want to keep the baby at first," she said. "I thought it was because I wanted to show the world that a child and his natural mother belong together, no matter what. Maybe I have grown up a little since then, but not enough to help a child meet the world. I wish I could try—believe me." Mikki's voice was low. "By parting now the suffering is mine alone. If I keep him, both of us may suffer."

"Do your parents know?"

"I told mother my baby was due in November. Now she thinks it was stillborn. We haven't told my father; he has been ill. When I have my degree I may tell him. I don't know yet."

I had just one more question I wanted to ask: "Why did you choose a private adoption?"

Mikki laughed a little. "I *am* Japanese," she said. "It might not be so easy for the agency to place my baby right away. I wanted to be sure he had a good home. I went to a Japanese lawyer and, as it happened, he and his wife were looking for a baby to adopt. I was lucky."

"I wish I knew what is the right thing to do!" I said. Mikki nodded.

"I know what you mean, but there are no guarantees. You must be strong enough to act without being sure that what you do is absolutely right."

"I came to say good-bye," I said, "and thank you. I am going to a wage home this afternoon." Mikki reached out and took my hand.

"Whatever you do, Jean, make up your mind now," she said. "You have all the facts and you need time to strengthen your conviction. What you decide will be with you for the rest of your life. Your reasons must be strong enough and clear enough to withstand doubt." Mikki smiled and squeezed my hand. "I didn't mean to lecture you. But I know what you are facing. I even wrote my thoughts down. I could look them up when I got emotional."

"Thanks," I said. "I'll try to remember—and good luck!"

"Good luck to you." I saw her open *The Prophet* again and settle back against the pillow, but her eyes were on the old Russian gardener below the window, watering his flowers.

Thursday evening

I'm waiting for Mr. Duncan to pick me up. I had already packed my things when Mrs. Duncan called and said her husband would be late. I didn't feel like eating supper and came downstairs to the smoking room instead. Marian was in a corner staring at the dirty concrete wall and crying without a sound. She didn't turn her head when I came in.

"Chow time," I said. "Aren't you going to eat?" She shook her head without looking away from that wall. Maybe she was sick.

"Anything I can do?" I said and she turned to me, her eyes swollen from crying for a long time.

"My boyfriend just called," she said. "He wants me to come back and marry him. He's borrowed money for my ticket."

"So what's the problem?" I said.

"Mother doesn't want us to get married. She says people will talk, if we have a baby five months after the wedding." Marian saw the look on my face and blushed. "Mother loves me," she said quickly. "She doesn't want me to get hurt." I kept thinking it was none of my business—it was Marian's problem. I had my own to think about.

"Known your boyfriend long?" I said, and the glow came back in Marian's eyes the way it always does when she talks about him.

"Ever since I was a little girl," she said. "He's in graduate school now. He'll have his master's degree in chemistry in two years. Mother says I can marry him then if I still want to." Her voice suddenly lost its eagerness and she stared at me darkly. "That is, if Chris still wants me after I've given away our baby."

"Have a cigarette," I offered, but she shook her head. I lit one for myself, and noticed that my hands were shaking quite a bit.

"What should I do, Jean?" Marian looked at me but I knew she was talking to herself. My opinion wouldn't matter.

"Since Daddy died Mother doesn't have anybody else," she said. "But the baby—Chris and I will be parents together whether we keep it or not—we're responsible, aren't we?" I puffed on my cigarette and nodded; Marian was looking at me intently.

"We are responsible for the child first, aren't we? Say something, Jean. Agree with me—I need someone to agree." I wanted to tell her yes, but I shook my head instead.

"What difference does it make," I said, "if anyone agrees?"

Her eyes went blank for a second. Then she suddenly jumped up.

"Got a dime?" she asked, her hand already stretched out. "I'm going to call Chris collect and tell him I'm coming home. I've spent half my life waiting around for other people to make up my mind for me. Mother, Chris, anybody who'd listen. By God—" she smiled a little—"what difference does it make? I've got to do what's right for me whether someone else agrees or not." She took the dime I found in my pocket and was gone. I heard her run down the hall and slam the phone-booth door shut after her.

So there is one of us finding her way out.

At the Duncans', Saturday the 26th

It is nearly midnight and I don't have to go to bed. Over the hill hangs a full moon; I have turned off the electric light and lighted a red candle on my table.

My room is small, with a bed, a chest of drawers, a table and a chair. I have room to walk one step in one direction and two steps in the other, that's all. But it is all mine. I thought I would feel lonely and the white walls would seem too close. Instead, I feel a peace inside that is an unexpected contrast to the restlessness I've always felt before when I was alone. But then, of course, I am not alone here. There is a little somebody inside me and I am beginning to get used to the thought.

I have hung two pictures on my wall. One is a woodcut of three boats sailing into the sunset, done in brown, rust and black on unbleached coarse sailcloth. I bought it in a small gallery in Greenwich Village a few years ago. The other is a reproduction of a painting by Diego Rivera that I tore out of the art section of *Time* magazine. It is called "Mexican Child" and is of a small girl sitting with her hands in her lap and staring ahead with large, solemn brown eyes. I love her eyes. It is as if she says: I am not afraid—you will care for me.

Most of my books are stored in Dorothy's attic, but some I couldn't bear to leave behind. They stayed in my suitcase in the locker at the Home but in this little room they are with me. A. A. Milne's *Winnie-the-Pooh*, Kenneth Grahame's *The Wind in the Willows*, Antoine de Saint-Exupéry's *The Little Prince*, and of course, *The Prophet*. They are all loyal old friends.

So this is my little kingdom; my room with a view.

Monday the 28th

The house rests in the valley surrounded by rolling hills dotted with clusters of fine old trees. The blacktop road leading to the city goes along the rim of a hill high above us. A dirt road winds its way down the hill to our house and then on past a grove of trees and around a bend to our nearest neighbor, half a mile away.

The traffic on the blacktop road is light. The mailman comes once a day in his red-white-and-blue truck and leaves mail in the two boxes by our driveway. Three times a week the milk truck and the bakery truck come down in a cloud of yellow dust.

We are three miles from the highway where the buses go to town, and fifteen miles from the city itself. I get a day off once a week. Mr. Duncan will take me to town when he leaves for work in the morning and bring me back when he comes home in the evening. But I have nowhere to go, so I will only leave here once every two or three weeks when I go to the Home for my medical checkup.

The house is only a year old, quite large, with seven bedrooms, four baths and three fireplaces, no less! Four of the bedrooms, with two baths and a playroom, are in the children's wing, and that's really all I have to worry about. Josephine, the colored maid, comes every Tuesday and Friday, sometimes on Saturday, to do all heavy cleaning and ironing. I just look after the children, straighten up their rooms and feed them whenever Mrs. Duncan is away.

Kids have always made me feel awkward; I never knew what to say to them. I've never even been a baby-sitter. But Peter and Lori are nice. They don't ask for a lot of attention and they do as I say. Peter is eight and in the third grade. He is in school most of the day and when he is home he's got all kinds of projects going. His room is full of things I always thought little boys ought to have. Like rock collections and an abandoned bird's nest, an old steering wheel, a homemade slingshot, and Alexander the turtle in a cardboard box.

Lori is only four and plays alone most of the day. She has brown eyes below blond bangs and lives quite often in a world of pretend. I hear her talk to her make-believe friends and pets; sometimes she sings to them. Maybe it's because there are no other four-year-olds in the valley.

The new baby is already part of the family. Mrs. Duncan is knitting a little white baby-sweater, and Lori rocks her teddy bear to sleep and sings about the baby. Peter works in spurts on his project; he is building a car for his new brother (Peter is sure it will be a boy), and that's what the steering wheel is for.

My presence doesn't seem to make much difference to the household. When Mrs. Duncan is home, I do my work quickly and go to my room or for a walk in the hills. Sometimes in the evening I am invited to join them watching television, but I enjoy the solitude of my room so much I'd rather stay here. Also, I don't want to be with the Duncans more than I have to. I don't want to be tempted to talk about myself. Watching the family doing things together hurts a little bit, too. I am just plain envious, I think, and it makes me feel more restless and alone.

Tuesday the 29th
Late evening

Mikki's words, "Make your decision early," have been bothering me every day. Last night I wrote Dorothy and told her to look around for an adoptive family, just in case. I haven't made up my mind yet, but if I am going to part with this baby I must start making plans now. Just because it's growing in me doesn't mean it belongs to me. I know that. It would be like saying that a flower belongs to the soil.

It is strange how the love between mother and child develops from one-ness to separateness—independence. And the love between man and woman develops the other way.

There is the daylight coming over the hill. My candle is burning low and dripping. When I blow it out, the window frames a square of light gray pre-dawn.

OCTOBER

Monday the 5th

I put Lori down for her after-lunch nap and ran barefoot up the steep dirt road. I still don't look pregnant when I wear a loose shirt over my dungarees. Running uphill takes my breath away. I'll probably have to give that up soon.

The view from the rim road is beautiful. The grass on the rounded hills has dried to a rich yellow, and the clusters of trees range in color from a deep green to orange, yellow and rusty brown. Yellow and red wildflowers grow by the wayside. I picked enough for a bowl in my room.

I saw the mail truck coming and stopped to watch it. The heavy beating of my heart wasn't from running. It was about time for a letter from Dorothy. The mailman smiled and waved at me.

"Are you Jean Thompson? Staying with the Duncans?"

I nodded and he handed me the bundle of mail, several magazines and letters, and on top an airmail envelope addressed to me in Dorothy's strong, slanting handwriting.

"Just want to make sure when there's a new name that somebody didn't get the wrong address." The mailman grinned and waved again as he took off down the road.

I walked back slowly, feeling the gravel under my bare feet. I looked at that envelope addressed to Jean Thompson; it seemed strange it should have anything to do with me. I ate my lunch before opening it, trying to let my mind go blank. Letting the thoughts wait makes me feel as if I have a choice. Dorothy wrote:

> I am proud of you and think you are wise in making the arrangements for the baby's adoption this soon.
>
> A good friend of mine, who lives in the city where you are, knows a young couple there who adopted a baby three years ago. They would like to have another child now. My friend says they are fine people. He is a high school teacher. If you are interested, I will let them know about you and their lawyer will get in touch with you.
>
> I miss you, and you've had two phone calls. I told them you were in New York for a couple of days. What are you going to tell your family about Christmas plans?
>
> Let me know if there is anything I can do for you.
>
> Why don't you want an agency adoption?
>
> > Love,
> > Dorothy

How typical of her. She is matter-of-fact and to the point, outspoken and a stickler for details. I don't know what I'd do without her. Now, why couldn't Mother be like that? Blow her stack when I do something she disapproves of but accept me for what I am. Oh, I know she means well, but we just don't talk the same language. She'd die of shame if she knew what I am doing. She belongs to the Salvation Army Auxiliary back home and I've helped her wrap Christmas gifts for those "poor misguided, unfortunate girls." She never believed it could happen to the daughter of anyone she knew, especially her own! In her mind those girls were "different."

The couple Dorothy wrote about—are they the right family for my baby? How can I be sure? I wish the baby were here to talk to. I wish I didn't have to decide alone what is best for both of us.

Tuesday the 6th

The letter I've written Dorothy is right here, sealed and stamped. I can still tear it up.

I am telling her to write that young couple. To tell them I want to see their lawyer as soon as possible—and then I want to meet them. Maybe it will hurt more that way, but how else can I be sure they are the right family for my baby? I've got to make sure. Am I doing the right thing? Am I going against a natural law that says a child belongs with its natural mother?

In my letter to Dorothy I say I am sure. From now on I must act as if I am sure—even if I can never be. When I mail the letter, I have committed myself. From then on my fears and my doubts must be mine alone.

Must it be this final? Dear God, what have I just done?

Later . . .

I ran all the way up to the mailbox and flipped up the little red flag on the side, so the mailman would be sure to pick up my letter. I could see his red-white-and-blue truck up the road.

Then I came back to my room and tried to sit in the chair by the window, my hands touching the white painted window sill. The afternoon sun was slanting through the trees along the edge of the hill. I moved my fingers over the smooth surface of that sill, trying to put my whole being into touching the wood, trying to stop the thoughts, the fear. I closed my eyes and tried a desperate wish—let me get out of here, out of this waiting for something I can't anticipate—except that it will hurt. I try to fill the time with simple surface thoughts and, for a little while, I can almost make believe that is all there is.

And then something goes wrong inside. I am afraid this time it will break and carry me away out there to drown in the oily smooth blackness. I mustn't scream. I mustn't let go! God! I say it out loud and my voice is calm, still under control.

Give me anything but this quiet waiting, this stillness and loneliness. People—but I don't want people. I'm sick of them, the shells that are people and the empty voices coming out of them.

Mrs. Duncan knocked on my door and peeked in. She looked concerned.

"Jean, are you all right?"

I made myself smile and nod; my throat was too choked up to talk. Mrs. Duncan was pretty in her new maternity dress.

"We're going out for supper—give the children hamburgers and don't let them watch too much TV before bedtime."

Later . . .

I can't let myself go like that again. I'm walking a tightrope and I've got to keep my balance, so I've taken a stand. That's that. Alone, I could afford to wallow in self-pity, but others are involved and I'm committed to them. Help me hold off my emotions just a few more months—till I've fulfilled my commitment to the baby and the adoptive family. I'm on my own after that and I can only hurt myself.

These months are the real thing. I can't pretend otherwise. I was always a dreamer. I thought my dreams were real and my actions not so important. Dreams are easy; they never leave scars.

You're never stuck with consequences of your bad dreams. Just dream another one.

Wednesday the 7th

A note from Dorothy—enclosed was a letter from Patrick. Dorothy wrote:

I'm enclosing a letter for Jean Thompson from someone I've never heard of—how come he knows that name and not your whereabouts?

Surprise! My thoughtful husband thinks I should go to California to visit Aunt Helen before Christmas. Wouldn't it be grand if I can come to see you? I'll let you know more about it later. . . .
                                                      All my love.

I made myself an extra cup of coffee and curled up on my bed before opening Patrick's letter. He wrote:

Dear strange girl from the train . . .

I have a terrible problem. You may be the girl of my dreams, and I let you go without trying to find out. Now if I rush back to see you, you may not be my dream girl. Then I won't even have that dream to keep me company.

The red leaf isn't in the envelope by accident. It stuck to my foot when I walked home from class in the rain, an autumn greeting to you. . . . I am coming back east on my Christmas vacation. Will you meet me then, or don't you like my dream?

I wish I could tell him everything. But maybe he wouldn't write to me then. He is on the outside, where people put labels on each other and don't look back of the labels. I can't tell Patrick that I'm going to be an unwed mother soon. What about his dream then? Would he still send autumn leaves?

Saturday the 10th

Karen just phoned; it was really good to hear her voice again.
She said she's discovered a small café down the street where they
have the best coffee in the world; it's a truck stop, and the guy
who owns it makes great hamburgers, too.

"Let's go there Tuesday when you come in for your checkup."

Karen said Marian has gone to a wage home. She'll only be
there a month and then go home to get married before Christmas.
Cora had her baby and didn't even want to see it, Karen said.
She left the home yesterday looking very slim and very striking
in a new suit and with a new fluffy hairdo. Karen said she was
going to Hollywood to get a job. Lucy has delivered and gone,
too. Lisa was moved downstairs to the small dorm early this week.
Karen said the other girls had been teasing her.

"And you," I said, "how do you feel?"

"Couldn't be better!" Karen laughed. "I've been having some
real sharp dropping pains lately. The more it hurts the sooner it's
over!"

Lori came rushing into my room screaming at the top of her
voice, "The bird bit me, the bird bit me!" I left the typewriter
to take her in my arms.

"Birds don't bite. They don't have teeth," I said.

"This one does," Lori sobbed. "It is a red bird and it has giant
black teeth." I said perhaps it was a pretend bird, and she
stamped her foot. "That doesn't make any difference. Pretend
birds can bite too." She looked at me with tears rolling down
smudgy cheeks.

"I know they do, but now you're safe and maybe we can find

a big pretend dog to chase the bird away?" That made her laugh
and she ran outside to look for the dog. In Lori's little world real
and pretend flow together.

In my world I'm just learning to keep them apart.

Later

I heard the phone ring again and Mrs. Duncan came to my
door. She had a funny look on her face when she said the call
was for me, and I wondered why. The man who called said his
name was Mr. Borton, attorney for the young couple who want to
adopt my baby.

"I hope I haven't embarrassed you," he said. "I forgot you are
living under an assumed name. I'm afraid I used your real name."
I could feel my cheeks burning, but I told him it didn't really
matter. He asked how soon I could come to his office, and I said
Tuesday, when I go to town for my checkup. He said, "See you
then," and I hung up and turned to face Mrs. Duncan.

"Isn't Jean Thompson your real name?" It sounded like an
accusation. I just stood there staring at her, like a fool. All I
could think of was that Miss O'Connor had told me the wage-
home mother wouldn't ask questions.

"Don't you trust us, Jean? We want to be your friends." I
could only nod and stammer, "I—I know you do—of course I
trust you," but I couldn't make myself tell her the truth, and I
just stood there till she finally smiled and said, "We know it must
be hard for you."

I smiled back as well as I could and turned to go to my room.
I hope she never gets back on that subject. Maybe I can trust her
—maybe I can't. But she would be one more person who knows
the truth, and she would tell her husband. I can't take chances.

Near midnight

Maybe this was the wrong time to do it, but I wrote Patrick anyway. I have to have someone to talk to—even if it is only on paper. I didn't tell him where I am and why, but I did write about how I feel. About being alone and afraid. About how hard it is when there are no absolutes, no easy answers. How hard to grow up to the big world, the excitement, the new horizons, ideas, people, unlimited hopes, unlimited dreams—unlimited reality.

And then you can't go back to the security of being very young, assuming that grownups know all there is to know, even if you don't. And you can't go back to wipe out your mistakes and what you've learned and done. You're so damned alone—you can't share your innermost thoughts, even if you know them. You can never quite reach the soul of another person, and you're even afraid of coming close—afraid you might get hurt, lose something of yourself.

It is the sort of letter I never send if I wait till the next day to read it again. But I won't read this one again. I want to share something with someone.

Tuesday evening, the 13th

What a day this has been. So much has happened in a few short hours, and I had grown so used to the peaceful solitude of this valley. Today shattered that peace and I'm really not sorry.

To begin with, Mrs. Duncan drove me to the Home this morning. We didn't say much on the way; there is tension between us and I don't know how to ease it without telling her about myself.

She stopped the car outside the Home and handed me a check for the money I have earned. My cheeks got red.

"I'm sorry," I said. "I haven't got any identification, I can't cash a check."

"Not even in there?" She looked surprised and nodded toward the Home. I shook my head, and without a word she gave me twenty dollars from her purse.

"My husband will pick you up at six," she said.

"Thank you, I'll be ready." I got out of the car and waved good-bye. She didn't look back.

I could hear laughter from the second floor of the Home. The windows were open and the old house sounded like a happy place. I walked slowly up the steps and through the green door. A new girl was waiting on the couch in the hall, her hand on the handle of a worn suitcase. She looked up at me quickly with that guarded look we all carry in here from the outside.

"Poor kid," I thought, and smiled at her. She smiled back. It felt good to be a visitor, to nod to the girls I saw passing in the hall and watch them grin when they recognized me as one of them. Then Mrs. Warren stuck her sour face out the window from the inner office.

"Go straight to the hospital floor, Jean," she said sternly. "No outsiders in the dorms, you know." I felt cheated and left out. "The hell with her," I told myself, and marched right upstairs and into the green dorm, where Karen was knitting on her bed.

"Hi, there!" I yelled, so loud she jumped. Her face lit up when she saw me.

"Hi, stranger, join the party." Karen waved a chocolate bar in my direction and then she noticed that I was wearing my blouse loose over my skirt instead of tucked in and with a belt.

"Why Jean," she said with mock seriousness, "if I didn't know you better I'd suspect you were pregnant." We laughed and

Karen patted her own big belly. "Guess what, the doctor says I'm engaged, I'm going to be two soon."

"Wow!" I said, playing along. "Who's the lucky guy, anyone I know?"

"Stupid!" Karen laughed. We all use the old joke about being engaged. Actually it is the term the doctor uses to say that the baby's head has come down into the upper part of the birth channel during the last stage of the pregnancy. I sat on the edge of Karen's bed and munched on the chocolate bar. The noises of the dorm—two radios playing at once, voices talking and laughing—seemed pleasantly familiar.

"You missed seeing Marian," Karen said. "She left yesterday and she'll be married Saturday. She said to tell you good-bye. You never saw a happier bride-to-be."

We sat quietly with our own thoughts for a minute. I thought how hard it must have been for Marian to make her decision to go home. How she had to come all the way out here to a home for unwed mothers to get away from the pull of those who love her and want to make up her mind for her.

"Don't forget our date," Karen said. "Coffee at Toni's."

The intercom made noise: "Jean T., Jean T., you're wanted on the hospital floor." I ran down the hall where Nurse Simpson was holding the white hospital gown for me.

"Doctor can't wait, hurry up!" She didn't sound mad, so I guess she knows how it is to come back and meet friends after being alone in a wage home.

The doctor listened to my heart and then put the stethoscope against my tummy, listening intently.

"He's there, all right," he said. "A good, strong heartbeat." I felt quite excited.

"When will it be?" The doctor smiled a little at my eagerness. "It's a bit early to tell yet. When are you due?"

"In March."

"Maybe you'll be just a little bit early." He smiled.

"Thanks a lot." I jumped off the table and headed for the door.

"You're welcome," he said after me, "but don't blame me if you're late."

Shucks, I said to myself, I won't be late.

Karen was waiting for me, all ready to go, but I had something to do first.

"Why don't you go ahead?" I said, ignoring the question mark written all over her face. "Tell me how to get to Toni's and I'll meet you there."

"Can't miss it," she said. "It's on your left when you walk down Main Street. There are always a couple of big trucks parked in front."

"O.K." I waved her out the door and walked down the hall to Miss O'Connor's office. She looked up and smiled when I opened the door.

"Come right in, Jean," she said, pushing away a stack of papers on her desk. "What's on your mind?" I dumped down in her red chair and pulled on the cigarette she offered me as if there were some kind of hidden courage in the smoke.

"I'm on my way to see a lawyer and I need some advice," I said. Miss O'Connor watched me calmly.

"Oh?" she said.

"I've decided to have the baby adopted, and I want an independent adoption," I said, watching her face for a reaction. But she just kept on looking at me with that quiet smile of hers.

"So?" she said. "What do you want me to tell you?"

"The people who want my baby—I'm seeing their lawyer for the first time today—they've already adopted one baby three years ago. I thought—I mean, they've already been approved by the state." I broke off, feeling angry at my own clumsy speech. "Why don't you tell me an agency adoption is better and safer?" I said, hoping she'd say something, try to change my mind or something. "Why don't you tell me I run all sorts of risks with a private adoption? Oh, and I haven't told you the clincher yet—I want to meet them to make sure. . . ." Miss O'Connor smoked in silence, watching me punch out my cigarette in her ash tray.

"I'm not here to tell you what is better for you," she said quietly. "I'm not here to make up your mind for you, even if you'd just love to have someone tell you what to do. However, I can tell you what is involved in what you want to do, once you have made up your mind to do it. Why do you want an independent adoption, by the way?"

"I want to make sure the baby has a mother to go home to right from the start. I just know a baby needs a mother right away," I ended lamely.

"Of course, you are aware of the risks," Miss O'Connor said briskly. "You, the natural mother, are actually legally responsible for that baby until the court closes the case six months after placement. The adoptive parents could change their minds, you know, in case something unforeseen develops."

I nodded. "That's why I wanted to meet the couple," I said, "to be sure they were the kind who would go ahead regardless." I moved uneasily on the chair. "Is it common for natural mothers to meet the adoptive parents?"

Miss O'Connor took a book from her shelf. "This is the California law governing such cases," she said. "Actually, in independent or direct placement adoptions, the natural mother has a right to know the names of the adoptive parents and to assure herself, either through a third party or by personal contact, that the adoptive parents satisfy her requirements."

"But agency adoptions are safer, aren't they?" I don't know what made me ask. Miss O'Connor smiled.

"That depends on what you're looking for," she said. "The agency *does* take over full legal responsibility for the child until placement is made, and in an agency adoption the family is thoroughly evaluated by the welfare agency before placement of the child . . . just to give you an idea," she said. "A few years ago, of nearly ten thousand adoptions in California alone, nearly seventy per cent were independent, and fifty per cent of those were open agreements—that is, the natural mother met the adoptive parents. Risk or no risk"—she smiled—"you aren't the first one to take it." I got up to leave.

"I came to get some moral support, if nothing else," I said. "I'm scared to death of making this thing final!"

"I bet you are," Miss O'Connor said. "You wouldn't be normal if you didn't have some serious thoughts about doing this. But I will say one thing before you go. I am confident that you will do the right thing for all parties involved. Come back and see me soon." She reached her hand across the top of the desk and shook mine.

"Good luck, Jean," she said, and in spite of myself I had to smile back. "Thanks," I said. "See you later."

I found Karen at Toni's. She lifted her coffee cup in greeting when she saw me and said, "My fifth. What kept you?"

"Nothing much." I tried to sound casual. For some reason I couldn't come right out and tell her about my talk with Miss O'Connor. Karen shrugged her shoulders, but her smile was the old friendly one. "You keep your secrets, I keep mine," she said. "Nine months of secrets and for me it's almost over." She nodded toward the Coke-calendar on the wall.

"See that?" she said. "I've been sitting here staring at it. I can hardly believe my due-date is this close. You know, sometimes I wake up in the middle of the night thinking I'm going to stay pregnant forever. The baby won't come out or I'll be discovered or something."

"I know," I said, wondering if March would ever come. Toni

brought another cup and the coffee pot. He is short and bald.

"This is Jean," Karen said. "She's a new one on the Hill and she'll be drinking your coffee after I've gone, won't you?" I nodded and smiled, and Toni grinned all over his round face. "You girls are always welcome here," he said. "I've got plenty of coffee." When Toni had left us Karen stirred her coffee absent-mindedly.

"You know, now that it is almost over, I think the worst part of it has been the damn loneliness," she said. "I've adjusted pretty well to the hiding and the lying to the outside world, but I've just never gotten used to being all alone inside." She shook her head, then straightened up and smiled. "But a lot of good has come out of this, too, you know," she said. "I've discovered who my friends are. You find out when you're in trouble. Some people you thought would stick with you always simply walked away, and others, the ones you'd never even thought would care, want to help."

"I used to wonder how you could laugh and joke all the time," I said. "The day I met you and Lucy, I was almost shocked."

Karen laughed. "All the new ones go through that stage," she said. "I did, too. But after a while you find that crying isn't going to help any. You know you've got all that time to wait before you can go out and do something else, and you might as well laugh."

"I know," I said. "But it still upsets me. I think maybe if you learn to live with something that hurts and almost ignore it, then you're not going to try to make it better."

Karen looked at me and shook her head sadly. "You can't do much about it now, Jean. And don't try to be a crusader. Wait till you're out of here, anyway."

"It's just that I keep wondering why I did it in the first place," I said, "and just putting the whole thing out of my mind isn't going to answer the question."

"Forget it, Jean." Karen sounded almost angry, then she smiled and put her hand on my arm. "Look, kid," she said, sounding like a big sister. "This isn't the time to do all that analyzing of yourself and everybody else. It will only drive you nuts and you won't be any wiser. Believe me, I've been the route." She sighed. "But maybe you've got to find out for yourself—is that it?"

"I don't know." I shrugged my shoulders.

"Well." Karen sounded resigned. "I've thought about it a lot, too, and I've only figured out one thing for certain. That the bunch of us in here got pregnant because we had some other big problem we just didn't know how to handle. All of us had a different problem, but one that had us in a corner and pretty miserable." She lit another cigarette. "Of course, I may be all wrong." We smoked in silence. I wondered how many lonely hours and how many cups of coffee and cigarettes it had taken Karen to get to that point. Then I noticed the time—it was nearly one o'clock and I would be late if I didn't hurry.

"I've got an appointment with a lawyer downtown," I said. "Gotta run."

"Lawyer?" Karen looked curious.

"Independent adoption," I said, and the look on her face made me glad I'd said it. Karen held out her hand and I took it.

"Good luck to you," she said. "Give me a call soon."

I watched her go up the sidewalk, her head high and her shoulders straight under the trench coat. She walked with an easy stride in spite of her heavy stomach; she looked very sure of herself. I turned and walked slowly the other way, toward downtown. There was a faint smell of salt from the ocean and I was suddenly aware of how much I had missed the sea breeze in the hills. I've never liked big cities. I get a feeling of being trapped among those big buildings and all the people rushing around for no apparent reason. But this afternoon I didn't mind it. I was an outsider, and what I saw and heard and smelled had nothing to do with me. I thought it was like listening to a great symphony orchestra. The listener can turn and walk away at any time. But if he is one of the musicians he can't, and his little sound is indistinguishable from all the other sounds. (Unless, of course, he plays off key. Then he gets all the attention his little ego might want.)

I found the lawyer's name on the directory in the lobby of one of the big downtown buildings. I couldn't think of another excuse to keep from facing the interview. Seventh floor. In the elevator I stared at all kinds of necks in front of me—thick and thin ones, close-shaven ones and long-haired ones. I've always looked at people's necks. We are all so clever at making masks you can't tell much from faces anymore. Even eyes lie shamelessly. But hands and necks say a lot.

I suddenly had a ridiculous thought. There we were, bodies in a small cubicle, our minds somewhere else. I thought of invisible lines going from each of us to parts of the city and all over the world. What if the elevator fell down and killed us all? Would our thoughts still be floating around somewhere, without purpose, and nowhere to come back to?

"Seven," called the elevator operator. I pushed past the necks and followed a plump lady with tinted red hair down the corridor. She walked straight past the door with the legend, RICHARD E. BORTON, ATTORNEY, and I had to go in alone. The carpet was thick and green, and the young well-groomed lady behind the mahogany desk looked at my shabby trench coat and my only pair of low-heeled walking shoes splashed with muddy rain.

"I think Mr. Borton is expecting me," I said, fighting the impulse to turn and run out the door again.

"Oh, you must be Miss Thompson," she said, and flipped a switch on the little box on her desk.

"Miss Thompson is here to see you," she said in a warm

smooth voice. The door to the inner office was opened quickly and Mr. Borton came toward me with outstretched hand and a tremendous smile. He was wearing a tweed suit and red tie, and looked about forty. There were discreet streaks of silver in his thick black hair. His voice was booming.

"Hel-lo, Miss Thompson. I'm so glad you could make it. Come on in." I smiled weakly and he grabbed my hand, almost pulling me into his office. I sank into a huge, soft, leather chair and Mr. Borton sat down behind his gleaming desk in his red leather swivel chair. I waited for him to start the conversation. He cleared his throat several times, tapping his finger tips lightly together.

"Let me make it clear from the start," he said, a bit awkwardly, and I suddenly felt like laughing. "I don't hold your present situation against you . . . it can happen to the best of us." I smiled and thought his clients had better not be anything like their lawyer or I'd call the whole thing off.

"Well, then," Mr. Borton continued after a slight pause, "my clients have informed me that you are interested in making arrangements with them for the placement of your child." I nodded.

"I want everything settled as soon as possible," I said, "so that when the baby is born there will be nothing further to discuss."

"I can understand that," he said, "and I'm sure the adoptive parents will agree." He reached for a pad and a silver pencil on his desk.

"Some questions. The adoptive parents would like to know your age, occupation, the father's age, race and occupation." I rattled off the answers; I'm getting used to them by now.

"I'd like to meet them," I said, and Mr. Borton stopped taking notes to stare at me.

"I—I really don't know," he said. "I've only met them over the phone—they may not agree to a meeting." I drew in my breath sharply and felt the nervous quivering in my stomach. "It's very important to me." I tried to keep my voice calm. "And it is quite common here in California." I nodded toward his bookshelf where I could see the book on the California code Miss O'Connor had quoted. "It's in your book there"—I spoke quickly—"that in independent adoptions the decision is made after the two parties—the natural mother and the adoptive parents—have obtained a thorough knowledge of each other and have come to a complete agreement." I could hear how stilted my own words sounded, but Mr. Borton was listening intently.

"As the natural mother I have a right to know the name of the adoptive parents," I continued. The nervousness had left my stomach entirely. "I saw some statistics in my social worker's office. A few years ago fifty per cent of the independent adoptions in this state were open agreements—the natural mother met the adoptive parents."

Mr. Borton was smiling a little. "You've done your homework, haven't you?"

"It's my baby and my life," I said. He leaned forward across the desk, his voice businesslike again. "I'll call the young couple today," he said. "I'll tell them what you have told me—I hope they will see it the same way."

"If they don't, I'm afraid I can't go ahead with it," I said. "I've got to be sure in my own mind that they are the right family for the baby."

"I'll do my best to convince them." Mr. Borton got up from his chair and held out his hand. I got to my feet. We shook hands and he said he will call me as soon as he has talked to the adoptive parents. I caught the bus back to the Home and got there just as Mr. Duncan drove up to pick me up.

It's way past midnight and I've written half a book, it seems. But I remember Mikki's words—write it down, then you can go back and read how you felt. I'm terribly forgetful. Is it a blessed forgetfulness? Or a dangerous one, just putting off facing things?

Wednesday the 14th

Another letter from Patrick came today. He writes as if he can read my thoughts: "Yes, you might get hurt if you share your innermost thoughts with someone. But without sharing you will never live fully—the way I believe we are meant to live. Our masks of lies and pretenses become so much part of us that two who could love each other may meet and pass by and never know this."

He is right, of course. But I don't dare share with him now. I have to write about little things, walking in the rain, a favorite book. I can't say where I am and what I'm doing. I am not lying to him. I just avoid the truth.

Friday the 16th

Late at night when the house is quiet, I talk to myself. Is it any different from writing to myself in these pages? Or I talk to my books or to the pictures of Mother and Dad. It's good to get thoughts off my chest, hear them spoken out loud, even if they can't hear me.

I remember last summer. I helped Mother clean the attic and we found the baby clothes she has saved all these years. Mother held the little dresses and shawls up for me to see and said I could have them for my first baby. I wonder how I'll feel when I put them on my second-born—if I ever have another child.

I've promised myself I will try not to think of things that may make me break down. I break that promise often.

Sunday the 18th

Last night I kept waking up to go to the bathroom. When I returned to my room after the last trip I could see the faint glow over the hills where the morning was about to happen, and suddenly I felt a light fluttering inside my stomach, a tiny movement, almost like a gas pain, only I knew it wasn't. I stood still and it came again.

My baby moved.

Friday the 30th

I'm halfway through the pregnancy, the calendar says. Four and a half months to go—that isn't all eternity, even if it seems that long since I first thought I was pregnant. I alternate between wishing it were all over and wishing it would go on and on and on. When I try to imagine what it will be like to give up a baby, it is still only in my mind, and that baby is safely inside me. Four and a half months from now it won't be imagination anymore. I believe that somewhere inside of me is the strength I will need to face that test, but I'm scared to death that I won't have the self-discipline to call on that strength. If I chicken out then, all this will have been for nothing.

I ask myself the same questions over and over again and repeat my own made-up answers. I must get off that merry-go-round and think of something concrete instead—sew the tear in my shirt, make a pot of coffee.

NOVEMBER

Saturday the 21st

Less than four months to go, and it's suddenly crowded inside my skin. My ribs are sore, and when the baby kicks I think maybe he or she is trying to tell me that two of us are just one too many inside a skin made for only one. I feel stuffed every time I eat, and I can't drink anything at night without having to go to the bathroom every couple of hours. If I could only walk in my sleep. Now I toss and turn and chase my thoughts in hopeless circles most of the night.

I don't want to be this tired. I can't think straight when I don't get enough sleep. I feel sometimes as if someone or something is trying to see how far they can push me before I break. But I'll get through this thing one way or the other!

And that's a rotten lie. I'll never be through with this; it will be part of me always. A child growing up somewhere—and my name on the adoption papers.

Later

The phone rang—for me. Mr. Borton called to say the adoptive parents have agreed to meet me. Their name is Carver, Martha and Don.

"They would like to have you come to their house tomorrow afternoon," he said.

"So soon?" I could barely whisper.

"You asked for it, didn't you? I had to work hard to convince them." Mr. Borton sounded impatient.

"Thank you. I appreciate it," I said, and felt as if a web were slowly closing around me. But that's what I wanted, to have it so tied up I can't chicken out.

"Mr. Carver will pick you up after church tomorrow," Mr. Borton said. "And by the way, I suggested he call you by your first name, and that you pretend you know each other—we don't want to embarrass you any further with the Duncans." The poor guy is probably sorry he made that silly blunder the first time he called.

Saturday night

I'm scared. What if I don't like them? Or, if I like them a lot, is it going to hurt more knowing what they are like and what their house is like?

Karen just phoned from the mothers' ward. "I made it," she said. She was bursting with excitement. "We get to make one phone call right after we get back from the delivery room. I just had to tell someone right away—did I wake you up?"

"Of course not," I said. "It's only ten thirty. I'm a night owl, you know—and congratulations!"

"Jean, I'm so happy!" Karen's voice trembled slightly. "You ought to see me—no tummy and I'll start exercising tomorrow morning. I'll be out of here in a week."

"That's great," I said. "I'll be coming in Tuesday for my

checkup—I'll expect you to be doing the twist by then." It was a silly thing to say but Karen laughed.

"I'll show you. And I'm gonna get a solid night's rest, on my tummy, starting right now. Goodnight, Jean."

"Goodnight, Karen."

So she's over the line now. I wonder if she had a boy or a girl. I didn't want to ask and I guess she didn't want to tell me.

Sunday morning, the 22nd

It's a lovely morning. The sun is gold over yellow and brown hills. I am all dressed up, which isn't so much—just the black skirt and my red-and-green top; it isn't as washed-out as the others. I've shined my one pair of shoes. I don't want to make an altogether bad impression on Mr. and Mrs. Carver. He ought to be here any minute now. Oh God, I know I wanted this. Give me strength to go through with it.

Sunday night

I am really too tired to write about it now, but I'm afraid of going to bed. I'm afraid of turning out the light and trying to go to sleep, and starting to think. So maybe I better talk about it, get it all down on paper and out of my mind.

Don Carver came to get me a little after noon. He is tall, blond and good-looking. I don't know what I had expected but I hadn't thought he would be so nice. He took my hand in a firm shake and his blue eyes looked at me calmly. Mrs. Duncan was watching us, so I smiled and said, "Hi, Don, nice to see you."

The Carvers live in a suburb on the other side of town and the ride took nearly an hour. I felt awkward at first, but Don

Carver must have felt worse. He was trying to make polite conversation.

"How do you like California?" he asked me, and then bit his
lip. I guess he thought it wasn't the thing to ask under the circumstances.

"It's nice," I said. "I'd like to come back on a visit some time."
I caught his quick glance and realized I'd said something wrong,
too. We rode in silence for a while and I was beginning to think
the whole thing was a terrible mistake.

"I'm sorry," I said. "I—I just had to see you."

"We understand," he said. "It took me a while, but my wife
said she thought she understood how you must feel—and we do
want another child very much."

"When this is over," I said, "try to believe me when I say I
will honor the decision we make together. I won't try to get in
touch with you again. I don't want you to get in touch with me.
I only want what is best for the baby." I could see Don's knuckles
whiten over the steering wheel.

"I believe you," he said, "because I want to believe you. We
know this is harder for you than for us. We have nothing to lose
—and a lot to gain."

Don turned into a quiet side street with trees lining the side-
walks and stopped in front of a brick house. The white front
door flew open and a little girl ran down the path to meet us.

"Daddy, Daddy!" She screamed with delight when Don lifted
her high in his arms.

"Hi, princess," he said. "Say hello to Jean. This is our Kathy."

"Hi, Jean," Kathy said politely and turned immediately to Don
again, her red curls dancing around her bright little face. "We're
gonna have cookies and tea—Mommy's got it ready." Don
laughed and put her down on the sidewalk. She held his big hand
and they walked together to the house. Martha Carver was standing in the doorway. I was almost afraid to look at her, but her

eyes were warm and when she smiled there was a dimple in her cheek.

"I'm glad to meet you." She took my hand and I could only smile and whisper, "Thank you." I didn't trust my voice.

The tea table was set for four in front of a blazing fire in the fireplace. Kathy's little rocking chair was there and she ran to sit down before we did. I glanced around the room—the books, the paintings lining the walls, the worn but comfortable furniture, the bay window full of potted flowers. Martha caught my glance.

"It's one of our hobbies," she said, "growing flowers."

"How about some tea?" Don pointed to a comfortable chair. "Sit down, Jean, make yourself at home." I did want to feel at home, and it would have been so easy in that friendly room with those nice people—if only I hadn't been the mother of their future child. Half a birthday cake stood on the tea table.

"Kathy's birthday was yesterday. We thought we would celebrate two days," Martha said.

"How nice," I said. "How old are you now, Kathy?"

"I was three yesterday," said Kathy, "and I'll be four soon."

Martha poured the tea and Kathy drank hers with half a cup of milk and sugar. Her dolly sat on her lap and had to be scolded for spilling crumbs on the rug. Over Kathy's head we talked about the weather, getting ready for Christmas and the latest news, carefully avoiding any mention of babies or related subjects. At last Martha turned to Kathy with a smile.

"Time to put baby-doll down for a nap, Kathy." Kathy looked reluctant but her mother's face was stern. She stood up with her doll in her arms.

"Baby-doll isn't very sleepy," she said. "But I'll read her a long story so she won't cry." We sat in silence till Kathy had left the room.

"We know your decision is a hard one," Martha said, looking directly at me. "We want you to be sure in your mind about us—

so ask any questions you like." I searched for words—what could I ask them? How could I even try to compare what I have to offer a baby with all they have to give?

"Now that I'm here, the questions don't seem so important," I said. "I wasn't concerned about your social or financial situation. I know you've already adopted one child and have gone through the state investigation. I just wanted to know what kind of people you are." I hesitated but Martha's eyes urged me on. "I really have no right to question you," I said. "I don't have anything to give the baby myself. But there are some things I wish I could give—maybe I'm selfish in wanting you to give them."

"Not selfish," said Martha. "You have a right to look for what you think is best for your child."

"I'm also asking for my own sake," I said, "so that if I have regrets in the future they will be for myself, not because I worry about the baby." I was beginning to feel terribly self-conscious. "Maybe what I really want to know is whether you're going to be good parents and love the baby. And how can you ask a question like that?"

Don smiled. "I can tell you that I think Martha is the best mother in the world. Or maybe you should ask Kathy. They sing together and read and grow flowers."

"No one is a perfect parent," said Martha. "We can't promise happiness for your baby. But we would love him—or her, perhaps even more than if we had had our own children, because then we would not have known how badly we wanted them. We would have taken them for granted." Tears kept flooding my eyes. I had been scared of coming, scared of finding out for sure, but now I knew.

"You're more than I had hoped for," I said, trying to keep my voice even. "My baby will have a wonderful home here with you." I could see the tears in Martha's eyes, too.

"Do you mean that?" she said. I nodded.

"I'm quite sure. And I'm happy, believe me. You need a baby and my baby needs a home. It is really the best for us all." I thought if I didn't get away from there I would break down.

"Tell Mr. Borton to draw up the papers and have them ready to sign as soon as the baby is born. I'll call you when it gets here. It should be around March seventeenth." I thought I sounded quite businesslike.

Martha dried her eyes. "I'll tell my pediatrician," she said. Don offered to drive me home but I thought I would like to be alone, maybe go to the movies and catch a bus back to the hills later.

We said good-bye at the door and I walked quickly down the sidewalk without turning to look back.

I walked the two miles to the business section, and when I got there I didn't want to see a movie after all. The two dollars in my pocket was all the money I owned. I can't get used to being broke all the time. I was broke before this all happened, but it never bothered me then. I knew I could always get a job. Now I'm trapped. I'm not free to earn my own keep. The ten dollars I get at the Duncans' feels like charity, not wages.

My feet began to ache, and inside I felt numb. I could see my reflection in a shop window—the trench coat doesn't quite hide the bulge of my stomach anymore. I wanted to keep on walking, keep from thinking about the baby and Martha and Don Carver and the things I had said to them. The nice noble things about wanting the best for the baby and how I thought they could give him that. It's true, but I don't want it to be.

I sat down on the bench by the bus stop and closed my eyes against the glare from the sinking sun. And then I heard a voice —a trembling old voice. I looked up and saw an old lady sitting next to me, her yellow cheeks painted bright red with rouge, her white hair in thin curls under a pale blue hat. As pale blue as her watery old eyes, so sad and lonely, staring straight ahead while she talked to no one.

"I'm so tired. Where I come from the altitude is so much higher—" Her voice trailed into a whisper and she turned her head slowly to look at me. I saw her hands, limp inside the clean white gloves in her lap. I couldn't make myself speak to her. From inside my loneliness I saw hers—and I got up and walked away.

I walked into the drugstore on the corner, where the juke box was blaring and some boys in leather jackets and high boots played the pinball machine while their girls—also in leather jackets and boots—were dancing with each other. I bought some chewing gum and read the titles of the paperback books on the rack. The monotonous beat of the music drove me out of there, and I went into a small Chinese restaurant right next door. On the wall was a bright poster advertising Coke as "The Friendliest Drink in the World." It made me feel very lonely and I wanted to cry. I ordered tea and the little Chinese woman brought fortune cookies with it. I broke the cookies and two of the slips of paper inside them said that I'm lucky in money matters and will soon hear pleasant news from an unexpected source.

I walked back to the bus stop and the little old woman had gone.

Tuesday night, the 24th

I went in for my checkup today.

At the Home they are getting ready for Thanksgiving. They make the most of every holiday to break the monotony for the girls. Gay streamers decorated the hall and on the chapel door someone had tacked up a copy of the first presidential Thanksgiving proclamation of 1789.

... It is the duty of nations to acknowledge the providence of Almighty God, to obey his will, to be grateful for his benefits, and humbly to implore his protection and favor. . . .

George Washington

I met Mrs. Warren in the hall and she wagged a finger at me. "No visiting on the dorm this time, Jean." I smiled and shook my head. There wasn't anyone I wanted to see in the dorm. Karen is in the mothers' ward.

Doctor Norwad was on duty again. I hope he'll be on call when I get ready to deliver. All the doctors who take turns serving our hospital are nice, but most of them make us feel like numbers on a production line when we jump up on the examination table, one after the other. Doctor Norwad is different. He makes you feel important. He cares. He even has time to answer our questions and explain how we are doing in words we can understand, instead of the mumbo jumbo the nurse puts on our charts.

He felt my tummy. "Long and narrow," he said. "Floating, dipping lower right quadrant," which means in plain English that the baby is in correct position, head down but not engaged yet. Doctor Norwad told me all about it, smiling, his blue eyes circled with dark from lack of sleep.

I'm holding my weight down, too. Nurse Simpson is pleased. Heaven knows I fight the urge to nibble all day long. Smoking isn't a healthy substitute but I can't stay off cigarettes, too.

I saw Karen in the mothers' ward. She's up already and looked slim in a housedress. But her smile wasn't as bright as it used to be and she joked about having the "after baby blues"—literally.

She told me she signed the papers yesterday and the baby will go to a foster home tomorrow to await placement in a permanent home.

"Thank God she's healthy," Karen said. "Healthy white babies find homes quickly." We joked about my big tummy, and I told her I met the adoptive parents Sunday.

"Good for you," Karen said, and we were silent for an awkward minute.

"Well, I'll be going back to the snow country the day after Thanksgiving," Karen said brightly. "It'll be good to try on skis again."

"Think of me when you go down that slope," I said, and Karen laughed. "How can I ever forget!"

We sat in silence again—it was hard to think of something to say. There was a wide gulf between us and nothing to bridge it with. I think we could have been good friends on the outside, too, but Karen never told me her real name or where she comes from, and I never told her mine. If we meet again it will be by accident—and we may not even want to admit we ever knew each other. I got up to leave.

"So soon?" said Karen, but in her eyes I saw the relief I felt, too.

"Mrs. Duncan is picking me up early," I said. I held out my hand and Karen took it.

"Good luck, Karen," I said. "It's been good knowing you." My throat felt funny.

"Good luck to you, Jean," Karen said, and the look in her face brought the tears to my eyes. I pulled her close and hugged her quickly, and then I ran out the door.

I think I understand now why we joke so much in the Home and don't get too close to each other. It hurts to be alone—but it's even worse to part from someone who could have been a friend.

Thanksgiving evening

The house has been full of the smells and sounds of Thanksgiving all day. Mrs. Duncan told me I could have the day off, but I have nowhere to go, so I went for a long walk among the hills and I've spent the rest of the day in my room reading. I borrowed Hemingway's *The Old Man and the Sea* from the shelf in the den. I remember reading it several years ago and thinking that it was very good, but now the story of the old man—alone with his pride and his pain and his giant fish, battling the sharks who nibbled his catch away—means so much more to me. Mrs. Duncan just knocked on my door and asked me to join them for Thanksgiving dinner.

The table was beautiful. It is tradition in the Duncan family that all members of the household help prepare the meal. Peter and Lori had helped cut up vegetables and decorate the pumpkin pies. Mr. Duncan had made the dressing and stuffed the turkey. Now they were dressed in their Sunday best, and the candles were lit. Mr. Duncan asked us all to join him in prayer. We bowed our heads and they all prayed together. It must be their traditional Thanksgiving prayer.

> Bless our house, Lord, and all in it.
> Bless the food you have given us.
> Bless those who suffer and those who are in need.
> For a wonderful year—we thank you. Amen.

"And bless Grandma and Grandpa and Jean," said Lori, peeking at me. I could feel the silly tears coming and I didn't want to make a fool of myself. I pushed back the chair and got to my feet. They all stared at me and I tried to keep my voice steady.

"I don't think I can eat—will you excuse me please?" I left

the room before anyone could say anything, and I felt like a heel. Why can't I accept kindness? Why do I turn away when someone wants to help? I have so much to give thanks for (or is that proud ego of mine too stubborn to say that sincerely?).

Thanksgiving last year—Mother and I were alone. My brother had joined the Air Force and Dad was caught in a snowstorm in the Midwest where he had been giving guest lectures at a college. What a miserable Thanksgiving it turned out to be.

I had come home from college and had hoped that the months I'd been living away from home had made things easier, but in the big house, that seemed so empty without the rest of the family, Mother and I ate our Thanksgiving chicken dinner in polite silence. I found that we still had very little to say to each other even if Mother always talked a blue streak. She bored me with her fussing over my looks—"You're too thin—do you eat regularly? Shouldn't you wear a heavier coat?" Maybe she meant well but I couldn't take it. Funny, now that I look back on the whole thing, I guess I missed Daddy. We sure do a lot of arguing when we're together and we clash on practically every subject in the book. But it's better than Mother's endless small talk.

Maybe I'm crazy, but right here, right now in my little room, I feel more like giving thanks than I did last year.

Saturday the 28th

The hills were different this morning. It is warmer. Clouds were drifting across the sky and their shadows moved over yellow dry hills. I stopped to wonder what the difference could be. The wind, maybe? It seemed to come from a different direction. There was waiting in the air—something like April in the north when spring comes. Except here it is November in the southwest.

When I went to get the mail the rain came. The drops fell with a rustle against the dry leaves and the heavy scent of dry grass rose from the earth like a soft wave. The drops fell on my face and my bare arms and I felt that, like the hills, I had been waiting for the rain.

I went back to my little room just to sit by the window and watch the rain and the mist drift through our valley. I was never able to just sit before. I would feel guilty. I would feel I ought to be doing something or going someplace.

Here I can sit and it is wonderful. I know this peace doesn't fill all of me, but I am grateful when I have it. It takes little to throw me off balance, but each week, here in the valley, I feel I am getting stronger.

DECEMBER

Tuesday the 1st

It is the first day of the Christmas month and already the holiday spirit is beginning to haunt me. I went in for my checkup today and the group social worker, Mrs. Horner, caught me in the hall to ask if I want to help on the Christmas Service project. This year the girls are going to repair and dress dolls for the Salvation Army Christmas Welfare.

"And of course you're welcome to join our Christmas workshop every afternoon this week and next," she said, holding on to my arm. "We have a wonderful selection of material to make gifts for your friends and relatives—jewelry, wallets, aprons, stuffed toys and lots more."

"I can't get transportation," I said. "I'm too far away to come by bus."

"Oh." She looked disappointed. "Well, you'll enjoy working in the crafts room when you come back to stay, I'm sure," she said, more to herself than to me.

Actually I *would* like to make some gifts for my parents. I used to make gifts for them when I was a little girl. I remember a pair of socks I knitted for my Dad—they were too wide around the ankles and too long between the heel and the toe—but Dad wore them every night during Christmas week. This year I would like to give them something special, and I don't even have the money yet to shop in a five-and-ten.

Friday the 4th

I walked the two miles to the crossroads where there is a small drugstore, a grocery store and a gas station. For my ten dollars I bought a scarf for Mother, a lighter for Dad and some Christmas cards. I've wrapped the gifts and written the few greetings I have to send. I hadn't thought it would hurt so much to write those greetings. Happy, easy words, and I wanted to say so many things I can't say.

I have this feeling of closeness to Mother and Dad that I can't remember ever having felt before. Sure, we haven't gotten along very well the last few years, but what was it Martha Carver said? "No one is a perfect parent—but we'll love our children," or something to that effect. I guess Mother and Dad in their own hardheaded way love me a great deal, and maybe I haven't been the easiest daughter to rear.

I think I'm getting overly sentimental. Those Christmas carols on the radio really get to me.

Sunday the 6th

Dorothy was here today! She didn't phone, just drove up to the house and rang the doorbell. I happened to answer it and my heart skipped a beat when I saw who it was.

"Hi, there," she said, her blue eyes laughing. "Aren't you going to ask me in?" Then she held out her arms and when she hugged me I wanted to burst with happiness. I didn't know how much I had missed her. I showed her to my room and she stood in the center of the floor, turning slowly, seeing the sunlit walls, the flowers in the vase on my table, my miniature Christmas tree hung with the balls I made from tinsel and yarn.

"This is nice," she said, and I saw tears in her eyes. She smiled. "You look wonderful, Jean." I remembered the day she came to my dark hole of an apartment.

"You don't know how I've worried," she said. "I've imagined you pale and panicky."

I said, "Let's have some tea and cookies," and she waited while I brought the tray from the kitchen. I baked the cookies yesterday, leaf-thin spicy ones, from an old recipe my mother taught me years ago.

"I must have known you were coming," I said. We talked for nearly four hours. I told her about the fumbling lawyer and about meeting Don and Martha Carver. It was wonderful to talk to someone without pretending, without having to watch my words.

"I'm glad you made the decision this early," said Dorothy. "I'm quite proud of you, you know." It made me feel good to hear her say it but I had to tell her that sometimes I feel very bad about it. Sometimes I still want to keep the baby even if I know that is all wrong.

"You've come a long way," Dorothy said. "You will find the strength. Don't worry." Dorothy's voice and laughter drove away the shadows of the months of loneliness and fear and lies. I had almost forgotten that it is normal to relax and to laugh and to say what I really mean. To be whole again instead of a split personality. I kept wishing I could stop the clock and hold on to these hours. With Dorothy here, my little room was suddenly no longer isolated from the rest of the world.

It was hard to say good-bye, to hug her and know that the loneliness will close in on me worse than before. Dorothy will be back

in March. She has promised to carry the baby from the Home to
Martha Carver. Then we'll travel back east together.

Meat loaf for supper. Peter and Lori emptied their plates and
I forced myself to eat. After dinner I did the dishes slowly,
stretching the time. I made dough for tomorrow's cookie baking.
The girl who was here from the Home before me, Cindy, will
come to say good-bye. She was like a daughter in the house, Mrs.
Duncan has told me often. Cindy had her baby a week ago and
she is going home the day after tomorrow. I know I can't measure
up to Cindy here, but then the Jean T. who is here is really no
one. It doesn't matter what they think of her.

I brought a cup of tea with me to my room, though I shouldn't
drink anything so close to bedtime. I know I'll get my punishment
during the night—countless trips to the bathroom and sleepless
hours tossing in bed, but right now I don't care. I can let my
hair down just for a while, let those tears roll—stupid, hopeless
tears flowing silently without any purpose. I can't stop them for
they come from somewhere deep inside me where I'm not the
master. It frightens me that I can build up my careful defenses
and watch them be shattered from inside myself.

It is time for my nightly ritual. I cross out another day on my
calendar and then count the days ahead. January, February and
half of March. I can see all the little black crosses and all the
days in one glance. But I sit here and stare at the calendar and
time doesn't seem to move at all, even if I stare for an hour.

Monday the 7th

We had a good day. I think I will sleep tonight. Cindy was
here and we made cookies, a golden mountain of cookies, filling
the house with their fragrance. Peter watched over the record

player and provided us with Christmas music. Our cookie mountain grew slowly because we had to taste every batch. Cindy looked slender and pretty—and a little tired. Her baby has already gone to his new home. She told me about him; he had dark hair and blue eyes and dimples.

"They told me not to hold him," she said. "But I don't want to run away from it. It was really a miracle, Jean. Nothing like it has ever happened to me." When Cindy leaves the Home tomorrow, another girl will be gone—and another child's life just begun.

It is such a great thing—the birth of a child, and I feel so small.

Thursday the 10th

A letter from my brother Tommy, and a twenty-dollar bill enclosed! I haven't been this rich for months. What a wonderful feeling. I should, of course, put the money away for the future. When I get out of this in March I won't be able to go to work right away. But I'd rather do something extravagant, something quite unnecessary. I'll have to think about it. I go in for my checkup Tuesday—I can shop then.

My brother writes poetically about love. He's met this absolutely wonderful out-of-this-world creature, he says. She's a teacher for the American children on the base. My brother says he doesn't mind our family being apart this Christmas, as long as he can be with her. The letter doesn't sound like my practical, down-to-earth, reliable little brother. I'm happy for him, of course. Just hope he doesn't get hurt too badly, but maybe he's more sensible than I ever was.

I remember the first time I thought I was in love—maybe it's really the only time. I was seventeen, and we spent a great deal of time walking through the park holding hands. I can't remember much of what we did or even what we said, only that we were either totally happy or totally in despair. There was never any in-between—or at least I can't remember.

How things have changed since then. Now I find these moments of quiet peace and joy, quiet happiness without the exhilaration I remember—but a happiness that doesn't go away with pain and hurt. I pray that I will never lose it again.

Tuesday the 15th

Today was checkup day again. I'm still holding my weight down and the doctor says I'm doing just fine. Christmas was everywhere in the Home. All this month the girls do special projects and have extra entertainment. Major Laski, the tall, skinny, Polish-born officer, was in the office when I arrived. Her friendly smile was a welcome change from Mrs. Warren's usual sour greeting.

"Are you coming in to spend Christmas with us, Jean?" the Major asked. I shook my head.

"No, I guess I'll stay in the hills," I said. I didn't tell her that I don't think I can stand to have a memory of Christmas in a home for unwed mothers haunt my Christmases in the future. To be alone in a small room with a candle is better.

"We'll miss you," said the Major. "Perhaps you can stay one evening for one of our programs instead." I said perhaps, and let it go at that. Tonight they are having a Christmas carol sing-along and Thursday they will hang greenery and lights all over the house and decorate the Christmas trees. They'll bake cookies Monday, so next Tuesday when I come in I'll have a treat in store.

I could hear a piano and someone singing "Silent Night." The door to the TV lounge was ajar and I looked in. I couldn't see

the girl at the piano but the singer was facing me. Her voice was
so clear and beautiful that I stood there without moving. She is a
new girl and looks about sixteen; she has braces on her teeth, and
short blond hair with bangs above large blue eyes. She wore a
pale blue smock and her hands were folded over her full tummy.
In her eyes was that faraway look of enchantment I've seen in
children's eyes every Christmas.

I went downstairs for a smoke before reporting on the hospital
floor. In the corridor the smell of turpentine and paint hit me,
and the smoking room chairs were piled up outside the door. I
thought to myself, that's great, the janitor must've softened with
the Christmas spirit. I stopped in the doorway. The old drab sanctuary had been painted a cool baby blue, and in the corner was a
girl, in jeans and a washed-out dungaree shirt, down on her
knees putting the finishing touches on the floor boards. She was
whistling while she worked—that old sea chantey, "What Will
We Do with a Drunken Sailor." When she came to the refrain
she started singing, moving her brush in time with the melody,
"Way, hay, there she rises, Way, hay, there she rises, Way, hay,
there she rises—Early in the morning." That finished off the last
of the floor boards and she sat back on her heels to look the job
over. I cleared my throat and she turned her head.

"Hi, there," she said. "You're just in time to help me move
the furniture back in." She jumped to her feet and I noticed that
her stomach was very large.

"I'm Peggy B.," she said. She lifted one of the heavy armchairs
with ease. "I'm due next month."

"I'm Jean T.," I said. "I'm just here for my checkup today—
I'm staying in a wage home. I like the color."

"Oh." Peggy wrinkled her nose, which was spattered with
baby-blue paint. "It fits the mood I'm trying to stay in—cool. I
spend a lot of time down here and I'm hoping the color will re-

mind me not to blow my stack quite so often." She laughed and tossed her short black hair.

"This is a crazy place, don't you know. I mean I thought the girls in here would be a bunch of rebels like me—you know, not caring about the way most people live. I mean they're all having babies and all. And they're not that way at all." Peggy lit a cigarette with slender paint-stained hands. "These kids are the worst conformists I've ever met! They're acting as if they're failures— as if they don't measure up. Me, I'm having a kid, it's a great part of life; then I take off again on the road."

"Is that where you come from, the road?" I said. I took hold of one end of the table; Peggy took the other end and we carried it to its place by the window.

"Well," said Peggy, "yes and no. I've got a home someplace but I've been on the go for the last three years, ever since I quit college."

"What were you taking?" I couldn't help being curious.

"Education and art." Peggy laughed again. "Believe it or not, I wanted to be a teacher, teach little kids in grade school about art. It was a great idea. Little kids are great artists before they get harnessed. I wanted to save some talents. Too bad it didn't work."

"What happened?"

"Those damn courses in education drove me out of my mind. Ever take any? There's nothing more boring, and I can't see that it's got anything to do with kids, real kids." The furniture was back in place. The rickety old chairs looked even shabbier now against the bright walls. Peggy shrugged. "Maybe some other crazy nut-head like me will come along and fix up the furniture," she said. "Not that you girls deserve it." She looked at me and her dark brown eyes sparkled. "Did you go to college?"

I nodded. "Yes, only I got pregnant during my summer vacation."

"Chicken!" Peggy spat out some tobacco from the loose end of her cigarette. "Didn't have the guts to just up and quit?" I had to laugh. Three months ago I would have stalked out in anger.

"That's about it, I guess," I said. "But you got pregnant for a reason, too, didn't you?"

"Sure," she agreed. "Honestly, I just thought I'd try it. I've tried just about everything else—waitress in Alaska, barrel-racing on the rodeo circuit. Last summer I worked a steamer on the Great Lakes."

"And how does it feel?" I said. "Is pregnancy all you thought it would be?"

Peggy's eyes darkened and she lit another cigarette before answering. "Nope," she said. "It ain't what I bargained for—there's more to it than I thought." She sat silently staring out the little window high on the wall.

"I think the difference is that I can't quit this if I don't like it," she said. "I can't just pack up and leave. I'm involved with all of me whether I want to be or not. I thought bearing a child was part of the experience of being alive, that it was something I could go through and then leave behind. I guess I hadn't really thought about the baby."

"That's honest enough," I said. "So where do you go from here?"

"I don't think I'm up to trying the 'mother-experience' yet," Peggy said, and smiled a little. "The baby goes out for adoption the way I always planned it, and I'll pack my bundle and jump a bus for the desert country. I'm going to spend a couple of months on the trail with a horse and some paints and a couple of canvases. I'm gonna have to do some thinking after this."

"Jean T. Jean T. You're wanted on the hospital floor." The voice over the intercom was Mrs. Warren's and she sounded plenty impatient.

"If I don't see you again—good luck," I said to Peggy, and

ran. I heard her start whistling before I reached the stairs: "What will we do with a drunken sailor." I hope I see her again next week.

Tuesday the 22nd

Only three days till Christmas, and the Home was decorated with lights and greenery everywhere. They even had Christmas music playing over the loudspeakers in every room. Mrs. Duncan brought me in before lunch and I ate at the Home. I had hoped to find Peggy and maybe talk her into going downtown with me after my checkup, but she wasn't in the dining room. A girl at my table, Cecilie—she was there when I first came to the Home— told me that Peggy left two days ago in a rage. It had happened during chapel. Lieutenant Stewart was holding the service, and while the girls sang "Throw out the Life line, Throw out the Life line," she threw Life Saver candy wrapped in paper with printed Bible verses on it. After the singing the Lieutenant asked each girl who had caught a Life Saver to stand up and read the Bible verse out loud. Peggy had caught one of the candies and refused to stand up and read.

"Why won't you stand up, Peggy?" asked the Lieutenant.

"Because we have freedom of religion in this country and I don't share your faith," said Peggy.

"You should have seen her," said Cecilie. "You know, many of the girls in here don't go along with the Salvation Army beliefs. But this is a private institution and we've got to go along with their rules—or leave."

"You may believe as you wish, Peggy," the Lieutenant said, "but as long as you stay under our roof you will follow our regulations."

"I'll sit quietly in your chapel," said Peggy, "but I don't have to participate in your service."

"Please do as you are told, Peggy," said Lieutenant Stewart. Peggy stood up.

"You leave me no choice," she said. "I can't compromise, so I shall leave."

"She walked down the aisle," said Cecilie, "and nobody said a word or did anything to stop her. When we got out of chapel she had left and we haven't seen her since."

The girls are going downtown tonight to see the Christmas lights. Cecilie said several of the girls from wage homes are going along but I told her I have other plans. Somehow the thought of fifty or sixty pregnant girls going in chartered buses to see the Christmas lights goes against my grain. I'd much rather spend my evenings alone in my little room anyway.

I had decided to spend my precious twenty-dollar bill on something as silly as a maternity dress for myself. I really shouldn't have done it. I mean, there's no one to dress up for and I'll have to leave the dress at the Home when I'm through. But I suddenly had this tremendous urge to look neat and well-dressed and—well, Christmasy. These washed-out hand-me-downs are so depressing. It's almost funny, but one of the things my parents used to complain about constantly was my lack of interest in how I looked. My favorite attire used to be washed-out jeans and denim shirts.

So I took a bus downtown from the Home and walked into a maternity shop, trying not to look self-conscious. There was only one customer ahead of me. She was trying on a very elegant-looking maternity cocktail dress and looked like one of those ads in a women's magazine (pretty as can be—mother soon to be). She was chatting with the saleslady about the baby and I wanted to say, "Hush, someone might hear you." When it was my turn the saleslady asked me how far along I am, and when I said six months she looked at me carefully and said, "You certainly carry it well. Is it your first, honey?" I nodded and she said, "I bet your husband is proud. Do you want a boy or a girl?"

"Oh, it really won't make a difference," I said.

"Why, of course not, honey. You'll be happy either way, won't you?" She smiled and chatted constantly while she picked dresses off the rack and held them up in front of me.

"You're too pale, honey—can't wear this blue one. How about green?" I nodded. Anything would be fine with me. I wanted to get out of there. The saleslady had the kind of smile I hate, the kind older women seem to lavish on young expectant mothers. As if they were saying, "How sweet. I can just see your little love nest and the baby's room all ready." She wrapped my dress and pushed a blank form across the counter.

"Won't you sign your name and address, honey, and have a chance on a baby crib? We always give one to a customer every month." For a second I panicked. I couldn't very well tell her I'm going to give away my baby (although it might have been worth it to see the look on her face). I wrote Martha's name and address. If she wins, the baby will enjoy it, I'm sure.

Wednesday the 23rd

Someone has said that the happiness you give to others no one can take away from you. I will make Martha and Don and little Kathy Carver very happy one day in March. Stated that way, it sounds so simple. Then why do I have to be so mixed up inside?

A pretty young actress was interviewed on television this afternoon. She sat in a swivel chair next to a huge Christmas tree, swinging her shapely legs this way and that. "The thing I love most in this world is to always be on the move," she said. "I love to go to a new place even if I like where I am. Oh, yes, I always

come back to Paris and I always fall in love there, just like that!"
She snapped her pretty fingers and laughed.

I've never been to Paris, but I know what she's talking about
when she says she loves to move on. Except that now I'm beginning to recognize the feeling as more like a need to escape. It
doesn't sound quite as nice. I haven't exactly been moving around
from place to place as much as I've been skipping from person to
person, interest to interest, project to project, idea to idea. I used
to think vaguely of myself as being dedicated to mankind, wanting
to make the world better. Yet I've never been able to settle down
to something specific and definite for any length of time. So I've
eagerly thrown myself into a new friendship or a new idea, and
when the newness wore off, when the moment came when I would
be expected to give of myself, commit myself, be responsible for
my share—well, then I'd find some excuse to drop the whole
thing. I did that with Gene, the father of my baby—I know it.

Later

Mrs. Duncan came into my room and said she had something
to say to me. Something she'd thought about for a while. "I don't
want you to ever have company again without asking me first,"
she said. She was talking about Dorothy. "You understand, don't
you? After all . . ." she let the sentence hang. I understood perfectly. I wanted to pack my things and leave immediately—but
where could I run to? Instead, I lowered my head and mumbled
that I was sorry.

"It won't happen again," I said. I don't know why she waited
this long to tell me, but I know what she's been worried about.
To her I'm an unwed mother from a Salvation Army home, who
won't even tell her my name. She has taken me into her home

and she trusts me with her children (and her silverware). I can't let it bother me. I've got to stick it out here whatever happens.

Thursday the 24th

The house is quiet. It is nearly midnight—Christmas Eve. The radio is playing "Silent Night" and I'm going to let myself get sentimental. The day has been a rat race. The doorbell rang constantly for deliveries—late mail, mysterious packages to hide away. Peter and Lori have climbed everywhere trying to discover secret hiding places; they finally went to bed about an hour ago when their father said Santa Claus absolutely won't come to a house where the children haven't gone to sleep yet.

How different from the Christmas Eves I remember as a child. Santa Claus came to our house in person on Christmas Eve. But first we always trimmed the tree; the rest of the house had been decorated days ahead, but the tree was left till last. In front of the fireplace was always a large tray of Christmas cookies and hot punch. We sang the Christmas songs as we worked and Daddy was always off-key.

When the tree was ready and lit, we turned off all the other lights in the room. Daddy sat down in the large chair by the fireplace and we sat on the rug around him. Mother brought the family Bible and we all listened to Daddy read the story of the birth of Jesus. As a child I used to wonder why my father's eyes always got moist when he read the part about the multitude of angels praising God and saying "Glory to God in the highest, and on earth peace, good will toward men" (St. Luke 2:13–14). Before I go to sleep tonight, I will take out my Bible and read for myself the second chapter of Saint Luke, verses one through twenty. I did it this morning, and I know that I'll probably want to cry again.

My father always had to go out on an errand on Christmas Eve after reading for us. And it always happened that Santa Claus knocked at our door while Daddy was gone. He carried a sack over his shoulder and spoke with the trembling voice of an old man. He asked each of us if we had been good children, and he knew exactly when we hadn't. Mother always asked him to taste our cookies and he took some and put them in his big pocket. I always wanted him to eat them right away to see if he really liked them, but he never did. Then he took a small gift for each of us out of his sack and promised to come back during the night, when we would be fast asleep, to fill our stockings. My brother always assured him that we would be extra careful to put out the fire in the fireplace before we went to bed. "So you won't get burned, Santa Claus." And Santa Claus Ho—Ho-ed and said that he would have an extra good present for an extra good boy.

After Santa left, Daddy always came back and said how sad it was that he had missed meeting him again, but that maybe next year he would come while Daddy was home. It took several years before my brother and I caught on. Even after that Daddy kept on playing Santa Claus and we went along with him without saying that we knew.

Those were the good years, before I started to grow up and have a mind of my own. Maybe some of my ideas were wrong, but my parents just couldn't understand that I had to live my own way. That I had to question the ideas they said were the only right ones, that I had to make my own mistakes. But then maybe parents always try to keep their children from making mistakes and getting hurt. I hope that when we meet again we can talk a little more calmly about things.

Daddy is working on a new book this year in Europe. It is about Christian ethics and the new morality. Even the title used to make me furious when I first heard it. Now I hope he gets it finished. I'll read it all the way through before starting to yell about it.

It is past midnight. Merry Christmas, Jean. Merry Christmas, little unborn baby. Christmas is all about birth, all about the hope and promise that came into this world with a Child. Hope and promise come into this world with each new child. You are a small miracle, little one.

Saturday the 26th

Holidays are hard on my equilibrium. I can't keep my mood even. I'd just as soon forget it's Christmas, yet I get sentimental over a candle and Christmas mail from Mother and Dad. They wish me happiness, of course, and all the best in the new year.

So I went for a quick walk up the road to calm myself, but even the hills couldn't do it for me today. Sometimes I wish they wouldn't be so calm and so beautiful. Maybe if a violent thunderstorm tore through our valley I would get my mind off my own navel for a little while.

Later

Something always hits you when you're low. Mrs. Duncan marched right into my room without knocking and said, "Why don't you answer when you're called?"

"I didn't hear anybody."

"Nonsense," Mrs. Duncan said. "You couldn't have helped hearing. Why do you lie about it?" Josephine is here to do the ironing and she had apparently called me to help fold some sheets.

"I don't lie," I said to Mrs. Duncan, but I could see in her face that what I said didn't make any difference. I couldn't keep the tears from coming, and when Mrs. Duncan saw me crying her voice softened.

"Don't cry, Jean. I understand. I sometimes don't feel like helping anyone either," she said. "But I must insist that you be honest with me as long as you live with us." I wanted to lift my head and scream in her face. Tell her I don't care a damn about what she thinks and I'm leaving right now! She thought my tears meant I was sorry, and put her hand on my arm.

"We won't talk about it anymore—try to relax now." She left the room and I threw myself on the bed and cried long and hard. Leave here? What would be the use of that? I would be miserable in the Home, too, and I can't afford to run up too big a bill there. If I tell Mrs. Duncan about myself, she may be nicer during the six weeks I've got to stay here. But I just can't tell her; I've got to guard against slip-ups in the future.

She called me a liar. Sure I am. That's why it hurt to hear it from her. I lie to her, to my parents, to the whole world.

Thursday the 31st

New Year's Eve. I'm home alone with the children. The Duncans are at a party and I've been watching television, all those wrap-up programs commenting on national and international happenings during the year. It's funny how they sound so much alike from one year to the next—little wars started here and there, a race riot, a strike, a government toppled in South America. An old statesman or a famous writer dies and they call it the end of an era. Eras always end and new ones begin.

This year certainly marked the end of an era for me. Last New Year's Eve I was at a party. It was a large one at the studio of a painter who'd "made it." I mean his paintings are selling for more than beans. We were dancing and laughing, toasting the new year—this year. I don't think I had any feeling of impending disaster. Not in my wildest imagination could I have thought I'd celebrate the end of this year here, under an assumed name, bulky with a child I'll never even know.

Where will I be a year from tonight? That, of course, will depend upon what I make of the year ahead. I hadn't quite thought of the future that way before, that the future depended upon what I would do. I used to think circumstances had a lot more to do with it. When I first got pregnant I thought of myself as a victim of circumstances I hadn't been in control of. I used to ask myself those big questions—I guess we all do—like *who am I, why am I living*. I haven't found the answers, but I think I have discovered one thing this year: I am responsible for what I do. I believe God created us with free wills, gave us the opportunity of choice, and so I believe that I am responsible for what I do. It doesn't sound like so much, but it is really an awesome thing, I think.

I used to blame so much of what I did on my parents. They didn't understand me, I used to tell myself. I am beginning to realize just how absurd that is. My parents may never understand me very well. But still I am the only one responsible for my action and I must take the consequences.

It's a thought to start a brand-new year on—a brand-new era. I don't know what it is going to be like, but I'm glad it's here. Happy New Year!

JANUARY

Tuesday the 19th

I can't think of anything nice to say about January. I can't stand this month. It always depresses me and this year it is worse than ever. Maybe it's because it is the letdown after the holidays. Maybe it's because it's the month I usually break all the good resolutions I made New Year's Eve. Or maybe it's just because it's the darkest month of the year and there isn't even a hint of spring to liven it up. Whatever it is, I feel I'm going to be lucky if I live through it. The hills look drab. I'm barely on speaking terms with Mrs. Duncan.

I went in for my checkup today and physically I'm in top shape, the doctor says. I'm glad he can't read my mind. I didn't see many girls I used to know. A lot of them have left and new faces are everywhere.

I did see Joan C. She delivered around Christmastime but her parents didn't want to take her home then. Cecilie told me all about it at lunch. She is just about the only girl I talk to nowadays. She's been around longer than I have and she seems to know everything about everybody. I never did find out anything about her, though. Maybe I will when I go in to stay.

Anyway, Cecilie told me that Joan had tried to talk her parents
into taking the baby home, but they refused. When Joan first delivered, she called her mother to tell her, and her mother said,
"Keep the news of your bastard to yourself," and she hung up.
Joan had turned to the girl in the next bed. "I've got to tell someone about my baby. I've got to tell someone . . ." Joan tried to
get her social worker to talk to her parents, but nothing worked.

Joan first came to the home in September, before I came here
to the hills. She had the bed in the corner, and I remember her
sullen face. She never talked much to any of us and we didn't try
to talk to her. She was sixteen, and had come from a juvenile
home. Her parents brought her, without luggage, to the Home;
they had told her they were taking her on a Sunday ride. And
then they dumped her here and said she'd get a beating if she
ever ran away.

She did run away, twice. She got her beating and she was returned; after that, she mostly just sat in her corner. Except once.
It was Sunday, and at breakfast time Joan came downstairs with a
smile on her face that made her look different, almost pretty.
She had washed her hair and brushed it till it shone, and she was
dressed to go out. Usually, on Sundays local girls go home on a
visit or for a ride with their parents or friends. All day long, cars
pull up in front of the Home to pick up or unload girls. That
particular Sunday morning Joan told us all that her parents were
coming to take her for a ride. She beamed with pride when she
told it and we were all really glad for her.

When the first cars began to arrive, Joan ran to the window to
look out. But it was never the car she was looking for. Half an
hour passed—an hour—two—then lunchtime. Joan's parents still
hadn't shown up and the smile on her face wasn't so bright anymore. But still she ran to the window when she heard a car stop.
At last, when most of the other girls had returned, Joan gave
up hoping. She came to stand by the window next to my bed. Her

eyes were dark and full of tears. Her mouth was trembling when she said—to no one in particular, "It must be nice to have parents you can trust. . . ."

Today I saw Joan dressed to go home, and crying on a green couch in the hall. Her baby is in a foster home and that's where he will stay, because Joan didn't want to sign his release for adoption. No one can force her. Maybe she hopes that one day she can get him back.

There are thousands of babies like Joan's little boy, and most of them grow up in foster homes and institutions because their mothers never manage to realize their dream of getting their child back. It is sad and I wish something could be done about it. A law isn't the answer, but maybe girls in homes like ours could get the counseling and guidance they need to see that their own despair isn't eased by keeping a child from getting a good home.

Saturday the 23rd

I've got to force myself to write letters nowadays. I'm afraid Mother and Dad are going to read between the lines that I'm not exactly happy. How can I write without telling anything about where I am and what I'm doing? I'm following the weather reports on television so I can write about the weather on the other side of the country as if I were there. I write about books and about news events and things like that, but I can't write about the job I'm supposed to be working at. I guess I could make one up. I'm afraid it's going to be too easy to check up on if I do say something about a job.

I have a hard time putting anything down on paper, even this sort of thing. I get so sick and tired of seeing my own stupid, hopeless thoughts that I could throw the typewriter out the window.

Walking is just about the nicest thing I do. I walk so fast and so far that my legs and my muscles ache all over. It's good exercise and it makes me tired enough to sleep.

About three more weeks to go—then I have to move into the Home. I'm counting the days.

FEBRUARY

Friday the 19th

I'm back in the Home with less than a month to go before my due-date. Wow, I didn't think I was going to last this long at the Duncans'. The strain was awful the last couple of weeks. We didn't have any big blowups, and when I left we said polite good-byes, but I used to get up every morning hoping I wouldn't lose my temper before the day ended. In my better moments I thought of it as an endurance game. Now that it is over I'm glad I didn't pack up and run earlier.

I saw Miss O'Connor, my social worker, today and she said, "I thought you might have come back earlier—you had some difficulties, didn't you?"

"It was all a misunderstanding," I said. "They expected me to confide in them and I didn't want to."

"You were only the second girl there," said Miss O'Connor, "and they had grown very fond of Cindy. They were hurt when you didn't get as close to them."

"It's all over now," I said. "Maybe the next girl will be more like Cindy."

Miss O'Connor looked at the cigarette she was getting ready to light. "There won't be a third girl," she said. "Not for a while anyway. Our policy is that girls do not have to confide in their wage-home parents, and if they expect them to do that the strain can be an unhealthy one, we think. You girls are already in a strained situation and extra pressure is something we are trying to help you avoid." Miss O'Connor smiled a little. "I have watched you every time you came in for your checkup. If you had shown signs of being upset I would have told you to move back here earlier."

"Upset!" I couldn't help laughing. "You didn't see me rant and rave at those hills. I was just too damn stubborn to admit I couldn't get along."

"Well, it's over," said Miss O'Connor, "and I've got a nice surprise for you. You are going to sleep in the five-bed dorm downstairs. You'll have some privacy there. The girls are older— with the exception of Lisa."

"Wonderful," I said. "Thanks a lot."

"By the way"—Miss O'Connor looked straight at me—"you are still going ahead with the adoption plans for the baby, aren't you?" I nodded and she smiled, relieved.

"Good. Any time you need to talk, you know I'm here."

It's good to be in the small dorm. I haven't met the other girls yet, but the bed by the window doesn't have any sheets so I guess it's mine. Anyway, I've unpacked my things. Half of the chest of drawers next to the bed is mine and there is room on top for a few of my books. I can lie down on my bed and see the sky between two large treetops. I stay awake much of the night now— I can look for my favorite stars.

Sunday the 21st

A cup of tea, a cigarette, on a red counter. Is it really four months since I was here last with Karen? Toni brought my teapot and nodded with a big grin, but I don't suppose he remembers me—or Karen. She looked at the calendar on the wall and could see her due-date. I remember I envied her and wondered if the day would ever come when I could see mine.

I had a letter from Karen before I left the Duncans', postmarked Colorado. She wrote that she's been skiing and it's grand. When we were here together Karen thought she'd never go down the slopes again. There was no return address on the letter, and I don't know Karen's real name, anyway.

I am here alone now. I can see my due-date on the wall and my stomach is hard as a blown-up football against the counter. March seventeenth isn't far away now.

I bought a small notebook on my way down here. It fits right in my pocket. I won't be able to write my thoughts down on the typewriter in the Home. That first afternoon, when I was writing in my room, one of the girls from the big dorm down the hall stuck her head in our door and said, "Hi, stranger." She came all the way into the room, and when she saw the pile of papers next to my typewriter I could see her face go rigid.

"You aren't writing a book, are you?"

I laughed and said, "I sure ain't," but her eyes didn't leave those papers, and she said, "We're all in the same boat in here and we sure don't want to get famous because of it. Leave me out, will ya?"

"It's just a letter." I grabbed a letter from Patrick that happened to be on my bed. The girl flopped down on the bed next to mine and looked at me carefully.

"Name is Katie S.," she said. "You sure write long letters."

"Sure," I said. "It's for my boyfriend." I put the bundle of papers casually down in my drawer, and Katie smiled.

"Gosh, I don't see what there is to write about in this place," she said. "Lousy food, nothing to do except a lousy movie every

Friday night, and the chairs are too damn hard to sit on all the way through the movie, anyway."

"Where are you from?" I asked.

"Milwaukee, a long way from home, thank goodness. What about you?"

"Chicago."

The closeness of our two cities made me feel a bit uncomfortable, and I noticed that Katie had that careful look in her eyes again.

I'm holding my breath. For eight months I've been lucky. No one has found out about me. What if something goes wrong now? Mother has sounded a little funny in her letters lately, as if she wants to come back *before* June, when they are due to leave France. I've tried to sound as cheerful as I can in my letters and keep telling her to see as much as possible while she is there—not to cut the trip short. I shiver at the thought that something may go wrong. . . .

The girls in my dorm are nice. Jane S. is the senior among us. She looks about sixty, with gray hair in a neat bun at the nape of her neck, her blue eyes deep in their sockets. She looks gaunt and worn but Cecilie says she is only in her mid-forties. She doesn't say much and walks around with her nose in a book most of the time. Cecilie says she teaches college and is working on her doctor's degree. Her parents live near here and come to take her for a ride every Sunday. I saw them from a distance today—both white-haired and small. I can't imagine how Jane ended up in the Home.

Lisa is due any day now although no one knows for sure when. She tags along after anybody who smiles at her. I think she has pains, because she often curls up on her bed next to mine, without a sound—only her eyes are wide and dark with long suffering. I want to reach out and take her pain and her fear away, and I get hot with anger when I think of the jerk who forced his way into her childlike world.

The other two girls in our dorm are German immigrants and speak English in a heavy accent. They are together most of the time, speaking rapidly in their own language. Their side of the room is immaculate. They aren't due till June and will go to wage homes next week.

Monday the 22nd

The Ladies' Auxiliary had gotten us some tickets to the symphony and several girls went last night. The bus came to pick them up as I watched from the window in the lounge. I love to go to concerts but I couldn't make myself go yesterday. I don't want to remember that once I went with my belly full of a baby. So I took a shower, and knitted before going to bed. The radiators in the house usually make a terrible racket but last night they hardly made any noise at all.

I was assigned to my new duty today. I'm in my last month now and the duty is easy; I do light everyday cleaning in the staff residence. The five Salvation Army officers who run the Home live in a small bungalow across the park from the big house. I make up their beds, run the vacuum cleaner, dust and keep the three bathrooms clean. I go there right after breakfast when the officers have gone to their jobs. I am all alone in the house and I like to pretend it's my own home. I dust off the knickknacks and the books on the shelves, straighten the pillows in the cozy living room and look at the pictures of their families. But even if I work very slowly my job only takes about two hours. I was through at eleven o'clock today and there was nothing more to do except sit around or go for a walk. I think I'll probably go down to Toni's more than anywhere else. Toni knows me now;

he brings the pot of tea before I have time to say anything, and he leaves me alone in my corner with my notebook.

Tuesday the 23rd

The doctor says I may deliver in two weeks. I called to tell Martha and she said everything is all ready and waiting for the baby. Her voice bubbled with happiness over the phone. We've been alone in this together, the baby and I, for so long now that it doesn't seem real that he is wanted and expected by someone else. He is so big inside me that I can't move without being aware of him. A few weeks from now he is supposed to be none of my business!

I go for my daily walk, and when one of the girls says she'd like to go along, I find some excuse. I don't want to talk to anyone. I'm in my own world and people on the outside don't matter. It is roller-skating time and the first flowers of spring are coming out on the lawns.

I walked down the main business street and the school kids were on their way home. They swarmed in large colorful flocks, full skirts floating over young girls' legs—bright chatter and much laughter. The sounds blended with the singing of tires over asphalt and the birds' chittering above. The girls have painted their young lips with pale lipsticks; their eyes are large and dark with heavy mascara. But even the masks can't hide how young they are.

I stop to browse through the rack of secondhand books outside the candy store on the corner. An old man owns the store; he shuffles behind the counter in his felt slippers, and his soft white hair is long and curling slightly. Round glasses rest halfway down his long nose, and his rusty old voice blends with the shrill voices of little boys who are always in the store buying candy and sec-

ondhand comic books for two pennies apiece. I like to listen to
their voices.

I walk down the sidewalk in step with the words running
through my mind: it's almost over, it's almost over, it's almost
over.

Wednesday the 24th

I'm alone in the smoking room. I get through with my work
before the other girls and get here in time for a quiet smoke all
by myself. The staff residence is so neat every time I get there in
the morning that I wonder sometimes what the officers do when
they are off duty. They don't make a mess, that's for sure.

We had pancakes for breakfast today and Tammy at my table
ate ten! I think about my weight now, and the baby seems to take
up so much room in my stomach that I can't eat very much anyway. Mrs. Coralis, the second cook, read the prayer this morning
and all I could think of was the soft clicking sound of her false
teeth slipping back in place after every few words.

The girls are coming; I hear them in the corridor. We all head
for the sanctuary when our morning duties are over. I should go
upstairs to read a book or write a letter, or maybe take a nap, but
I know I won't. I'll sit around here instead, listening to the gossip,
watching the girls play cards or embroider. Maybe somebody will
go into labor, and we can watch for the doctor's car and bet on
the time of delivery.

Sue delivered yesterday. She is our youngest; she was thirteen
last month. Sue's mother has eleven other kids at home and she
has told Sue that she can take her baby home. Some of the girls
have been to see Sue in the mothers' ward and they say she gets
to hold the baby.

We can't go out on a pass till after lunch and the time drags.

I can walk through the hall pretending I've got an errand somewhere but when I get there I don't know what to do and I turn
around to go somewhere else. I see other girls do the same; we
drift listlessly through the house.

I peeked into the pink dorm and Nancy was on her bed crying.
When she saw me she waved me into the room.

"See," she sobbed, holding out two snapshots. "My family,
aren't they wonderful?" I looked and saw a middle-aged chubby
woman and a balding man sitting in overstuffed armchairs with
a Christmas tree behind them. The other picture showed the
family at the table for Christmas dinner, three gawky little girls
and a fat little boy in a high chair. They didn't strike me as wonderful, but Nancy smiled proudly through tears and told me she
hasn't seen them in five months.

I walked upstairs and had to stop on the landing to catch my
breath. Peggy ran past me, taking two steps at a time. She is fourteen and looks as if she is having the time of her life, always
laughing or singing the latest hit song. There are several very
young ones here now—they don't seem to mind being here as
much as the older ones do.

Martha called. They will pick me up after chapel Sunday and
take me out for lunch. I should have bitten my tongue out rather
than say yes, but I said it anyway, in spite of myself. Martha
wants to give me the clothes the baby will wear when he goes
home from the hospital, but I don't think I can stand that. I'm
going to ask her to give the clothes to Dorothy when she gets here.

Thursday the 25th

The two German girls have left for their wage homes and a
young Negro widow moved into one of the empty beds today.
She has two little children at home; her husband died just three

months ago. Carrie has a wonderful big laugh and she talks about her little ones at home with such joy. She is due in three weeks but doesn't even look very pregnant. She told us she kept her job as a clerk in a department store till last week. She is staying at the Home because she has decided to give this baby out for adoption.

"I don't want my babies at home to know anything about it," she said. "They don't even understand that I'm expecting. I told them I had to stay away on a job for a few weeks." Carrie's husband was a Korean veteran and she gets a small monthly pension from the government now.

"But it isn't enough to raise three kids on," she said. "Colored kids got to have a good education to get ahead. I reckon I can manage to put two through college—I can't do it with three."

Friday evening, the 26th

The Ladies' Auxiliary are here entertaining us tonight. I enjoy the cookies and punch they bring but I can't say I'm thrilled by their performance. Tonight a fat lady in a tight corset gave a song recital, accompanied by a skinny, efficient-looking young matron at the piano. The fat lady sang in a quivering soprano, twisting a lace handkerchief while she sang. It's the sort of thing they make funny scenes of in the movies, but it wasn't so funny with fifty or so pregnant girls sitting on rows of straight-backed chairs while a small group of well-dressed matrons sat in a corner whispering and stealing glances at us during the performance.

I couldn't stomach it any longer. After the punch and cookies break, I stole away and came down here to the smoking room where I can be alone with my notebook for a few minutes. That is, almost alone. Jane from my dorm is over in a corner with her

nose in a book as usual; her gray head is bent and she didn't look
up when I came in. I know she's got to stay away when the
Ladies' Auxiliary comes. Some of the ladies live in her neighborhood.

I don't know why my stupid pride keeps me from being just
plain grateful when kind ladies make cotton smocks for us to
wear, and layettes for our babies, and curtains and bedspreads
for our "home-in-hiding." They give us all the materials for our
hobby room and workshop, too, and I know they must spend
hours of dedicated work to help us. Do I have a right to begrudge
them the sense of satisfaction they may receive from doing something like that? Couldn't it just as easily have been me—giving
and enjoying it—instead of receiving and resenting it?

Maybe what I really resent has nothing to do with the kind
ladies upstairs. Maybe I'm remembering the afternoons and evenings when my mother was too busy with her auxiliary work to
be home with us.

Saturday morning, the 27th

I'm alone in the smoking room, and the morning is gray outside. Everyone else has special duties on Saturday—scrubbing
floors and walls, windows and woodwork, pantry shelves and
stoves. There is nothing extra for me to do.

So much happens so quickly in here. Lisa had her baby last
night, and this morning Carrie went upstairs to the labor room.

No one noticed that Lisa didn't go to the lounge to hear the
program last night. When I came to bed I saw her bulky form
under the blankets on the bed next to mine and I thought she was
asleep. I woke up at the sound of her whimpering. The moon
shone right in our window and I could see Lisa rocking slowly

back and forth under the blanket. Jane was awake, too. She sat straight up in her bed across the room and her face looked pasty-white in the moonlight.

"Lisa is in labor," she whispered. "I'm sure—and the poor thing doesn't know what's happening to her."

I jumped out of bed and tried to lift the blanket from Lisa's head, but she held on and the whimpering stopped. Jane was beside me, a clumsy pale figure with a soft voice.

"Are you sick, Lisa?" We could see the head nodding under the blanket.

"Does your stomach hurt?" Jane asked, and this time we heard the muffled "Yes" and a sob. Jane looked at me.

"We've got to get her upstairs," she whispered. She patted the rocking form under the blanket with a gentle hand.

"Listen to me, Lisa," she said. "I'm going to take you upstairs and the nurse will give you medicine to make your tummy feel better." Lisa grabbed better hold of the blanket and held it over her head.

"She's scared—maybe we better get the nurse down here," I whispered, but Lisa heard me and her body grew tense.

"Go away—go away. . . ." Her voice was lost in a moan.

"Get the nurse, Jean—quick," Jane said.

I ran up the stairs two steps at a time and didn't even feel my big stomach in the way. I found Nurse Simpson in the office.

"Poor thing," she said, and ran ahead of me downstairs. We found Jane sitting on Lisa's bed. She held Lisa's head in her lap and was rocking slowly back and forth, stroking the tangled blond hair. She looked up at us with a quiet smile.

"I'm sure she's in labor," Jane said. With Nurse Simpson's help she gently got Lisa up and out of bed. The three of them walked slowly up the stairs and into the labor room. I followed just in case they needed more help. Lisa wouldn't let go of Jane's hand, even when she was put to bed. Her eyes were wide with pain and fright.

"Don't leave me, please," she sobbed. Jane looked at Nurse Simpson, who nodded slightly.

"I won't leave you, baby." Jane smiled at Lisa, and Lisa sighed deeply. Nurse Simpson gave her an injection.

"This will help," she said, "till the doctor comes. He will give the order to put her under complete anesthesia. Stay here till then, Jane." I watched them from the doorway, Jane's gray head and strained white face bent over the young blond girl tossing on the pillow. I thought, why, Lisa could have been her daughter.

Jane came downstairs at daybreak, her face drawn from lack of sleep. She tiptoed to my bed.

"Lisa's asleep now," she said with an even, almost toneless voice. "She had a little girl." Jane sat down on my bed and together we watched the white mist of dawn shimmer among the trees in the park outside our window.

"Little Lisa." Jane said it with a sigh. "She won't know what happened to her. She will go to a foster home now and I hope they'll be good to her. You and I will go on living, building a future on what has been. But Lisa isn't very bright; she is only trusting. Let's hope she won't always be let down."

Mrs. Larsen, the housekeepr, interrupted my quiet time in the smoking room. "What you doin' here? Get out till someone's cleaned up this mess." She nodded angrily toward the ash trays running over with yesterday's filth. I wandered out into the corridor and saw her go muttering toward the laundry. She muttered just loud enough for me to hear—I'm sure she meant me to. "Don't do nothin' but sit around smokin' all day—don't feel bad about what they've done. . . ."

Two girls came whistling toward her carrying a basket full of dirty linen between them. "No whistlin'—get on with your work," snorted Mrs. Larsen as they passed her. Behind her back the girls giggled and formed their lips again in silent whistling.

Late afternoon

I had to get away for a few hours. I have a pass for the evening, and I'll just have a cup of coffee here at Toni's instead of supper. The intrusion on your privacy isn't the only bad thing about the Home. It's the fact that I just can't help getting emotionally involved with the other girls. Maybe I shouldn't say that is bad, but right now it's upsetting.

Now I'm all upset over Carrie, the Negro widow from our dorm, and I shouldn't be. I didn't see the doctor's car come to the Home this morning, but the nurse on duty stopped me when I came from the dining room after lunch and said that Carrie wanted to see me in the mothers' ward. Carrie was sitting up in her bed, her lunch tray untouched.

"You made it in time for lunch, didn't you?" I smiled at her but she didn't smile back. When she spoke her voice was so low I had to strain to catch the words.

"Will you do me a favor, Jean?"

"Sure," I said. "Anything you want."

Carrie's dark hands fingered the sheet on her bed.

"I want you to call my sister and tell her the baby was born dead."

"I'm sorry. I didn't know." I didn't know what to say.

"You don't understand," Carrie said. "The baby isn't dead. He's doing fine. I just don't want my sister to know he's alive. It's bad enough for me to know." Inside, I wanted to cry.

"What's her number?" I said. "I'll call from the booth downstairs. What else do you want me to say?"

"Tell her not to come and get me. I'll take a taxi home Wednesday. And tell her to kiss my babies for me."

"O.K." I turned to go and Carrie called after me, "You see, I can't lie about it to my sister."

I dialed the number and the voice at the other end was so much like Carrie's, so deep and warm, that I almost hung up again. But I introduced myself and told her what I had to say. I heard the faint "Oh, no!" then silence. When she talked again her voice was low and muffled by tears.

"Was it a boy?"

"Yes," I said.

"Thank you for telling me, Jean," she said. "I am glad Carrie has friends there. Tell her that I pray for her. Tell her the good Lord must have meant it this way. It will be easier for her—later."

"Carrie is fine," I said. "She had an easy time. But I don't think she wants to talk about it when she gets home."

"I know."

"She wants you to kiss her babies for her," I said, and heard that muffled sob again on the other end of the line.

"Oh, I will, honey. I will. Tell her they're so good—and waiting for their mama."

"I'll tell her," I said. "Good-bye."

"Good-bye," said Carrie's sister, "and God bless you."

I walked slowly up the stairs again and found Carrie resting with her dark head buried in the pillow. She heard me coming and looked up; there was pain in her eyes.

"Your sister says your babies are good and waiting for their mama," I said.

"My babies," she said, glowing as I remember she used to do when she first told us about them on the dorm. "You know, this new one looks so much like them. That makes it easier." I nodded —there was nothing I could say.

"I found such a good family for him," Carrie went on. "A colored teacher. His wife can't have no babies of her own. They'll love my baby and give him all the things I can't give." She was silent and watched the gardener rake leaves from the driveway outside the window. She spoke without turning her head and I saw her hand tense on the sheet.

"What did my sister say when you told her the baby is dead?"

"She said it must have been the Lord's will," I said, and saw her hand relax again.

I almost ran from the mothers' ward and downstairs to get my coat and get out of there. The crisp air cooled my spirit, and I stopped at the drugstore on the corner to buy a candy bar for Carrie. Thank God for Toni's, somewhere where I can sit in a corner and watch people who aren't pregnant, and listen to conversations that have nothing to do with the agonies we live with in the big house on the hill.

Late evening

I took the candy bar to Carrie when I came home. I had to sneak past the nurse on duty—it was past eight o'clock and visiting hours were over. Carrie looked much better. She was talking to little Sue and laughing when I got there.

"Thanks, Jean," she said. She split the candy bar with Sue. "At least it won't make me as fat as I was yesterday." I sat down on the chair next to her bed, and soon Carrie's face turned sober and she stopped kidding around.

"Promise me one thing, Jean," she said. "Don't pick up that baby of yours. I know what I'm talking about. I've had two of them before and I know what it does to you." Carrie's eyes were distant. "You look down at that little baby snuggled so cozy and safe against you with his eyes closed. Something happens to you right there and then. You can't help it. . . . I had to pinch my-self to make sure it was really me lying there with my own baby." It hurt to listen to her. But I know that telling me about it was sort of a substitute for holding that third little one.

Sunday the 28th

Sunday is an empty day here, no duties. Many of the girls leave on day-long passes right after chapel. The rest of us wander through the nearly empty dorms, go for walks, watch television and have lousy cold cuts for meals. Today I'm not going to stick around. I almost wish I were. Don and Martha are going to pick me up to take me out for lunch.

Little Sue came to chapel this morning for the first time since she had her baby. She wore a pink sweater and a yellow skirt, and her brown face was streaked with tears. She sniffed her way through the service. The injustice of things made me want to go light a torch somewhere. We've all heard what happened. Sue's mother and her eleven kids are on relief and Sue came here from Juvenile Hall. When Sue's mother said she wanted to take the baby and Sue home and keep them both on relief, the matter went to the juvenile court. Sue and the baby were made wards of the court. Sue will go to a foster home when she leaves here and her baby will be placed in another home.

I agree that neither Sue nor her mother is fit to keep a baby and that the baby will be better off in another home. But how did it happen that Sue was allowed to hold that baby—was allowed to feed and dress him—for five days?

When she came here she was twelve. She was too young to attend the high-school classes but she loved to sew. She sat in the hobby room and made dolls' clothes while her body grew big under the bright cotton smock. Her case worker said her mother would let her take the baby home and so Sue began to make baby clothes instead of clothes for her doll. Soon her cardboard box was full of little blue, pink, yellow and white clothes, all a baby would need. Five days after the baby was born, the blue door to the nursery was closed and Sue stood there crying. "I want my baby—I want my baby." They haven't found a foster home for her yet and she will be moved downstairs to a dorm again—away from that blue door.

Sunday night

We drove around town, walked through a museum and had lunch at a restaurant with a view over the harbor. Martha's eyes were on me often. I think she wonders if I'll change my mind.

"When it's all over, after those six months of probation—I know *we* won't change our minds—" she said, "we'll take out a great big bottle of champagne." I thought, for me, that bridge will be burned and I'll have myself a good long cry. It was difficult to talk to them. I like them more the more I see of them, and I don't want to know them well or to have a great deal to remember about them. I think that if we had met under different circumstances we might have become friends. I didn't take the clothes Martha wanted to give me. I told her Dorothy will pick them up when she gets here.

They dropped me off downtown, as I didn't want to come back here yet. I saw a movie instead, Doris Day in a comedy. It was romantic in a silly way, and I cried.

I walked home; there were stars overhead. Cars whizzed by with blinding headlights. The night was cold and I walked with my hands deep in the pockets of my trench coat. I picked out the North Star, Stella Polaris. That made me feel foolishly secure. I talked out loud to the star as I walked, and Martha and Don and the baby were pushed far out of my mind for a while.

MARCH

Monday the 1st

My month is here! I used to think it never would come. But it did and today doesn't feel any different from yesterday—yet it is. Next time a new month rolls around it will be April and the world—my world—will have changed. Some of the question marks whirling around in my head will be gone.

I signed out for supper and came down here to Toni's just to celebrate the occasion by myself. I've got the booth in the corner and a steaming pot of tea and my notebook. Two truck drivers are sitting at the counter and Toni is reading aloud from *No Time for Sergeants*. Most of the time Toni is laughing so hard he can't read and the truck drivers are howling. The café smells of French fries and hamburgers frying on the grill, and outside dusk is turning into dark. I feel safe here and very much at home.

"Want another tea bag—on the house?" Toni grins and peeks under the lid of my teapot.

"Thanks, I'd love some more tea." I smile back, and Toni turns to the two truck drivers.

"Meet Jean, fellas, she comes from the Salvation Army Home on the hill, and fills up on my tea and scribbles in her notebook every day."

The drivers nod and smile and say, "Hi, Jean. Nice meetin'
you." There isn't a thing in their eyes or their faces to make me
feel embarrassed. They look as if they know the score and accept
it as something quite normal. It feels good to smile back instead
of hiding.

"Tough luck," one of the drivers says. He is tall, his dark hair
streaked with gray.

"Oh," I say, "it's almost over now."

"Jeez," says the other driver. "Anything like that happen to
one of my daughters I'd skin the guy alive!"

"Well," I say, and I can't help smiling because it feels so good
to talk about it this way without pretending or trying to defend
myself, "I guess it was my fault too—it takes two, you know."

"Yeah," the tall driver says. "But you gotta take the consequences alone. I sure wouldn't let the guy get off that easy."

"If I ever see him again I'll tell him," I say. "Thanks for taking my side, anyway."

"Jean will make it O.K.," says Toni and pats my shoulder.
"She knows what she's doing." Both drivers smile and nod.
"Good luck, kid," they say, and I smile back, feeling suddenly
strong enough to take on the whole wide world.

I don't have anything to cry about. I've got so many things
waiting for me and these months have made me stronger. They
had better!

We have two new girls in our dorm. Anne is from Minnesota
and she has told her parents she is working in New York. She
was in love with the father of her baby, she says. He had told
her he was in love with her and she thought he wanted to marry
her, but when she told him she was pregnant he said he was
sorry. Two weeks later he married another girl.

Diane is in Lisa's bed, next to mine. She is thirty-four and
acts as if she's on Cloud Nine. Her bed is cluttered with bits of

colorful yarn and cloth and she sings while she makes rag dolls and stuffed animals for her three kids at home. Diane is a widow and she will marry the father of her new baby as soon as his divorce becomes final. She is staying here in the Home to save on the expenses and to save her boyfriend embarrassment. Her eyes and smiling face have a glow that I guess goes with being an expectant mother in love with and loved by the father of her baby. She doesn't say "my baby"; she says "our baby." In here, the difference is to touch and feel. Diane's happiness affects us all. Her voice and laughter draw some of the girls like a magnet. They come to watch her make Raggedy Anns and hear her tell about her kids and her "honey" who loves them all. The pictures of her children and her boyfriend are admired and talked about. Every evening at eight fifteen her boyfriend calls. He is on vacation now, Diane says, and is spending his three weeks with Diane's kids.

"My honey will be so proud of his first baby," she says, patting her stomach. "His first wife didn't want any kids." The girls who come daily to sit with Diane and talk about her family want to hear again and again about her love. It is almost as if they are trying to submerge their own misery in her joy, as if they hope something will rub off on them.

The girls who don't come avoid Diane and don't even want to talk about her. "Ah," they say, shrugging their shoulders, "she's a fool. She's probably making up the whole story."

I think it is because Diane seems so *alive* in here, where most of us are walking around pretending we are just dreaming or something. That's why she affects us all, and no one can ignore it. She's shaking up the finely-balanced equilibrium we're all trying to preserve.

Tuesday the 2nd

The day started badly. The weatherman had predicted cold weather for last night and the furnace had been turned up. The heat was awful and nobody slept much. The weather was mild and I heard the rain against the window. I tossed and turned because of a million little aches, wishing one of them would turn into a real pain.

About midnight I heard Jane get up and go downstairs. Her slippers always trail along the floor. She looks horrible now, her cheeks sunken and her eyes hollow from lack of sleep. For her this must be living hell. I see some of the fourteen- and fifteen-year-olds run laughing up the stairs as if they're living a great big game, and I feel like shaking them. But they are perhaps better off than Jane who never walks down the middle of the corridor; she walks next to the wall, looking as if she would like to shrink into it.

After checkup today (I'm still doing fine) Simpson took us on a guided tour of the Hospital. Six of us are due this month. I like Nurse Simpson, and today she was smiling as she answered all our questions. I always had a feeling her stern face was just a front to keep us in line. I hope she is on duty when I deliver. With her and with Doctor Norwad around, I don't think anything could be too hard.

Simpson took us through the labor room and the delivery room and told us there is nothing to worry about.

"You're not going to be sick," she said. "Childbirth is a very natural thing and the pain is just your body helping to bring out the baby. And remember, someone will be with you all the time," she said.

We stood in a semicircle around the delivery table, and she

showed us the stirrups where our legs will be fastened, and the incubator all ready for the baby. Over the table are strong lamps and a mirror. Simpson's face looked stern again when she told us that we can ask to be blindfolded if we don't want to see our baby. A couple of the girls smiled and looked relieved.

I haven't made up my mind about it yet. After all these months of waiting and soul-searching, I don't know if I want to ask to be blindfolded. I'm going to pretend to others that I've never had a baby, but I'm not going to try to pretend to myself. I *think* I want to see the baby.

Lisa was taken to a foster home this morning. Carrie is alone in the mothers' ward now. All the dorms are filled to capacity and we hear that girls are on waiting lists outside. Miss O'Connor told me there are girls in the Salvation Army shelters and in rented rooms waiting to get in. About half the girls in here are due in March and early April. The nurses say it is always this way—a mad rush in March and then again in October. Now count back nine months from those two peak seasons and you get to June and New Year's. That makes sense, I guess!

After lights out

I can scribble in my notebook by the light from the lamp outside our window. It's getting harder to sleep every night, now.

Someone brought a portable radio downstairs to the smoking room after supper and some of the girls danced in the corridor. Their shadows jerked and swayed on the wall, grotesque and shapeless. The smoke in the room was so thick it burned our eyes and throats; most of us chain-smoke anyway. The talk drifted to "how we got here."

"Wow," said Cleo, a tall Negro girl from the pink dorm.

"I got so drunk at a party I don't even remember when it happened. I wasn't even sober enough to enjoy it!"

"For me it was wonderful," said Nancy, who is eighteen and a freshman in college. "I knew what I was doing. There couldn't be anything between us—marriage, I mean—but I don't regret it." Her face looked dreamy under the curlers. "We had one wonderful week together—it was worth every bit of what I'm going through now."

Wednesday the 3rd before dawn

I am alone in the smoking room, gray pre-dawn outside. I was tossing in bed after midnight when Jane whispered across the room. "Let's go down for a smoke." The smoking room was dark. Jane sat in a dark corner and her voice reached me, even and low.

"I went to a teacher's convention last summer and things didn't turn out the way I had thought," she said. "I guess I was desperate and I didn't care what happened. I wasn't quite sober that night and the man was married." The glow from her cigarette showed her pale face and thin wisps of gray hair across her forehead. She laughed, a sad little laugh. "And to think I could have gone to the Far East that month instead. Not much to joke about, is it? You see, I don't really mind the pregnancy—I mean the discomfort and all—it's just that I'm sure this is my last chance and I wish so much that I could keep the baby."

I sat there feeling guilty for being young, for having another chance waiting. There was nothing for me to say. I don't think Jane really wanted me to say anything; I was just somebody nameless to talk to on a sleepless night. After a while she put out her cigarette and shuffled upstairs. I heard the slow steps moving up.

Afternoon

This morning I found a small cardboard box at the staff residence. It was empty, just the right size for packing the things I need when I go upstairs to deliver. Major Laski came while I was dusting the living room and I asked her if I could take the box.

"Why, certainly, Jean," she said and smiled. "It's almost your time now, isn't it?" I said yes and thanked her for the box. Later I took it to the dorm and packed my things in it. I've seen other girls do that before. They keep the box under the bed and it's almost a status symbol. It means we're ready to go. I guess it's like the young expectant mother on the outside who packs a suitcase to go to the hospital.

But I was caught. Mrs. Larsen, the housekeeper, peeked in the door and when she saw the box she came all the way into the room. She looked angry.

"What do you think you're doing?" she said.

"Packing—to go upstairs," I answered.

"You know you're not allowed to keep luggage in the dorm. What if all of you started keeping boxes under your beds!"

"I've seen others—" I said. "Please let me."

"Don't 'please' me!" Mrs. Larsen looked as if she was enjoying the scene.

"You can keep it in the locker room if you wish—or I'll throw it out."

"But the locker room is locked at night, when I may need it." I was almost choking with anger.

"That's your problem," said Mrs. Larsen and left, slamming the door. I threw my things in a heap on the bed and ran downstairs to throw the stupid box away myself. I was so mad my hand was shaking when I lit my first cigarette in the smoking room. It doesn't take much to throw me into a fit nowadays. How am I going to stand up when the real test comes?

Thursday the 4th

I couldn't sleep last night and wandered downstairs to the smoking room. It was dark, but I saw the bulky outline in the corner and heard the muffled sobs.

"Is that you, Jean?" I recognized Jane's voice and turned to leave her alone. "Don't leave. . . ." The words were like a cry and I sat down. I had never seen Jane lose her composure before. I've watched her—she's always carrying a book around and she reads to keep from breaking. At least that's what I think she does. She reads, I write—for the same reason.

"I want this baby—but I can't, I can't." Her thin body shook with sobs. Then she straightened up and the words came tumbling out.

"I'm going to keep it with me the seven days I'm here," she said. "No one can take that away from me!"

"It will hurt more later," I said. Jane must have told herself the same thing again and again.

"I don't care." Her voice was defiant. "I'll cram it all into those seven days. If it hurts later, at least I'll have had that." We sat in silence. I wondered how she got her personal life so mixed up that the only way out was a home for unwed mothers.

Do we ever get to be free to do what we want to?

I'm not worried about being a fabulous success anymore. All I want is an ability to get along with myself and the world. Stability. How I used to hate that word. Now I want it. Stability—continuity—stick-to-it-ness, not to give up.

Friday the 5th

A new girl who calls herself Christine moved into our dorm yesterday afternoon. Early this morning she had a bloody show and was moved upstairs to Isolation. She is only six months' pregnant. Everybody is concerned for her. It is funny; most of us are unhappy about being pregnant, but we are all concerned if it looks as if one of us may lose the baby. Christine is in her late twenties, and she has been living with her parents and supporting them for the last five years. She is a secretary.

"They think I don't want to live with them anymore," she said, showing us the picture of her parents, a white-haired elderly couple sitting in a porch swing outside a small frame house.

"I don't know how they'll get along without me." Christine was blinking away tears. "I just couldn't tell them the truth. They are too old to be hurt this way."

Saturday the 6th at Toni's

I discovered a new road today, up a narrow winding side street, away from the main street with its busy Saturday traffic. The street climbed a steep hill and little houses stood in terraced gardens against the moss-grown gray cliffs. The tall crowns of old trees shaded the street and, above, white clouds raced by on a blue spring sky.

I could smell leaves burning, and somewhere someone was sawing with a handsaw making a singing steady rhythm. A small boy raced down the street on a bicycle, throwing newspapers on front porches with the sure aim of long experience. I saw a tree house in a big oak and heard children laughing. The street narrowed to a gravel road leading through a canyon with tall gray boulders, and there was the sound of water running in the deep ravine next to the road. The road wound its way around a boulder and there just ahead was a wooden bridge across the little creek. It led to a park.

I hadn't expected to find anything like that so close to the heart of the city—the tall trees, the paths covered by last year's fallen leaves, the picnic tables deserted this early in spring, and everywhere birds chirping and flitting around. Near the edge of the creek was a family of five kids; Mom and Dad were busy watching a small boy in blue jeans getting ready to put up his red and white kite. What a great day for flying a kite!

What a great day for doing anything, for walking down a path covered with last fall's brown leaves, crisp and dry in the sun, soft under my old shoes. A great day for leaning against an old rugged tree trunk, watching puffy white clouds in a clear blue sky reflected in the water of a small stream.

A great day to be alive, with a little someone alive and kicking inside me.

Sunday the 7th

The Major spoke about hope in chapel this morning. "Be of good courage, and he shall strengthen your heart, all ye that hope in the Lord" (Psalms 31:24). The Major said that in her opinion the word "hopeless" should be taken out of our language—it is the worst word, she said.

Jody is two weeks overdue and someone always asks her why she is still around. "'Cause I like it here!" she says, her brown eyes flashing below straight dark bangs. "I don't want to leave you all alone in your misery!" But when no one is looking Jody sits quietly just staring ahead. She looks tired today.

Last night some of the girls talked about inducing labor. We just got the news from upstairs—Suzanne took castor oil and is in labor right now. Suzanne is sixteen years old, chubby, blond and always giggling. Who would have thought she'd have the guts to do it? She isn't due for another two weeks.

Later

I took a walk through quiet Sunday streets. It is mild and sunny today and windows were open. I could hear radios or television sets in the houses. Lawns look spring-green, and I saw fathers playing with their children.

All is quiet in the Home. Many of the girls are out on passes, the others sit around talking, knitting, smoking.

Evening

I walked again after supper. It's getting so I can't sit still anymore. The moon is up now, so new and shining. Before it is full my baby will be born. He is all ready inside me: fingernails and hair, small and red and wrinkled and safe. I hope he is all right— he has to be, the way he kicks around.

I wonder what you'll be like. Will you ever wonder what your real mother was like, and why she wasn't ready to take care of you herself?

Tuesday the 9th

My name was left off the list of girls who go for checkup today. It was a mistake but I feel disappointed. It's just a week till my official due-date and I guess I was expecting some sort of a miracle, like having the doctor tell me the baby is ready to be born and I better hurry to the delivery room.

Cecilie was told she will have a breech birth. I wish she'd go ahead and tell her medical student that she is expecting his baby. She says she doesn't want to because then he'd probably quit school to marry her and not go on to get his degree. They've been engaged to be married for five years, Cecilie says, and all this time she has helped pay for his schooling.

I can't understand how she's kept this from him, or why she wants to give the baby up for adoption. But then maybe the story about the medical student is a lie. We all have lies in here.

I get a letter a day from Dorothy now. She is wonderful. Her small talk keeps me going. My drawer is piled with unanswered letters; each day I feel as if I'm drifting further away from the world I used to know. I wonder what this place will seem like when I look back from the other side?

Jody hasn't delivered yet. And I am the next one due. Some of the girls have started betting on which one of us will go first and they look at us as if we're two of a kind. Sure, we are both going to have a baby and maybe our babies will be born at the same time, but we are worlds apart. Her thoughts and her pain will be hers alone. I will have mine. When we go upstairs the girls will say to each other, "How wonderful, I'm glad she's through."

They will come to see us in the mothers' ward and between them and us will be a gulf no words can bridge. On their side is the waiting, the laughing and joking and quarreling and crying, the fighting about turns in the shower, the being together, sharing each other's lives—a little.

On our side will be the aloneness. They will look at us with something like envy and pity. There is something new in the eyes of the mothers and the girls shrink from it. Mothers don't come back to the dorm. They are still in the house, but almost forgotten. They are the reminders that the day all of us wait for and fear will come.

Last night in the smoking room the girls talked about carrying weapons. Some of them have switchblade knives; they say they need them for protection. Some of them have spent time in Juvenile Hall. I wonder what the knives have protected them from? Not from the boys who made them pregnant, obviously.

One of the knife-carriers is Lizzie, a bright Negro girl. I like talking to her, and she asked me if I want to go home with her tomorrow. She lives on the other side of town and I am really not allowed to go that far away. But maybe I'll go anyway. If I start in labor I can always get a cab—babies have been born in cabs before.

Wednesday evening, the 10th

We took a taxi across town, Lizzie and I. Riding in the taxi made me feel almost normal and the town looked just as it did when I saw it a month ago. Somehow I've felt as if the whole world has been changing with me.

Lizzie lives with her mother and grandmother in an apartment right above the Midnite Bar. Her father died in action in Korea. The street is wide and the old buildings are large. Once this was a refined residential neighborhood. Now the plaster is falling from the walls and the junk stores, bars, pool halls and grocery-liquor stores take up the first floors of the buildings.

The smell of stewing chicken met us in the steep hallway, where a lonely electric bulb threw a weak yellow shine over walls scribbled with names and dates and four-letter words. Lizzie's mother and grandmother met us in the kitchen, where the pot of chicken simmered on a stove in the middle of the room. The mother and the grandmother were both tiny and shrunken; Lizzie towered over them and they clung to her, crying.

"Meet Jean, from the Home." Lizzie introduced me and each shook my hand, showing a quick smile. In the living room plaster cupids crumbled from the tall ceiling. Lizzie put a stack of records on the corner hi-fi set, and just then we could hear the rumbling of many feet coming up the stairs. Kids started filing in and suddenly the room seemed full of them, laughing and talking, slapping Lizzie's back and glancing at me—white and very pregnant—on the edge of a chair.

"Jean is a friend of mine from the Home." Lizzie laughed and flung her arms wide. "Gee, but it's great to be out of that joint! Let's dance." Some of the kids nodded and smiled at me, but soon I was forgotten. Lizzie was dancing in the middle of the floor; it was obvious that she is the leader. In a loose sweat shirt over a tight skirt she didn't look pregnant. Her brown eyes were sparkling and her teeth very bright in a wide, happy smile. The whole room seemed to sway with the music—Lizzie was home again.

The door to the kitchen opened and grandma peeked in, beckoning to me. I went to her room on the other side of the kitchen. Here the dark red and white wallpaper had been left intact from former days. The lace curtains were pulled to hide the view of the scarred buildings on the other side of an alley. A bird cage hung by the window and on the dresser were rows of family pictures. The large four-poster bed was covered by a beautiful hand-embroidered quilt. The sound and beat of the dancing reached us faintly through closed doors but in grandma's room was an aura of timelessness, far from the rock-'n'-roll age. The room smelled faintly of something I couldn't recognize, except that it made me think of fields of poppies in spring.

Grandma pulled her shawl closer, and sat down in her red

velvet platform rocker. I sat on the edge of the only other chair in the room, a straight-backed wooden yellow one, and wondered what the shrunken old woman with the bright peering eyes wanted to talk about.

"We miss her so," she said finally, meaning Lizzie. "She is such a lively one." I nodded and waited.

"She is such a bright one, too, you know. First in class in school even if she never studies. She's too restless—just like her Daddy used to be."

"She'll grow out of it," I said, and grandma nodded.

"If she goes to college she'll get a pension," grandma went on, "since her Daddy died in the war." Lizzie's mother stuck her head in the door.

"Dinner's ready," she said. Grandma nodded again, staring straight ahead as she rocked back and forth.

"She's not a bad girl, just young."

"We all like her at the home," I said. "She'll be all right, I'm sure." I wondered if that was what grandma wanted to hear.

The kitchen was full of people talking and laughing and eating. The pot held enough chicken and dumplings for everyone, and it was delicious. I hadn't eaten like that for weeks.

After dinner Lizzie showed me her room and said I could take a nap while she went with the gang to the drugstore. She made me feel very old and tired, but I guess I wouldn't have been able to keep up with the rest of them for long. I lay on the big four-poster bed and stared at the books filling the shelves on the walls. Shakespeare, Plato, Nietzsche, James Baldwin, anthologies of Negro literature, pocketbooks on crime and passion, poetry—volumes of poetry.

On the dresser was a large notebook. The cover was scribbled full of boys' names and drawings of faces and trees. I opened it, feeling guilty, but too curious to leave it alone. Across the top of a page Lizzie had written:

Elizabeth—picture of a young woman . . .

Yesterday a girl—strange—longing, mind full of dreams. To run up a grass-clad hill—sing from the top.

Laugh in the face of the world.

Lonely, nights of wondering.

Different. Not just drifting along. Cutting off—cutting out—to be herself.

Seventeen—black skin—black hand—white skin—white hand—heartbeats in rhythm together.

The world is mine also. I want it.

Today—a woman. Woman's body. Mind—bright, alert, aware, knowing. And because of the knowing—crying.

Elizabeth—a girl's dream—a woman's secret.

Cry, Elizabeth. . . .

Last night in the smoking room she talked about carrying a knife and almost getting hooked for dope-peddling. Today here is her room with shelves full of books and her words, "The world is mine—I want it!" And a baby. What will you do, Lizzie? With your bright and restless mind—will you be bad? Or will you be very, very good? In the next few months you may make the choice.

One of Lizzie's friends drove us back to the Home.

"He's crazy," Lizzie said later. "He isn't the father of my baby but he wants to marry me anyway." She laughed. "But who wants to be married? Not me."

Later, after chapel

The Major spoke about Hidden Sins in chapel tonight. It almost made me laugh out loud.

They tell me Tina took castor oil and went into labor this afternoon. She is only fourteen and has been held in Isolation for two weeks for stealing from the girls in the dorm.

I haven't had a letter from Mother and Dad in nearly three weeks. Haven't written either, for that matter. I hope everything is all right with them and that they don't think there is anything wrong with me. My letters haven't been too cheerful lately.

Latest flash from the hospital floor—Tina's labor was false. "Serves her right," says Tammy, and puffs big clouds of smoke. Tina took twelve dollars from Tammy and has already spent it on a movie and candy.

I have piercing dropping pains and my stomach is hard as a wooden ball.

Thursday the 11th

Several months ago I dreamed one night that my baby would be born on March eleventh. I saw the date clearly in my dream and woke up thinking that it would be true, but I guess dreams don't come true often.

At breakfast Lieutenant Stewart led us in prayer. She asked the Lord to help us not to burden today with the sorrows of yesterday and the problems of tomorrow. I wish I had her faith.

The word went around at the table—Carolyn is in labor five weeks early and the doctor says it is twins.

There was a new girl at my table at breakfast. Her name is June and she is pretty in an all-American-girl-next-door way. Afterward, in the smoking room, she chain-smoked and talked very fast and very much. "Maybe this is tough," she said. "But it will sure make a girl think. There can't be much after this that'll scare me." Later she talked about love and said, "If we had loved the guy with the right kind of love none of us would be here. Maybe we'll be better judges next time." June is a psychology major from a Midwestern university.

Later, at Toni's

I've checked out for supper. Toni is boiling an egg for my supper and the pot of tea is on the red counter before me. This place is saving my life.

Tammy came back from town all upset this afternoon. She had gone down to celebrate her birthday; she's eighteen.

"My God," she said, pacing the narrow floor in the smoking room. "I ran into the bastard who's the father of my baby. I told him we was quit and the idiot says he's got a Reno divorce and wants me to move in with him again." Tammy flipped the ashes from her cigarette on the floor. "But I told him, 'You got no divorce when you should have so I don't need you no more.' And do you know what that self-lovin' fool had the gall to tell me? 'Sure Baby,' he says, 'Soon's I get you in bed with me you'll wanna shack up again.' " Tammy shook her head. "I hate his guts!"

"So I fell for him once," she went on after a while. "So I was mad at Mom and had to get away. That bastard came through town and I went north with him to a lumber camp. When we come back my mom says to him, 'Get the hell outa here and don't come back till you're single,' but he didn't get no divorce then and I'm glad, 'cause he's rotten. He gave me fifty bucks today and that's all I'll ever get outa him, that louse!"

Tammy talks tough but I like her. She's always the first one to volunteer when a girl is sick and needs someone to do her work. Tammy doesn't have an ounce of self-pity (some of the girls do) and I think she'll go on from here walking straight and with her head up high. Red hair and laughing green eyes and a way about her that makes people turn to watch, even when she's pregnant.

Another cup of tea, a cigarette, and I'll stare a hole in the calendar on the wall. Every night I hope I'll wake up and have to go upstairs. When I have little pains I wish they would grow stronger. When I have an occasional strong pain I'm not quite so brave. But I wish I could get it over with.

Carolyn's labor stopped and they moved her into Isolation. She'll have to stay in bed for a while, the doctor says. But Carolyn is happy anyway. Her boyfriend is coming home from the Army in June and they'll be married. He has been paying her expenses at the Home, and when she leaves here Carolyn will take an apartment with her babies and wait for him.

"I can't go home," she says. "My foster parents and his foster parents won't let us have kids now—they'll try to make us give 'em up." Carolyn has been sewing on the layette for her baby since she came. Now, with twins coming, she is sewing in bed, they say. Her boyfriend is a mechanic and Carolyn has had a job since she was sixteen. She is nineteen now.

"I've known Don since I was thirteen," she told us once in the smoking room. "He was fifteen then and when I got to be seventeen I got pregnant. Don had just joined the Army and didn't know about it, and I was scared to tell him. My foster parents made me sign an agreement to give the baby up for adoption. They were gonna get a thousand dollars for it and they said they could sure use the money. But I lost the baby when I was five months along. My foster parents were mad but I was sure glad it happened. Nobody can take our babies from us now. We won't have a fancy home, but it'll be nice and solid." Carolyn's had the hard breaks but she's coming out ahead.

Miss O'Connor told me eleven girls are waiting to get in the Home now. The mothers' wards have empty beds waiting and we're crowded in the dorms. The bets are going strong about Jody and me—sure, we'll hurry!

The sunset is red over the dark rooftops of the city. I've spent two hours at Toni's counter; I don't know how many cups of tea I've had.

Two college boys are in for coffee. Their books are stacked on the counter and they wave their hands as they talk eagerly. Next year I'll be back in school. I'll talk with boys like those about art and philosophy and current events.

All this will be like a dream, but I'll always know it was my world for a while. And that I shared it with others—sweet girls, ugly girls, kind ones and tough ones with knives hidden under their leather jackets. But in the house on the hill we were women all, fulfilling the biological function of our kind. The rest of our functions would have to wait.

Friday the 12th

I wandered through the corridor, walked in and out of the dorm, picking up a book I ought to have read, putting it down again to wander around some more. Finally I checked out and came down to Toni's.

"You still around, kid?" Toni said, handing me a cup of tea before I had time to ask for it.

"I've got five days till my due-date," I said.

My stomach is hard against the counter and I watch two young couples in for quick hamburgers and Cokes on a Friday afternoon. The smoke curls up from my cigarette; I have nothing to do but watch it. When I curl my bare feet in my shoes I can feel a nail right under my left big toe—my only pair of flats and they're almost worn through. I can't afford to buy new ones. I can hardly afford to buy my little ten- and fifteen-cent notebooks. To make them last longer I write small and don't use a margin.

I shouldn't skip supper so often. Maybe I better go back for it tonight. But we can't sign out for a walk after supper, so if I stay in to eat I've got to stay there all evening.

I know what I'll do first when I get out of here. I'll walk all over the city one early morning. Climb the hills and watch the harbor, the fishing boats coming in from the sea, the big ships at anchor and at dockside, feel that fresh salt morning breeze come in from the ocean.

Later

Four of us were talking in one corner of the smoking room after supper. In the other end the regular poker gang was playing.

"Is this the way it feels when you're on dope?" said June. "Your senses so dull you only exist from day to day, happy you're not going mad?"

"And yet if you believe life has a meaning you've got to believe we're doing something important, waiting for new life to be born through our bodies," said Cecilie.

"Maybe I believe there's a meaning," said June, "but I sure don't know what it is—-why we are born, live and learn through hard knocks, just to die one day. If God didn't mean for us to know why, why the heck did he make us bright enough to worry about it?"

I said, "Maybe at one time in our lives we fulfill whatever it is we are meant to do, only we don't know it."

"Whatever it is," said Cecilie, "I think a woman gets close to it when she gives birth to a child."

"That's something to be grateful for, anyway," said June. Madeline, who had been knitting all the time, looked up and laughed. "You are naïve fools," she said. "I've had three children and there is nothing beautiful or meaningful about it. Not even when you're married. It is ghastly and disgusting—the swollen bodies and the pain and all the blood." Madeline looked at each of us in turn and then went back to her knitting. None of us found anything to say in answer.

The doctor's car just pulled up. That settles the bets. Jody went to the labor room two hours ago. She certainly isn't wasting her time.

Getting ready for bed is the best part of the day. Everyone feels better at night. We've all put little marks on our calendars and counted one more day gone. Then to bed, stretching under the covers, searching for a comfortable position, not so easy to find now. But it is good to lie there, the restlessness of the day gone.

The window is open every night now, and the breeze is fresh and fragrant. I shift around and feel my stomach harden in contraction and wonder if I shall have pains before morning. But always the gray dawn comes and another long day of idle waiting ahead.

Saturday the 13th

I sneaked in to weigh myself in the nurse's office today. I've lost two and a half pounds this week—a good sign, say the girls who've had babies before.

There is a new girl in the smoking room. She sits fiddling with a package of cigarettes and hasn't even taken off her coat. Her short blond hair needs combing.

"How can you be so cheerful?" She interrupts the girls who've been laughing and talking as usual over their cards. "How can you joke about the babies?" Some of the girls stop talking and look at her. She goes right on. "It's cut-and-dried, isn't it? We're all in here to have babies we don't want. We're hiding it from the world and we'll leave here pretending it didn't happen. I hate those lies—and you just laugh!"

Tammy speaks first, and she smiles. "Cool it, kid—you'll get the hang of it soon." The new girl gets up to leave without a word. I see the tears flooding her eyes. By the door, June reaches out to touch her arm.

"We know we're in the same boat," she says soothingly. "We all cry sometimes and I don't think anyone likes to lie, but the tears don't help and we laugh to keep them away." The new girl looks straight at June.

"Maybe you don't like the lies," she says slowly, "but what about those poker players in the corner? Thanks for trying anyway." She removes her arm from June's hand and is gone. I feel sorry for her. I felt that way once and the adjustment hurts. I wish we could get more help with our adjustment in here. The social workers are mostly concerned with arrangements for adoption. We need someone who can help us understand ourselves better, and why we got into this mess in the first place. What we really need is a psychiatrist or a psychologist who could give us individual or group therapy. Since we have all demonstrated our problem in pretty much the same way, group therapy might be very effective here.

Sunday the 14th

Stella, the new girl, went into labor in a state of shock and was rushed upstairs right after chapel today. She was almost "discovered" in the kind of freak happening all of us are scared to death of.

Stella is a nurse and she had told her family she has a job here. Her sister happens to be visiting in town and phoned here yesterday. Stella talked to her, said she would be on duty all weekend and couldn't meet her. But her sister decided to come anyway. She came just as the girls were leaving chapel after the service this morning, and someone had left the front door open by mistake. Stella's sister was standing in the corridor. The Major saw the stranger and had the sense to pull her out of the hall and close the door before Stella walked by and the sisters didn't see each other. The Major explained that Stella was working in the lab and couldn't be disturbed, and the sister left without suspecting that Stella is one of us girls.

The front door was locked again and the Major called Stella to tell her what had happened. She came back downstairs to the smoking room and sat here pale and shaking. And then the pains came. Now she is upstairs in Isolation. They've given her sedatives to stop the labor, and she is safe from visitors. But we are all a little shaken. It could happen to anyone.

Monday the 15th

Last night the moon was almost full. I remember my first night in this dorm—a full-moon ago. I thought that by this full moon my baby would be born. I woke up in the middle of the night and the fog was thick against the window. I sat on a wooden stool in the bathroom and read about the true love of Elizabeth Taylor just to keep from having to go to bed.

The fog is still here this morning; we can't see the city from our hilltop. I walked across the park to my morning duty in the staff residence and thought how lucky I am. I had a letter from Mother Saturday and she says she will come home in May. That suits me fine. I'll have time to get organized after I leave here.

June just came into the smoking room, mad and ready to yell at someone. "I met that snotty Mrs. Horner—the group social worker—in the hall upstairs and she wanted me to take up a hobby. I said I didn't want to fool with it, and she told me I'm no better than the rest of them or I wouldn't be here." June lit a cigarette with a shaking hand. "Who the hell does she think she is, anyway?"

Later

The first session of the girls' council met this afternoon. There are two representatives from each of the three large dorms, one from our little one. I wanted to go but girls who are in their last month can't be members of the council. The council doesn't have any power other than to air grievances and make suggestions, but it is still a good idea. A Salvation Army staff member and one of the social workers are standing members. The girls' representatives are elected from the dorms, and the council will meet once a week. I think maybe the housekeeping staff ought to be included also since most of the problems come from our frictions with them.

Diane was representative from our dorm and said that the first meeting didn't accomplish much. They appointed a food committee to suggest more appetizing menus and avoid waste. Someone also brought up the point that certain girls make a practice of standing outside the door to the delivery room listening during deliveries. All the dorm representatives brought complaints about the heating system; it always gets too hot or too cold at night.

Tuesday the 16th

One day till my due-date. I went to the clinic this morning hoping the doctor would tell me it's coming, but he just said the baby is still floating, is not even engaged, and I was so upset I started crying later in the smoking room. Diane happened to come by with an armload of colorful yarn the cooks had given her and asked me what was wrong. I lost my temper and screamed at her, "Nothing's wrong! Can't you see I'm happy?" She didn't look hurt, just went on her way. I'm glad I didn't run into someone I don't like—I might have hit her!

It's drizzling rain outside. Just the kind of weather to suit my mood, but I can't get a pass till after lunch.

Later

Greasy spaghetti for lunch. I drank a glass of skim milk instead and then felt tired enough to lie down on my bed. I fell asleep and when I woke up my eyes were swollen from crying. But the sun was shining.

Cecilie wanted to go out with me, and we walked in the warm breeze with our coats open. I felt like smiling, and then I saw my reflection in a shop window, pale drawn face, dark circles around puffed-up eyes. I look awful!

After the second cup of tea at Toni's Cecilie said, "I worry about you, Jean."

"What do you mean? You don't even know me."

"Oh, yes, I do." Cecilie looked straight at me and I felt my stomach tighten—could she possibly?

Cecilie smiled and shook her head. "Don't worry," she said. "I don't know your real name and I don't care. But we've been here together now, since October, and I think I know a little bit about what you're like."

"Oh," I said, and wondered what she was talking about.

"You're a smart girl," she continued. "I bet you're filling those little notebooks of yours with thoughts about what is happening to you and why." She was stirring her coffee and didn't look at me. "I know I'm talking about something that's taboo around the Home."

"That's O.K." I wondered what she was aiming at.

"When you leave, don't try to forget." Cecilie's voice was urgent. "Don't try to 'make up for it.' Go someplace where you can be alone and think, and listen to what's inside you. Accept what is you and what has happened. If you don't, you'll be running away and you'll just run in a circle right back to where you started from."

"Get pregnant again?" I had to smile, it sounded so silly.

"Yes, that has happened to girls before." Cecilie lit another cigarette and we both stared in silence at the red counter.

"I'm going to break a promise," Cecilie said, not looking at me. "I think maybe you ought to know."

"Go on," I said.

"Jane in your dorm had another baby eleven years ago—here in the Home. She gave it away for adoption without even seeing it."

"No!" I felt as if I was going to be sick. I remembered Jane's drawn face, the thin wisps of gray hair and her voice: "For seven days I want that baby. I'll cram it all into those seven days. I won't have another chance."

"Oh, yes," said Cecilie. "She told me herself. She never did get over feeling guilty. Feeling like a failure. And she always kept looking for that baby . . . wondering every time she saw a child that age." I found it hard to look into Cecilie's face.

"Just being intelligent won't keep you from making the same mistake twice," Cecilie said. "You've got to learn to accept yourself and the world around you as they really are. Jane couldn't."

We walked home under a sky colored red by the sunset. Cecilie didn't say any more but my head was full of confusing thoughts.

I've thought so much up to the point when I will leave here, and then maybe about how I must keep from letting myself ever interfere with the baby and with Martha and Don. But somehow my thoughts haven't gone on much from there, to how I will live with myself and the world around me, what I will actually do. I've been vague about it. I've never thought that it might be too hard, that I couldn't somehow do it. To think that Jane, who has accomplished so much, couldn't!

Tuesday night

Jane and I were both moved upstairs to Isolation tonight, to give room to new girls. I share a room with Stella and Jane is alone next door. Nurse Simpson told me that Jane will be allowed to stay with her baby in that room, after she delivers.

Stella still looks pale and shaken after the near run-in with her sister. "I'm glad you're here," she said when I came in. "I can't stand these thoughts and the time dragging endlessly. Six more weeks to go. There are some people right now who know they only have six more weeks to live, six weeks to do what they want to do before they die . . . and we are just waiting, wasting our time." Stella has deep dark circles around her eyes and she's grown frightfully thin.

"It shouldn't be possible to just waste time," she said. "I can't help it. I can't help feeling how horrible it is to waste all this . . . and then not know where to go and what to do when it is over. I don't have any money to go home on. My family thinks I have a job and am well off. Even if I'm lucky, and strong enough, to get a job the day I leave here, what do I live on till my first payday comes around?" Stella hides her face in her hands and I can hear her sob. But what can I do about it? I'm in the same boat. I don't have a penny to share.

Wednesday the 17th

I've circled today on my calendar and now that it is here it doesn't seem so important, my due-date. What will happen will happen in its own time. I can't push or postpone it.

Cecilie went along on my walk again this afternoon. "Can't let you go alone anymore," she said, and for a moment I didn't know what she was talking about. But of course—the baby may come any time now.

Toni greeted us and brought our coffee. "On the house today— your day," he said and winked at me. "Let me know when the baby gets here."

Tina left yesterday and it was discovered that she had stolen money from all the dorms. Not much, but then the girls don't have much. She took the six dollars Jody had saved for bus fare home, and Jody is due to leave tomorrow.

Sunday the 21st

It is almost midnight, but I can't sleep. I'm alone in the smoking room, and outside is the steady sound of rain beating against the ground.

I have a feeling deep inside as if something terrible is about to happen. I am scared. Is it the baby I'm scared of? I don't know, but I have never felt anything like this—not any pain, not anything physical, but as if I were trapped and helpless and something was closing in on me. I wish I could hide in a dark corner and give birth to my baby—just the two of us alone, no hands and thoughts of others intruding on our world. . . .

Monday the 22nd

This can't be true—it's like a nightmare! Mother is coming! She's arriving in New York tomorrow and thinks I'll be at Dorothy's to meet her the day after!

I cried hysterically after I read the letter, but at least I'm calm enough now to smoke and to write. Mother says she can't stay away any longer; she's flying home ahead of Daddy. "We'll have a wonderful week together," she writes, "and then I'll have to go back to New York to open up the house and get things in order for your father. Tell your wonderful friend Dorothy I'm looking forward to meeting my little girl's 'second mother.' "

What am I going to do? I'm stuck. I'm sitting here in the basement, smoking and staring at the pipes on the ceiling. My belly is swollen with an unborn baby. Why? Why? Why? I can accept the pregnancy. I needed to learn my lesson. But Mother! Must she know this? I've got to think of something. Ask somebody to help. To do what?

Later

I called Dorothy and made a mess of myself crying over the phone. She sounded so calm, so sure. She said not to worry, it will work out. She'll stall Mother—tell her I've gone skiing in New Hampshire or something, that I'm staying in a cabin with friends and can't be reached by phone. She'll tell Mother I'll come to New York to meet her there after I get back.

"That'll give you at least a week," Dorothy said. "Something will happen soon, don't worry. The baby can't wait much longer. It is overdue already." Maybe Dorothy is right, but on the other hand I've heard of babies being born several weeks late. Mother is bound to think something's up. And even if the baby is born right away, how can I face my mother seven days after I've had a baby and pretend I've been skiing in New Hampshire?

June is sitting here with me in the smoking room and says I ought to talk to the chief of the medical staff. He is here at a conference today. Maybe he could check me and see if I'm ready; maybe they can induce labor.

The word is out. Everyone knows by now and everyone is full of sympathy and good advice. I can see the fear in their faces. They're as scared of being discovered as I am. Mrs. Tebbits, the first cook, just brought me a cup of tea and said she is praying for me. Funny, but her clicking teeth didn't sound so bad, and I am really glad for her prayers.

Later

I've been upstairs and the chief of the medical staff will look me over in half an hour. Nurse Simpson told me to be ready. My stomach is hard as a rock. God, make me ready. Let that little baby be ready. We've gone through this much, we've got to make it through the last stretch now.

Later

Nurse Simpson stood by while the doctor examined me. He gave me a pelvic examination, and it hurt. Then he told me to sit up, and he patted my knee and looked at me with kind eyes. I heard his voice from far away.

"Sorry, young lady, I'd like to help but you aren't ready yet."

"How long?" I said.

"It's impossible to tell. The baby is still floating. It could happen anytime or maybe not for two weeks." Nurse Simpson took my hand and squeezed it tight.

"That's all right," I said. "I understand." But inside I wanted to scream and rage at the unfairness of it. I stood up and felt my knees shaking. I had to lean against the table and I wished I could just pass out, lose consciousness, lose myself. I remembered to thank the doctor for spending his time with me, and I walked without feeling my legs down the corridor to my room, where I got out a textbook I should have studied a long time ago. I took the textbook downstairs to the smoking room. The girls didn't have to ask me what had happened; it shows all over my face.

I took the cigarette June gave me and opened my book, an outline of American literature. I saw the letters and the words, and behind my eyes they collided with the thoughts that are tumbling around, making my head swim. It's no use. My stomach is hard again, and it is resting on my lap as if it were something separate from me. It is. I can't control it. I have no power over it. I am trapped by the inside of that stomach of mine.

Suppertime

I have only half-hour passes now, since it is past my due-date, but I don't give a damn. June walked with me to Toni's through the rain and I'm not going back to that place on the hill till it's bedtime.

Toni said, "Hi, you still around, kid?" when we got here, and I said yes and smiled automatically, as I've done every day this week. The Coke-calendar with my meaningless due-date hangs on the wall.

June spent her money on the juke box, and told me about the father of her baby. He is married and she is in love with him.

He wanted to get a divorce when he found out she was pregnant, but June's father threw him out of the house and told him never to come back. "So," said June, shrugging her shoulders, "this baby goes out for adoption because we weren't ready for it. Maybe some day he'll get a divorce and we'll meet again."

June has kitchen duty today and had to go back for supper. I took a walk by myself in the rain. My shoes got soaked and the rain seeped through my coat. The drops rolled down my face and neck and mixed with the tears I couldn't hold back any longer. I talked out loud to the rain and the trees and the passing cars. All will be well, I told myself, as long as I don't lose my head. I walked as quickly as I could, carrying my big stomach. Every step hurt but the pain was good to feel. The rain poured into little streams that ran along the sidewalk, and the lawns smelled fresh and clean. Dusk turned to dark and I kept on walking.

How did I ever get into this mess? I've had nine months of crazy luck, and now when it's almost over, the whole thing blows up. My thoughts went round and round.

Back at the red counter, Toni looked at me with serious brown eyes. "What's wrong, kid? Don't go sick on me in this weather." Toni is a great guy. I ordered a soft-boiled egg for supper. I've got to keep my health through all this or I'll never make it.

June is back again. She is all upset because the kitchen was a mess. She tried to hurry and spilled a whole bowl of gravy all over herself. The way she told it, it sounded so funny I had to laugh, and we both laughed till our stomachs cramped.

After lights out

The girls were all excited when we came back. Peggy had called her father, who is a doctor, and he told her that inducing labor at this stage in a pregnancy shouldn't present a problem. Everyone thinks I got a rotten deal from the chief. Another girl has a boyfriend who is a mate on a ship leaving for Hawaii in a couple of days.

"I can get you some postcards tomorrow and you can write them with different dates. My boyfriend will mail them from the Islands to your mother," she said. Most of the girls are in favor of that scheme and they were full of ideas about things I could write on the cards. Nobody talks about anything else and the excitement has everybody in a frenzy. All the girls can remember how others have been in tight squeezes before and they tell me and each other that no one has ever been discovered yet. We're all in this together, and the girls act as if somehow we can work together and find a way out, too. This feeling of solidarity in a crisis is real enough to touch. It has even spread to the staff. June told me that the Lieutenant prayed for me at the supper table.

Tonight I feel there must be a way. I don't know how, but I think all will be well. I am tired—tomorrow I will face what comes.

Tuesday the 23rd

I feel as if I'm floating in a happiness greater than anything I've ever known, beyond the range of words I know.

My baby was born four hours ago! A beautiful, perfect, live little boy, born through me. That such a miracle could ever happen to me!

People say newborn babies are ugly. Not my son. The nurse held him upside down, a bright red, naked little human being, screaming furiously. Who can blame him? He's been pushed and squeezed and handled, and then dangled upside down in a brightly lit, strange world.

How silly my fears have been. If I had only known how wonderful it would be to see him alive and perfect, to know that he has grown inside me all this time, I would have longed for it instead of dreading it. Even the lies, the loneliness and the hiding —today I feel they were worth it just to be alive to this moment. He is someone else's son, but to me was given the miracle of giving birth.

I feel as if all my life has only been a prelude to this, that I could die now, fulfilled.

Later

I called Dorothy and told her the good news. She didn't sound surprised at all. "I was awake most of the night," she said, "and toward morning I felt that something had happened. I knew all would be well."

Dorothy will stay home till Mother arrives to make sure she doesn't get worried about me. "I'll tell your mother you'll be coming to New York in ten days," she said. "I'll fly out to see you Saturday and we can go home by train to give you time to collect yourself."

Then I called Martha and Don to tell them they have a son. "He is perfect and very good-looking," I said. Inside I felt a swelling pride that almost choked me.

"A son!" said Martha and her voice rose with excitement. "How wonderful, how wonderful! I can't wait to get him home!"

"Next Tuesday, on our seventh day," I said, "he can go home." Not even the thought that he belongs to Martha can mar the joy of today. I won't let it. My body is so light, so relaxed. My stomach is so flat; it is funny not to have a little someone kicking around in there.

I am going to sleep now—on my stomach.

Just to think—he was inside me. . . .

Wednesday the 24th, First Day

They call the day the baby is born Zero Day, so this is our First Day. I slept most of the night but I am tired. I guess I was too excited to feel anything yesterday. The nurses are so sweet, so different now that I'm a mother. They are stricter with the girls. Grumpy would be a better description.

Jody and I are the only ones in the mothers' ward and we can hear the babies crying across the hall. I imagine I can recognize the cry of my little boy. We are being waited on like queens. Yesterday the cook even put a small vase of flowers on my tray.

June came by to say hello from Toni. She said the girls talk about my delivery as a "miraculous escape" from discovery.

"I guess from now on you will be one of those stories that will be told from girl to girl for years to come," said June. "Like the story about the girl who got out of here only two hours before her mother was due to arrive in the city." Unwed mothers must have a protective saint somewhere looking after them, I guess. Labor wasn't really hard, and not as long as I had feared. At first I couldn't even believe it was anything other than severe gas pains. Nurse Simpson was on duty and I shuffled down the hall to ask her for a pain pill. She took one long look at me and said, "You better go to the labor room and let me see how you're doing."

"But the chief said it might take two weeks," I protested. "I just have a few cramps, that's all."

"Babies have a way of ignoring doctors' predictions," said Nurse Simpson. "You better get in bed." She checked me and said I wasn't far along yet, but it was labor all right. I kept telling her she was probably wrong because this wasn't at all the way I had thought it would be.

"Won't hurt to get you ready," she said calmly, going about her preparations. She gave me an enema and I thought the baby was going to come popping out while I was sitting on the stool. But it didn't, and when I got back into bed Nurse Simpson told me to relax and to remember that the pains served a good purpose. Each of them would open up the birth channel a little more for the baby. Then she left me alone.

"Push the button when you need me—I'll be in the next room," she said. I had been afraid of labor mostly because it was something no one could tell me about. Now the pain was just something to go through. I could duck headlong into each new pain-wave knowing that it brought me closer to the moment of birth.

Sure it hurt—I can't even remember how much, except that each time it came I knew that I was made to take it. The pains came close, about three minutes apart, from the very beginning. I guess that's how come I thought they were only gas pains. I had heard so much about timing pains. Now I know there are exceptions to every rule. After just a couple of hours the pains got so bad I had to push that button. I was a little bit ashamed because the nurse had told me the baby wouldn't come for a long time yet.

But when Nurse Simpson examined me again she looked surprised. "Time to call the doctor," she said. "You've opened up quicker than I thought." I kept hoping it would be Dr. Norwad, and when I saw his eyes surrounded by dark circles above the surgical mask, I remember I thanked him for coming.

When it was all over I felt like laughing and dancing, and yelling from the rooftops for all the world to hear that I'm a mother. I remember I told Dr. Norwad I wanted to have lots and lots of children one day. He laughed and said, "Great. Just don't come back here to have them!" It sounded like a funny joke then.

Today I feel sore all over. My muscles are aching from the

strain they've gone through. The nurse says that's only natural, that the First Day is always worse than Zero Day.

Here is another new mother. It's Stella; she had a little girl five weeks early. Stella is sleeping; the nurse says the birth wasn't easy but the little girl is doing pretty well in the incubator.

Thursday the 25th, Second Day

Two new mothers today—I guess the ball is rolling and the late March rush is on.

I feel fine today. I weigh five pounds less than when I first got pregnant and my stomach isn't flabby. I think I can leave here and look pretty much my normal self.

Of course I have been putting off thinking about leaving. I don't know how I'll feel when I see Mother, but I know I can't give myself away, not now that it is all over. I must think of getting a job right away too, and get back to studying. I can't let this feeling of emptiness creep in—it is hovering on the edge of my mind now. I've got to wrap up this experience, know what it has meant and then go on my way. I needed these nine months. Now I've had them and I must go on.

There is a brand-new little boy and his family is waiting for him. He is no longer a concern of mine. I have served my purpose. So I couldn't be a mother for you, little boy, but you will have a mother. You will be loved very much. You have helped me, but someone else will meet your needs now.

Friday the 26th, Third Day

The doctor says I can leave next Tuesday. I'm in fine shape, he says. Dorothy will get here tomorrow and she'll call Martha then. They will make arrangements to meet Tuesday morning and Dorothy will bring the baby's clothes here. Then she will carry the baby out of the hospital to Martha. Dorothy will stay here and we will leave together Tuesday afternoon. It is all neatly planned.

I can get up and walk around now. When I had my shower yesterday it felt wonderful to be able to bend down and wash my feet without having to stretch around a big stomach. Tomorrow I will start taking my meals in the diet kitchen and I will have a job—rinsing out diapers before they go down the chute to the laundry.

Friday afternoon

One of the nurses came in to tell me that my little boy has been sick. He ran a slight temperature on his second day, yesterday.

"His temperature is normal now," said the nurse, "but this may mean that he can't go home Tuesday. He may have to be under observation a while longer." The nurse smiled and patted my arm. "Don't worry, hon," she said. "I just thought you'd like to know about it."

I haven't called Martha yet. He isn't sick anymore so maybe they'll let him go home Tuesday anyway. I can't believe that something will go wrong now. I walked across the hall and peeked in the door to the nursery. I saw that his crib has been moved behind a screen, separate from the others. I tiptoed in to look at him more closely. He was sleeping peacefully with one fist jammed into his mouth. Poor little one. I hope he isn't hurting. What would it mean for all of us if he is really sick?

I've got to get some sleep. Maybe tomorrow I can speak to the doctor.

Saturday the 27th, Our Fourth Day

Dorothy called. She is staying with her aunt; after all, that is the excuse she is using for coming here in the first place. She said my mother is fine and not at all worried about my being away for a couple of weeks.

"She said she knew you weren't expecting her home now, so how could you possibly have known," said Dorothy. I told her about the baby's temperature and she said I ought to call Martha.

"Don't get upset over it," said Dorothy. "It's probably nothing serious, but they ought to be told." I called Martha right away and heard the catch in her voice when she said, "Is he all right?"

"Don't worry," I said. "He doesn't have a temperature anymore, and he sleeps well and is gaining weight. It will be all right."

The pediatrician gets here Monday to check the babies and then he'll call Martha's doctor to talk it over with him. The nurse tells me he doesn't have a big appetite yet, but he is improving all the time.

Just two days ago I wrote in my notebook that he is no longer a concern of mine. Now I am being forced into caring much more than I had planned to. It will be harder to forget this way, if forgetting is what I want. But he is my concern until the moment I know he is safe in his mother's arms.

I have been to see him several times today. He looks so content and so healthy. His hair is a fine reddish brown and his eyes clear blue. There is a dimple in his chin. I am sure he'll be a real heartbreaker one day. I could stand by his crib just watching him forever. He wrinkles his nose and stretches his arms way up. Then his face gets all puckered up and he yawns or he cries, and I don't know what to do about it. Sometimes when he is asleep he mutters and moves his tongue as if he is searching for the nipple.

I am sure he smiles sometimes but the nurse says it is only gas pains. I pretend it is a real smile. I'll never see the way he'll smile some day. I must see in him today all he will be in the future. I feel so close to him now, in a different way, not just because he came through me, but he has become someone entirely his own. I can't let him down, for *his* sake.

What if Don and Martha won't take the chance? For a moment I feel a surge of excitement. He would be mine then. But of course they'll take the chance. And they have everything to offer him—I have nothing.

I'm going in to say goodnight to him now.

Sunday the 28th, Fifth Day

I watched the nurse feed him and change his diapers today. She cuddled him and talked to him and I was allowed to stand close. He is so beautiful.

You just have to be all right, little man. It is a little bit up to you, so drink all that good milk in your bottle. With a burp in the middle of your mealtime, you ought to make it.

Grown-up people will decide your future soon. Oh, but I know they will decide the right thing for you. Had you been born to them they wouldn't hesitate.

Monday the 29th, Our Sixth Day

The nurse told me to come to the doctor's office. "It's about your baby," she said, and the words shot through me, *your* baby.

He is my responsibility. The doctor said he can't release the baby for adoption now.

"I must be sure he is perfectly healthy before I can sign him out," he said, "and I can't be sure until we have observed him for at least several months. A fever may not mean anything, but it could mean brain damage. Of course, if the adoptive parents are willing to take the chance, they may take him home at their own risk in an independent adoption." He looked at me steadily. "The advantage of being adoptive parents is that they may choose," he said.

"But a slight temperature," I said. "How much of a risk is that?"

"Probably none," said the doctor. "If this weren't an adoption case we might not even mention it to the mother. Perfectly healthy babies sometimes have a little cold and run a temperature right after birth.

"The other alternative," said the doctor, fingering a paper on his desk, "would solve all your problems at once. You could sign here and release him to an adoption agency. They will be legally responsible for him and you don't have to give it another thought."

"And what would happen to him?" I felt suddenly very angry at this smug doctor who talked about not giving my child another thought.

"He would go to a foster home for six months," said the doctor. "Then if he is found to be healthy he will be placed for adoption. If he is not healthy, he will be placed in a proper institution under proper care and you will not have anything to concern yourself with in either case."

My hands were folded tightly in my lap and I heard the words come out of my mouth before I knew what I was going to say.

"It will be either the adoptive parents or myself," I said. "There can be no other alternative." As I heard my own voice, I knew it had to be that way. I couldn't send that little boy on to an uncertain future.

"You are talking about a full-time responsibility," said the doctor. "Are you prepared for all that that implies?"

"No," I said, "I'm not prepared, but my son needs a mother and he's going to have one—even if it's only me." The doctor looked at me for a long time. Then he put the form he was holding in his briefcase.

"I'll call the Carvers' pediatrician and inform him of your decision then," he said. "He will talk with the adoptive parents and you will know their decision tomorrow."

"Thank you," I said. "I will be waiting for their call."

On my way from the office I stopped in to look at my little boy. He was asleep in his crib, so unaware of the turmoil he is causing in several lives. But the turmoil is all of my making. I am responsible for bringing him into this world. Somehow I must see to it that he gets an even chance. If worst comes to worst and Martha and Don say no, I guess I can manage somehow. I think perhaps I am better prepared to be a mother now than I was months ago before I was willing to let him go out for adoption. When you give up your life it shall be given to you—isn't that what it says in the Bible somewhere?

But if he is to be mine, there is much to consider, a name to protect him, and my family. But now—not to think, not to get too involved, because surely Martha and Don will call to say they want him. Am I glad this is happening? I don't know. But at least I am kept from taking the easy way out, from just waking up after the delivery thinking that in seven days I will be putting on a new dress, new lipstick, and trying to forget.

Monday night

The nurse came to ask me if I would like to feed him. They all know what is happening and I can see in their faces their concern for the baby and for me. It was strange and wonderful to hold him at last, his body such a light weight on my lap, his head small enough to rest in the palm of my hand, little hands groping, little feet kicking. He has been so long inside me—and now to hold him, feel his soft skin smelling of baby powder. He drank all his milk and the nurse said that is good. Then she showed me how to burp him, how to support his back and neck, his downy head resting against my cheek.

He is so tiny, and yet a whole world in my arms. His eyes are drooping—he's so sleepy. Goodnight, baby. Tomorrow you go home with your mother.

Tuesday the 30th, Seventh Day

I am waiting for Martha's call. She should have called an hour ago. Dorothy will be here soon and we are scheduled to leave with the baby before noon. It is ten o'clock already. Is something wrong? I pray for the baby's sake that all is well. I don't worry about his health. I know he is all right. He must be. When I look at him, hold him, he is so alert, so quick to turn his eyes toward the light. When he is on his stomach, he tries to raise his head up high.

Is it too much for Martha and Don to take the chance? I know they must consider Kathy, too. Is it safer if he stays with me? I'm already attached to him. What if he goes with them and they find that he is sick? I don't know. I can only wait.

11:30 a.m.

The phone rang, but it wasn't for me. Hope rushed to my heart, and then came disappointment. I wonder what is keeping them? Have they talked to their doctor? Do they have to discuss it some more? Are they perhaps afraid of hurting me? How silly. They don't know how much they have done to make me grateful already. Whatever they decide won't change that.

I'm still wearing my housecoat. My things aren't packed yet. I feel exhausted. I wish they would call.

2:00 p.m.

I've talked to Dorothy on the phone and she has tried to call Martha and Don to find out what is happening. She called back to say their line is busy but she will keep on trying. She says not to worry, but how can I help it?

My little boy is fast asleep. I almost wish he were back inside me where nothing can happen to him. I feel so terribly helpless right now, and I shouldn't be, now that I have the responsibility for him also.

4:00 p.m.

Still no word from Martha and Don. We are supposed to leave here today and we'll have to go before evening. But I can't go before I know what is happening with Martha and Don. Dorothy called; she will be here before five o'clock. She will rent a motel room with a crib and a hot plate in case we need it. If we take the baby along, they'll give me twelve hours' supply of formula in four bottles and a complete layette with diapers and clothes. The nurse told me the Ladies' Auxiliary always gives a layette to the girls who keep their babies.

4:30 p.m.

Don called and his voice was so strained I almost didn't recognize it. "The doctor and the lawyer warn us against taking the baby home now. . . . I can't bear to see Martha suffer. . . . You understand, don't you?"

"Sure," I said. "I understand." I felt absolutely numb.

"Would you agree to have him placed in a foster home, under close observation by our pediatrician—we'll pay the bill—till we know for sure if he's all right?" Don sounded apologetic. "Martha doesn't want to do it that way but the doctor says we should."

"No!" I said, and the anger inside gave me strength to speak. "When that baby leaves here he goes with his mother—whether she is me or Martha. I chose you deliberately so that he wouldn't have to go to a foster home or an institution."

"I see," said Don in an empty sort of voice. "I guess there isn't anything more to say then, except thank you—and forgive us. We know this must be hard on you, Jean."

"Not as hard as on you," I said, and I meant it. "You lost a baby—I just got one." I put down the phone and went to lie on my bed. I could feel tears welling up but there was no time for them. I stared at the trees outside and tried to keep my mind a blank for just a minute, before the new thoughts came rushing in . . .

5:00 p.m.

The phone rang; it was Martha. "I can't bear it," she said. "If you don't want him in a foster home, I don't either. He needs a mother—and I need a baby. I don't care what happens." Her words came tumbling out. "I wouldn't have cared if he had been born to me. Please, Jean—will you let us have him?"

I could only feel a soreness inside—a horrible, dull ache. I saw the baby in his crib, so safe, so secure in his lack of knowledge of the world around him.

"What if he isn't all right?" I said.

"What if a son born to us hadn't been all right?" said Martha. "We will love him and give him what he needs, and we will never, never let him down."

"He needs you," I said, "more than he needs me. Please take him home." It was hard to keep from crying.

Martha said, "Now I feel that God is giving me a new chance to be a mother, for better or for worse." She was silent for a moment. "Don wants it this way, too, believe me, Jean. He just didn't want me to get hurt." Martha was crying openly now and laughing at the same time. "Oh, Jean," she said, "now I know how a mother feels. It isn't important that the baby suits us—but that we must try to be good for him."

"Thank you, Martha," I said, feeling a wave of exhaustion flooding me. "Your baby is ready to go home."

5:30 p.m.

I looked at him for the last time. He was asleep. I didn't want to hold him, and I suddenly remembered Carrie's words: "Don't hold him if you're going to give him away." But I'm not giving him away. He was never mine. I've just been responsible for him for a little while.

EPILOGUE

That was six years ago. Now I am married and have children of my own. Each day they grow to be more and more themselves, each one of them unique—each one wonderful, I think. And I am reminded of the lesson I learned several years ago; your children are not your children—they dwell in the house of tomorrow. What a blessing it is to be a guardian of their growth.

I know now also that a lesson once learned isn't always a lesson remembered. Only by self-discipline and will power does it become a lesson applied. My father once told me happiness comes not from doing what you like but from learning to like what you have to do. I know that now. I *try* to live it.

On her son's first birthday, Martha wrote Dorothy a card. He could walk then, and say a few words. "He is absolutely perfect in every way," wrote his mother.